T4-ALC-656

Education and Development of Infants, Toddlers, and Preschoolers

Education and Development of Infants, Toddlers, and Preschoolers

George S. Morrison
Florida International University

Scott, Foresman/Little, Brown College Division
SCOTT, FORESMAN AND COMPANY
Glenview, Illinois   Boston   London

Library of Congress Cataloging-in-Publication Data
Morrison, George S.
    Education and development of infants, toddlers, and
preschoolers.

    Includes index.
    1. Education, Preschool — United States.   2. Child
development — United States.   3. Child care — United
States.   I. Title.
LB1140.23.M67   1988   372.973   87-23531
ISBN 0-13-1177451

Copyright © 1988 by George S. Morrison

All rights reserved. No part of this book may be reproduced in any form or by any
electronic or mechanical means including information storage and retrieval systems
without permission in writing from the publisher, except by a reviewer who may
quote brief passages in a review.

    2 3 4 5 6 7 8 9 10 — RRC — 93 92 91 90 89 88

Printed in the United States of America

To Betty Jane, who is faithful in all things.

Preface

Education and Development of Infants, Toddlers, and Preschoolers presents points of view, philosophies, and real-life program vignettes relating to teaching, caring for, working with, and parenting children from birth through preschool. Concepts, ideas, research, and applications assist readers in acquiring the knowledge and skills for working with young children. The intended audience includes child-care providers and students in early childhood education, nursing, social work, psychology, and home economics. Parents and prospective parents will discover implications for parenting as they learn about the developmental process.

Throughout the text, current research supports new trends and classic studies clarify traditional practice. Research is used to heighten interest, illustrate concepts, clarify content, and provide a basis for decision making. Quotations from studies relate research to a particular topic. When care-givers act on the basis of evidence, they increase the chances that they will contribute positively to children's development and education.

Child development and early childhood topics are part of everyone's life, whether or not he or she is a parent. Many contemporary magazines contain articles about the care and education of young children. These articles sometimes emphasize the bizarre and the sensational. The public is more aware than ever of child development issues. I show how contemporary issues, practices, and ideas relate to and, in many instances, grow out of current knowledge about young children.

Another theme is the public attitude toward the very young. Public policies resulting from specific state and federal legislation affect how people rear and educate children. Laws relating to child abuse, compulsory school attendance, adoption, and education of the handicapped are just a few examples of public policy in action. These and other public policy programs are discussed in light of their effects on people and institutions and their resulting influence on practices relating to educating and developing young children.

People need information and knowledge about young children in order to conduct quality programs, create good environments, and be effective care-givers and service providers. The text does not advocate "one best way" of caring for or working with young children. Instead, different philosophies, models, and points of view are described to help readers understand the many opinions about what is "best." Real-life vignettes assist the reader in understanding how theories and ideas are translated into practice.

Implications for Care-givers sections throughout the text provide reasonable and practical suggestions that enable those who work with the very young to conduct *developmentally appropriate* practices. Indeed, a hallmark of the text is the application of theory to everyday interactions with young children. Considerable attention is given to how people such as parents, teachers, siblings, and peers interact with developing children. The influences of environmental settings — home, school, peer group — are also emphasized.

Special Features

Reality-Based Discussions. The text is based on the realities of care-giving at all levels from birth through preschool. Specific techniques and activities are identified that care-givers can use with young children and their parents. The program vignettes in particular add a realistic focus to the text.

Comprehensive and Extensive Coverage. This text integrates both development and curriculum. As a result, readers understand developmental concepts and theory as well as the applied curriculum and care-giving implications of theory. Comprehensive coverage of the major topics relating to the education and development of young children are included: involving parents, meeting young children's special needs, and guiding behavior.

Current and Up-to-Date Information. The latest thinking of professionals in the field for the 1980s and '90s is presented. Material on infant care-giving provides theory and care-giver activities for this fast-growing area of early childhood education.

Chapter-Opening Questions. Study questions help readers develop a learning set as a prelude to their reading. They alert readers to chapter content and help focus purpose and intent. In addition, they provide a basis for review and reflection.

Program Vignettes. Vignettes of real-life programs spark the reader's interest and illuminate textual material. They add a realistic base to theory and assist readers in seeing what life is like for children and care-givers in varied settings.

End-of-Chapter Activities. Each chapter ends with thought-provoking and challenging activities designed to help readers enrich and extend their knowledge and understanding about what is involved in being a good care-giver.

End-of-Chapter Readings. The suggested readings provide direction for readers who want to pursue a topic in greater detail. The readings are interesting and informative and will contribute to readers' professional growth. The annotations also provide insights and additional useful information.

Readability. The text is presented in an orderly, logical, and interesting manner. Visual materials such as charts and tables summarize and highlight important information and concepts.

Acknowledgments

Many people are responsible for any worthwhile endeavor, and they should be publicly thanked. I am always impressed with the way professional colleagues help me learn about the education and development of young children. Individuals who made this book possible are Odalys Figueroa, Chris Holicek, Silvia LaVilla, Beatrice Taylor, Marcia Orr, Joann Anderson, Virginia Milano, Shirley Rice, Debbie Steadman, Betty Williams, Anne DeHaan, Joan Lessen-Firestone, Harriet Jo Midgett, Constance Kamii, Harriet Wasserman, Cristina Fernandez, Marcia Orvieto, Mary Wilson, Cindy Genovese, Debbie Anderson, Lois Madison, Rosalyn Saltz, Christine Boesen, Judith LaVorgna, Nancy Bacot, Shirley Raines, Pam Boulton, Jackie Larus Conway, Patricia Vicenzi, Virginia Hayes, Joncee Feakes, Cynthia Warren, Janet Speirer, Kyo Miller, Judith Burch, Jill Valent, Dianne Draper, Maritza Bosh, Muriel Lundgren, Silvia Casanova, Thomas Kermes, and Margo Siegenthaler.

Marie Westlake, permissions editor, ably assisted with the many permissions details and made that task easier. Andrea Cava, book editor, made the editing and production processes pleasant and rewarding. I appreciate her facilitative manner and attention to detail.

Photographs were taken at the following locations: Miami Dade Community College Child Care Center–North Campus, Mt. Sinai Hospital Child Care Center, Holy Cross Child Care Center, Park Road Baptist Church Child Development Center, and Mount Carmel Child Care Center. I would also like to thank the reviewers, Elizabeth Goetz, University of Kansas; Margery Kranyik, Bridgewater State College; Deborah Stone, University of New Hampshire; and Sue Stuska, Front Range Community College.

Contents

Chapter 5

Programs for the Education and Development of the Children We Care For   175

Chapter 6

**Methods for the Education and Development of the
Children We Care For** 217

Chapter 9

Involving the Parents of the Children We Care For 319

Education and Development of Infants, Toddlers, and Preschoolers

Chapter 1

Who Are the Children We Care For?

Questions to Guide Your Reading and Study

- What views do care-givers have of young children?
- How do care-givers' views of young children influence how they educate and care for them?
- Why is it important for care-givers to develop a personal, comprehensive view of young children?
- How are young children defined and why is it important to define them?
- What is Sigmund Freud's psychoanalytic model and how does it influence the care of young children?
- What is Erik Erikson's psychosocial model of development and what implications does it have for the education and care of infants, toddlers, and preschoolers?
- What is Arnold Gesell's maturational model and in what ways does it influence child care?
- What is the behaviorist model and what implications does it have for child care?
- What is Jean Piaget's cognitive-developmental model and what are its implications for care giving?
- Why is there so much interest in the very young?

INTRODUCTION

Early childhood educators give many different answers to the very interesting question "What are young children like?" There is no one "right" answer. People's answers depend on their points of view and beliefs about children. We all carry around with us the baggage of images accumulated from experiences as children, students, parents, care-givers, and teachers. Views are passed on through study, word of mouth, and the interactions of parents and children. How your parents treated and reared you influences your views of children. Some images of children are narrow and limiting. Other images are better since they dignify the very young and recognize them as unique individuals in their own right.

Physical Characteristics

Sometimes, people see the very young merely as the sum of their physical characteristics. They base their understanding of children on physical appearances. They see a chubby, blue-eyed, smiling infant and label her as cute and content. Physical comparisons of the young with their parents are very common. You've probably heard someone say, "Oh, you have your mother's smile." Unfortunately, some people don't go beyond the physical characteristics. What they see is what the infant is.

Clichés and Misinformation

Misinformation, lack of knowledge, and clichés shape images of the very young. Care-givers who believe young children are not capable of much don't expect much from them. The children they care for may be victims of stereotypical sayings such as "Learning doesn't begin before two" and "I've heard twos are terrible." Children are losers when interactions with adults are based on such false beliefs.

Alike, Yet Different

All too often some care-givers look at children as though they are all alike. They categorize children into a generic whole. When people view all children as being alike, their expectations about what children are capable of are limited to the average. As a result, they expect too much from some children, not enough from others, and very little from the rest. The "sameness" view is detrimental when it is the basis of children's programs.

A healthy and humanistic way of looking at infants, toddlers, and preschoolers is to acknowledge commonalities and to look for, recognize, and encourage individuality and uniqueness. All care-givers need to celebrate through words, actions, and interactions the ways all children differ from the norm and from each other.

Who are the children we care for? They are alike yet different in many ways. Their individuality and uniqueness merit quality programs and developmentally appropriate curricula. What can you do as a care-giver to meet the unique needs of children?

In this book, the themes of individuality and uniqueness pervade all the discussions of the very young. At the same time, emphasis is placed on understanding normal developmental processes and the ages and stages at which they typically occur. All children are alike in many ways. We discuss these common characteristics and document the comparable ways children look, behave, and develop physically, intellectually, socially, and emotionally. Care-givers must recognize these norms and use them as guides as they plan, nurture, and educate. Thoroughly understanding average development enables care-givers to recognize the uniqueness of children, and it enables students of the very young to approach their study of children with open minds attuned to the reality that children are simultaneously alike and different. Recognition of the wonderful differences among children provides the basis for quality and developmentally appropriate early childhood programs.

DEFINITIONS

Young Children Defined

Early childhood means the years from conception to age eight. *Early childhood education* (ECE) is the education of children from birth to age eight. Historically, early childhood professionals concentrated their efforts on children in the five-to-eight age range. Our attention has more recently focused on infants, toddlers, and preschoolers.

The term *neonate* is used by health professionals and people who specialize in child development to designate the child in the first month of life. "Neonate" is derived from the Latin *neo* for new and *natus* for born.

Infants are children from birth to the beginning of walking. The *average* child reaches this milestone at twelve months. The term "infant" comes from the Latin word *infans*, which means "speechless." The term *baby* in this book is applied to the same age span, from birth to twelve months. The public, however, frequently uses the term to refer to young children in general. "Infant" and other age groups may be defined differently in different states.

Toddlers are children from one year of age, or the beginning of walking, to age three. The toddler period is further divided into two categories: *junior toddler*, from one year to eighteen months, and *senior toddler*, from eighteen months to two years.

Preschoolers are children from age three to the beginning of kindergarten or first grade. Many preschoolers are enrolled in preschool programs operated by private individuals, religious organizations, universities, public schools, or child-care programs. Once children enter kindergarten or first grade, the *primary years* begin.

With the growing interest in infants, toddlers, and preschoolers, the generalized and nonspecific term "early childhood" no longer meets our needs for designating this younger age group. Indeed, "early childhood" and "early childhood education" are not suitable terms to accurately describe the many programs and children in the birth-through-age-eight age group. A changing profession like early childhood education needs new terminology to clearly designate particular age groups. Therefore, *the very young* is the term used in this book to categorize and describe children from birth through preschool.

Some professionals prefer to talk about children in terms of continuous development as they mature from birth through childhood to adolescence and adulthood. They believe categories such as "infants" and "toddlers" are restrictive and discourage people from seeing the very young as unique individuals and developing persons. Nevertheless, as defined here, the categories are an aid in the study of children. It is helpful to think about and study children as representative of particular groups that have certain characteristics. Think of the definitions as identifying "sets" of children that belong to a larger domain. The set "infants" belongs to the larger universe "developing children." In this manner we can still use the definitions but will not be tempted to stereotype and categorize children.

Care-giver Defined

A *care-giver* is any person who provides care, education, and protection for the very young in or outside the home. Defined in this way, "care-giver"

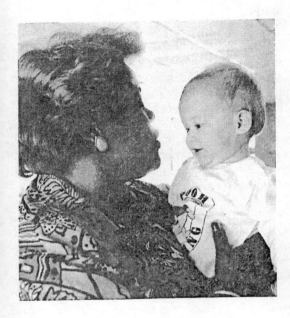

A care-giver is any person who provides care, education, and protection for young children. What special qualities and attributes do care-givers need?

is a comprehensive term and includes child-care workers, home-care providers, and preschool teachers. Given the current status of early education and child-care programs, where children are in the care of others beginning as early as six weeks, an inclusive term like "care-giver" is necessary to designate all those who fulfill the important roles of nurturing, educating, and developing.

Just as they have definitions for children, most states have preschool and child-care licensing standards and regulations that define "care-giver." These definitions usually list minimum qualifications such as age and educational background. Because of the recent increase in awareness and reporting of child abuse, many states now include mandatory fingerprinting and absence of a criminal record as further prerequisites for assuming the care-giver role.

EXPERTS' VIEWS OF CHILDREN

The theories and beliefs of psychologists and child-rearing experts can and should play a major role in care-givers' understanding of young children and their behavior. Learning how to educate and develop the very young must include developing a personal and comprehensive view of children. Such a view enables care-givers to confidently make day-to-day decisions about how to provide quality programs.

Children According to Freud: The Psychoanalytic Model

According to Sigmund Freud (1856–1939), *libido*, or general sexual energy, is the driving force that influences children's behavior. The *id* controls this energy and releases it through instincts, innate drives, and reflexes. The id's primary function is to bring pleasure associated with the *erogenous zones*. In childhood, these zones are the mouth, the anal area, and the genitals. Children derive pleasure from the release of this sexual energy. The primary means for releasing this sexual energy are through oral gratification (eating and sucking), warmth, love, elimination of body wastes, and pleasurable body sensations that result from fondling, massaging, and being held.

The current popularity of baby massage indicates an acceptance of the idea that parents not only relieve infants' tense muscles but contribute to their psychic well-being through erogenous gratification. As a result, infants learn to trust their parents as reliable sources of gratification and love.

However, constant pleasure seeking must be brought under control. The *ego* (the Latin word for "I") provides an adaptive function for children and acts as a mediator, controlling behavior in relation to the realities and mores of everyday life. It permits the child as much pleasure as possible within the constraints of what is right and wrong. According to Freud, children are *amoral* and have no knowledge of good or evil, right or wrong. Parents have the responsibility to establish the parameters of right and wrong and provide guidance and direction for right behavior. As the child matures under the direction of the parent, the *superego* develops and becomes the child's conscience, the determiner of right and wrong.

According to Freud, children progress through a series of psychosexual stages. During the oral stage, which begins at birth, the libido or sexual energy is directed toward gaining gratification through the mouth. Pleasure results from sucking the breast, bottle, thumb, or pacifier, from biting, and from orally investigating objects. Generally, this stage lasts until the time of weaning from breast or bottle. This is when children encounter their first conflict with social and parental norms, for they desire to continue sucking indefinitely. How the parent handles this developmental crisis helps shape the child's adult personality. According to Freud, too aggressive and harsh weaning leaves the baby feeling rejected and unloved. The key is to help the baby resolve the conflicts associated with weaning while showing love and affection.

Freud's view of children focuses attention on the importance of the early years. Childhood experiences are seen as critical determiners in the continuum of human development. His theory underscores the importance of the encounters between parent and child and the role these interactions play in personality growth. Much of what children are like — their personalities — results from how their needs are met in the cultural and family environment in which they are reared.

Children According to Erikson: The Psychosocial Model

Erik H. Erikson (b. 1902), an influential developmental psychologist, was a student of Sigmund Freud. He built on and extended Freudian theory to develop his theory of psychosocial development. According to Erikson, ego development occurs in response to social institutions, including family and school. The social contexts of children, then, are important determiners of development. Children's needs, in interaction with the qualities of the environment, set the direction for personality development. Parents and other care-givers in particular are critical environmental influences in children's lives as children create their unique personalities.

Erikson's theory has eight stages or *ego qualities*, which occur throughout the human life span. These are depicted in Table 1-1. For Erikson, the ego, not the id, is the major driving force in development. The stages postulated by Erikson are invariant. Therefore children — and adults — must progress from one stage to another and deal with the particular crisis of each stage in their development through life.

During each stage of development, Erikson says, individuals experience an *ego crisis* or *basic conflict*. The conflict or crisis must be successfully resolved, which enables a positive quality — for example, trust rather than mistrust — to be incorporated as part of the personality. Ideally, the individual will resolve all conflicts with a minimum of crisis, resulting in a positive ego state.

Stage 1: Basic Trust vs. Mistrust (Birth to Eighteen Months). During this stage, the child learns to either trust or mistrust care-givers and the environment. Trust results from having basic care needs met in consistent, predictable, and loving ways.

Stage 2: Autonomy vs. Shame and Doubt (Eighteen Months to Three Years). During this stage children become more independent and want to do things for themselves. Care-givers must provide opportunities for them to do so. Overprotection and lack of opportunities encourage self-doubt and lack of achievement. As a result, instead of feeling good about their accomplishments, children come to feel ashamed of their abilities. Toilet training and walking are two critical developmental accomplishments of this period and provide many opportunities for care-givers to enable children to develop autonomy or shame.

Stage 3: Initiative vs. Guilt (Three to Five Years). During the preschool years, children are independent and active initiators of events. Erikson believes children need opportunities to respond with initiative to activities and tasks. When children are allowed to demonstrate initiative and are greeted positively by care-givers and others in their demonstrations of initiative, then a sense of purposefulness and accomplishment results. Guilt, on the other hand, results when children are discouraged from initiating

TABLE 1-1
Erik Erikson's Eight Ages of Man

Stage	Age	Psychosocial Stage	Care-giver Tasks and Roles	Intended Outcome
1. Oral sensory (similar to Freud's oral stage)	Birth to 18–24 months	Basic trust vs. mistrust	Children learn to trust when their basic needs are met with consistency, continuity, and sameness.	Children view world as safe and dependable.
2. Muscular-anal	18 months to 3 years	Autonomy vs. shame	Encourage children to do what they are capable of doing. Avoid shaming for any behavior.	Children learn independence and competence and develop confidence to deal with the environment.
3. Locomotor genital (similar to Freud's phallic stage)	3 to 5 years (to beginning of school)	Initiative vs. guilt	Encourage children to engage in many activities. Provide environment in which children can explore language development.	Children are able to undertake a task, be active and involved; are not hesitant, guilty, or afraid to do things on their own.
4. Latency	Elementary years	Industry vs. inferiority	Help children to win recognition by producing things. Recognition results from achievement and success.	Feelings of self-worth and industry; the ability to accomplish.
5. Puberty and adolescence	Adolescence	Identity vs. role confusion	Help teenagers develop independence from parents. Resolve confusion about sex role and occupation.	Adolescents must develop an ego identity of their own.
6. Young adulthood	From the end of adolescence to middle adulthood	Intimacy vs. isolation	Support efforts at establishing intimate relationships.	Intimate relationships.
7. Adulthood	35–45 years	Generativity vs. stagnation	—	
8. Maturity	Midlife	Ego integrity vs. despair	—	

Source: E. H. Erikson, *Childhood and Society*, rev. ed. (New York: Norton, 1963).

activities and attempting to do things on their own. As we will discuss later, the key for the care-giver during this stage is to provide freedom within limits.

Stage 4: Industry vs. Inferiority (Elementary Years). During this stage children display an industrious attitude toward life. They want to build things, discover, manipulate objects in their environment, and find out "how things work." Productivity is important during this stage. Children want recognition for their industrious attitudes and nature. The responses adults give to this productivity help in the development of a positive self-concept. If children's growing abilities are harshly criticized, if children are unfairly compared to each other, and if children constantly fail — or are made to fail — then inferiority results.

Stage 5: Identity vs. Role Confusion (Adolescence). The fifth psychosocial crisis occurs during the adolescent years as individuals search for a self-identity as persons and as members of society. Career decisions play an important role in this process as adolescents decide what they want to do with their lives. Answers to questions such as "Who am I?" and "What do I want to do?" are integral to the search for identity. According to Erikson, teenage romances play an important part in identity development since they provide an opportunity for individuals to clarify who they are. Difficulty in dealing with the search for identity results in the individual taking a long time to "grow up" and end his or her "childish" behavior.

Children According to Gesell: The Maturational Model

One of the most widely accepted and persistent views of children is that they are similar to growing plants. This view has its roots in the ideas and practices of a German educator, Friedrich Froebel (1782–1852), who is considered the father of the kindergarten ("garden of children"). Froebel likened children to plants and parents to gardeners whose main task is to nurture and care for children so they can mature according to their genetic inheritance and maturational timetable. This view maintains that given the right amounts of attention and care, children will become what they are able to become and parents and teachers should not hurry or rush this development.

Arnold Gesell (1880–1961) was the founder of the *maturational approach* to early childhood. Gesell made fashionable and acceptable the idea of inherent maturation that is predictable, patterned, and orderly. Biological forces provide the impetus and direction for development. In fact, maturation is so orderly that Gesell constructed a number of tests to measure development. Based on the results of these tests, he developed a series of norms or standards that chronicle in detail children's motor, adaptive, language, and personal-social behavior.

Gesell coined the concept of *developmental age* to distinguish children's developmental growth from their chronological age. A child who is four years of age chronologically, for example, can be immature for his age and have a developmental age of three years. In this case, the developmental age of three would indicate that the four-year-old child responds to items on a behavior test as a three-year-old would respond.

The work and efforts of Gesell are continued by his followers at the Gesell Institute of Human Development in New Haven, Connecticut. Here, Gesell's ideas are further developed and refined. Table 1-2 shows the Gesell Developmental Schedules for children aged two through five.

For Gesell, orderly, predictable maturation was the underlying foundation for all development. As he explained it,

> All things considered, the inevitability and surety of maturation are the most impressive characteristics of early development. It is the hereditary ballast which conserves and stabilizes the growth of each individual infant. It is indigenous in its impulsion; but we may all be grateful for this degree of determinism. If it did not exist the infant would be victim of a flaccid malleability which is sometimes romantically ascribed to him. His mind, his spirit, his personality would fall a ready prey to disease, to starvation, to malnutrition, and worst of all to misguided management. As it is, the inborn tendency toward optimum development is so inveterate that he benefits liberally from what is good in our practice, and suffers less than he logically should from our unenlightenment.[1]

As viewed by Gesell, then, the worst mistake a care-giver can make is to interfere with the normal growth and development of young children.

Gesell's theory has two major implications. One affects parents and the other primarily affects teachers.

For parents, the implication is that nature guides children's growth and development. Children develop best without any interference. Gesell believed that children were inherently good and that their development was orderly and good, also. Parents can make their greatest contribution to the child-rearing process by providing a climate in which children can grow without interfering with each child's innate timetable and blueprint for development. This viewpoint is very well stated in *The Gesell Preschool Test Manual*.

> A question which often arises is how much, if anything, can a parent or teacher do to increase or improve a child's maturity. Parents often report that the school has labeled their child immature, and ask what they, as parents, can do to increase their child's maturity. (During the summer months is the time when many plan to accomplish this miracle.) Though growth and development can on occasion be uneven, in general the rate of any child's maturing *seems* to depend much more on genetic or internal factors than on anything that others can do to or for him.[2]

The second implication primarily affects teachers and the schooling process, but also has implications for parents. This is the concept of *readi-*

ness, which is widely and popularly interpreted to mean children's ability to accomplish school tasks and succeed at the process of schooling. According to the Gesell point of view, if the results of a readiness test reveal that a child is not physically or behaviorally performing at the norm for his age, then this indicates he is not "ready" for school. Time is the best cure or antidote for immaturity and lack of readiness, as attested by the quotation just given. Nothing cures or counteracts a lack of readiness like time, which enables the natural maturation process to work. Accordingly, the best cure for being developmentally delayed at four years of age is to become five.

The maturational model states that development consists of behavioral components that emerge according to a specific timetable. The presence or absence of these maturational milestones at certain times indicates a child's rate of development. The basic determiners of development are genetic background, biology, and time.

In later chapters there is additional material on the concept of readiness and tests that purport to measure it. In particular, in Chapter 6, we consider the "play school–nursery school" approach to implementing maturational ideas.

Children According to Skinner: The Behaviorist View

The behaviorists provide us with yet another, albeit different, way of looking at children. Their theories are opposite from those of the maturational model. For the behaviorists, the critical factors in growth and development are not biology and time but the environment and opportunity to learn. They see development as a continuous set of changing behaviors governed by the principles of learning, rather than as a series of age-bound behaviors. Age and stage descriptions of development are irrelevant because development results from children's interactions with the environment and the reward system inherent in the environment. Change is a function of learning, not age.

From the behaviorist point of view, there are limitless possibilities for development. When the learning environment and experiences are controlled, the direction of behavior is controlled. J. B. Watson (1878–1958), a psychologist and one of the popularizers of behaviorism in the United States, made the following classic statement:

> Give me a dozen healthy infants and my own specified world to bring them up in, and I'll guarantee to take any one of them at random and train him to become any type of specialist I select — doctor, lawyer, artist, merchant chief and, yes, even beggarman and thief, regardless of his talents, penchants, tendencies, abilities, vocations, and race of his ancestors.[3]

The popularizer of behaviorism and the person who inspired the application of behaviorist principles to parenting and teaching is B. F. Skinner

TABLE 1-2
Gesell Developmental Schedules*

Age (year)	Motor	Adaptive	Language	Personal-Social
2	Walks: runs well, no falling Stairs: walks up and down alone Large ball: (no demonstration) kicks Cubes: tower of 6–7 Book: turns pages singly	Cubes: tower of 6–7 Drawing: imitates vertical stroke Formboard: places blocks on separately (G) Formboard: adapts after 4 trials Color Forms: does not identify any	Speech: jargon discarded Speech: 3-word sentence Speech: uses *I, me, you* Picture Vocabulary: 2+ correct	Toilet: may verbalize needs fairly consistently Play: domestic mimicry Play: hands cup full of cubes Play: parallel play predominates Feeding: inhibits turning spoon Dressing: pulls on simple garment Communication: verbalizes immediate experiences Communication: refers to self by name Communication: comprehends and asks for "another" Temperament: gentle, easy
2½	Stands: tries, on 1 foot Cubes: tower of 10 Drawing: holds crayon by fingers	Cubes: tower of 10 Cubes: aligns 2 or more, train Drawing: imitates vertical and horizontal strokes Drawing: scribbles to circular stroke Incomplete Man: adds 1 part Formboard: inserts 3 blocks on presentation Formboard: adapts repeatedly, error Color Forms: places 1	Interview: gives first name Interview: tells sex (G) Prepositions: obeys 1–2 Picture Vocabulary: 7 correct Action Agent: 3 correct	Play: pushes toy with good steering Play: helps put things away Communication: refers to self by pronoun "me" rather than by name Communication: repetition in speech and other activity Self-help: can put on own coat (not necessarily fasten) Temperament: opposite extremes

3	Walks on tiptoe, 2 or more steps Stands on 1 foot, momentary balance Skips: tries Rides tricycle using pedals Stairs: alternates feet going up Jumps down: lands on feet (G) Broad jump: distance 12" Pellets: 10 into bottle in 26 seconds (G); 24 seconds (B)	Cubes: adds chimney to train Cubes: imitates bridge Copy Forms: copies circle Copy Forms: imitates cross Incomplete Man: adds 3 parts Formboard: adapts, no errors or immediate correction of error Color Forms: places 3 Counts with correct pointing: 3 objects Pellets: 10 into bottle in 26 seconds (G); 24 seconds (B)	Speech: uses plurals Interview: tells age (G) Interview: tells sex (B) Prepositions: obeys 3 Digits: repeats 3 (1 of 3 trials) Picture Vocabulary: 11 correct Comprehension Question A: answers 1 Action Agent: 6–7 correct Picture Vocabulary: 11 correct	Feeding: feeds self, little spilling Feeding: pours well from pitcher Dressing: puts on shoes Dressing: unbuttons front and side buttons Communication: asks questions rhetorically Communication: understands taking turns Communication: knows a few rhymes Temperament: cooperative
3½	Stands on 1 foot 2 seconds or more Jumps: both feet leave floor Broad jump: distance 19" Jumps down, lands on feet (B) Hops on one foot: succeeds (G) Pellets: 10 into bottle in 23 seconds	Cubes: builds bridge from model Copy Forms: copies cross Incomplete Man: adds 4 parts Incomplete Man: eyes better than a scribble Pellets: 10 into bottle in 23 seconds	Interview: gives number of siblings Prepositions: 4 correct Digits: repeats 3 (2 of 3 trials) Picture Vocabulary: 12 correct Comprehension A: answers 2 Action Agent: 12 correct	Dressing: washes, dries, hands, face Play: associate play replaces parallel Communication: calls self "I" Communication: asks "How" questions Toilet: seldom has "accidents" Temperament: vulnerable

(continued)

TABLE 1-2 (*continued*)

Age (year)	Motor	Adaptive	Language	Personal-Social
4	Stands on 1 foot 2–7 seconds Stairs: walks down, foot to a step Skips: on one foot Jumps: running or standing broad jump Broad jump: 20" Bean bag catch: any method Pellets: 10 into bottle in 23 seconds	Cubes: imitates gate or better (G) Copy Forms: imitates square or better Incomplete Man: adds 5 parts Incomplete Man: arm straight out from body or better Pellets: 10 into bottle in 23 seconds Counts: 4 objects	Interview: gives own age (B) Prepositions: 5 correct Digits: repeats 3 (3 of 3 trials) Digits: repeats 4 (1 of 3 trials) Picture Vocabulary: 14 correct Comprehension B: 1 correct Action Agent: 14 correct	Dressing: buttons clothing Dressing: washes and dries face and hands, brushes teeth Dressing: dresses and undresses, supervised Dressing: laces shoes Dressing: distinguishes front and back Play: cooperates with other children Play: builds buildings with blocks Development: goes on errands outside home (no crossing streets) Development: tends to go out-of-bounds Communication: asks "Why" questions Temperament: expansive
4½	Hops on one foot: succeeds (B) Broad jump: 24" Bean bag: overhand throw: succeeds (G) Bean bag catch: hands vs. chest or better (B) Pellets: 10 into bottle in 20 seconds	Cubes: makes gate from model Copy Forms: copies square recognizably Copy Forms: divided rectangle — ladder design, lines straight Incomplete Man: adds 7 parts Letters: 1–2 recognizable Numbers: 1–2 recognizable Counts: 4 objects and answers "How many?" Pellets: 10 into bottle in 20 seconds	Articulation: not infantile Interview: gives names of siblings Digits: repeats 4 (2 of 3 trials) Comprehension A: 3 correct Action Agent: 16 correct	Communication: calls attention to own performance Communication: relates fanciful tales Play: shows off dramatically Temperament: unpredictable

5	Stands on one foot 9 seconds or more Walks on tiptoe: 5 or more steps Skips: using feet alternately Broad jump: distance 27" Pellets: 10 into bottle in 18 seconds	Cubes: 6 cube steps with demonstration Copy Forms: copies triangle more or less adequately Copy Forms: all forms on 1 page Copy Forms: divided rectangle ladder design, side lines slanted Incomplete Man: adds 8 parts Name: prints first name Counts: 10 objects correctly Calculates: within 5 Pellets: 10 into bottle in 18 seconds	Interview: gives first and last names Picture Vocabulary: 15 correct Comprehension B: 2 correct Action Agent: 17 correct	Dressing: ties a bow knot Dressing: dresses and undresses with little assistance Communication: asks meaning of words Play: dresses up in adult clothes Temperament: gentle, friendly
5½	Stands on one foot 12 seconds Bean bag overhand: succeeds (B) Bean bag catch: hands vs. chest or better (G)	Cubes: 10 cube steps with or without demonstration (G) Copy Forms: copies triangle recognizably Copy Forms: divided rectangular horizontal line crosses vertical, angled lines may cross vertical Copy Forms: diamond — 1 or 2 sides correct Incomplete Man: eyes match in size Incomplete Man: arm points upward Counts: 12 objects correctly	Interview: knows month of birthday Action Agent: 18–19 correct Digits: repeats 4 (3 of 3 trials)	Money: identifies pennies and nickels Play: understands games like tag and hide and seek Temperament: breaking up

(continued)

TABLE 1-2 (continued)

Age (year)	Motor	Adaptive	Language	Personal-Social
6	Stands on each foot alternately Broad jump: distance 32" Bean bag: advanced throwing Bean bag catch: hands only Pellets: 10 into bottle in 16 seconds	Cubes: 10 cube steps with or without demonstration (B) Copy Forms: divided rectangle 3 lines may cross center vertical line Copy Forms: copies diamond, oddly shaped (good shape not until 7 years) Incomplete Man: adds 9 parts Incomplete Man: adds 2 or 3 parts at neck Name: prints first and last (G) (normative at 6½) Adds and subtracts within 10 (normative at 6½) Pellets: 10 into bottle in 16 seconds Counts: 13+ objects Calculates: within 10 (6½ years)	Interview: knows day and month of birthday (normative at 6½) Digits: repeats 5 (1 of 3 trials) Picture Vocabulary: 16 correct Action Agent: 19 correct	Dressing: ties shoe laces Communication: differentiates A.M. and P.M. Communication: knows right and left (3 of 3 or complete reversal) Communication: recites numbers to 30s Temperament: oppositional, emotional

*B = boy; G = girl.

Source: Jacqueline Haines, Louise Bates Ames, and Clyde Gillespie, *The Gesell Preschool Test Manual* (Lumberville, Pa.: Modern Learning Press, 1980), 67–68.

We must keep in mind that individual children make up the so-called average child. These children are all three and a half years old. When we say a child is "average," what does it mean?

(b. 1904). One of his inventions, which captured public attention, was the "baby box" or Aircrib that mechanized child care. Skinner built an enclosed, quiet space in which his second child, a daughter, wore only a diaper. The temperature was regulated by a fan blowing air through a woven plastic sheet. This environment enabled the baby to move about in a safe, comfortable environment. She experienced a normal childhood and grew up a physically and emotionally healthy person who now has children of her own.[4]

Behaviorists see development as a gradual and continuous process that parents and care-givers control in several ways. The first is by arranging the environment so it facilitates, shapes, and rewards desired behavior. Behavior is influenced by the physical setting and by the expectations for behavior in that setting. An infant program with a reading center that contains books, pillows, soft carpeting, and a care-giver who reads to children conveys the notion that reading is important. Parents who organize children's rooms with low shelves and easily accessible drawers support the expectation that children will take care of their own environment.

Second, care-givers control behavior by providing appropriate and immediate rewards for desired behavior. Children like and respond to rewards of verbal praise, affection, food, and use of toys and materials. All these are used to promote desired behavior.

Third, care-givers model and demonstrate behavior they want children to imitate. It is a case of "children see, children do."

Children are the products of the behaviors for which they are rewarded. The key to good parenting is to determine the kind of child desired and provide the proper rewards to reinforce and condition the behaviors necessary to achieve that goal. Viewed from the behaviorist model, the child is seen as a reactor to environmental stimuli, lacking purposeful intention of actions. Learning is the product of reinforcements.

Albert Bandura (b. 1925) used behaviorist ideas to develop a *social learning theory*. Bandura and other social learning theorists believe learning occurs through modeling, observation, vicarious experiences, and self-regulated behavior.[5] Bandura explains the role of modeling in learning this way:

> Learning would be exceedingly laborious, not to mention hazardous, if people had to rely solely on the effects of their own actions to inform them what to do. Fortunately, most human behavior is learned observationally through modeling: From observing others, one forms an idea of how new behaviors are performed, and on later occasions this coded information serves as a guide for action.[6]

In Chapter 7, there is an in-depth discussion of how young children learn through modeling.

Behaviorist theory has a rather wide following, particularly in the applied areas of parenting, child care, and teaching. Many care-givers have been trained to use "behavior modification techniques." Also, curricula and programs have been specifically developed to utilize the ideas and concepts of behaviorism.

Critics of behaviorism believe it is too simplistic in its rationale of how learning occurs. They believe the theory does not have enough substance to account for the full range of learning. They also believe learning involves more than stimuli and responses. Behaviorists counter, though, that such criticisms reflect lack of understanding of behaviorist principles and their applications.

Children According to Piaget:
The Cognitive-Developmental Model

Jean Piaget (1896–1980), perhaps more than any other person, has had a profound effect on our understanding of how children acquire and use knowledge. According to the developmental-cognitive model, development occurs in an orderly, sequential manner, with each stage qualitatively different from the next. One of the unique features of this model is that it emphasizes the active role children play in their own development.

Piaget was trained as a biologist, and he used a biological model to describe human intellectual development. In biology, it is the structure that changes and adapts. For Piaget, *scheme* became the cognitive correlate for biological structure. The earliest schemes are sensorimotor schemes such as sucking and grasping, which are reflexive in nature. However, these schemes change in response to the environment, experiences, and the active involvement of the child. Sucking soon becomes differentiated between nutritive and nonnutritive sucking and changes in form to accommodate to cup and spoon. The first two years of life are characterized by sensorimotor schemes.

Cognitive schemes are cognitive structures in which an individual assimilates information. Acquired from approximately two years of age on, they become the concepts by which children organize and classify their world. Cognitive schemes include our number system, concepts of space and time, and the laws of logic. Cognitive schemes help children know their world by helping them understand how objects, experiences, and events are related. These cognitive schemes form an individual's *cognitive structure*. Just as our skeletal structure organizes our physical appearance and grammar organizes language, cognitive structures organize cognitive development.

How are new or more complex schemes developed and old ones changed? This cognitive process occurs through the *cognitive functions* of *organization, adaptation, assimilation, accommodation,* and *equilibration.*

Organization is essential to cognitive activity. Organization is innate and entails the interaction of physical, maturational, and psychological processes. It enables the child, for example, to combine the initially separate sensorimotor schemes of grasping and looking into the coordinated scheme of intentional looking at what is grasped.

Adaptation is the basis for any developmental change in intelligence. As Mary Pulaski says,

> Adaptation is for Piaget the essence of intellectual functioning, just as it is the essence of biological functioning. We have been familiar with adaptation in the Darwinian sense of "survival of the fittest." But to Piaget, the word means more than just survival; it means modifying the environment to our own ends. He believes that an essential part of our biological inheritance is a mode of intellectual functioning which remains constant throughout life. This functioning is characterized by the ability to organize the myriad sensations and experiences we encounter into some kind of order, and to adapt ourselves to our surroundings.[7]

It is through this process of interaction with and adaptation to the environment that the child organizes sensations and experiences. *Intelligence* is the result.

Piaget believed that adaptation is comprised of two interrelated and simultaneously operating processes, *assimilation* and *accommodation*. These processes make adaptation possible. As Peter Richmond explains,

> Every experience we have, whether as infant, child or adult, is taken into the mind and made to fit into the experiences which already exist there. The next experience will need to be changed to some degree in order for it to fit in. Some experiences cannot be taken in because they do not fit and are rejected. Thus the intellect assimilates new experiences into itself by transforming them to fit the structure which has been built up. This process of acting on the environment in order to build up a model of it in the mind, Piaget calls assimilation.[8]

Accommodation, on the other hand, occurs when individuals change their present way of thinking, behaving, and believing to fit incoming information. Richmond explains accommodation this way:

> With each new experience, the structures which have already been built up will need to modify themselves to accept that new experience, for, as each new experience is fitted into the old, the structures will be slightly changed. This process by which the intellect continually adjusts its model of the world to fit each new acquisition, Piaget calls accommodation.[9]

Equilibration is the process of maintaining the balance or equilibrium between the processes of assimilation and accommodation. Children are intrinsically motivated to restore equilibrium to their cognitive systems through the processes of assimilation and accommodation. Cognitive development is a continuous process of developing schemes through transitions from disequilibrium to equilibrium. Using the process of equilibration, children develop through a series of four stages, as depicted in Table 1-3.

Piaget believed that the stages of cognitive development are fixed and invariant for all children and that stages of development cannot be skipped. The ages at which children develop through stages vary, however; some children develop more or less rapidly than other children. Consequently, the ages that Piaget attaches to each stage are only guidelines.

Whereas Gesell's description of development is physical and behavioral, Piaget emphasizes the *processes* that occur at each stage. Piaget ascribed primary importance to spontaneous physical activity in the process of cognitive development. He believed that children are active in their development, not reactive as the behaviorists believe.

Piaget's beliefs represent an *interactionist* view of how children develop. Rather than saying that a child is governed primarily by biological maturation (Gesell) or only by environmental stimuli (Skinner), interactionists believe development results from maturation and the *transactions* or interactions between the child and the physical and social environments. For Piaget, activity counts.

TABLE 1-3

Piaget's Stages of Intellectual Development

	Stage	Age	Characteristics
I.	Sensorimotor	0 to 2 years	Intelligence based on perceptual experiences.
	1. Reflexive	0 to 1 month	Reflexes become more efficient; lack of differentiation.
	2. Primary circular reactions	1 to 4 months	Repetition of certain pleasurable behaviors and the formation of habits, coordination of reflexes.
	3. Secondary circular reactions	4 to 10 months	Intentional repetition of events discovered through chance, notion of cause and effect.
	4. Coordination of secondary schemes	10 to 12 months	Application of old schemes to new situations, object permanence, first clear signs of intelligence, instrumental activity.
	5. Tertiary circular reactions	12 to 18 months	Discovery of new means and repetition with variation for novelty's sake, experimentation on cause and effect situations, hypothesis testing.
	6. Symbolic representation	18 to 24 months	Internalizes actions and begins to think before acting, represents objects and images through imagery, invention of new ideas.
II.	Preoperational	2 to 7 years	Onset of sophisticated language system, egocentric reasoning, thinking is perception-bound.
III.	Concrete operational	7 to 11 years	Thought is reversible, and ability to solve concrete problems develops; conservation becomes operative; logical operations develop; thinking is experience-based.
IV.	Formal operational	11 years to adulthood	Formulation and testing of hypotheses, abstract thought, deductive reasoning, hypothetico-deductive reasoning, thought no longer perception-bound.

Source: Neil J. Salkind, *Theories of Human Development*, Copyright © 1985, John A. Wiley and Sons. Reprinted by permission of John A. Wiley & Sons, Inc. (196–197).

Implications for care-givers. Too often, care-givers don't articulate their views of young children. This is unfortunate, since articulating views helps clarify beliefs by making them open to discussion and examination. Even though care-givers don't state their beliefs, the beliefs become manifest in practice. What we do with the very young is a statement of our views of them. Care-givers must analyze their private views of children and, at the same time, determine other views they are willing to adopt as their own. Most important, all care-givers, through study, discussion, reading, and experiences must work out and synthesize their own views of children. These views must make sense, be defensible, and dignify the children entrusted to their care. Through such a process quality programs will result.

REASONS FOR THE CURRENT INTEREST IN THE VERY YOUNG

The study of young children is the fastest-growing area of early childhood education. As luck or timing would have it, you are studying and learning about this field at the height of its popularity. Interest in the education and care of very young children will remain strong over the next several decades. Baby boomers, upwardly mobile parents, and the ever-increasing belief that the early years are important years will all contribute to continuing fascination with the very young.

Children from birth to age four are a very "in" group. Early education topics are discussed more frequently and fervently than at any time in the history of education. How do infants learn? What should we teach them? What environments provide optimum growth? How can we prevent child abuse? How can we teach — and reach — very young children? How can parents, who are fascinated and frustrated with their children, become better parents? All of these are frequently asked and discussed questions.

The Importance of the Early Years for Learning

The 1960s ushered in a renewal of interest in research relating to young children. Many research studies focused on the importance of the early years for learning. Two of these studies are classic works and had a long-lasting influence on the field of early childhood education. They caused early childhood educators and parents to reconsider the role early learning plays in lifelong learning.

J. McVicker Hunt, a researcher and author, analyzed research and information relating to learning in animals, general learning theory, and computer programming. He concluded that "the assumptions that intelligence is fixed and that its development is predetermined by the genes are no longer tenable."[10] Hunt further observed that, based on the concept that intelligence is not fixed at birth, the advice parenting experts and early childhood educators gave to parents to let young children alone while they grow up was not in the best interest of children.

Benjamin Bloom, a noted educator and researcher, reached an equally remarkable and influential conclusion. He maintained that intelligence is a developing function and the stability of measured intelligence increases with age. Let's suppose that a person at age seventeen was given an intelligence test and scored 100. (An IQ of 100 is generally considered average.) Bloom said that 50 percent of the development of the measured intelligence takes place between conception and age four, about 30 percent takes place between ages four and eight, and 20 percent develops between ages eight and seventeen.[11]

Hunt's and Bloom's research helped focus attention on the years before school. The results have been far-reaching. Parent education programs have become very popular, especially programs that teach parents how to promote learning in young children. In addition, early childhood programs now provide curricula that emphasize early learning and cognitive stimulation, in addition to traditional play-oriented programs.

In summary, research and the application of research findings to early childhood programs contributes greatly to the public's knowledge of the early years. Research results help create interest in the very young. Research guides our thinking and helps us develop visions of good programs.

Babies have been rediscovered. Over the last decade, people have changed their minds about what babies are capable of doing. They are remarkably competent individuals who are capable of a wide range of behaviors. What are some behaviors this baby is capable of?

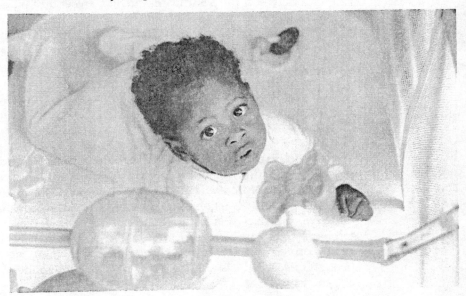

Without research, the world of children would not be the exciting, vibrant place it is.

Babies Rediscovered

Babies are "in." Parenthood is fashionable. In the last decade, research has revealed a great deal about babies' mental, physical, and emotional capacities. Previously, parents thought babies were human organisms waiting for development. Some parents believed that not too much happened in the mind of the infant. Maturation alone drove the infant to intelligence and learning. Babies were tender plants, parents the gardeners who protected them while they grew. This view was and remains a powerful force in early childhood education and parenting. Fortunately for parents and children, this view is changing. Now parents want to know about their babies before birth and are bombarding obstetricians, pediatricians, and child development experts with questions such as "What does my baby know?" and "How can I make sure my child will grow up smart?" These questions and many like them are prompted by the "rediscovery of babies."

What Do Babies Know? Because parents and professionals have been asking so many questions about babies, researchers are busy trying to find the answers. The overall results of much of the research are encouraging and enlightening. Studies reveal that infants are fascinating individuals who are much more competent than anyone suspected.

Some examples will help illustrate their capabilities. Babies can discriminate between different tastes such as sweet and bitter. Although babies seem to prefer a sweet taste, they will drink salty and bitter fluids. There have been tragic cases in which babies were fed formula made with salt instead of sugar. These mistakes usually resulted in death.

Babies at four days old can detect the odors of asafetida (a gummy substance with a strong garlic odor), lavender, and valerian (an herb with a strong odor). This olfactory ability is put to good use. When presented with the breast pad of the mother and the pads of other mothers, a baby will turn its head toward the mother's pad, indicating a preference for her odor.

How do researchers discover what babies know? The modern technology of 16 mm film, videotapes, and computers makes answering such questions easier. Microanalysis of data regarding how infants react reveals what they know. Reactions are measured by increases and decreases in heart rate, pupilary dilation, eye movement, and respiratory rate. Two researchers, for example, used sound film to record interactions resulting from "conversations" between mothers and their newborn babies.[12] Through microanalysis of each frame of film, they found that babies move

Parent→Interaction———→Baby   **FIGURE 1-1**
                              Limited View of Care-giver–Infant Interaction

Parent→Interaction———→Baby   **FIGURE 1-2**
Parent←Interaction←———Baby   **Expanded View of Care-giver–Infant Interaction**

their bodies in correspondence to their mothers' speech. They labeled this interaction *synchronization*. This discovery has many implications for parenting and care-giving. Parents can stimulate responses in their babies by talking to them. Babies, in turn, are active participants in conversations by their behavioral response.

Such findings underscore the importance of the dyadic (two-person) interaction between baby and care-giver. Whereas we always thought that the interaction between baby and care-giver was like that depicted in Figure 1-1, we now see the interaction as that depicted in Figure 1-2.

Utilizing modern technology, researchers can probe further and further into the world of babies. William James (1842–1910), the philosopher and psychologist, said that the baby feels that all the world is one great booming, buzzing confusion. This is not true. Research and practice verify that babies are competent, capable individuals who exercise a great deal of influence over themselves and others. Continued research findings serve to fuel further interest in babies and whet the public's appetite for even more information.

Changing Parents

Significant changes are occurring in the attitudes, practices, life-styles, work habits, economic status, and expectations of parents and prospective parents. These changes influence attitudes about young children. They direct attention to topics and practices surrounding child rearing and education.

What are some of these changes? First, 55 percent of women over the age of sixteen are in the work force. This creates demand for child care and increasing interest in the effects child care has on children. Also, working parents are beginning to look to their employers to provide child care as an employment condition or supplement.

Second, couples are postponing having children in order to concentrate on their careers. When such upwardly mobile parents decide to have children, they are more affluent. They spend more on early education, designer clothes for infants, and upscale nurseries. Money creates interest and new programs. Joan Barnes of California was one of the first entrepreneurs to capitalize on parents' willingness to pay money to play with their children. Gymboree, a national, franchised program of play and movement activities for parents and children, was the result.

Third, child-rearing is becoming more goal-directed. As many young professional parents combine career and child-rearing, they are more demanding of the services provided for their children. They want the best. This, in turn, encourages the creation and maintenance of high-quality programs. Just as parents have plans for their careers, so too do they plan for their children's careers. Parents want to start early to assure success and advancement for their children.

These parents also want to make sure the time they spend with their children is time well spent. As these parents combine career and child rearing, they want quality child-care services for their children soon after the baby's birth. Twenty years ago, it was the exception rather than the rule for parents to leave their six-week-old infants in a child-care center. Since there was little demand, there were few programs. Today, the demand for good infant child care far exceeds the supply.

Fourth, primarily as a result of the high divorce rate, there are more single parents than ever before. Seventeen percent of all white children and 50 percent of all black children live with single parents.[13] Single parents need help with child rearing and child-care services.

Also, as a result of divorce and massive cuts in federal support for social services, poverty has been feminized. More women are falling below the federal poverty line of $11,000 for a family of four (1986 figures). This places more demands on social service agencies and at the same time creates more demand for low-cost child care.

The field of early childhood is changing because the life-styles, habits, and child-rearing attitudes of parents and families are changing. These changes in early childhood programs are for the better when children, parents, and child-care and early childhood professionals benefit. Changes bring increased attention and the need to improve practices and procedures.

SUMMARY

This chapter discussed some of the major reasons for interest in the very young and why there is more discussion today about children's welfare than at any other time in our history. It is likely that this interest will continue. Some of the topics discussed will fade into the background, but other topics as interesting and perhaps even more controversial will emerge to take their place. Others will remain in the forefront and continue to generate interest in young children. In particular, the further refinement and definition of the legal and ethical rights of children is one of the unexplored frontiers of early childhood.

The very young have entered center stage in the drama of life. The support cast of early childhood professionals, care-givers, and parents is working hard to assure that the show has a long run.

PROGRAM VIGNETTE

Park Road Baptist Church Child Development Center
Charlotte, North Carolina

It seems as though every mother in Charlotte wants to enroll her preschool child in Park Road Baptist Church's Child Development Program. The waiting list is so long it takes two years to get in. Marcia Orr, administrative assistant at Park Road, is quick to point out that "parents go to the doctor to see if they are pregnant and then they come to Park Road to get on the waiting list! We even have people call and say 'I'm thinking about having a baby, can I put my name on the waiting list?' We tell them they have to be pregnant before they can apply."

But Beatrice Taylor, director of Park Road Baptist, won't put parents' names on the waiting list until they have personally visited the program. "Parents have to see what our program is like and what they are getting themselves and their children into. They have to see if our program is right for them and what we do agrees with their child-rearing practices. A visit validates the program for parents. Parents have to see a program so it is more than something they just hear about from their friends. This way they see and experience what we do."

Karen Spieler, mother of nine-month-old Kathryn, enrolled the day she knew she was pregnant. "Even though I registered early I still didn't get Kathryn in until she was three months old. She had to stay with her grandmother. I really wanted her to go to Park Road. They have a low teacher-child ratio so they have more time to spend with the kids. There are three teachers to eight infants. They give them a lot of individual attention and it is a homelike atmosphere. I also like the way the program teaches the children. It is not just a baby-sitting service. The other day they took the two-year-olds across the street, bought fruit, and then came back and prepared it. They do a lot of very educational things that other programs might think you couldn't do with that young a child."

At Park Road there is a loving, caring atmosphere. "We work hard at being close to the children and the parents," says Virginia Milano, lead teacher in the infant program. "We give the infants a lot of individual attention. We're not a baby-sitting service and the parents appreciate that. We hold every child when they get a bottle. In some programs, a care-giver will just prop a baby up with a bottle, but we never do that. When children have difficulty going to sleep, we rub backs and rock them. We hold them when they cry so no child ever cries very long. We also keep the children out of their cribs as much as possible. They're usually only in their cribs when they are sleeping."

The close relationship with parents is evident at drop-off and pick-up time. When Anita Price comes to pick up Will, teacher Betty Williams spends about five minutes sharing events of the day. She tells Anita everything about Will and reviews his activity and health charts with her.

As Virginia Milano emphasizes, "We all want to keep on a good relationship with each parent and make them comfortable with our program. We talk to each parent as long as they want to talk about their child. We also try not to make parents jealous of our relationship with their children. We make a big fuss with the children when their parents come. We'll say, 'Look! Here is your mom! Let's give her a big hug!'"

Park Road's program begins at 7:45 A.M. and ends at 5:45 P.M. Sara and seven other infants, ages three to thirteen months, spend their day in a pleasantly arranged and decorated room. During this time they are provided with a full range of activities and services. Each infant has his or her "own" assigned crib. This is one of the features Kathryn's mother likes about Park Road. "A lot of day-care programs will enroll children on a daily basis and if your child is sick, they will put another child in her crib. Not here. I don't want other children sleeping in my child's crib."

Sara arrives at 8:00 A.M. and begins playing with three other infants who are also about a year old. Virginia has organized the room with an arrangement of manipulable toys, dolls, and books. She and the other staff members sit on the floor with the children and talk to them about what they are doing. Props such as toy telephones are used to encourage language development.

Sara spends about five minutes talking to Virginia. Teacher assistant Shirley Rice sits in a rocking chair and gives four-month-old Jonathan his bottle. Teacher aide Debbie Steadman sits on the floor and "reads" a cloth book to the older infants when they are finished playing with the toys. Five-month-old Brandon sleeps soundly in his crib while Virginia teaches the children a finger play, "Twinkle, Twinkle, Little Star." "These infants love to sing," Virginia points out. "They like the finger plays and they can put their index fingers together to make a star."

Adults and infants are happy and content. Virginia explains why. "This group doesn't fuss about playing together. They get along pretty well for being one year old. This age child usually wants to play independently, but these children play together without any trouble. We try to duplicate good home care and we play around with the infants just like you would if they were at home. They like it a lot. I think this is why they are so compatible."

Following a snack of fruit sticks and milk, Virginia and Debbie take six infants on a stroll. All Virginia has to say is, "Let's go for a walk" and six infants in a line crawl out the door to the strollers parked in the hall. It is a scene out of *Make Way for Ducklings*! With four children in one stroller and two in another they leave the center for the great outdoors.

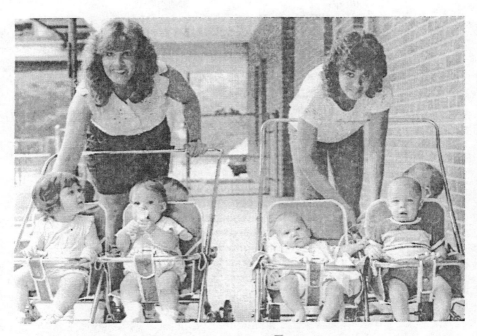

Outside activities are an important part of the Park Road curriculum. Here caregivers and children are preparing for a tour of the school grounds. What important benefits result from such experiences?

Virginia believes it is important to take children outside. "We try to go out every day it is fit to do so. The covered walkways of the church make it nice on rainy days. While the infants and toddlers don't leave the school grounds, the older children do because we believe that the school grounds, the neighborhood, and the community are learning environments. You can teach children just as much, if not more, outside a classroom as you can inside. We're constantly talking to the children about what they are seeing and hearing and where we are going."

Lunch is a family affair. While the younger infants hungrily suck their bottles, the older infants eat noodle soup and cheese sandwiches in their highchairs. After lunch, the children are put down for a nap. They usually sleep until 3:00 P.M. Nap time is followed by bottles, snacks, and play. Learning centers are arranged by the staff and are changed once or twice a week to provide novelty and toys appropriate to developing skills. Depending on how well the infants participate in the learning centers and the mood of the group, they may go for an afternoon walk. By 5:45 P.M. all infants have left for the day.

Children "graduate" from the infant room to the young toddler room at about thirteen months. The criteria for "graduation" are that the infants are able to walk by themselves to the playground and drink from a cup. Joann

Anderson teaches a group of five older toddlers between the ages of eighteen and twenty-four months. She is a gregarious woman who believes children learn best in an environment that promotes language development and independence. "I work hard on language development, because when a child can tell me his needs I can help more. I've had parents say to me, 'Joann, do you think children understand what you say to them?' and I say 'Yes.' They understand more than what we give them credit for. I'll say to Kathryn, 'Please go to the sink and get me a paper towel' and she's able to go and get it. I try to stimulate language development all the time. If Ryan comes up to me and points to something, I say, 'Tell me what you want.' He usually can tell me in a word or two. This group also loves books. I read to them every day. Reading is a great way to stimulate language."

Joann also supports the toddlers' quest for independence and accomplishment. "I let them do all they can for themselves. They like to use the abilities they have to accomplish things. I let Kathryn put on her shoes even if they are wrong. Later, I'll put her on my lap and change them around."

The other children's groups in the Park Road program in addition to the infants and young toddlers include older toddlers (eighteen to twenty-four months), young twos, two-and-a-half-year-olds, threes, fours, fives, and an "after school" group of up to age nine.

Park Road is unique for a number of reasons. First, the low teacher-child ratio permits individual and caring attention. This is the feature parents like most about the program. This low ratio is possible because the church subsidizes the program by donating space, utilities, and custodial services. The church supports the program as part of its service to the community.

Second, as Marcia Orr explains, "We have teachers who care and they are professional. At Park Road, we make child care an honorable profession by paying teachers decent wages and providing benefits. We feel it is an important job to take care of someone's child eight to ten hours a day."

Third, the care-givers believe parent and staff communication is essential. There are two formal parent-teacher conferences a year. Brown-bag lunches offer parents a chance to informally discuss the program and meet with child-rearing experts. Evening parent meetings provide an additional opportunity for parent involvement. One parent, happy about the evening programs, remarked, "I can't bring my daughter in or pick her up because of my work schedule. This way I have a chance to meet her teachers."

Fourth, everyone at Park Road has a positive attitude about providing the best program for each individual child. This philosophy is articulated very well by Betty Williams, teacher of the young toddlers. "I have goals for each one of my children. For example, when Ronnie came to me, he was shy and wouldn't mingle with the other children. I worked with him. When we were on the playground, I would hold him in my lap and encourage him to play with the others. Within two weeks he could leave me and go play. It's the same way for all children, regardless of how smart they are. You can do something for everyone."

With teachers like Virginia, Shirley, Debbie, Joann, and Betty, it is little wonder Park Road has a long waiting list. Parents are attracted to quality programs. Park Road has features that contribute to quality child care: a caring staff, a homelike atmosphere, parent involvement, and a low child-staff ratio.

ENRICHMENT THROUGH ACTIVITIES

1. Listed below are some beliefs people have about the very young. Read each belief statement and choose the one you agree with the most and place a 1 beside it. Place a 2 beside your second choice. Continue rating each belief. The view you agree with least should be rated 8.

Belief about Children	Rank
Miniature Adults: Children should be encouraged to dress, behave, and think like adults.	
Sinful: Children are prone to misbehavior and therefore need careful supervision and must be taught "right" behavior.	
Good: Children are basically good and are quite capable of controlling their own behavior. They learn best in an environment of freedom and choice.	
Blank Tablets: Children are born with generalized tendencies, but the environment and experiences really determine what they will become.	
Growing Plants: Children mature according to an innate timetable, and it is important to time learning activities with the "readiness" of children for learning.	
Property: Children are "owned" by their parents, who have a legal right to exercise control over them as they would anything else they own.	
Future Investments: Children are their parents' and a country's future hope. Investments in children will pay off in the future.	
Persons with Rights: Children have basic rights and these rights need to be upheld, enforced, and extended.	

2. Ask parents and early childhood educators about their views of the very young. How do their views differ from your own? What implications do your data have for parenting and child care?

3. List at least five social, political, and economic conditions of modern society and explain how these conditions influence how people view, treat, and care for the very young.

4. Use specific descriptions to illustrate how views discussed in this chapter influence care-giver practices.

5. Interview five professionals from the areas of early childhood education, pediatric nursing, social work, and child care. Collect the following information from each person:
   a) How do they define early childhood education?
   b) Why is knowledge of young children important in their job? Gather specific examples of how this information is used.
   c) What has on-the-job training taught them about young children?
   d) What topics do they recommend that early childhood students study before they graduate?
   e) Which model or models of child development discussed in this chapter do they use to guide their work and thinking?

   Analyze your data by occupation category. What implications do your data have for your study of the very young?

6. Interview parents who take their children to infant stimulation and awareness programs such as Gymboree (a national, franchised program of play and movement activities) to determine
   a) Why they take their children to such programs.
   b) The values and benefits of the programs for parents and their children.
   c) Parents' suggestions for improving such programs.

7. What reasons can you give to explain why middle-income parents are more inclined than low-income parents to send their children to a preschool?

8. List at least five significant contributions you believe good early childhood education programs can make in the lives of young children.

9. Over a period of several weeks or a month, collect articles from newspapers and popular magazines relating to infants, toddlers, and preschoolers and then
   a) Categorize these articles by topics, e.g., child abuse. What topics were given the most coverage? Why?
   b) What are the emerging topics or trends in early education, according to newspaper and magazine coverage?
   c) Do you agree with everything you read? Can you find instances in which information or advice may be inaccurate, inappropriate, or contradictory?

10. The emphasis on early education has prompted some critics and experts to charge that parents and early childhood educators are making children grow up too soon too fast.
   a) Interview parents and preschool teachers to determine their views on this topic.
   b) How do you agree or disagree with the data you gathered?

11. Recall your own childhood. Do you think your parents pushed you through childhood too quickly? Or did you have a relaxed, unhurried childhood?

12. Tell which model or models of child development presented in this chapter you agree with the most. Why?

ENRICHMENT THROUGH READING

Elkind, David. *The Hurried Child: Growing Up Too Fast Too Soon*. Reading, Mass.: Addison-Wesley, 1981.
> Elkind explores the current concern of many early childhood educators that parents and society are putting too much pressure on young children to grow up too soon too fast. Provides evidence on how parents and society hurry children and shows how children's fears of failure result in stress.

Postman, Neil. *The Disappearance of Childhood*. New York: Delacorte, 1982.
> Postman is one of the leading critics of making children miniature adults. He maintains that childhood is disappearing at a "dazzling speed." Most of the blame for the disappearance of childhood is placed on the electronic media. Television has opened the Pandora's Box of adulthood to children, and there are no more secrets. With no secrets, there is no childhood.

Raines, Shirley C., ed. *The Wesleyan Papers: Keeping the Child in Childhood*. Arlington, Va.: Eric Document Reproduction Services, 1983.
> These eight papers focus on the general theme of allowing children to have a childhood. The first paper urges educators to communicate their beliefs about young children and act on the principles of child development. The second points out how schools deprive children of childhood through such practices as excessive testing. The third paper urges educators to respect the rights of children in their quest to teach reading. The fourth, fifth, and sixth papers suggest ways to use television to enhance language development, discuss play as a strategy for learning, and provide suggestions for implementing Piaget's and Kohlberg's theories of moral development, respectively. The seventh paper stresses the importance of treating hearing-impaired children as children. The final paper discusses child advocacy and the goal of keeping the child in childhood. Informative and challenging reading.

Salkind, Neil J. *Theories of Human Development*. 2nd ed. New York: John Wiley, 1985.
> This readable and informative book expands on the views and theoretical ideas presented in this chapter. In particular, a chapter on Gesell merits reading; the next chapter, on ethology and sociobiology, stresses the role of biology in development.

Weber, Evelyn. *Ideas Influencing Early Childhood Education: A Theoretical Analysis*. New York: Teachers College Press, 1984.
> From Plato to Piaget, this book is about the ideas that have stimulated the thoughts, aroused the emotions, and shaped the ideas of generations of early childhood educators. The contributions of the philosophers and psychologists will enable readers to begin the important process of redefining and reconceptualizing their views of children and the profession.

White, Burton L.; Kaban, Barbara T.; and Attanucci, Jane S. *The Origins of Human Competence*. Lexington, Mass.: D.C. Heath, 1979.
> A very interesting and informative account of the interactive nature of the relationship between child-rearing practices, early experiences, and the development of abilities in the first three years of life. The authors are "convinced that much of the anxiety, stress, and ill feeling experienced by families raising young children is avoidable." This book tells why and how.

Zelizer, Viviana, A. *Pricing the Priceless Child: The Changing Social Value of Children.* New York: Basic Books, 1985.

The author traces the economic and sentimental value of children from the 1870s to the 1930s. She shows how children developed from economically valuable to economically "worthless" and emotionally priceless individuals. This transformation occurred, in part, as a result of the sentimentalizing of childhood. Child labor laws and compulsory schooling also helped make children economically nonproductive. This fascinating account of childhood examines in detail the cultural factors that have redefined the value of children in the United States. The last chapter explains how the current "death of childhood" is an indication that parents and some segments of society, such as the legal profession, are no longer willing to keep children economically nonproductive. There are many attempts — not always popular or successful — to return children to useful economic roles.

NOTES

1. Arnold Gesell, *Infancy and Human Growth* © 1928 by Gesell Institute of Human Development, New Haven, Ct.
2. Jacqueline Haines, Louise Bates Ames, and Clyde Gillespie, *The Gesell Preschool Test Manual* (Lumberville, Pa.: Modern Learning Press, 1980), 2.
3. J. B. Watson, *Behaviorism* (New York: Norton, 1925), 104.
4. B. F. Skinner, *Particulars of My Life* (New York: Knopf, 1976).
5. Albert Bandura, *Social Learning Theory* (Englewood Cliffs, N.J.: Prentice-Hall, 1977).
6. Bandura, *Social Learning Theory*, 22.
7. Mary Pulaski, *Understanding Piaget* (New York: Harper and Row, 1971), 6.
8. P. Richmond, *An Introduction to Piaget* (New York: Basic Books, 1969), 34.
9. Richmond, *Piaget*, 34.
10. J. McVicker Hunt, *Intelligence and Experience* Copyright © 1961, The Ronald Press Company. Reprinted by permission of John A. Wiley & Sons, Inc. (p. 363).
11. Benjamin S. Bloom, *Stability and Change in Human Characteristics* (New York: John Wiley, 1964), 88.
12. W. Condon and L. Sander, "Neonate Movement Is Synchronized with Adult Speech: Interactional Participation and Language Acquisition," *Science* 183 (1974): 99–101.
13. Arlene F. Saluter, "Marital Status and Living Arrangements: March 1983," in *Population Characteristics* Series P–20, no. 389 (Washington, D.C.: Bureau of the Census) (March 1983): 4.

Chapter 2

Who Are the Infants We Care For?

Questions to Guide Your Reading and Study

- What are the characteristics of normal physical growth and development during infancy?
- What can care-givers do to promote normal physical growth and development in infants?
- How do infants develop intellectually according to Jean Piaget's cognitive-developmental model?
- How can care-givers apply Piaget's model to child-care programs, homes, and preschools?
- What are the major theories of language development?
- What can care-givers do to promote language development in infants?
- How does social development occur in infants?
- How can care-givers promote social development in infants?
- How does personality develop in infants?
- What are the functions of attachment and bonding in social and personality development?
- Why is it important for care-givers to know about infant physical, social, emotional, and intellectual development?

INTRODUCTION

Infancy, the first year of life, is a time of new beginnings and significant firsts: the first breath, first smile, first word, and, at the end of the infancy period, first steps. All these "firsts" play an important role in normal growth and development. While the experiences, events, and maturation of infancy may not entirely *determine* the direction of development, they do *influence* later development. We must first learn about infants to provide quality care for them, and also to help us understand human beings. Just as life begins in infancy, our understanding of the very young begins with infants.

Although television and magazines encourage us to believe that infants are born into the world as miniature adults, this is not so. Many people think all infants are like those they see in magazine advertisements: cherubic, healthy, and dressed in designer clothes. Human infants are remarkably well developed at birth. They are competent and capable of many things, as we will learn. But, compared to other animals, children have to participate in many more processes of development to achieve their full potential.

PHYSICAL DEVELOPMENT

Developmentally, human infants are born "early." If all the development necessary for survival took place prenatally, babies would be too large to pass through their mothers' pelvic openings. The brain, for example, is only one fourth (23 percent) its adult size at birth, but it develops to about 80 percent of its adult size by age two. After age two the growth rate slows and development toward full adult brain size progresses at a much slower rate. Thus, much of human development takes place after birth. This explains why it takes years for growing children to become independent and able to care for themselves.

This prolonged period of dependency is one of the factors that makes humans unique among animals. The long period of dependency gives humans the time they need to develop to their fullest potential so they will be able to achieve remarkable things.

Further evidence that infants are not miniature adults is found in body proportions. Look closely at an infant. The infant looks out of proportion to the adult, as Figure 2-1 indicates. To achieve adult proportions, the developing infant will progress according to the 2-3-4-5 rule. The head will double in size, the trunk will triple in size, the arms will grow four times in length, and the legs will increase to five times their infant length. The numbers on Figure 2-1 indicate the number of times the size of an infant's body part must increase to reach adult size.

FIGURE 2-1
Relation of Infant-Adult Body Proportions

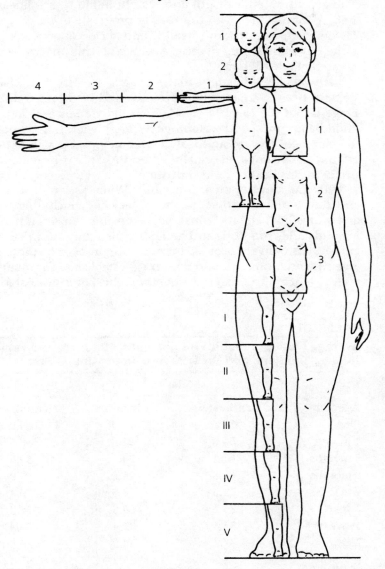

Source: From *Man in Structure and Function* by Fritz Kahn. Copyright 1943 by Fritz Kahn and renewed 1971 by Alfred A. Knopf, Inc. Reprinted by permission of the publisher.

Height and Weight

The growth rate for height and weight in humans is linear toward the genetic potential. That is, the rate is progressive, based on environmental factors such as nutrition, health, and socioeconomic status, and is determined by genetic inheritance. Average heights and weights for infants are given in Tables 2-1 and 2-2.

Always keep in mind that averages are just that. Height and weight depend on sex, genetic background, and environmental factors. The average is not the ideal toward which individuals develop; rather, it is the "middle ground" of development. Care-givers should not attempt to force development toward an ideal or become upset if a child does not develop toward the average, especially when the child is provided with the appropriate care, health, and nutrition. Care-giver concerns about normal growth and development are valid. When assessing this normal growth and development, however, the total child, including background, sex, and nutritional habits, must be taken into consideration. Good parenting and child-care skills and habits are also contributing factors. When parents and care-givers provide infants with proper nutrition, health care, and love, the environment and context is established for infants to reach their own potential. The result is development that is normal for them.

TABLE 2-1

Average (50th percentile) Height Norms for Male and Female Infants, Toddlers, and Preschoolers in the United States

Age	Males		Females	
	Centimeters	Inches	Centimeters	Inches
Birth	50.5	19.9	49.9	19.6
1 month	54.6	21.5	53.5	21.1
3 months	61.1	24.1	59.5	23.4
6 months	67.8	26.7	65.9	25.9
9 months	72.3	28.5	70.4	27.7
1 year	76.1	30.0	74.3	29.3
1½ years	82.4	32.4	80.9	31.9
2 years	87.6	34.5	86.5	34.1
2½ years	92.3	36.3	91.3	35.9
3 years	96.5	38.0	95.6	37.6
3½ years	99.1	39.0	97.9	38.5
4 years	102.9	40.5	101.6	40.0
4½ years	106.6	42.0	105.0	41.3
5 years	109.9	43.3	108.4	42.7

Source: P.V.V. Hamill et al., "Physical Growth: National Center for Health Statistics Percentiles," *The American Journal of Clinical Nutrition* 32 (1979): 607–629.

TABLE 2-2

Average (50th percentile) Weight Norms for Male and Female Infants, Toddlers, and Preschoolers in the United States

	Males		Females	
Age	Kilograms	Pounds	Kilograms	Pounds
Birth	3.27	7.21	3.23	7.12
1 month	4.29	9.46	3.98	8.77
3 months	5.98	13.18	5.40	11.90
6 months	7.85	17.30	7.21	15.89
9 months	9.18	20.24	8.56	18.87
1 year	10.15	22.38	9.53	21.01
1½ years	11.47	25.29	10.82	23.85
2 years	12.59	27.76	11.90	26.23
2½ years	13.67	30.14	12.93	28.45
3 years	14.69	32.39	13.93	30.71
3½ years	15.68	34.57	15.07	33.22
4 years	16.69	36.80	15.96	35.19
4½ years	17.69	39.00	16.81	36.98
5 years	18.67	41.16	17.66	38.94

Source: P.V.V. Hamill et al., "Physical Growth: National Center for Health Statistics Percentiles," *The American Journal of Clinical Nutrition* 32 (1979): 607–629.

A parent who discovers at a weekly infant-stimulation program that her daughter is smaller than the other infants should not conclude that the child is abnormal or that the parent has provided poor care. This is an area where care-givers can help. They can reinforce such parents when they give good care and provide all parents with information about good child-care and parenting skills.

For males, the average length at birth is 19.9 inches. At the end of one year the infant has grown 10.1 inches to 30 inches. Again, keep in mind that the figures in Table 2-1 are average and are intended as guidelines.

Table 2-2 indicates that average birth weight for females is 7.12 pounds. By six months, the infant has grown to 15.8 pounds, and by a year, to 21 pounds. Normal average infants should approximately double their birth weight by six months and triple it by one year.

Dental Development

Teeth are made of calcium phosphate and are much harder than bone. Development of the teeth brings about changes in the shape of the face by filling out the jaws and giving the baby an "older" look. It also means that infants join the rest of the human race in being able to chew their food.

The first tooth (lower incisor) emerges or erupts in the front of the lower jaw at about six months. The second tooth, also a lower incisor, erupts at seven months. Again, the average needs to be balanced by reality. Some babies are born with teeth, whereas others may take many more months than the average for the first tooth to emerge.

Humans have two sets of teeth. The first is the baby, "milk," or *deciduous* set. ("Deciduous" means "to fall out.") This set consists of twenty teeth. Most children have all their deciduous teeth by thirty to thirty-three months.

The second set of teeth is the permanent set. There are thirty-two permanent teeth. The first permanent tooth is the "six-year" molar, which can erupt when the child is between four-and-a-half and eight years old.

Motor Development

Motor development pervades all infant behavior, and accomplishments based on motor development contribute to intellectual development, as when the active child operates within the environment, and to social development, as when the infant attracts a parent or care-giver by smiling. Human development is inherently connected with motor development. It would be difficult to think of an area of development that does not involve some aspect of motor movement.

Although human motor development is not complete until adolescence, many of its important features are apparent in the developing infant. A knowledge of motor development milestones helps care-givers and parents provide experiences that will stimulate and promote motor development. Just as importantly, this knowledge enables care-givers to detect motor development lags, which may signal a need for the child to be evaluated further for a possible handicapping condition. Awareness of motor development also facilitates referrals to physicians and social service agencies, which can provide help and support to children with handicapping conditions and their families.

The following principles of motor development are helpful guidelines in understanding and caring for infants:

1. Motor development is sequential. The sequences of development for motor behaviors and skills are the same for all infants. This sequence is depicted in Table 2-3. Certain motor behaviors occur simultaneously, such as reaching for objects and rolling over, but infants cannot pull themselves to a standing position before they can sit with support.

2. The age ranges at which infants accomplish motor tasks vary from infant to infant. Table 2-3 shows the ages at which 90 percent of infants accomplish a task. The right-hand column shows the age ranges for accomplishing a task. Part of the variability in age ranges has to do with maturation, which is controlled by such factors as heredity, environment, and nutrition. Muscles, nerves, and the skeletal system must develop to the

TABLE 2-3

Motor Milestones of the First Year

Accomplishment	Age of Accomplishment for 90% of Infants	Age Range for Accomplishment
Chin up momentarily	3 weeks	Birth to 3 weeks
Follows to midline, eyes or head	5 weeks	Birth to 5 weeks
Arms, legs move equally	7 weeks	Birth to 7 weeks
Smiles responsively	2 months	Birth to 2 months
Head up 45°, 30 seconds	2½ months	Birth to 2½ months
Head up 90°, long time	3 months	5 weeks to 3 months
Sits with support	4 months	1½ to 4 months
Props self up on arms	4 months	2 to 4 months
Holds hands together	4 months	5 weeks to 4 months
Reaches for object	5 months	3 to 5 months
Smiles spontaneously	5 months	1½ to 5 months
Rolls over	5 months	2 to 5 months
Sits without support	8 months	5 to 8 months
Pulls self to stand	10 months	6 to 10 months
Stands holding on	10 months	5 to 10 months
Gets to sitting by self	11 months	6 to 11 months
Inferior pincer grasp	11 months	7 to 11 months
Walks holding on to furniture	13 months	7½ to 13 months

Source: N. Bayley, *Bayley Scales of Infant Development* (New York: Psychological Corporation, 1969). W.K. Frankenburg et al., "The Newly Abbreviated and Revised Denver
Developmental Screening Test," *The Journal of Pediatrics*, vol. 99, no. 3 (December 1981):
995–999.

point where a particular motor activity is possible. In addition to maturation, opportunity for practice is also a factor. An infant who is mature
enough and whose environment and care-giver encourage development
may accomplish a skill at an earlier age than a child who is less
advantaged.

3. Maturation of the motor system proceeds from gross activities to fine
motor coordination. When learning to reach for objects, for example, the
infant sweeps toward an object with his or her whole arm. Gradually, this
gross reaching behavior is replaced by a more specific reaching and grasping movement. The young infant, when given a new toy, expresses delight
by shaking all over, kicking legs, and waving arms. The older infant, on
the other hand, expresses pleasure over a new toy by smiling and
reaching.

4. Motor development, like physical development, proceeds from the
head to the lower parts of the body. This is called *cephalocaudal* development, from the Greek *kephalē*, head, and the Latin *cauda*, tail. This principle

implies that the head is the most developed structure at birth and the feet the least. Infants hold their heads erect before they sit, and they sit before they walk.

5. Motor development and physical development proceed from the *proximal*, or central part of the body, to the *distal*, or parts of the body at the extremities. Consequently, infants control arm movements before they control digital or finger movements.

Head Control. Developing control over the whole head takes about four to six months. When you consider how large the head is in relation to the rest of the body, it is remarkable that infants gain control over the head as quickly as they do. In a prone position at one month, infants can briefly hold their heads up, but they quickly lower them. At three months, infants can hold their heads and chests up at a forty-five-degree angle for about half a minute. By four months, infants can hold their heads and chests at a right angle off the floor indefinitely. At six months, they can hold their heads erect and turn them by using the shoulders and upper trunk.

When the infant is lying in the supine position (on the back) and moves her head or has it moved from one side or the other, her body will arch away from the side to which the head is turned. At the same time, the arm on the side to which the head is turned extends and the other arm flexes toward the ear. This is frequently referred to as the "fencing position" and is the result of the asymmetrical tonic neck response, which usually lasts until about three months. This reflex may help with early looking, reaching, and learning to use one side of the body separately from the other. This reflex also prevents the infant from rolling over.

Implications for care-givers. Care-givers should (1) provide infants with opportunities to be on their stomachs as well as their backs, and (2) when infants are in the crib or on the floor, place stimulating objects to the side to accommodate the infant's asymmetrical tonic neck reflex.

Smiling. What a wonderful thing a smile is. Everyone likes to smile and have someone smile in return. First smiles are reflexive. At two months, most babies smile responsively when someone talks to them. At five months, the infant smiles at the sight and sound of others. This spontaneous smiling encourages interaction on the part of parent or care-giver and lays the foundation for social interaction.

Crawling and Creeping. Between four and seven months, infants can hold their heads and chests up off the floor. They are still not able to get their stomachs off the floor, but they use their arms to pull and legs to push. This results in the form of locomotion known as *crawling*.

Creeping begins between nine and eleven months. This is possible when infants can support themselves on their hands and knees. *Creeping* occurs by alternating arm and leg movements. This is infants' preferred method of movement even during the beginning-to-walk stage, which is

Creeping is one of the motor milestones of infancy and major locomotion achievements for children. How does creeping influence a child's cognitive and social development?

not too far in the developmental future once creeping begins. Creeping enables infants to cover large areas at a pace that care-givers often find hard to match.

Vision

Where would we be without vision, our primary sense? We use vision more than any other sense and it plays a predominant role in our lives. At birth, infants can track the movement of people and objects with their eyes, but the focus of vision in the newborn is fixed at about seven-and-a-half to eight inches, so they do not see much detail in their environment. Parents almost instinctively hold their faces this close to babies when talking with them.

Visual acuity, the ability to distinguish clearly near and far objects, ranges from 20/150 to 20/400 in the newborn, depending on the method used to test their vision. Visual acuity at four months is about 20/200, at one year about 20/50; normal vision, or 20/20, develops at eighteen months to two years.[1] (When we describe normal visual acuity at 20/20, we mean that a person can clearly see at 20 feet certain letters on the Snellen Letter Chart, the chart you have your vision checked with in the doctor's office. When someone has vision of 20/150, that means she is able to see clearly at 20 feet what a person with 20/20 vision could see clearly at 150 feet.)

Table 2-4 summarizes the visual characteristics of the newborn.

Infants prefer to look at or attend to complex stimuli. The human face fits this criterion. In turn, babies' eyes and faces have a strong attraction for others. Parents say they have a strong interest in looking at their babies.

TABLE 2-4

Characteristics of Newborn Vision

Characteristic	Definition	Degree of Development in Infants
Acuity	Clarity of vision at a specific distance	Infants can clearly define the edges of one-eighth- and one-sixteenth-inch stripes at 9 inches and 12 inches, respectively.
Fixation	Ability to direct eyes at same point in space for a specific amount of time	Newborns have binocular fixation and convergence; can fixate 4–10 seconds and refixate every 1.0 to 1.5 seconds.
Discrimination	Demonstrated preference for particular sizes, shapes, colors, or patterns	Newborns can discriminate between large and small pictures of the same thing and between colors of medium, high, and dim intensity.
Conjugation	Ability of the eyes to move together	Adult and newborn conjugation differ only in how often refixation is required and how far the eyes travel before refixing the object on the center of the retina.
Scanning	Ability to move over the visual field and focus on the most satisfying image	Newborns search or scan the visual field, settling on the most desirable element of the stimulus. They prefer areas of sharp, dark-light contrast.
Accommodation	Adjustment of the eye for distance	Before one month of age, the infant cannot adjust to changes in focal distance. Median focal distance for the newborn is about 8 inches. At 4 months, ability to adjust is at the adult level.

Source: Susan M. Ludington-Hoe, "What Can Newborns Really See?" *American Journal of Nursing,* vol. 83 (September 1983): 1288.

Most parents try to hold their babies so they have direct eye contact. Parents' fascination with babies' faces in turn satisfies infants' desires to look at complex stimuli.

Many experts believe that when newborn babies look at the human face, they do not see all the features of the face, such as the nose and mouth, but attend more to the outline. At about two months, infants begin to see internal facial features such as eyes, nose, and mouth. Two researchers, however, report that infants one hour old can copy adults sticking out their tongues.[2]

Implications for care-givers. Susan Ludington-Hoe, founder of the Infant Stimulation Education Association, has these suggestions for how care-givers can use infants' visual abilities to help them see all they are capable of seeing:

1. Make mobiles that have a variety of shapes in black and white and medium-intensity colors. Place the mobile low enough so that the infant can touch it with his or her hands and feet.
2. Give infants ample opportunity to look around. Prop up infants with pillows so they can see. Place toys in the crib. Make sure infants can see beyond their cribs.
3. Change infants' scenery every few weeks, including the ceiling. For the ceiling, use a checkerboard, followed by a drawing of a human face and then concentric black and white circles.
4. Place stimulating objects within infants' range of vision. Use mirrors and objects such as silver decorations that reflect light.
5. Rotate the infant's bed.
6. Put small amounts of food coloring in infants' bath water.
7. Don't overdo the stimulation. Care-givers should spend time stimulating infants, but when they have signaled that they have had enough by turning away, shutting their eyes, or becoming fussy, the stimulation should be reduced or stopped. It is better to stimulate moderately and consistently than to give the infant occasional bursts of excessive stimulation.[3]

Hearing

The sense of hearing is rather well developed at birth. Newborn infants seem to prefer the human voice — especially their mothers' — to other sounds. The implications for parents and care-givers are clear. Talk, talk, talk to babies and infants. Since infants prefer the human voice, this should be the primary means of auditory stimulation. In addition, auditory stimulation also aids in language development.

A summary of infants' perceptual abilities is shown in Table 2-5.

INTELLECTUAL DEVELOPMENT

Piaget and Cognitive Development

In Chapter 1, you read about Jean Piaget and his theory of cognitive development. His theory is the standard in discussions of infant intellectual development. Piaget's theory was known in Europe long before it became popular and widely applied in the United States. During the last thirty years researchers all over the world have refined his theory. Educators are constantly seeking ways to apply his ideas to parenting, preschool settings, and elementary classrooms.

Piaget was trained as a biologist, and many of his ideas have their basis in biological theory. Biological theory suggests, for example, that the phys-

TABLE 2-5

Developmental Landmarks in Infant Perception

Age	Capability
Neonatal period	Sound-vision-motor linkages — indicated by turning head and eyes toward sounds Tracks movement of objects and people Discriminates mother's smell from smell of others
1 month	Recognizes different speech sounds
2 months	Has two-color vision Begins to respond to relationships among parts — not just the parts themselves
3 months	Has binocular vision and peripheral vision Recognizes mother's face from a photograph Hears and imitates a variety of high- and low-pitched sounds
4 months	Links mother's voice with her face and the sounds of a familiar object with the actual object Discriminates mother's and father's voices from a stranger's Discriminates between objects in upright and nonupright positions Discriminates between flat pictures and three-dimensional objects
5 to 6 months	Discriminates different nonupright positions — such as upside down from sideways
6 months	Discriminates mother's face from that of a stranger. Achieves size constancy
6½ months	Prewired visual-motor system is activated to aid in depth perception as infants begin crawling
8 to 10 months	Achieves shape constancy
10 to 12 months	Recognizes objects by touch — without looking at them Discriminates by touch between familiar and new objects in the dark

Source: From *Child Development and Relationships* by Carol Flake-Hobson. Copyright © 1983 by Newbery Awards Records, Inc. Reprinted by permission of Random House, Inc.

ical structure of an organism changes and adapts to environmental conditions and circumstances. Piaget believed the same process helps promote intellectual development. He used the term *scheme* for the cognitive structures or units of knowledge that change and adapt as a result of experiences and maturation.

The first schemes are the *sensorimotor schemes.* At birth, infants do not know that there are objects in the world. Also, according to Piaget, infants do not have internalized thought processes or "thoughts of the mind." Rather, infants come to know their world by acting on it through their senses and motor actions.

Infants *construct* (as opposed to absorbing) schemes using their innate sensorimotor reflexive actions. Sucking is an innate sensorimotor scheme. This scheme involves turning the head to the source of nourishment, closing the lips around the nipple, sucking, and swallowing. All these actions are the behavioral manifestations of the sucking scheme. As an infant matures, and in conjunction with sucking experiences, this basic sensorimotor scheme *adapts* to include anticipatory sucking movements and nonnutritive sucking such as sucking the pacifier or blanket.

New schemes are constructed or created through the processes of *assimilation* and *accommodation*. Piaget believed children are active constructors of intelligence, assimilating or taking in new experiences and accommodating or changing existing schemes to fit new information. He thought that infants are constantly in quest of *equilibrium*. Equilibrium is a balance between assimilation and accommodation, between new experiences and old ideas, between what the world is really like and a person's view of the world. In this sense, humans are programmed to develop their intelligence through active involvement in the environment.

Sensorimotor schemes help infants learn new ways of interacting with the world. These new ways of interacting promote cognitive development. One infant sensorimotor scheme, for example, is grasping. At birth, the grasping reflex consists of closing the fingers around an object placed in the hand. Through experiences and maturation, this basic reflexive grasping action becomes coordinated with looking, opening the hand, retracting the fingers, and grasping. In this sense, the scheme develops from a pure reflexive action to an intentional grasping action. As the infant matures, and in response to experiences, the grasping scheme is combined with a releasing scheme, which leads to a purpose such as the delightful activity of grasping and releasing things.

Infants begin life with only reflexive motor actions. These are used to satisfy biological needs. By using these reflexive actions on the environment and in response to specific environmental conditions, however, the reflexive actions are modified and *adaptations* to the environment occur. Patterns of adaptive behavior are used to initiate more activity, which leads to more adaptive behavior, which in turn leads to more schemes.

Infants are not capable of engaging in reflective action, mentally representing and manipulating objects. The first stages of intellectual growth occur through the senses and innate reflexive actions. As the infant continually engages in reflexive action, behavior becomes more predictable. The baby demonstrates incidents of "knowing" how to do certain things. The first sensorimotor actions become the basis for later *adaptive* behaviors, which are more organized. The reflexive motor action of sucking is adapted to many instances of nonnutritive sucking through which the neonate explores objects. In this way, a scheme or model is developed about the objects sucked. These early schemes are the foundation for cognitive development. The neonate builds a foundation on which the accomplishments of the infant are built. Accomplishments accumulate from one stage of in-

TABLE 2-6

Stages of Sensorimotor Development During Infancy and Toddlerhood

Stage	Age	Cognitive Development and Behavior
I. Reflexive action	Birth to 1 month	1. Infant engages in the reflexive actions of sucking, grasping, crying, rooting, and swallowing. 2. Reflexes are modified and become more efficient as a result of experiences, e.g., infant learns how much sucking is required to result in nourishment. 3. Reflexive schemes become adaptive to the environment. 4. Little or no tolerance for frustration or delayed gratification.
II. Primary circular reactions	1 to 4 months	1. Acquired adaptations are formed. 2. Reflexive actions are gradually replaced by voluntary actions. 3. Beginning of understanding of causality, evidenced when infant tries to repeat action that prompted response from caregiver. 4. Circular reactions result in modification of existing schemes.
III. Secondary circular reactions	4 to 8 months	1. Infants increase responses to people and objects. 2. Intentional activities increase. Infant able to initiate activities. 3. Beginning of object permanency.
IV. Coordination of secondary schemes	8 to 12 months	1. Increased deliberation and purposefulness in responding to people and objects. 2. First clear signs of developing intelligence. 3. Continued development of object permanency. 4. Actively searches for hidden objects. 5. Comprehends meanings of simple words.
V. Experimentation (tertiary circular reactions)	12 to 18 months	1. Active experimentation begins, as evidenced through trial and error. 2. Toddler spends much time "experimenting" with objects to see what happens. Toddler is literally "a little scientist." Insatiable curiosity. 3. Toddler differentiates self from objects. 4. Realizes that "out of sight" is not "out of reach." 5. Can find hidden objects in first location hidden. 6. Beginning of understanding of space, time, and causality of spatial and temporal relationships.
VI. Representational intelligence (intention of means)	18 to 24 months	1. Mental combinations evidenced by thinking before doing. Development of cause-effect relationships. 2. Representational intelligence begins. That is, the toddler is able to mentally represent objects. 3. Engages in imitative behavior, which is increasingly symbolic. 4. Beginnings of sense of time. 5. Aware of object permanence regardless of the number of invisible placements. 6. Searches for an object in several places. 7. Egocentric in thought and behavior.

tellectual development to another. In this way, the actions and scheme development of the neonate help give meaning and order to environmental objects, people, and events.

Stages of Cognitive Development

The sensorimotor stage of intellectual development consists of six stages, as shown in Table 2-6.

Stage I. During this stage, infants suck and grasp everything. They are literally ruled by reflexive action and are not in control of their behavior. Through the practice of these reflexive actions, however, infants assimilate, accommodate, and build schemes. During this stage, an infant cannot perform a mental act; rather, all acts take place through the basic reflexive actions. Freedom from complete dependence on reflexive actions comes with maturation and development of schemes. Reflexive responses to objects are undifferentiated and infants respond the same way to everything. Objects are assimilated through reflexive actions and infants accommodate to the environment as a result of experiences with objects.

During this stage, infants are totally self-centered and do not differentiate between themselves and the external world. Indeed, infants are not "aware" that external objects exist, but treat them as part of themselves.

Implications for care-givers. Because infants must create their own intelligence by interacting with the environment, it is important for care-givers to provide many objects to suck, feel, grasp, and look at. Piaget believed that activity and the child's quest for equilibrium between the old and new, the known and the unknown, fuel the process of intellectual development

Infants explore their world through their senses and reflexive actions. They literally suck and grasp everything. Why is it important for infants to have opportunities to have objects in their environment to suck, feel, grasp, and look at?

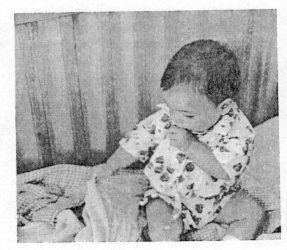

through assimilation and accommodation. Consequently, a rich social and physical environment plays a major role in intellectual development by creating disequilibrium.

A rich social environment depends in part on how care-givers and parents interact with infants. Care-givers are the best toys infants have, and there is no substitute for an attentive care-giver. There is no substitute for spending time with infants. Infants need positive and stimulating human environments.

Although Piaget believed the environment plays a role in development, the environment alone does not determine intelligence. The active child in an enriched environment assimilates and accommodates. Care-givers have to provide for, encourage, and be a part of this interaction. Meeting infants' basic trust needs is also important, since they will accommodate more in an environment they can trust. (See Table 1-1.)

Stage II. The milestone of this stage is the modification of the reflexive actions of Stage I. Sensorimotor behaviors not previously present in the infant begin to appear: habitual thumb sucking (which indicates hand-mouth coordination) and tracking of moving objects with the eyes and moving the head toward sounds (which indicate the beginnings of the recognition of causality). Infants begin to direct their own behavior rather than being totally dependent on reflexive actions. The first steps of intellectual development have begun.

Primary circular reactions begin during Stage II. A circular response occurs when an infant's actions cause a reaction in the infant or another person that prompts the infant to try to repeat the original action. The circular reaction is similar to a stimulus-response cause-and-effect relationship.

Piaget classified three kinds of circular reactions: primary, secondary, and tertiary. The *primary circular reaction* characteristic of Stage II is indicated when infants use their bodies to initiate and repeat many actions such as thumb sucking, leg kicking, and staring at the hands for extended periods of time because of the pleasure it brings. These reactions are called "primary" because they are reactions involving the infant's own body. An infant's behavior, by chance or accident, leads to a pleasurable or interesting result. The infant attempts to repeat the action. When the sequence is repeated a number of times, the behavior becomes habit.

Implications for care-givers. Care-givers can continue to provide many interesting and varied activities that provide a context for the infant to grasp, manipulate, and look. Crib mobiles and objects hung within the infant's reach promote and support eye-object and eye-hand coordination. Speaking, singing, and playing records promote aural stimulation. Infants can be held or placed so they can look at sources of sound.

Stage III. Piaget called this stage the stage of "making interesting things last." Infants manipulate objects, which indicates the ability to coordinate vision and the tactile senses. An infant reproduces events with *intention* or with the purpose of sustaining and repeating acts. These actions become goal directed and the infant repeats acts that are interesting to him or her.

The intellectual milestone of this stage is the beginning of *object permanence.* When infants in Stages I and II cannot see an object, it literally does not exist for them. It is a case of "out of sight, out of mind." During the later part of Stage III, however, there is a growing awareness that when things are out of sight they do not cease to exist.

Secondary circular reactions begin during this stage. These reactions are characterized by the infants' repeating an action with the purpose of getting the same response from an object or person. They will repeatedly shake a rattle, for example, in order to repeat the sound. Repetitiveness is a characteristic of all circular reactions. The name "secondary" implies that the reaction is elicited from a secondary source rather than from the infant. The infant interacts with people and objects to make interesting sights, sounds, and events last. When the infant is given an object, he or she will explore it using all available schemes, such as mouthing, hitting, and banging. Should one of these schemes produce an interesting result, the infant will continue using the scheme to elicit the same response. This explains why Piaget gave this stage its name. Imitation becomes increasingly intentional as a means of prolonging an interest.

Implications for care-givers. Care-givers can continue to provide objects for infants to grasp and manipulate. Place objects on strings or elastic and hang them over the crib and play area at the infants' level so they can strike them and participate in repetitive actions. Provide materials and activities that permit the infant to repeat actions. Activities that involve imitation are also good. Vocalization games are simple, effective activities in which the care-giver verbalizes and performs actions, the infant responds, and the care-giver, in turn, responds to the infant.

Stage IV. During this stage, the infant uses means to attain ends. Infants move objects out of the way (means) to get another object (end). The shape and size of objects become stabilized concepts for the infant. Infants begin to search for hidden objects, although not always in the places hidden, which indicates a growing understanding of object permanence. Infants become aware that objects cause actions.

Implications for care-givers. Care-givers can play hide-and-seek games with infants by hiding objects under a blanket or diaper. Provide activities that encourage ends and means, such as push and pull toys. Placing a pillow in front of an object the infant wants, for example, will encourage the infant to crawl around the pillow or move it to get the object.

Stage V. This stage marks the beginning of truly intelligent behavior and is the climax of the sensorimotor period. Physically, it is also the beginning of the toddler stage with the commencement of walking. The toddler is capable of a great deal of coordinated behavior involving the arms, legs, and hands. This physical mobility, combined with the growing ability and desire to "experiment" with objects, makes for fascinating and frustrating child rearing. At this stage, toddlers seem to be into everything. They are excited explorers, determined to touch, see, and feel everything. Although some early childhood professionals once used the term "terrible twos" to describe this stage, we now know that there is nothing terrible about toddlers exploring their environment as a means of developing intelligence.

During this stage awareness of object permanence continues to grow, as evidenced by toddlers searching for objects in the *last* place they were hidden.

Tertiary circular reactions are characteristic of this stage. Novelty is interesting for its own sake, and the toddler will experiment in many different ways with a given object. A toddler may use many items — a wood mallet, a block, a rhythm band instrument — to hammer the pegs in a pound-a-peg toy.

Implications for care-givers. Care-givers and parents must child-proof the environment so toddlers can explore and experiment in a safe environment. Quite often, care-givers want to restrict toddlers so they cannot get in or to anything. It is appropriate to restrict on certain occasions, but an active child in a well-prepared environment is the goal toward which care-givers should direct their planning. Toddlers cannot fulfill their tendency to be explorers and experimenters in an overly restricted and sterile environment.

Water and sand play activities help toddlers experiment with a variety of materials. Care-givers should continue playing hide-and-seek games and provide materials such as push-pull toys and jack-in-the-boxes that provide action and demonstrate cause-effect relationships.

Stage VI. This is the stage of transition from sensorimotor thought to symbolic thought. Toddlers' behavior is characterized by improved memory, which enables them to try out new actions that they have seen others do. This is not always welcomed by parents, who sometimes wish their toddlers would not repeat what they have seen others do.

During this stage, toddlers can solve problems internally, without depending on sensorimotor actions. Thus, they are liberated from sensorimotor action as the *only* means of intellectual development. The continued construction of representational thought enables toddlers to search for and find hidden objects they have not seen someone hide. Since toddlers can now "think" using mental representations involving mental images and memories, they can engage in "pretend" activities.

Implications for care-givers. Care-givers can provide many props for dress-up, pretend-play, and make-believe activities. These activities encourage and promote language development, which accelerates rapidly during this stage. Songs, finger plays, and movement activities encourage toddlers to mentally represent actions. Also, care-givers need to provide dolls, stuffed animals, trucks, cars, and small sets of building blocks or construction sets to encourage pretend activities, which strengthen mental representations.

Important Concepts

In summary, there are several important concepts to keep in your developing scheme about infants' intellectual development.

1. The ages of the sensorimotor stage are only approximate. Care-givers should avoid treating the age ranges Piaget specified for the stages of intellectual development as though they were etched in stone. The behavior and developmental progress children demonstrate gives a clearer understanding of their intellectual development. Sensorimotor schemes are internal and are manifested in the actions of the infant. These schemes are in infants' heads but operate and are observable through sensorimotor actions. This explains why Piaget named the first stage of intellectual development "sensorimotor."

2. Infants do not "think" like adults. They know their world by acting or operating on it with action-based schemes such as sucking, grasping, pulling, shaking, listening, and looking. Infants think as they move and observe objects and people.

3. Infants, like all humans, are actively involved in developing or *constructing* their own intelligence. Activity plays an important role in intellectual development. As infants act, they are stimulated mentally, which leads to the development of schemes. Infants' primary way of learning about the world is by interacting in and with it. Sensorimotor involvement establishes a foundation for future learning. Consequently, physical handicaps that restrict the child from being actively involved in the environment have implications for learning as well as for parenting and child-care practices. Care-givers must bring activities to handicapped infants, adapt activities to their ability levels, and make special efforts to see that they are not excluded in any way from appropriate activities.

4. Parents and care-givers need to provide the environment and opportunity for infants to use their reflexive actions, which are modified during the first weeks of life. This is especially important since, as we have discussed, these are two important conditions for intellectual development. Reflexive actions form the basis for assimilation and accommodation, enabling the development of cognitive structures. Infants construct the world of objects through their experiences with it. Care-givers must

assure that infants have experiences that will enable them to do a good job of intellectual construction.

5. At birth, infants do not know that there are objects in the world, and, in this sense, have no knowledge of the external world. They do not and cannot differentiate between who they are and the external world. For all practical purposes, the infant *is* the world. All external objects are acted on through sucking, grasping, and looking. It is precisely this acting on the world that enables infants to construct schemes of the world.

6. The concept of causality, or cause and effect, does not exist at birth. An infant's concept of causality begins to evolve only through acting on the environment.

7. As infants and toddlers develop from one stage of intellectual development to another, the previous stage is not replaced by the new. Rather, later stages develop out of earlier ones. Schemes developed in Stage I are incorporated into and improved on by the schemes constructed in Stage II. So it is with all stages of intellectual development.

Unlike the child Gesell describes (Chapter 1), who is biologically driven to "mature," the child Piaget describes is driven by physical and mental activity. The implications for parenting and care giving are clear. The neonate and infant need many and varied opportunities to act on objects and interact with people because the development of intelligence is dependent on the mental actions that these behaviors promote.

LANGUAGE DEVELOPMENT

Have you ever thought about the consequences of a life without language? What would happen in a child-care or preschool program without language? We are so accustomed to language that we take for granted its function and use in our daily lives. We also take for granted the process by which language develops.

Language is the most remarkable of human abilities. It helps define our humanness and sets us apart from all other species. Only humans communicate with language. No other event in the developmental process, with the possible exception of walking, is as eagerly awaited by parents as an infant's first word. With language, children become new and different persons, fully capable of interacting with parents and care-givers in ways considered truly human. Language is a common denominator between child and care-giver, student and teacher, and parent and care-giver. Language and its use is a yardstick of success and achievement. How well children learn and use language determines in large measure their success in school and life. Much that happens to the infant, toddler, and preschooler depends on language. Life and language are fundamentally entwined.

What Is Language?

Language has these essential features:

1. Language is a system of agreements about what particular sounds and words mean. Users of the English language agree that the word "book" means a volume of printed pages bound along one edge. Without such arbitrary agreements chaos would result.
2. Language is a system of sounds. We call this system of sounds "speech." Speech is the way we express ideas and emotions. Sometimes people use language and speech as synonymous terms, but speech is a subset of the process of language.
3. Language includes the processes of *encoding* (speaking and writing) and *decoding* (listening and reading). Much of language development involves deriving meanings from words. Meanings are important in oral language development. When children enter school, deriving meaning from the written word plays a major role in their lives. Self-image and future success depend on how well this task is accomplished.
4. Language is patterned and orderly. This orderliness results from the application of grammar, the rules of language usage. In the English language, adjectives usually come before nouns, and tense governs agreement of subject and verb. All languages have this orderliness.

These four features define language and distinguish it from other means of communication. Language and communication are not synonymous, although they sometimes are used in that manner. This confusion results in discussions about whether or not apes and dogs can talk and if they have the same capacity for language as humans. Animal communication is quite different from human language. By the same token, other forms of communication, such as sign language, nonverbal communication, and body language, are frequently labeled "language." These are all effective means of communication.

How Does Language Develop?

Behaviorism. There is universal agreement that the majority of children develop language, but authorities disagree about *how* children develop language. A traditional theory of language development uses *behaviorism* and *learning theory* to explain the process. This theory maintains that language is acquired through associations formed as a result of stimuli and responses. Language is learned because parents and the environment reward children for their efforts at language production. Parents, for example, reward children for their first sounds by constantly talking to children and making sounds in response to children's sounds. First words are treated the same way, with parents and care-givers constantly praising and encouraging. So it is with the rest of language development, including first sentences, correct pronunciation, and grammar.

Imitation plays a major role in behaviorist learning theory. Children imitate the sounds, sentences, and grammatical patterns they hear modeled by other children and adults. After repeated imitations, children have literally learned the language.

Behaviorist ideas help explain much of what humans do. Nevertheless, the behaviorist approach to language development is too simplistic and fails to adequately explain, by itself, the marvelous process of language acquisition. The behaviorist view, for example, cannot account for *generativity* and *novelty*, two characteristics of all users of language. Generativity is the ability of children to generate words and sentences without first having heard or purposely learned them. Think what language would be like if all the words and sentences you used had to be learned first through a process of reinforcement! What would life be like in a child-care program if children only learned words and sentences you rewarded? What would your language be like if you could only speak those words, phrases, and sentences taught you by others?

Consider also the novelty factor. You have the ability to generate a sentence that no one but you ever said. Consider the following sentence, for example: Teaching is caring. I have never seen this sentence before, yet I wrote it. It is new or novel for me. Everyone has this ability to create new sentences. Behaviorist learning theory by itself cannot explain generativity and novelty regardless of how tempting it is to believe otherwise.

Researchers are continually extending the horizons of our understanding of the precise process of language development. Although we don't know all we would like to know, and much remains beyond our current ability to comprehend, the current view of language development suggests that heredity, biology, maturation, the environment, and social interactions are all influential.

Heredity. Heredity plays a role in the development of language in a number of ways. First, humans are born with a brain that makes language possible. The left hemisphere of the brain is the center for speech and phonetic analysis. This hemisphere is the main language center of the brain, although it has other functions as well, such as helping us process time concepts. The left hemisphere does not have exclusive responsibility for language processes. The right hemisphere plays a major role in our understanding of the intonations of speech by which we distinguish the differences between declarative, imperative, and interrogative sentences. Nevertheless, the major language processing occurs in the left hemisphere. Without a brain that enables us to process, language as we know it would be impossible.

Second, some scholars theorize that the ability itself to learn language is innate and hereditary. Collectively, such theories are said to belong to the "innatist" or "nativist" school of language development. A major proponent of innatist theories is Noam Chomsky (b. 1928), a linguist and political activist. Chomsky takes exception to the behaviorist view of language acquisition. Although he recognizes that reinforcement plays some role in language development, he believes humans have within them an internal mechanism for language acquisition. He hypothesizes that children have an innate *language acquisition device*, or LAD, which helps them naturally learn language. Children receive the raw materials of language, such as sounds and general grammatical rules, from their parents and caregivers. These are processed into language through the LAD. The LAD is a "fixed nucleus" that consists of the propensity to learn language. This entails learning vowel and consonant sounds; learning basic syntactic structures common to all languages such as sentence structure and noun-verb agreement; and such factors as infants' preference for the human voice.

The existence of a LAD seems plausible and helps explain in an understandable way how language develops. One caveat is in order when discussing the LAD theory, however. So far, no research data confirm the existence of such an innate language learning device.

Biological Propensity. Eric Lenneberg (1921–1975), a biologist, believed that language acquisition develops according to biological schedules that appear when the time is right or as a result of maturation. According to Lenneberg, language development occurs in a definite sequence and on a definite time schedule. Children are biologically programed to learn language. He states:

> All the evidence suggests that the capacities for speech production and related aspects of language acquisition develop according to built-in biological schedules. They appear when the time is ripe and not until then, when a state of what I have called "resonance" exists. The child somehow becomes "excited," in phase with the environment, so that the sounds he hears and has been hearing all along suddenly acquire a peculiar prominence. The change is like the establishment of new sensitivities. He becomes aware in a new way, selecting certain parts of the total auditory input for attention, ignoring others.[4]

The best time for language learning would be during these sensitive periods, which Lenneberg believed exist between the ages of two and twelve. He maintained that

> language cannot begin to develop until a certain level of physical maturation and growth has been attained. Between the ages of two and three years language emerges by an interaction of maturation and self-programed learning. Between the ages of three and the early teens the possibility for primary language acquisition continues to be good; the individual appears to be most sensitive to stimuli at this time and to preserve some innate flexibility for the organization of brain functions to carry out the complex integration of subpro-

cesses necessary for the smooth elaboration of speech and language. After puberty, the ability for self-organization and adjustment to the psychological demands of verbal behavior quickly declines.[5]

The idea of a biological propensity for language learning and sensitive periods makes sense. The idea of sensitive periods has been recognized and utilized by great educators. Maria Montessori (1870–1952), the renowned early childhood educator, based her system of educating young children in part on sensitive periods for learning. A sensitive period, according to Montessori, is a genetically programed period of time when a child is better able to master a task than at any other time. She describes a sensitive period as "a special sensibility which a creature acquires in its infantile state, while it is still in the process of evolution. It is a transient disposition and limited to the acquisition of a particular trait. Once this trait or characteristic has been acquired, the special sensitivity disappears."[6]

The concept of the sensitive period played a major role in Montessori's educational philosophy. She believed all children are possessed with an *absorbent mind* that enables them to literally absorb sounds, words, grammar, and sentence structure from the environment. The first sensitive period for learning language begins at birth and lasts until about three years. During this time, the infant unconsciously absorbs language from the environment. The second sensitive period for language development begins at three years of age and lasts until about six years. During this time the preschooler is a conscious, active participant in language development and spends a great deal of time happily learning how to use his or her newly acquired power of communication.

Montessori believed so strongly in the innate ability of children to develop language prior to entering first grade that she said of their language-learning abilities, "all this happens without a teacher. It is a spontaneous acquisition. And we, after he has done all this by himself, send him to school and offer as a great treat, to teach him the alphabet!"[7]

An important implication of the concepts of sensitive periods and the absorbent mind is for parents and care-givers to create an environment for language development early in life, during its most rapid period of growth.

Environmental Influences. Finally, social interactions and environmental settings contribute to language development. To learn language, the child must hear language, be stimulated to produce language, and be provided an environment that supports language use.

Susan Curtiss's account of Genie, a modern-day "wild child," is graphic in its account of what happens when parents deprive a child of the opportunity to learn language. Her father isolated Genie in a small room from the time she was two until she was thirteen. She spent her days harnessed to a potty seat and her nights in a sleeping bag that restrained her movements. During this time she had minimal human contact; her father and brother barked at her like dogs instead of using human language. Genie did not have a chance to learn language until she was thirteen years and seven months old. At this time social workers discovered her and began language and social therapy. The effects of language deprivation on Genie's language development were devastating. Even after prolonged treatment and care, Genie remained basically language deficient. Curtiss described her this way: "Genie fails to acknowledge questions, statements, requests, summonses, and so forth, much of the time. She can, of course, and does at times acknowledge communication addressed to her (especially if the topic holds some special interest to her). Genie very often acts as if she had not been spoken to, however. In fact, Genie's appropriate sociolinguistic behavior is extremely limited."[8]

Genie remained "conversationally incompetent." Curtiss summarizes by saying, "It is not surprising, I think, that Genie displays incompetence in this area. Her failure to perform many of the behaviors requisite for successful interaction is probably a result of her social and psychological deprivation."[9]

Social Interactions. Care-givers and parents play major roles in the development of language by being conversational partners with infants. Care-giver-child interactions can precipitate many rich and rewarding conversations. The key is to treat babies as human beings who are capable of participating in the process of language.

Catherine Snow and her colleagues conducted a cross-cultural study of English and Dutch mothers to determine how mothers' ideas about child-rearing affect their interaction with their babies. One very interesting conclusion underscores the nature of the care-giver/infant conversational process. Mothers who believe their babies are potential communicative partners talk to them in ways that serve both to strengthen that belief and make it come true. The fact that the mother talks in predictable ways about recurrent events undoubtedly helps the child to structure his or her world, segment events, distinguish different types of activities, and anticipate future events.[10]

Two very common activities involving infants and parents encourage communication. First, infant behaviors such as smiling, laughing, burping, sneezing, coughing, vocalizing, and looking intently at something prompt mothers to converse with babies. In these cases, the baby's behaviors act as the initiators of conversation.

Second, care-givers communicate with their babies when they interact with them in some way, such as picking them up, putting them down, giving toys, checking their diapers, or taking something away. Care-givers who converse with their babies as partners also treat them as partners in the actions, not as unresponsive objects.

Game playing that involves turn taking and has a beginning and ending provides a context for conversational episodes between parents and

TABLE 2-7

Games Played by Mothers and Their Babies at 3 and 6 Months

Age	Games
3 months	
Tickling	Playing kicking games
Lifting baby in air	Facial imitation
Jiggling baby's feet	Showing baby self in mirror
Stretching, moving baby's limbs	
6 months	
Lifting baby in air	Blowing on stomach
Looking and approaching	Showing baby self in mirror
Tickling and poking	Vocalization: "a-e-i-o-u"
Bouncing	Playing "catch" with soft object or ball
Pulling to sit and stand	Patty-cake
Peek-a-boo	Tug-of-war

Source: Adapted from Catherine Snow et al., "Talking and Playing with Babies: The Role of Ideologies of Child Rearing," (Table 5, Chapter 13) in *Before Speech: The Beginning of Interpersonal Communication,* ed. Margaret Bullowa (London: Cambridge University Press, 1979), 282.

babies. Table 2-7 illustrates the types of games most frequently played by mothers with their babies.

Implications for care-givers. Care-givers must believe that children are individuals who are capable of being involved in conversation. How you view children makes a difference in how you talk to them. If you view them as unresponsive objects, interaction will not be spontaneous and interactive. The conversation will be one-way rather than two-way. The care-giver will also tend to ignore infants' contributions to the process.

Infants exhibit a range of behaviors that promote the "conversation process." Care-givers who are in tune with their infants respond to them as a means of promoting conversation. Care-givers must respond sensitively to a baby's visual, aural, and physical signals.

"Conversations" or interactions between infants and their care-givers are the building blocks for language development. Good care-givers use every opportunity to converse with their infants. The best stimulator of cognitive and language development is the caring, attentive, interactive primary care-giver. Toys or media are no substitute for a responsive care-giver.

When working with young children, care-givers must be aware that there are several kinds of communication and language. Humans express (send) and receive language. Examples of *expressive language* include crying, vocal sounds (such as whimpering and humming), body language, sign language, and speaking. *Receptive language* takes the form of listening (receiving), responding, and understanding. Care-givers can help infants learn to receive and express language.

Normal child-care routines provide excellent opportunities to engage in social interactions and conversations with infants. Such encounters, however, should not be limited only to these times. Follow these guidelines:

1. Always use the infant's name in conversation. This personalizes the encounter and helps the infant build a self-identity.
2. All encounters with infants should involve conversation. For example:

> Come, precious Patte, it is bath time. Miss Marcia has your bath water ready. First, let's take off these clothes. You help me do it. That's right, first this leg then the next. Oh! You really like to kick when your diaper is off, don't you? Now let's enjoy this nice warm bath water. It's been so hot this morning a nice bath will relax you. My goodness! It looks like your nails need attention again. I'll take care of that when you're sleeping.
>
> Okay, Patte, that's enough splashing for today! I can tell your arms and legs are getting stronger by the way you splash the water. Let's dry off now. This towel is extra soft just for you. I got a sample of a new softener, and it really works. The label said it's nonallergic and won't irritate your skin. It's important for my precious to have a soft towel!
>
> You like this lotion, don't you, Patte? It makes you smell nice. You like me to rub your body with it. I can tell by the way you're kicking. Let's do something different with your hair. Yesterday you looked like a Kewpie doll. How would you like to look a little "punky" today? I'll just brush your hair back like this. Oh that looks cute! We'll see what your mom thinks of it when she comes. She'll probably say you look different. I think she's going to prefer it au naturel!

3. Resist the temptation to avoid talking to infants simply because they don't talk to you. Infants are very responsive individuals and will be responsive to your conversation as you engage them in it. Child-care workers sometimes say they feel "foolish" and "embarrassed" about talking to babies when they began caring for them. Later, when they see the benefits that accrue to babies and to themselves as care-givers, they feel quite natural with the conversational process. Remember that in interactions with infants, care-givers provide all the conversation. Infants can and do communicate nonverbally, but they need to develop their conversational roles with the help of linguistically competent role models.
4. Use a variety of means and situations to promote language. Read books and sing songs to infants. Play records of songs and stories. Take infants on trips both inside and outside the home or center. Use these occasions to talk with the infants and comment on what they are doing and seeing.
5. Respond verbally with enthusiasm and praise to the infant's accom-

plishments and behaviors. Accomplishments and actions are a ready-made context for verbal interchanges. In addition, your responses make the child feel good and contribute to a positive self-image.

There is a great deal of interest in the social contexts in which children learn language. Heredity and biology may program children's language development, but they don't learn in a vacuum or entirely on their own. Children learn language with the assistance of others and within a context of mutual support and encouragement.

The Emergence of Language

Language development is stage-related. The rate of development through these stages varies for individual children, but the stages apply to all children, regardless of culture. There are literally hundreds of languages (some estimates range as high as three thousand) used by different cultures in the world. Children of one culture master the same language patterns as children from another culture who speak a different language. This universal sequence of language development occurs in spite of different environments and child-rearing patterns. This sameness of language development is one of the reasons given as evidence for the innateness of language development.

Table 2-8 illustrates receptive and expressive language and its *normal* development in infants.

Crying. Language development begins at birth with the infant's first cry. Crying represents the first form of communication between child and care-giver. Although crying cannot be called language, it is a prespeech vocalization and is important for the beginning of language. Crying is common in infants, especially the newborn, who may cry from 7 to 22 percent of the time.

Peter Wolff, a researcher and psychologist, analyzed cries of babies and found there are distinct phases of a cry.[11] These are a short cry, a rest period, intake of breath, another rest, and another short cry. The amount of time between the phases distinguishes one cry from the other. Cries of infants have different meanings, as most parents know. Wolff identifies three kinds of cries: the basic cry that signals hunger, an angry cry, and a pain cry.

Care-givers must not consider crying a negative act and should avoid responding to it in negative ways. Crying is a signal that merits response. The care-giver should respond to crying and investigate the conditions that may cause it. Wolff found that inexperienced mothers responded differently to the cries of babies than did experienced mothers. Experienced mothers, for example, responded to the hunger cry by also checking for a wet diaper, and they tended to ignore the hunger cry if the baby had just been fed.

TABLE 2-8

Language Development in Infants

Age	Receptive	Expressive
Birth	Startle reflex	Crying
1½ months		Social smile
3 months		Cooing
4 months	Orients to voice	
5 months	Orients to bell (looks to side)	"Ah-goo" Razzing
6 months		Babbling
7 months	Orients to bell (looks to side, then up)	"Da-da" and "ma-ma" (used inappropriately)
8 months		
9 months	Gestures	"Da-da" and "ma-ma" (used appropriately)
10 months	Orients to bell (turns directly toward bell)	
11 months		One word
12 months	One-step command (with gestures)	Two words

Source: Arnold J. Capute and Pasquale J. Accardo, "Linguistic and Auditory Milestones During the First Two Years of Life: A Language Inventory for the Practitioner," *Clinical Pediatrics*, vol. 17, no. 11 (November 1978): 847–853. Reprinted by permission of J. B. Lippincott Company, Pennsylvania.

Smiling. The social smile infants develop in the second month is a powerful signal and serves to attract attention and promote social interaction with the care-giver. In this sense, smiling is a form of communication. It promotes reciprocal communication — usually speech in the care-giver — and consequently plays a role in language development.

Cooing. Cooing is a positive, noncrying vocalization. Cooing is usually pleasant, a sign that the infant is not distressed. Cooing can be stimulated by social interaction, speech, and toys.

Babbling. Babbling is a combination of consonant and vowel combinations repeated over and over again, such as "babababababababa." Babbling helps strengthen the tongue, throat, and lips. Care-givers may respond to infants by repeating the babbling sounds as a sign of approval and to develop a sense of conversation between infant and care-giver. At this stage, it is the attention and reinforcement that count as much as the actual conversation. Imitating the cooing and babbling of infants is a good game to play with them, one that care-givers derive pleasure from, also.

"Ma-ma" and "Da-da." "Ma-ma" and "da-da" are sounds that are natural and easy for infants to make. All infants make these sounds, regardless of culture, although these parental names are common in many cultures and languages, including French and Japanese.[12] Infants make many sounds not needed in the language being learned. Through hearing, use, and reinforcement over time, only those sounds used in the language are retained.

First Word. At about one year, the time of the infant's birthday, the first word is spoken and the symbolic functioning of words begins. Words are essentially labels for things, and infants need help in the labeling process. Care-givers can help in several ways. First, they can verbally label objects through naming and conversation. For example, say to the infant, "Here is your cup. The cup is red. Can you say 'cup'?" Second, words that describe action are learned best when accompanied by the action. The word "drink," for example, is learned best using the word when the infant is drinking. "I bet Hector wants a drink! Let's drink from your cup. You like to drink from the cup, don't you?"

From the first cries at birth, the infant begins the process of language development. Language is one of the most essential of human abilities. All care-givers must do all they can to empower infants, toddlers, and preschoolers with the ability to learn and use language to its fullest. This empowerment begins in the first year of life.

SOCIAL AND EMOTIONAL DEVELOPMENT
Social Behaviors

Social relationships begin at birth and are evident in the daily interactions between infant and care-giver. Infants are social beings with a repertoire of behaviors they use to initiate and facilitate social interactions. *Social behaviors* are used by people to begin and maintain a relationship with others. Regardless of their temperament, all infants are capable of social interactions and benefit from interactions with others.

Crying is the neonate's primary social behavior. It attracts the caregivers and promotes a social interaction of some type and duration, depending on the skill and awareness of the particular care-giver. Crying has a survival value. It alerts care-givers to the presence and needs of the infant. However, merely meeting the basic needs of infants in a perfunctory manner is not sufficient to form a firm base for social development. Caregivers must react to infants with enthusiasm, attentiveness, and concern for them as unique *persons*.

Imitation is also a social behavior infants perform. They have the ability to mimic the facial expressions and gestures of adults. When a mother sticks out her tongue at a baby, after a few repetitions, the baby will also stick out its tongue. This imitative behavior is satisfying to the infant. The mother is also pleased by this interactive game. Since the imitative behavior is pleasant for both persons of the dyad, they continue to interact for the sake of interaction, which in turn promotes more social interaction. Social relations develop from social interactions.

Bonding and Attachment

Bonding and *attachment* play major roles in the development of social and emotional relationships. *Bonding* is the process by which parents or other care-givers become emotionally attached or bonded to infants. It is the development of a close, personal, affective relationship. *Attachment* is the emotional tie between the infant and the parents and other primary care-givers. It is "a unique relationship between two people that is specific and endures through time. Although it is difficult to define this enduring relationship operationally, . . . indicators of this attachment [include] behaviors such as fondling, kissing, cuddling, and prolonged gazing — behaviors that serve to both maintain contact and to exhibit affection toward a particular individual."[13]

As this quote indicates, attachment is a behavioral system or construct and is characterized in its early stages by sensory behaviors. Attachment, then, is that special relationship that exists between infant and care-giver, usually the mother. Lay persons frequently use the terms "attachment" and "bonding" interchangeably.

Attachment behaviors serve the purpose of getting and maintaining proximity. They form the basis for the enduring relationship of attachment. Care-giver attachment behaviors include kissing, fondling, caressing, holding, touching, embracing, making eye contact, and looking at the face. Infant attachment behaviors include crying, sucking, making eye contact, babbling, and general body movements. Later, when the infant is developmentally able, attachment behaviors include following, clinging, and calling.

Touching is the first physical encounter parents have with their children and is one of the principal means of developing attachment. Touching includes such contact as massaging and palmar stroking, which is a rubbing or massaging with the palms of the hands.

Baby massage is growing in popularity. Many towns across America have at least one program for helping parents — usually mothers — learn how to rub their babies the right way. Baby massage is not to be confused with the stereotypical pounding of flesh, grunting, and groaning seen in films and television. Rather, it entails stroking, gentle pressing, rubbing, and communicating through touch. Baby massage provides parents the opportunity to more fully enjoy their children. It is also a great way for hesitant parents to develop a closer relationship with their babies. Some parents and professionals think there are other benefits as well. They believe it stimulates the mind, improves alertness, helps develop other senses, and promotes general relaxation in infants. Most parents engage in some kind of massage while diapering and bathing their babies. Now,

Parents engage in many attachment behaviors, such as eye contact, with their babies. This mother delights in looking at her baby. She intuitively holds her face about 18 inches from her baby's. What other maternal behaviors are important for attachment?

however, instructors and books are teaching the fine art of massage to parents who want to get in touch with their babies.

Eye contact is also an important attachment behavior. Most new parents are visually attentive to their babies and hold them so they can have direct eye contact. Perhaps you have seen parents almost instinctively hold their faces about eight inches from their babies' faces. This distance is compatible with infants' limited range of vision.

Adult speech has a special fascination for infants. Interestingly enough, given the choice between listening to music or listening to the human voice, infants prefer the human voice. This preference for the human voice plays a role in attachment by making the baby more responsive to the care-giver. Infants attend to language patterns they will later imitate in their process of language development.

Babies move their bodies in rhythmic ways in response to the human voice. Babies' body movements and care-giver speech synchronize to each other. Care-giver speech triggers behavioral responses in the infant, which in turn stimulate responses in the care-giver, resulting in a "waltz" of attention and attachment. Ten years ago, researchers focused almost exclusively on the role of the mother in the attachment process. This view that the interaction is one way is no longer popular with early childhood educators, who now recognize that infants greatly influence the social interaction process by their behavior. Today, the focus in studying infant social development is on the care-giver–to–infant relationship, not on the individuals as separate entities.[14]

Multiple Attachments. Increased use of child-care programs inevitably raises questions concerning infant attachment. Parents are concerned that their children will not attach to them. Worse yet, they fear that their baby will develop an attachment bond with their care-giver rather than with them. They need not be so anxious. Research to date indicates that "both across cultures and within the broader culture in American society, children experiencing early day care form primary bonds with their parents, just as home-reared children do. Further, there is no evidence that day care 'dilutes' or 'weakens' attachment bonds that have been previously established."[15]

Care-givers and early childhood educators must realize that parents may need help in forming the primary bond with their children. Furthermore, the quality of the care-giving program, be it baby-sitting, family child-care at home, or a child-care center, should be high, so that parents will be supported in their roles as primary care-givers of their children.

Children can and do attach to more than one person, and there can be more than one attachment at a time. Infants attach to parents as the primary care-givers as well as to a surrogate. The latter attachments are not of equal value. Infants show a preference for the primary care-giver, usually the mother. Parents should not only engage in attachment behaviors with their infants, they should select child-care programs that employ care-givers who understand the importance of the care-giver's role and function in attachment.

It is natural and desirable for child-care workers to form attachments with infants. It is not at all uncommon for care-givers to have feelings of loss when "their" infants leave their care and go to the toddler room. One care-giver said, "I've gone home many nights and cried about losing my infants to another teacher." Better by far for a care-giver and infant to have a relationship that the care-giver can cry about when the attachment must physically and emotionally end than to have a care-giver indifferent to the importance of attachments and the need to let go.

Surrogate care-givers should handle the weaning of infants from their care with compassion, understanding, and concern for the well-being of all parties involved, especially the child. The transition from home to child-care setting can occur gradually, a little at a time over a period of time. Likewise, the transition from infant room to toddler program can be done a little at a time, with the infant spending an hour or two in the toddler room and then returning to the infant room. In this way, a gradual transition results with opportunities to create an attachment to the new care-giver while "breaking away" from the attached care-giver.

Good child-care programs help mothers maintain their primary attachments to their infants in many ways. The staff keeps parents well informed about infants' accomplishments. Parents should be allowed to "discover" and participate in infants' developmental milestones. A care-giver, for example, might tell a mother that today her son showed signs of wanting to take his first step by himself. The care-giver thereby allows the mother to be the first person to experience the joy of this accomplishment. The mother may then report to the center that her son took his first step at home the night before.

Some perceptive mothers initiate a supportive parent–care-giver relationship. One mother explained it this way: "Almost every morning I told the teachers at the child-care center that if my son did anything great during the day, such as say his first word or take his first step, not to tell me about it because I wanted to be the first to know."

The Quality of Attachment. The quality of infant-parent attachment varies according to the relationship that exists between them. A primary method of assessing the quality of parent-child attachment is the "Strange Situation" developed by Mary Ainsworth and her colleagues.[16] The Strange Situation consists of observing and recording children's reactions to several events: a novel situation, separation from their mothers, reunion with their mothers, and reactions to a stranger. Based on their reactions and behaviors in these situations, children are classified into one of three groups. These groups are illustrated in Table 2-9.

The importance of knowing and recognizing different classifications of attachment is that care-givers inform parents and help them engage in the specific behaviors that will promote the growth of secure attachments.

Stages of Attachment. John Bowlby, a pioneer in the articulation of attachment theory, proposes four phases or stages in the development of attachment, as shown in Table 2-10.

Bowlby believes that during Stage 1, infants use basic reflexive actions and crying to initiate interactions. During this stage the ability to discriminate one care-giver from another is absent and, according to Bowlby, it is the attention received that is important, not who provides it.

Importance of Attachment. We can talk about attachment all we want, but sooner or later we have to ask what purpose attachment serves. Attachment plays a role in the development of competence. As researcher L. Alan Sroufe so eloquently states,

> The infant who uses the care-giver as a base for moving out into the world, and as a haven when threatened or distressed, develops motor skills and a sense of himself as effective. In sharing his play with his care-giver at a distance, the infant evolves a new way of maintaining contact while operating independently. The infant is free to invest himself in challenging the environment because he is confident that he can maintain his tie with his care-giver even while he is widening his world.[17]

TABLE 2-9

Individual Differences in Attachment Behaviors

Attachment Classification	Behavioral Characteristics
Group A: Anxious-Avoidant	Avoids contact with mother after separation. Ignores attempts of mother to initiate interaction.
Group B: Secure	Presence of mother supports exploration and facilitates return to exploration after separation.
Group C: Anxious-Resistant	Resists contact with mother during reunion. Is not comforted by the presence of the mother after separation. Lack of exploration prior to separation.

Source: Mary Ainsworth et al., *Patterns of Attachment* (Hillsdale, N.J.: Erlbaum Associates, 1978).

Fathers and Attachment. Fathers are "in" in early childhood education. Many fathers have played important roles in child rearing and have engaged in shared and participatory parenting. Today, however, there is an increased emphasis on ways to encourage fathers to become even more involved in child rearing.

TABLE 2-10

Bowlby's Stages of Attachment

Stage	Age	Behavior
1	Birth to 8 weeks	Infant responds to and attends to any person—parent, care-giver — that is nearby. Looks at and listens to person(s).
2	8 weeks to 6 months	Infant discriminates between familiar people — parents and care-giver — and unfamiliar people. Is more responsive; smiles and vocalizes more to familiar people than to unfamiliar people.
3	6 months to the 2nd and 3rd year	Infant/toddler maintains contact or stays near attached person(s) — parent, care-giver — by creeping to, walking to, and following person(s). Also uses vocal signals — crying and words — to maintain contact.
4	3 years and older	Toddler or preschooler engages in the "formation of goal-corrected partnerships" with the attachment figures. Child plans how to get parents and care-givers to change their behavior to conform to child's wishes.

Source: John Bowlby, *Attachment* (New York: Basic Books, 1969): 266–267.

Fathers who feed, diaper, bathe, and engage in other care-giving activities demonstrate increased bonding behaviors such as holding, talking, and looking. Early childhood educators can encourage fathers to participate in all facets of care giving. Child-care programs can conduct training programs that will help fathers gain the skills and confidence they need to assume their rightful places as co-parents in rearing responsible children.

Michael Lamb, a leading authority on fathering and child development, maintains there is no biologically based sex difference in responsiveness to infants and that fathers can be as responsive to babies as mothers.[18] Nevertheless, custom and practice provide mothers with a larger role in child rearing, which necessitates the further encouragement of fathers to be involved in the parenting process.

Sensitive Periods for Attachment. Marshall Klaus and John Kennell, pediatricians and researchers,[19] popularized the "sensitive period" view of mother-infant bonding. According to the Kennell-Klaus theory, bonding of infant and mother occurs in the minutes and hours after birth through close skin contact. This view has popularized the concept of "love at first touch." It also encourages expectant parents to believe that if they don't have physical contact with their babies immediately after birth they will "fail to bond." This theory further maintains that failure to bond early results in a later breakdown in the mother-child relationship and may even contribute to parental child abuse.

Follow-up studies of the Kennell and Klaus research do not support their theory.[20] There is not universal agreement about the existence, length, and duration of a sensitive period for bonding, although fascination with and belief in early bonding remains strong. The early attachment theory has had a beneficial effect on childbirth and hospital maternity practices. This is reflected in an increase of natural childbirth practices, family-centered birth, and a general humanizing of childbirth practices.

The idea of early attachment has also promoted an increase in the popularity and practice of breast feeding, which is seen as one way of initiating and maintaining early contact. The return to breast feeding would seem, on the surface at least, to be a reaffirmation of Freudian theory (see Chapter 1), which emphasizes oral gratification. Freud believed that feeding promotes attachment and that when too many people feed an infant, he or she fails to attach and therefore fails to learn how to love.

Early parent-child contact is only one of many constellations of behaviors that influence attachment. Attachment is a developmental process that occurs over time and within a social environment. Factors involved include the quality and nature of the infant–care-giver relationship, basic nutrition and health care, the quality of the child-rearing environment, economic factors, and the time, opportunity, and desire for effective parent-child interaction. Although early contact is desirable and should be encouraged, the practice, by itself, is no substitute for effective parenting across the life cycle.

Good maternal care contributes to attachment. Such care is characterized by a quality of responsiveness and sensitivity to the infant as a person. Alan Sroufe offers the following advice about the care-giver's role in promoting attachment:

> Good maternal care involves responding to the infant's signals promptly and effectively. When during face-to-face interaction the infant turns his head away, signaling that he needs less stimulation, the sensitive care-giver relaxes and waits. Not until the baby signals his readiness does she reengage him. When the infant cries, the sensitive care-giver responds promptly, and effectively puts an end to the infant's distress. When the baby seeks contact, the sensitive care-giver responds warmly and affectionately, teaching the infant that his signals are effective. The sensitive care-giver provides smooth transitions and meshes her (or his) stimulation or assistance with the infant's behavior. She does not thrust interaction on an unresponsive infant. Sensitivity requires that the mother respond to the individual needs and nature of her infant. This is why sensitive care generally promotes healthy emotional development in vastly different babies.[21]

Temperament and Personality Development

Children are born with individual behavioral characteristics that, when considered as a collective whole, constitute temperament. This temperament, what the infant is like, helps determine his or her personality. The development of personality occurs as a result of the interplay of the particular temperament characteristics and the environment. The classic study undertaken to determine the relationship between temperament and personality development was conducted by Alexander Thomas, Stella Chess, and Herbert Birch.[22] They identified nine characteristics of temperament: level and extent of motor activity; rhythm and regularity of functions such as eating, sleeping, regulation, and wakefulness; degree of acceptance or rejection of a new person or experience; adaptability to changes in the environment; sensitivity to stimuli; intensity or energy level of responses; general mood, e.g., pleasant or cranky, friendly or unfriendly; distractibility from an activity; and attention span and persistence in an activity.

Thomas and his colleagues developed three classes or general types of children according to how these nine temperament characteristics clustered together. These types are the "easy" child, the "slow-to-warm-up" child, and the "difficult" child.

Easy children present few problems in care and training. They are positive in mood, regular in body functions, have a low or moderate intensity of reaction, and show adaptability and a positive approach to new situations.

Slow-to-warm-up children have a low activity level, are slow to adapt, withdraw from a first exposure to new stimuli, are somewhat negative in mood, and respond with a low intensity.

Difficult children are irregular in body functions, tense in their reactions, tend to withdraw from new stimuli, are slow to adapt to changes in the environment, and are generally negative in mood.

The interplay between temperament and environment plays a role in personality development. Consequently, care-givers need to consider the nature of this interaction for children in their care. Even the easy child who adapts readily to various child-rearing styles, for example, may have difficulty adapting to an authoritative-restrictive parenting style after having adapted to a laissez-faire style characterized by freedom and independence. Parents with a difficult child may intuitively treat the child in an authoritative, restrictive, and punitive manner. Nevertheless, as Thomas and his colleagues point out, "If parents are inconsistent, impatient, or punitive in their handling of the child, he is more likely to react negatively than other children are."[23]

One key to good child rearing with slow-to-warm-up children is to allow them to develop at their own pace. This does not mean leaving them alone to do whatever they want to do. They need encouragement and support — not pushing — to participate in new activities.

The importance of developing a match between children's temperament and the care-giver's child-rearing style cannot be overemphasized. This is particularly true in child-care programs. In this sense, parenting is a process that extends beyond the natural parents to include all those who care for and provide services to infants. It is reasonable to expect that all who are part of this parenting cluster will accommodate their behavior to take infants' basic temperaments into account.

Psychosocial Development

The first of Erikson's psychosocial stages, Basic Trust vs. Basic Mistrust, begins at birth and lasts until about one-and-a-half to two years. For Erikson, basic trust means that "one has learned to rely on the sameness and continuity of the outer providers, but also that one may trust oneself and the capacity of one's organs to cope with urges."[24] The key for children developing a pattern of trust or mistrust depends on the "sensitive care of the baby's individual needs and a firm sense of personal trustworthiness within the trusted framework of their culture's life-style."[25]

Basic trust occurs when children are reared in an environment of love, warmth, and support. An environment of trust also reduces the opportunity for conflict between child and care-giver. More will be said about the other stages of Erikson's theory in later chapters.

SUMMARY

Development in the first year results in many remarkable changes and accomplishments. What a joy and reward it is for care-givers to look back over the infant's first year through pictures and journals and smile with satisfaction and pride at all that has happened. A year is such a short period of time when measured by the rest of the human life span. Many of infancy's milestones are possible because of the interaction of infants with their care-givers.

Physical development and the accomplishment of physical tasks such as locomotion would not be possible without care-givers' physical nurturing, which maximizes positive environmental influences and minimizes detrimental ones. Developing cognitive abilities are supported by care-givers' interactions as infants begin with basic reflexive reactions, develop through Piaget's Stage IV (coordination of secondary schemes), and end their first year with clear signs of developmental intelligence. Socially, care-givers provide the supportive environments and interpersonal relationships that enable the infant to become trusting, confident, and ready to be gloriously independent.

Infants are interesting and remarkably competent individuals. As care-givers we cannot treat them with benign neglect. Rather, we must utilize all our wisdom, understanding, energy, and care so that we can look at the first year of all the children we care for and say, "I did my best — I helped make it happen."

PROGRAM VIGNETTE

Mount Carmel Child Care Center
Detroit, Michigan

The Mount Carmel Child Care Center, Detroit, Michigan, provides child care for 110 infants and toddlers, the children of employees of Mount Carmel Mercy Hospital.

The program is child- and parent-centered. "We try to be as flexible and accommodating to parents as we can," says Anne DeHann, the Center's director. "We are fortunate that the center is located close to the hospital. Ideally, all parents should have the option of child care so easily accessible to their work site. It takes only about two minutes to walk from the hospital to our Center. This allows us to operate a program that is flexible and accountable to parents' needs. A mother who is nursing her child may call and say, 'Try to hold off feeding my baby his bottle, I'll be right over to do it.' We are happy to meet that kind of request. We accommodate parents' opportunities to be with their children. There are times we can't do what they want, and when we can't they try to understand because we have a good working relationship."

Harriet Jo Midgett, head teacher of the infant program, is a firm believer in working closely with parents. As she points out, "By working with parents we make the program better for everyone. We want to support parents' child-rearing practices as much as possible. For example, we try to put the babies to sleep, the way the parents put them to sleep at home. In some centers they do it only their way, which may mean putting the baby in a crib and letting her put herself to sleep. If a mother puts her child to sleep by rocking him and patting him on the back then that is how we try to put him to sleep here."

The Mount Carmel staff believes in a developmental approach to child care. Although children are cared for in groups, they receive individual attention and developmentally appropriate activities. Lesson plans provide for individual developmental needs. "Simply because infants are in the same group does not mean that they all can or should do the same things," says Harriet Jo. "The teacher assistant and I write weekly lesson plans for the group. [See Figure 2-2.] We also write a weekly lesson plan with daily activities for each child. [See Figure 2-3.] We keep developmental records and daily records for each infant. This provides us with a basis for planning and for sharing information with the parents." (See Figures 2-4 and 2-5.)

The care-giving environment, room arrangements, and learning activities support the developmental nature of the program. The infant room, for children aged six weeks to a year, is organized into learning centers. Each center has materials with common learning properties. These learning centers are devoted to such subjects as toys that roll; soft, multitextured toys; and blocks. There is also a modified shelving unit that contains learning materials that change biweekly. One week the shelf may have pots and pans, two weeks later, large wooden puzzles. The first week the materials are out, the children basically just explore them. The second week, they begin to really manipulate the materials and solve problems with them.

Decisions about how and when children make the transition from the infant to the toddler program are also developmentally based. One child may move from the infant room (six weeks to twelve months) to the toddler room (one year to two years) as early as 11 months, whereas another infant may not make the transition until 18 months. Transition decisions are based on such things as frequency of attendance in the program, home background, parents' input, maturity of the infant, and developmental status. As Harriet Jo explains, "The majority of the developmental milestones for a one-year-old have to be in place before children are moved from the infant to the toddler room. I want to be able to explain to Anne, the program director, the basis for my decision recommending that a child be moved on to the toddler room."

Once the placement decision has been made, the transition is made as easy as possible for infants, parents, and care-givers. The staff discusses the placement decision with the parents and then determines how to handle the transition. Some children need little or no time and support to make the tran-

FIGURE 2-2
A Lesson Plan for the Week of the Opening of the Major-League Baseball Season

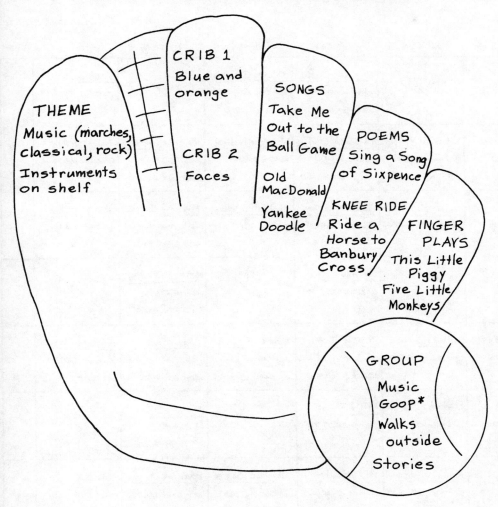

sition. For others, the transition must be made gradually, with infants spending part of their day in the infant room and part in the toddler room.

"There is a lot of two-way communication between staff members," says Harriet Jo. "I discuss with Sherry, the toddler teacher, facts about a child's development and temperament. We want the transition to be successful for everyone. This is just another part of our philosophy of helping children feel good about themselves."

---

* "Goop" refers to a mixture of cornstarch and water.

FIGURE 2-3
Week Plan of Daily Activities for Infants

Dates _Mar 31 – Apr 11_

Name and age	Monday	Tuesday	Wednesday	Thursday	Friday	Initials
Aaron 6 mo.		Pat-a-Cake *fine motor* *language*	Blow Bubbles *social emot.* *imitation*		Cushion Roll *gross motor*	
Andrew 4½ mo.	Sit with Help *gross motor*	This Little Piggy *language* *body awareness*	Water in Walker *sensory*	Whisper in Ears *language* *social emot.*	Rowboats *gross motor*	
Carrie 4½ mo.	Rowboats *gross motor*	Read Stories *social emot.* *language*	Shake Rattles *fine motor*	Pat-a-Cake *body awareness* *language*	Airplanes *gross motor*	
Chelsea 5½ mo.		Cushion Roll *gross motor*		Water in Walker *sensory* *social emot.*		
Jeffrey 5½ mo.	Pull to Stand *gross motor*	Music Time *auditory stim.* *cause & effect*	Knee Rides *language* *social emot.*	Stories *language* *social emot.*	Texture Toys *fine motor* *sensory*	
Katie 10½ mo.	Stories *language*	Fill & Dump *fine motor*		Water Play *sensory* *language*		
Kyle 9 mo.	Knee Rides *gross motor* *social emot.*	Pop N Pals *cause & effect* *object perm.*	Stroller Rides *social emot.*	Peek-a-boo *object perm.* *imitation*	Music *auditory stim.* *fine motor*	
Sam 11½ mo.	Crayons *fine motor* *cause & effect*	Music *language* *social emot.*	Stack Blocks *fine motor* *eye/hand coord.*	Help Push Stroller *gross motor* *self-esteem*	Goop *sensory*	

FIGURE 2-4
Infant Developmental Record

Name ___Joe_____   Date of birth ___11·12·85_____

COGNITIVE
Week 1. 3/1 watches toys
     2. 3/14 tracks
     3. 4/1 coos & plays w/voice
     4. 4/15 glance lingers where
     5.   object falls
     6.
     7.
     8.

SOCIAL/EMOTIONAL
Week 1. 3/1 predictable routine
     2. 3/14 smiles
     3. 4/1 recognizes familiar face
     4. 4/15 verbalizes for attention
     5.
     6.
     7.
     8.

GROSS MOTOR
Week 1. 3/1 lifts head up
     2. 3/14 lifts chest
     3. 4/1 rolls front to back
             back to front
     4. 4/15 sits alone briefly
     5.
     6.
     7.
     8.

FINE MOTOR
Week 1. 3/1 N/A
     2. 3/14 hands not in fists
     3. 4/1 holds toy briefly
     4. 4/15 explores toy, tries
             to hold own bottle
     5.
     6.
     7.
     8.

COMMENTS AND RECOMMENDATIONS:

FIGURE 2-5
Daily Infant Record

Name _Joe M._	Date _April 7, 1985_

ATE	7:00 ½ jar pears & cereal, 6 oz formula 10:00 6 oz juice 12:00 1 jar carrots, ½ fresh banana, 6 oz formula 3:00 6 oz formula
SLEPT	7:45 – 9:30 12:30 – 2:30
DIAPERED	7:30 wet 9:40 wet 11:30 wet & bm 2:45 wet
OTHER INFORMATION	Joe can start crackers, cheerios, and fresh banana.

In the Mount Carmel program, infants and toddlers are given many interesting things to play with in an environment designed to promote learning. Here, a young child is able to look through a shelf that separates learning centers. How can a child-care environment support a child's learning?

The following daily schedule of events and activities for four-month-old Nicholas Jefferson reflects the developmental and individualized care each child receives.

- 6:20 A.M. Amanda Jefferson, Nicholas's mother, brings him to the center in time to change his diaper and give him his morning bottle.
- 6:35. Harriet Jo involves Nicholas and two other infants in music activities. She ties bells around their wrists and they sing songs and use drums and rattles to make "music."
- 6:45. Nicholas is put in a play crib that has soft toys. Mobiles are hung so they move when Nicholas kicks or moves his arms.
- 7:10. Nicholas is held on Harriet Jo's lap while she feeds other infants. "I believe in involving the children in real-life events," explains Harriet Jo. "It is a good way to provide stimulation and involvement. So, as far as possible, I involve all the children in many activities we have to do such as caring for the children, cleaning up, going on errands within the building, and greeting visitors."
- 7:30. Nicholas has his diaper changed and is placed on the floor in the play area in front of a mirror while Harriet Jo changes other children's diapers. The play area floor contains a mattress that provides variety and a safe surface.

- 7:45. Harriet holds Nicholas and he falls asleep. He is placed in his own crib for his morning nap.
- 10:30. Nicholas wakes up, and Renee, an assistant teacher, changes him and gives him a bottle.
- 11:00. Nicholas is placed in the play area with some of the other children. Lori, an assistant teacher, plays with them, and they sing songs and read stories together.
- 11:30. Nicholas is put in a play crib while Harriet Jo changes diapers. She then changes Nicholas's diaper and bounces him to sleep. "Nicholas likes body contact, so I sometimes hold him while I'm doing other things and usually he goes to sleep this way."
- 1:30 P.M. Nicholas wakes up, Lori changes and feeds him.
- 1:45. Nicholas and other infants are put in strollers and are taken for a walk either inside or outside, depending on the weather.
- 2:15. Harriet Jo involves Nicholas in his individual daily activity based on his developmental growth and needs. Today, Harriet Jo uses texture toys to involve Nicholas in reaching, grasping, and sensory activities.
- 2:30. Nicholas has his diaper changed and goes to sleep while Harriet Jo rocks him.
- 3:45. Amanda comes to pick up Nicholas. She and Harriet Jo talk about Nicholas and his day. "Amanda is not an in-and-out mom," says Harriet Jo. "She is always anxious to talk about Nicholas. She usually asks me questions that relate to child rearing in general. I look forward to talking with her."

Unique Features of the Mount Carmel Program

A number of features and practices make Mount Carmel unique among child-care programs. First, "The program and curriculum are developmentally based," states Joan Lessen-Firestone, administrative supervisor of the Mount Carmel program. "We provide developmentally appropriate activities for all children in all areas — physical, social, emotional, and intellectual. In the intellectual area, our program is Piaget-based. All children — infants, toddlers, and pre-schoolers — are involved in open-ended activities and have a wide range of materials to explore and manipulate. Also, the children have choices of what they want to play with."

Second, the parent-involvement philosophy of the staff provides for a co-operative working relationship not often found in other programs. "Parents want to and should be involved," says Harriet Jo. "After all, if I left my child with someone, I would want to have some feeling of control over my child and the program."

Parents appreciate the close working relationship, too. According to Karen Falahee, "Having my daughter, Kate, cared for by Mount Carmel's Child Care Center staff has been a very positive and stimulating experience for both of us.

The staff has considered my needs as a new parent as well as my child's, and has encouraged my daily involvement in the program during my lunch hour. They follow my lead in determining Kate's schedules and recognizing her milestones and experiences. The very highly trained staff is caring and supportive and actively nurtures a cooperative, interactive relationship with each child's family."

Third, "Staff qualifications and teamwork are the keys to our success," states Anne DeHann, program director. "Teachers have bachelor degrees in early childhood education and the assistants have child-development training and experiences with young children. The staff is educated and knows how to plan and implement a program that is developmentally appropriate for young children. Teamwork exists at all levels, from within each classroom to the cooperation between the administrative supervisor and the director. We all work together to maintain a quality program for young children. When problems or concerns arise we handle them in a way which is professional, constructive, and growth-producing."

ENRICHMENT THROUGH ACTIVITIES

1. Do you think baby massage is a good idea? Would you take your baby to a class that taught parents how to massage their babies? If a parent asked you for your advice about attending such a program, what would you tell her?
2. Identify five key behaviors parents and care-givers should demonstrate toward infants aged between one and six months and between six and twelve months. Justify why you selected the behaviors. How do the behaviors differ between the two age groups?
3. List five ways in which babies are dependent on parents and care-givers.
   a) How can care-givers best meet these dependency needs?
   b) Does it make a difference how these dependency needs are met? If so, how?
   c) What advice would you give care-givers about how to meet these needs?
4. You have been asked to speak at the next meeting of the Parents' Preschool Association. Your topic is "Attachment and Its Role in Care-Giving." Develop an outline for your presentation.
5. Why are some parents better than others at developing attachment bonds with their children?
6. Interview parents, university professors, social workers, and child-care–givers to determine their ideas about how language develops. How are their views similar to or different from each other? Do their beliefs have any implications for child care?
7. Develop an argument for or against the following statement: "The period of infancy will not determine future child development, but will influence it."

8. If you were training a group of child-care workers, what would you tell them are their key roles in language development?
9. Do you think children are active participants in their language development? If not, why not? If so, how?
10. Write a paragraph supporting the following statement: "It is obvious that a child cannot learn language unless he or she is exposed to it."
11. Explain why it is important for child-care workers and other care-givers to have knowledge and information about normal growth and development. Defend your answer.
12. Identify at least five ways care-givers can meet the basic trust needs of infants.
13. Why is it important for care-givers to know about Piaget's theory of cognitive development? How can care-givers use this model to develop better programs for infants?
14. What features of the Mount Carmel Child Care Program do you most agree with? Would you want Harriet Jo Midgett and her colleagues to take care of your child? Why?
15. List five ways care-givers can support the physical development of infants.

ENRICHMENT THROUGH READING

Beck, Susan M. *Baby Talk: How Your Child Learns to Speak.* New York: New American Library, 1979.

Billed as a parent's guide to language development, this book provides background about how language develops and what care-givers can do to promote the language development process. Although the author has attempted to simplify her explanation of children's language, it is technical and tedious reading in places. A good first book to understand how children learn language.

Bloomgarden, Dave. *Stimulation Activities Age Birth to Five Years,* reprint no. 19. Washington, D.C.: Peace Corps, Information, Collection, and Exchange, 1983.

This is a collection of stimulation activities that encourage children's physical and mental growth. The activities were field tested with children in the Jamaican National Day Care Program. Emphasis is placed on activities that can be supported with low-cost or scrap materials.

Curtiss, Susan. *Genie: A Psycholinguistic Study of a Modern-Day "Wild Child."* New York: Academic Press, 1977.

This is an interesting book for several reasons. First, it tells about one of the most severe cases of abuse and neglect that is known and discusses the effects this has on normal language development. Second, it demonstrates the role of environment and human interaction on the process of language development. Although it is rather technical and analytical for the beginning student, reading selected portions of the book will add to the reader's understanding of how language makes us human and what is involved in the language-learning process.

Foss, B. M., ed. *Determinants of Infant Behavior.* London: Methuen, 1969.

Although dated, these chapters are still relevant and interesting for the insight they give regarding how maternal behavior influences infant development. Many of the authors of various chapters are regarded as pioneers in the study of bonding, attachments, separation, and parent-infant interactions. The first section is devoted to bonding and the effects of maternal behavior in animals. Animal studies provide researchers with much useful information about and insight into human behavior. The second section deals with crying and mothers' responses, attachment and exploratory behavior, and infants' responses to strangers. Very interesting reading.

Kagan, Jerome. *The Nature of the Child*. New York: Basic Books, 1984.
The seven chapters of this book are really a set of essays. Written over a seven-year period, they are intended to "offer a critique of many favored premises" of child development, e.g., that the events of infancy seriously influence the future mood and behavior of the adolescent. This book can be read on several different levels, so the beginning student as well as the graduate student will find many provocative and challenging ideas. Kagan's views will introduce some disequilibrium into the reader's views of children and care-giving. The resulting equilibration is, of course, up to the reader.

Klaus, Marshall; Leger, Treville; and Trause, Mary Anne, eds. *Maternal Attachment and Mothering Disorders: A Round Table*. Johnson and Johnson Baby Products, 1975.
Even though it is ten years old, this is a helpful and revealing book for anyone interested in learning more about attachment. The case studies paint a vivid picture of the behavioral and emotional consequences of failure to attach. The studies also describe life events and child-rearing patterns that contribute to successful and unsuccessful attachment.

Leach, Penelope. *Babyhood*. 2nd ed. New York: Knopf, 1983.
This is a very thorough and comprehensive book packed with useful information for parents and other care-givers. Leach gives the what and why of development during the first two years (three-quarters of the book is devoted to the first year). She also has a very refreshing attitude about being practical and realistic in the tasks of child rearing.

LeBoyer, Frederick. *Loving Hands: The Traditional Indian Art of Baby Massage*. London: Collins, 1977.
This book is a natural extension of the ideas in LeBoyer's book *Birth Without Violence*. Many parents who attend exercise and "natural" childbirth classes before birth believe baby massage is a natural extension of the concept of fulfilling all their babies' needs. LeBoyer says of infants, "We must gorge them with warmth and caresses just as we do with milk. Being touched and caressed, being massaged is food for the infant." An excellent book for learning how to massage infants and for use in parent training classes.

Lief, Nina R. *The First Year of Life: A Guide for Parenting*. New York: Dodd, Mead, 1982.
The major purpose of this book is to provide parents with practical information about child rearing. Each of the twelve chapters deals with a month of infant development in the first year of life. Much of the content comes from discussions about child development between parents and staff of the New York Junior League's Early Childhood Development Center. The format and content make for interesting reading and provide sound parenting information.

NOTES

1. L. F. Whaley and D. L. Wong, *Nursing Care of Infants and Children, Third Edition* (St. Louis: C. V. Mosby, 1987), 249.
2. Andrew N. Meltzoff and M. Keith Moore, "Imitation of Facial and Manual Gestures by Human Neonates," *Science*, vol. 198, no. 4312 (October 1977): 75–78.
3. Susan M. Ludington-Hoe, "What Can Newborns Really See?" *American Journal of Nursing* (September 1983): 1288–1289.
4. Eric H. Lenneberg, "The Biological Foundations of Language," in *Readings in Transformational Grammar*, ed. Mark Lester (New York: Holt, Rinehart and Winston, 1970), 8.
5. Eric H. Lenneberg, *Biological Foundations of Language*, Copyright © 1967, John A. Wiley and Sons. Reprinted by permission of John A. Wiley and Sons, Inc. (158).
6. Maria Montessori, *The Secret of Childhood*, trans. Joseph Costelloe (Notre Dame, Ind.: Fides Publishers, 1966), 46.
7. Maria Montessori, *The Absorbent Mind*, trans. C. A. Claremont (New York: Holt, Rinehart and Winston, 1967), 115.
8. Susan Curtiss, *Genie: A Psycholinguistic Study of a Modern-Day "Wild Child"* (New York: Academic Press, 1977), 233.
9. Curtiss, *Genie*, 233.
10. Catherine Snow et al., "Talking and Playing with Babies: The Role of Ideologies of Child Rearing," in *Before Speech: The Beginning of Interpersonal Communication*, ed. Margaret Bullowa (London: Cambridge University Press, 1979), 269–288.
11. Peter Wolff, "The Classification of States," in *The Competent Infant*, ed. L. J. Stene (New York: Basic Books, 1973).
12. J. G. de Villiers and P. A. de Villiers, *Early Language* (Cambridge, Mass.: Harvard University Press, 1979), 23.
13. Marshall H. Klaus and John H. Kennell, *Parent-Infant Bonding*, 2nd ed. (St. Louis: C. V. Mosby, 1982), 2.
14. Eleanor E. Maccoby and John A. Martin, "Socialization in the Context of the Family: Parent-Child Interaction," in *Handbook of Child Psychology*, ed. Paul H. Mussen, vol. IV, *Socialization, Personality, and Social Development*, ed. E. Mavis Hetherington (New York: John Wiley, 1983).
15. Ellen A. Farber and Byron Egeland, "Developmental Consequences of Out-of-Home Care for Infants in a Low-Income Population," in *Day Care: Scientific and Social Policy Issues*, eds. Edward F. Zigler and Edmund W. Gordon (Boston: Auburn House), 105.
16. Mary Ainsworth et al., *Patterns of Attachment*, Figure 9. Copyright 1978 by Lawrence Erlbaum Associates, Inc.
17. L. Alan Sroufe, "Attachment and the Roots of Competence," *Human Nature* 1 (October 1978): 52.
18. Michael E. Lamb, *The Role of the Father in Child Development*, 2nd ed. (New York: John Wiley, 1981).
19. Marshall H. Klaus and John H. Kennell, *Maternal-Infant Bonding: The Impact of Early Separation or Loss on Family Development* (St. Louis: C. V. Mosby, 1976).
20. Susan Gold, "Parent-Infant Bonding: Another Look," *Child Development* 54 (December 1983): 1355–1382.

21. Sroufe, "Attachment," 57.
22. Alexander Thomas, Stella Chess, and Herbert Birch, "The Origin of Personality," *Scientific American* 223 (August 1970): 102–109.
23. Thomas, Chess, and Birch, "Origin," 106.
24. Erik Erikson, *Childhood and Society,* 2nd ed. (New York: Norton, 1963 (first pub. 1950), 249).
25. Erikson, *Childhood,* 249.

Chapter 3

Who Are the Toddlers and Preschoolers We Care For?

Questions to Guide Your Reading and Study

- What are the characteristics of normal physical growth and development for children ages two to five?
- What are the milestones of motor development during the toddler and preschool years?
- What are the behavioral characteristics of toddlers and preschoolers?
- How does Piaget's theory of intellectual development apply to toddlers and preschoolers and what are its implications for care-givers?
- How does language develop in toddlers and preschoolers?
- How does Erikson's theory of psychosocial development influence child-rearing practices and what are its implications for child care?
- What developmentally appropriate strategies can care-givers use to enhance the physical, intellectual, social, and emotional growth and development of toddlers and preschoolers?
- Why is it important for care-givers to know how infants and toddlers grow and develop?

INTRODUCTION

All children, unless neurologically or physically impaired, experience the major developmental task of learning to walk. It is easy for care-givers to treat this achievement lightly and take it for granted, yet walking upright on two feet is an accomplishment that contributes to the uniqueness of human beings.

Unassisted walking, which for most children occurs between the twelfth and fifteenth months, brings freedom and independence. Toddlers are freed in space to go where they please, to touch things previously untouchable, and to discover things previously out of sight. Hands are no longer necessary for locomotion and can now be used in other, more interesting ways. Once they begin unassisted walking, every toddler is a Columbus. The new world is there for them to explore, and they are determined explorers.

Toddlers also have the privilege of participating in another of life's great milestones, the beginning of rapid language development. Although, as we have seen, the genesis of language begins at birth and preparation for language development occurs during infancy, significant language development begins during the toddler period. The toddler, to use Maria Montessori's phrase, "bursts into language."

Mobility and language are harbingers of autonomy. Toddlers pass from almost total dependency to a desire to use their emerging skills to be independent. Not all care-givers are willing or able to be partners with them in this adventure. Preschoolers soon develop the skills that enable them to accomplish many things without the interference and constant supervision of adults. The responses care-givers make to encourage or discourage toddlers' quest for autonomy help determine how well they achieve autonomy, master their environment, and relate to the world. It is not surprising, then, that for parents, a key test of care-giving skills occurs during the toddler period.

What a combination — mobility and speech! Is it any wonder that the toddler years are considered the most exciting of childhood? At the end of the toddler period, children are very independent in thought and action.

Next come the preschool years, the years from three to five. During this period, children extend and benefit from the independence gained during the toddler period to learn more about their world. Parents, teachers, and society view these years as a time in which children get ready for school. This process of preparing for school is critical for children. Teachers and other professionals believe the occurrences of these years, how and if the child gets ready for school, are the cornerstones of all learning.

A revolution is occurring in the preschool years and a battle is being waged by school districts and other agencies over who will educate the very young. The likely winner? School districts, who with increasing frequency are providing programs for four-year-old children. There are two issues in this war for control of the early years. First, should four-year-old children be in school? An allied issue is whether *all* four-year-old children or just the disadvantaged should be in school. Second, what is the most appropriate curriculum for children during this period?

It is to be hoped that the ultimate winners in this dilemma will be young children, especially those who without preschool experience would enter school lacking skills necessary for success.

Many parents and a growing number of professionals think the preschool years should be unburdened by formal learning. Nature should take its course and children should be allowed to play and enjoy life, unfettered by pressures to succeed. Many middle-aged adults view the preschool years as the last opportunity for children to enjoy life without the burdens of adult responsibilities. According to this point of view, the preschool years are the last time for a period of at least thirteen years that children's lives will not be dominated and molded by schooling.

PHYSICAL DEVELOPMENT

Weight and Height

At twelve months, the beginning of the toddler year, the average male weighs twenty-two pounds and is two feet six inches tall. The average female weighs twenty-one pounds and is two feet five inches tall, as shown in Table 3-1. (See also Tables 2-1 and 2-2 in Chapter 2.) At the end of toddler period, the average child has gained about five pounds and five inches. (See Table 3-2.)

During the preschool years from three to five, gains in height and weight are steady but not as large as in the second year. Average gains in weight and height for ages one through five are shown in Table 3-2. A number of things are significant about these data. First, the average weight

TABLE 3-1

Average Weight and Height for Toddlers and Preschoolers

Age (years)	Weight (pounds)		Height (inches)	
	Males	Females	Males	Females
1	22.4	21.0	30.0	29.3
2	27.8	26.2	34.5	34.1
3	32.4	30.7	38.0	37.6
4	36.8	35.2	40.5	40.0
5	41.2	38.9	43.3	42.7

Source: Adapted from P.V.V. Hamill et al., "Physical Growth: National Center for Health Statistics Percentiles," *The American Journal of Clinical Nutrition* 32 (March 1979): 607–629.

TABLE 3-2

Average Annual Weight and Height Gain for Toddlers and Preschoolers

	Males		Females	
Age (years)	Weight (pounds)	Height (inches)	Weight (pounds)	Height (inches)
1–2	5.4	4.5	5.2	4.8
2–3	4.6	3.5	4.5	3.5
3–4	4.4	2.5	4.5	2.4
4–5	4.4	2.8	3.7	2.7

Source: Adapted from P.V.V. Hamill et al., "Physical Growth: National Center for Health Statistics Percentiles," *The American Journal of Clinical Nutrition* 32 (March 1979): 607–629.

gains for the preschooler are less than they are for the infant and toddler. The weight gain of the infant in the first nine months is mostly fat to provide insulation and extra calories in case developmental factors such as teething or environmental interferences with good health should curtail normal nutritional intake. This accounts for the "chubby" appearance of most infants, who are characterized by fat cheeks, round face, protruding stomach, and general body fat.

Once enough fat has been accumulated, weight gains are primarily in the form of bone, muscle, and tissue. As bones grow, children lose their baby fat and assume a "slimmed down" appearance. The four- and five-year-old may even look skinny compared to the three-year-old. The slimming down makes it easier for the toddler to walk. Think what would happen if toddlers kept gaining weight as rapidly as they did in their first year. They would weigh more and have more weight to carry around. As toddlers learn to walk better, the slimming down permits more and easier mobility.

Infants are hearty eaters. They need many calories to put on fat. At the end of the first year or early in the second year, however, the toddler's appetite diminishes. As walking begins, weight gains decrease and eating habits change. Preschoolers are notoriously picky eaters, as most care-givers learn. Problems with eating result when care-givers do not understand the nature of and reason for the slowing down of the appetite.

Implications for care-givers. Many parents respond to picky eating by nagging children to eat. They tell children to clean their plates and generally worry themselves and their children about food and eating. Many mealtimes are ruined for all involved because parents insist on pushing unwanted food on toddlers and preschoolers. Such unwarranted pressure on children to eat also changes their attitudes toward food. Some parents become so alarmed that they consult a pediatrician, who tells them that this "picky eating" is normal. Parents need to provide their children with balanced meals and give their children smaller portions of food, rather than filling their plates and insisting, to everyone's displeasure, that they eat everything so they can be members of the "Mickey Mouse Clean Plate Club." It is always much easier to give children seconds if they want more food, and care-givers are much more likely to feel better about children's eating habits this way.

Generally, children will have an appropriate appetite when (1) they have opportunities to be active, (2) they are on a regular daily routine, (3) they get enough sleep, (4) they experience mealtimes as pleasant events, (5) they have balanced meals, and (6) they have care-givers who model good eating habits.

Preschoolers have changing tastes, whims, and desires about food. Their favorite food today may not be their favorite food two weeks hence.

Vision

Visual development is a continuing maturational process throughout the toddler and preschool years. The part of the eye where vision is the sharpest, the *fovea*, is not completely developed until about six or seven years of age. Consequently, toddlers and preschoolers are *farsighted* — they can see better at a distance. They cannot see well up close and have difficulty focusing on what is considered normal-size print. Farsightedness continues until age five or six. Because of young children's farsightedness and to reduce eyestrain, publishers use large print in children's books.

Implications for care-givers. To avoid placing undue strain on children, care-givers should be judicious in selecting tasks for the very young that involve close visual attention. Also, care-givers should be alert to symptoms of possible visual problems. Children who are suspected of having a visual problem should have a thorough examination.

Teeth

During the toddler and preschool years, children have their full set of "baby" teeth. During this period, they lose their baby teeth and the first of the thirty-two permanent teeth, the "six-year molar," erupts.

Implications for care-givers. Care-givers have two major responsibilities to children regarding dental health during the toddler and preschool period. First, they should teach good dental habits and provide the time and opportunity for children to practice good dental health. Good dental habits and care of the teeth begin with the emergence of the first tooth. Children should be taught how to brush their teeth and encouraged to develop the habit of daily brushing. Many child-care and preschool programs teach such practices by having children brush their teeth after each meal or snack.

Not all parents practice good dental health themselves. They may need to be prompted to know when to begin and how to promote good dental health with their children.

Second, care-givers should provide snacks and other foods that lessen the possibility of tooth decay. Much attention is focused on preventing tooth decay by providing children with snacks that do not contain sugar. Sometimes, however, care-givers go to extremes and provide only "natural" snacks, thinking that if it is "natural" it has to be good. Recent articles point out, however, that such foods as raisins contribute to tooth decay because they stick on and between the teeth. Does this mean that care-givers shouldn't give children raisins? No. It simply means that when care-givers know about the characteristics of snacks they can be more aware of what they have to do as a result. In this case, they can have children rinse out their mouths or brush their teeth after a snack of raisins.

Chapter 10 provides detailed information on young children's nutritional development and its implications for care-givers.

Motor Development

Motor development is classified according to the types of muscles involved in movements. *Gross motor activities* are accomplished by the use of the large muscles of the body. Behaviorally, gross motor activities include creeping, crawling, walking, climbing, jumping, hopping, skipping, and throwing. *Fine motor activities* are accomplished by the smaller muscles of the body. Many fine muscle activities are associated with the hand and fingers. Such activities include grasping, releasing, manipulating objects, marking, scribbling, and writing.

Motor skills develop along a continuum that is sequential from reflexive responses in infancy to specialized skills in adolescence, as depicted in Figure 3-1.

Walking. Crawling and creeping are the methods of locomotion for infants. Walking is the primary gross motor activity and method of locomotion for toddlers. The name "toddler" is aptly applied to one-year-olds, since they really toddle; that is, they shuffle, lunge, and propel themselves forward with short, unsteady steps. There is no mistaking the toddler gait and stance: the feet are spread wide at a forty-five-degree angle and firmly planted for balance and stability. But stability and balance are not characteristic of toddlers' first attempts at independent walking: there is much tripping, falling, and lunging into things. Toddlers are undaunted, however. They try again and again and the development toward walking overcomes all obstacles. Adults should be possessed of such self-confidence and determination! The toddler is propelled by nature and biology to walk. The feat itself results from the interaction of heredity, maturation, and environmental factors.

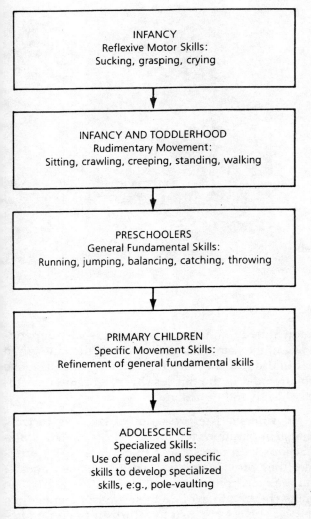

FIGURE 3-1
Sequence of Motor Development in the Very Young *Source:* Leonard D. Zaichkowsky et al., *Growth and Development: The Child and Physical Activity* (St. Louis: C. V. Mosby, 1980), 31–32. Used by permission of the author.

When walking, toddlers usually like to pull and push toys along with them. It is common to see toddlers with a block or other toy in their hands as they walk.

The exact time at which unassisted walking occurs is not as important as the reality of the achievement. The time varies from child to child. A sibling of one of the children in our preschool stood while holding on to the furniture at six months and walked unassisted at nine months. Such early walking is rare. The average child walks at twelve months, and those who cannot walk unassisted at that age can walk holding on to furniture or with one hand held by the care-giver. Published accounts of the devel-

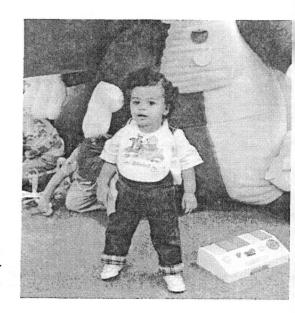

Unassisted walking is one of the major developmental milestones of the toddler. Toddlers need a safe, well-equipped, and well-supervised environment to explore. What do toddlers learn by being able to explore their environments?

opmental ages at which individual children accomplish tasks vary depending on the children from whom the data were gathered and the time when the data were gathered. Children in the seventies and eighties achieve milestones earlier than children did in the thirties due to enhanced maturation resulting from better health and nutrition.

Implications of walking for children. The processes of learning to walk and walking have a number of implications for young children. First, walking promotes social interactions with peers and adults. Such social interactions are important since they provide children with valuable information about themselves and their environment.

Second, walking permits children to explore their environments — to go farther away from their care-givers but also to return to them for support, reassurance, consolation, and encouragement.

Third, learning to walk and walking promote intellectual development because the child is now able to be actively involved in and with the environment. Piaget stressed the fundamental importance of activity in the development of cognitive schemes. Walking is one of the motor activities that empower children to act directly on objects, which in turn promotes cognitive development.

Implications for care-givers. Before and during the early learning-to-walk stages, some care-givers use an infant walker to assist children with walking. The walker consists of a seat suspended from a metal frame that has wheels. Infants are placed in the seat and their feet touch the floor so that they can move themselves along. Such walkers can be a source of injuries. Two physicians, Carol Kavanagh and Leonard Banco, decided to research the extent of injuries resulting from the use of infant walkers after they noted that a number of their patients had suffered such injuries. Their study provided evidence that infant walkers result in a significant risk of injury.[1] Thirty-one percent of all infants who used a walker suffered injuries, which included lacerations, skull fractures, and loss of teeth. Caregivers need to weigh the values of the infant walker with the potential for injury. An injury risk of almost one-third indicates a need to seriously consider if the walker should be used at all.

Since toddlers want to go wherever they want, they need a safe, spacious, well-equipped, well-supervised environment. Toddlers, in particular, want to touch, pick up, feel, carry, and play with every object available. They use this natural exploratory behavior to learn about their world and themselves. Within reason, this exploratory behavior needs to be encouraged and supported.

Once children learn to walk well, toward the middle of the second year, they are seldom still. The ability to engage in large motor activities with more facility during the preschool years is due in part to maturation of the skeletal system and the slimming down of preschoolers. Most of the preschool years are spent in play that involves a wide variety of large motor skills, such as riding tricycles or bikes, running, and climbing.

Fine Motor Abilities. The fine motor abilities of the toddler period include the ability to build a two-block tower at fifteen months and a four-block tower at eighteen months. Writing progresses from banging and jabbing at twelve months to scribbling at eighteen months. The toddler cannot completely master the release of objects. Grasping in infants is accomplished with the whole hand. This is called the *palmar* grasp and begins as a basic reflexive action. When infants grasp, it is hard for them to let go. By the end of the toddler period, the grasping movement is more voluntary, but the toddler still has difficulty coordinating the release of objects. The *pincer* grip or grasp using the thumb and forefinger is developed at the end of the infant period and in the beginning of the toddler period. This pincer grasp is put to good use by toddlers — it seems as though they want to use it on everything from stove controls and lamp switches to television knobs and drawer handles.

Handedness. Hand preference is really part of *dominance*, preference for one side of the body or the other. Most people develop a preference for using one side of the body over the other. People who are right-handed also kick with their right leg and prefer using the right ear to hear and the right eye to see. The left hemisphere of the brain controls the right side of the body. Some people, but not many, are *ambidextrous* and can use either hand equally well.

The preference for one hand or the other is usually indicated by the age of two. Children should be allowed to determine their own hand preference. When a preference for the right hand is demonstrated, its use should be encouraged. Children should not be allowed to vacillate between handedness. Unless a clear preference is shown for the left hand, the use of the right hand should be encouraged. Ninety percent of humans are right-handed. Why do 10 percent of all children have a preference for the left hand? It is partly a result of heredity. Left-handedness is familial and is more frequent in families in which at least one parent is left-handed.[2] A genetic model is not sufficient to explain all instances of left-handedness, however. Handedness can be attributed in part to practice. In any event, children who show a preference for the left hand should not be forced to change their handedness.

Implications for care-givers. The preschooler's fine motor skills cover a wide range, including tying laces, holding a pencil, buttoning, and pouring. Skill in fine motor activities is a function of maturation, opportunity, and training. Two-year-olds who lack digital dexterity because their hands are still too fat will probably not benefit from training in how to tie. On the other hand, three-year-olds who have matured more will readily accomplish such tasks. Opportunities to practice a skill plus training in how to perform it are also factors. Children who have a water table to practice pouring and an attentive care-giver to instruct and encourage them will master the skill of pouring earlier than those who lack such assistance.

Importance of Motor Skills. Why are motor skills important? The development of motor skills is important for a number of reasons.

First, motor development is like many other abilities in life: you use it or lose it. This is known as the *physiological law of use.* The human body grows and develops through use. As one author put it, "the body has its own built-in system of growth, repair, and even spare parts. But growth and renewal are available only on demand. Muscles grow big and strong in use, but develop atrophy in disuse."[3]

Young children are active because their bodies demand activity for motor development. Motor activity is necessary so children can develop their motor systems. The use of these developing motor skills brings competence and social approval.

Second, many early childhood educators see a relationship between motor development and academic achievement. A partnership exists between the use and development of fine and gross motor skills and the ability to accomplish traditional school tasks such as reading and writing. Quite often, children who are not able to perform well the gross motor tasks of running, balancing, skipping, hopping, and jumping also have learning problems. Fine motor skills are needed for writing and reading. It is difficult to think of a learning task that does not require motor skills, particularly the fine motor skills.

Diagnosis of children with learning problems often reveals difficulty with fine and gross motor abilities. Remediation of learning problems often includes teaching and reteaching the use of gross and fine motor skills. Helping toddlers and preschoolers develop motor skills helps them learn and gets them ready to learn more and at higher levels of achievement.

Third, motor activity contributes to learning. Young children learn by doing. This core concept has been supported and advocated by the great educators from Froebel and Montessori to Dewey and Piaget. Motor activities provide the basis and the context for the learning activity. Motor activity in and of itself provides a basis for learning, but it is obvious that motor activity in an enriched environment is the key to providing opportunities for learning. Providing an active child with an enriched environment is still the best way to help children learn and to promote readiness for learning.

Fourth, motor skills contribute to social development. As children use their developing motor skills, they gain self-confidence, which contributes to their mastering the developmental psychosocial stages of autonomy and initiative.

As children become competent at motor activities, they also gain approval from their parents and peers. This confidence and expanded ability to perform motor skills contributes to children's feelings of self-worth and promotes a feeling of well-being.

Implications for care-givers. The development of motor skills has a number of implications for parents and other care-givers. The first and probably most important involves the growing independence of the toddler. The toddler period is a stressful time for both parents and children. This stress is caused by the toddler learning to walk and being into everything. Stress, of course, affects the mother and other family members as well. Parents have to find a balance between giving the toddler unrestricted freedom (which is not possible in most homes and apartments) and being overly restrictive. Recent parenting information has probably done a great deal to cause anxiety and guilt in parents by overstressing their need to "child-proof" the home so toddlers can roam and explore at will. Such information includes the admonition that playpens and other restrictive equipment are "bad" because they thwart the toddler's basic desire to explore and be independent. As with anything else, however, there has to be a balance. Unrestricted freedom is neither possible nor practical. Parents can child-proof their homes by doing such things as putting away antiques and bric-a-brac, covering electrical wall outlets, and putting gates up in hallways and at stairs. Toddlers can and should be restricted at times when the care-giver has an important task to do or when he or she needs a break. At these times, playpens are entirely appropriate. What care-givers need to avoid is restricting toddlers for long periods of time without any opportunity for unrestricted activity. Table 3-3 shows some of the ways parents and care-givers in child-care programs can child-proof the environment.

TABLE 3-3

Child-Proofing Homes and Child-Care Environments

Home		Center
1. Remove throw rugs so toddlers don't trip.	6. Take knobs off stoves so toddlers can't turn them on.	1. Cover toddler-area floors with carpeting or mats.
2. Put breakable objects out of toddlers' reach. This may mean storing away antiques and family heirlooms for several years.	7. Purchase medicines and cleaners that have child-proof caps.	2. Make sure storage shelves are well anchored and won't tip over. Store things so children cannot pull heavy objects off shelves onto themselves.
3. Cover electrical wall outlets with special covers.	8. Store all medicines and cleaning agents out of toddlers' reach. Remove all toxic chemicals from low cabinets to high ones. Even items like mouth wash should be put in a safe place.	3. Use only equipment and materials that are safe — no sharp edges and broken materials.
4. Remove electrical cords. Toddlers love to pull on electrical cords, and the lamps or appliances can be pulled down.	9. Place safety locks on bathroom doors — the kind that can be opened from the outside. More than once toddlers have locked themselves into the bathroom.	4. Store all medicines in locked cabinets.
5. Install gates in hallways and stairs. Make sure gates are federally approved so the toddlers cannot get their heads stuck and strangle.		5. If there are sharp corners, cushion them with foam rubber and tape.

(continued)

Care-givers need to provide young children with the opportunity and environment for motor activity through play. One of the great attractions of programs such as Gymboree is that they provide a place, a time, an environment, and equipment for children to play with other children. All these ingredients are significant in that they contribute to motor development. One of the reasons for early attendance at child care or preschool is that it provides the opportunity to engage in play activities that promote motor development.

Toilet Training

Toilet training is a milestone of the toddler period that causes many parents — and consequently their children — a great deal of anxiety. Many parents

TABLE 3-3 (*continued*)

Home		Center
10. Cushion sharp corners of tables and counters with foam rubber and tape. Cotton balls can also be used to cushion corners.	14. Place guards over the hot water faucets in bathrooms so toddlers can't turn them on unless supervised.	6. Keep doors closed or install gates so toddlers can't wander off.
11. If there are older children in the home who use toys with small parts, beads, etc., have them use these when the toddler is not present or in an area where the toddler can't get them.	15. Keep wastebaskets on top of desks. Toddlers can fall over and in them.	7. Fence all play areas.
12. When cooking, turn all pot handles to the back of the stove.	16. Keep the doors to the washer and dryer closed at all times.	
13. Avoid using cleaning fluids while children are present because of toxic fumes.	17. Keep all plastic bags, including garbage bags, stored in a safe place. Better yet, use paper bags for garbage.	
	18. Shorten cords on drapes. If there are loops on cords, cut them.	
	19. Immediately wipe up any spilled liquid from the floor.	

want to train their children as early as possible, usually because of considerations for convenience and cleanliness. The American tendency, it seems, is to toilet train efficiently, cleanly, and quickly.

Toilet training is precisely that: training. Bowel and bladder elimination in the infant involve reflexive actions. When the bowel and bladder are full, the anal and urethral sphincter muscles open. Thus, care-givers are training an involuntary reflex. The goal of training is a child who voluntarily and independently uses the toilet when needed. As with anything else, training involves timing, patience, modeling, preparing the environment, and establishing a routine and partnership. Above all else, toilet training involves maturation. This is where timing comes into play. Bowel control is achieved earlier than bladder control.

Parents who have their children on a routine are able to anticipate by time and a child's actions when he or she is ready to defecate. By taking children to the toilet at these times, they are able to help them associate bowel movements with going to the toilet. This occurs before full training. Although some children are "trained" in the first year, it is probably the parent who is trained rather than the child. Toilet training that begins shortly before or after the second birthday is most successful. A general rule of thumb is that later works better than earlier for both care-givers and children. Many child-rearing experts such as Berry Brazelton[4] and Benjamin Spock[5] advocate waiting until the toddler is about two before toilet training.

Implications for care-givers. Patience and positive reinforcement as opposed to nagging and impatience are the rule when toilet training. Since patience is a varying attribute with care-givers, starting later when the chances of success are greater works best.

A partnership needs to exist between care-giver and child. Toilet training is not something care-givers do *to* the child, but one that they do *with* the child. Toilet training can bring feelings of accomplishment and pleasure to care-givers and children when care-givers approach it in a positive manner.

Another level of the partnership involves the parent and surrogate care-giver. Parents and care-givers have to be in tune with each other concerning when to begin toilet training and how it should be conducted. Conflicts can also arise between parents and grandparents about how and when the toddler should be toilet trained. Sometimes care-givers, especially those who see themselves only as baby-sitters, don't want the responsibility or work involved in toilet training. Similarly, parents with children in child care need to coordinate their efforts with the efforts of the child's primary care-giver. Generally, parents want to start toilet training earlier than child-care staff want to begin. The time to discuss such matters is when children are enrolled.

Many of the tasks and accomplishments of the infant and toddler stages take place in a context of motor activities. Motor development has great importance in the lives of the very young. Motor accomplishments cannot be divorced from children's intellectual and social development. Supporting and promoting motor development is as necessary as promoting intellectual and social development.

INTELLECTUAL DEVELOPMENT

Toddler intellectual development covers the two last stages of sensorimotor intellectual development: Stage V, Experimentation (also referred to as Tertiary Circular Reactions) and Stage VI, Representational Intelligence (also known as Symbolic Intelligence). See Chapter 2 for additional information on these two stages.

Stage V: Experimentation

Stage V, from twelve to eighteen months, is the stage of experimentation. Toddlers experiment with objects to solve problems. This experimentation is characteristic of intelligence that involves *tertiary circular reactions*, in which toddlers repeat actions and modify behaviors over and over to see what will happen. This repetition develops an understanding of cause-effect relationships and leads to the discovery of new relationships through exploration and experimentation. Here is Piaget's observation of Laurent, the "experimenter":

> Laurent is lying on his back but nevertheless resumes his experiments of the day before. He grasps in succession a celluloid swan, a box, etc., stretches out his arm and lets them fall. He distinctly varies the position of the fall. Sometimes he stretches out his arm vertically, sometimes he holds it obliquely, in front of or behind his eyes, etc. When the object falls in a new position (for example, on his pillow), he lets it fall two or three times more on the same place, as though to study a spatial relation; then he modifies the situation. At a certain moment the swan falls near his mouth; now he does not suck it (even though this object habitually serves this purpose), but drops it three times more while merely making the gesture of opening his mouth.[6]

Mobility increases the opportunities for experimentation and new experiences. Toddlers, therefore, act on their environment with a higher frequency than do infants. They learn by the effects their actions have on objects and the environment. Through such experimentation, toddlers learn the consequences of their behavior and cause-effect relationships.

Object Permanence. The development of object permanence continues during this stage. The child who has acquired *object permanence* knows that objects occupy space, have an existence of their own, and continue to exist even when not seen. You know that a ball hidden under a diaper still exists as a ball. Infants do not. Much of what we, as adults, take for granted as common sense is not common sense for the infant and toddler. Care-givers must constantly keep in mind that the thought processes of adults are not the thought processes of children.

A beginning understanding of object permanence begins in sensorimotor Stage IV. Awareness of object permanence continues to develop in Stage V. Toddlers are not confused by a change of location when an object is moved. They will search for an object in the last place hidden. But during this stage, toddlers still have to see the object being hidden. They do not yet have object permanence to the extent that they know an object is hidden without seeing it hidden.

Implications for care-givers. In addition to the suggestions provided for Stage V in Chapter 2, this stage has several implications for care-givers.

First, all three stages involving circular reactions have a great deal of significance for children. As indicated in Chapter 2, a circular reaction is

TABLE 3-4

The Development of Object Permanence

Stage	Age (months)	Level of Object Permanence
I	0–1	Infants do not differentiate objects from themselves. They look only at what is in their field of vision.
II	1–4	Infants still do not differentiate objects from themselves. They are able to follow an object and will look at the point where it was last hidden. Infants begin to coordinate seeing and hearing, but there is no visual or manual search for hidden objects.
III	4–8	Infants search for objects that have vanished from their grasp. They will search for a partially hidden object, but not a completely hidden object.
IV	8–12	Infants will search actively for completely hidden objects. When an object is moved from one hidden place to another, infants will look for the object in the first place hidden.
V	12–18	Toddlers in Stage V will search for an object in the last place they saw it hidden. They will, for example, watch the care-giver hide a ball under a blanket and then in a box, and they will then look for the ball in the box. They have no problem with this task as long as they have actually seen the object being hidden. At this stage, however, they cannot account for what Piaget called "invisible displacements." Piaget put a potato in a box, placed a rug over the box,

(continued)

the repetition of a sensorimotor action. The activity is the context for learning. These sensorimotor acts are necessary for and facilitate adaptation (the end product of assimilation and accommodation). Circular reactions serve to increase the range and kinds of experiences of the very young. The breadth of experiences all children have is critical because it increases opportunities for assimilation, accommodation, and scheme development. A broader range of experiences with which to adapt is more conducive to intellectual development than a narrow range.

Second, if, as Piaget and others maintain, activity is the context for intellectual development, then care-givers are the ones who must provide the context for the activity. Care-givers are the ones who control the environment in which children have opportunities to engage in sensorimotor acts.

TABLE 3-4 (*continued*)

Stage	Age (months)	Level of Object Permanence
		and turned the box upside down, leaving the potato hidden by the rug. When he brought the box out from under the rug, his daughter, Jacqueline, looked for the potato in the box; "it did not occur to her to raise the rug in order to find the potato underneath."*
VI	18–24	Toddlers achieve object permanence. They realize objects exist apart from themselves and that the objects can move in space. This cognitive achievement is possible because toddlers are now capable of forming mental representations. Piaget writes the following about Jacqueline at nineteen and a half months: "Jacqueline watches me when I put a coin in my hand, then put my hand under a coverlet. I withdraw my hand closed, Jacqueline opens it, then searches under the coverlet until she finds the object. I take back the coin at once, put it in my hand, and then slip my closed hand under a cushion situated at the other side (on her left and no longer on her right); Jacqueline immediately searches for the object under the cushion."†

*Jean Piaget, *The Construction of Reality in the Child*, trans. M. Cook (New York: Basic Books, 1954), 68.
†Ibid., 79.
Source: Adapted from Robert B. Sund, *Piaget for Educators: A Multimedia Program* (Columbus, Ohio: Charles E. Merrill, 1975), 19.

Stage VI: Representational Intelligence

Stage VI, from eighteen months to two years, is the stage of symbolic representation. Representation occurs when toddlers can visualize events internally. They can maintain mental images of objects not present. Representational thought enables toddlers to solve problems internally, without having to always solve them in a sensorimotor way through experimentation and trial and error. Representation enables toddlers to more accurately predict cause-effect relationships.

During this stage, true object permanence develops. This reflects toddlers' representational intelligence. Toddlers can not only search for hidden objects, they can now search for objects in the last place hidden. More importantly, they can search for objects they did not actually see hidden. The toddler is liberated, in a small way, from relying only on perceptions.

Object permanence also includes person permanence, and toddlers know their care-givers exist even when absent. The development of object permanence is a significant achievement. Table 3-4 summarizes the development of object permanence in the sensorimotor stage.

Once they have achieved object permanence, toddlers understand the rudiments of property *identity*, that is, that objects have an identity of their own and exist when the toddler is not present. Later, as preschoolers in the preoperational stage of intellectual development, they will learn other properties of identity — for example, that when clay is rolled out in a long piece, it is still clay. Having achieved property identity, toddlers begin to understand the properties of objects.

Representational thought is evidenced by the pretend play that is characteristic of this stage. Toddlers' representational thought does not necessarily match with the real world and their representations of things are not necessarily others' representations. This accounts for a toddler's ability to have other objects stand for almost anything. A wooden block is a car. A rag doll is a fairy princess. This type of play is also known as *symbolic play* and becomes more elaborate and complex in the preoperational period.

There is considerable difference, then, between the Stage I infant and the Stage VI toddler. Through the process of assimilation and accommodation, children have developed many schemes of the world. These schemes help them distinguish many objects and animals. They know that a ball is not a cat and that their mother is different from other mothers.

Stage VI children are no longer dominated and controlled by reflexive actions as infants are. The Stage VI child is capable of symbolic thought and is ready to manipulate the environment by use of symbols through language. The toddler is ready to enter the world of preoperational intelligence.

The child entering the preoperational stage is also different in another way. Sensorimotor children do not distinguish between themselves and external objects. Preoperational children can. This intellectual distinguishing between self and others and self and objects plays a role in the child's discovery of self. As children are able to distinguish themselves from others, they are able to understand themselves as persons.

Implications for care-givers. Since toddlers now have object permanence, they may become more upset by missing a favorite toy or parent. The obvious way to solve this with toys is to make sure the child has the toy present. A better way is to keep toddlers involved in a wide range of activities and not provide a chance for them to dwell on the missing item or person.

Care-givers should keep in mind that children's thoughts are not adult thoughts and that the way children see or represent things is not the way adults do. Therefore, care-givers should not emphasize "right" answers as much as they should emphasize helping children have meaningful experiences to enable them to discover the right answers through the process of living and maturation. The idea that children don't think as adults is one of the best reasons for making education child-centered rather than adult-centered.

Preoperational Intelligence

Preoperational thought as designated by Piaget is typical of children two to six years old. The most significant feature of this period is the use of symbols — language — to represent the environment. The preoperational child can rearrange experiences without actually physically manipulating the environment. The preoperational child is not yet capable of *operational* thought. An *operation* is a reversible mental action whereby an object or experience that is transformed can be returned to its original form. An example of a mental operation is that $1 + 2 = 3$ and that $3 - 2 = 1$. The process of addition is reversible through subtraction. You know this, but the preoperational child does not.

Preoperational thinking has certain other characteristics. Preoperational children cannot *conserve*; that is, they cannot mentally understand that amount (mass), quantity, and volume stay the same even though appearance (shape, size, and dimensions) changes. In a test of conservation of number, for example, a child is presented with a row of objects, paper dolls, as in Figure 3-2 (Row A). She is then asked to make a second row to exactly match the first. This she can do as in Row B. When the spacing is changed between the first row and the second (transformation by expanding) as in Rows C and D and the child is asked which row (C or D) has more dolls, the preoperational child will answer, "The second row" (Row D). When asked why the second row (Row D) has more dolls, the child will respond, "Because it is bigger" (or longer). The child really believes that there are more dolls in the second row (Row D) because she confuses length with number. This reflects the inability to conserve.

The preoperational child is still egocentric, but in different ways than the sensorimotor child. This egocentrism is illustrated by preoperational children's being unable to assume a perspective other than their own. Their view of the world is the only view they take and is the only one that matters to them.

The egocentrism of the preoperational child is illustrated by Piaget's three-mountain experiment. A model of three mountains is placed on a table as in Figure 3-3. The child is then shown drawings of views that other children would see if they sat at the other positions around the table. The preoperational child is unable to choose the mountain scene that other children would see if they sat at other places around the table. From this, Piaget concluded that preoperational children do not yet have the cognitive ability to understand that others can see things from a perspective other than theirs. The preoperational child thinks others see what she sees.

The preoperational child also uses language in the literal sense. This is

FIGURE 3-2
A Conservation of Number Test

Row A

Row B

Row C

Row D

termed *egocentric speech*. It is characterized by the child talking *at* others as opposed to talking *with* them.

Preoperational children are egocentric in the application of rules as well. They are not afraid to make up rules as they go along, and to them, their rules are all that matter. They are not aware of and therefore are unconcerned with and unaffected by external rules.

FIGURE 3-3
Piaget's Three-Mountain Experiment

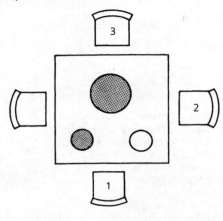

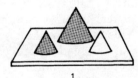
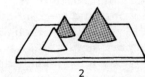
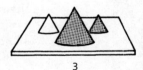

Source: Bernadine Chuck Fong and Miriam Roher Resnick, *The Child: Development Through Adolescence,* 2nd ed. (Palo Alto, Calif.: Mayfield Publishing, 1986), 210.

Implications for care-givers. Piaget believed that an active child is a developing child. Or to put it another way, the developing child is active. This inherent capacity for action is reflected both physically and mentally. The child wants to be active in the environment, and in so doing is mentally active in striving for equilibrium. Children need care-givers who will allow them to be active in an environment that provides many activities and opportunities to experience new things. Action contributes to intellectual development.

Symbolic representations can be encouraged in a number of ways. First, since children are in the period of rapid language development, the use of language can be supported and encouraged. For most children, language is the major form of representation.

Second, art work of various kinds can also be used to help children represent their internal thoughts and ideas. Drawing and painting pictures, modeling with clay, cutting and pasting, and construction activities with wood and styrofoam are all meaningful ways to promote and en-

Language development is an important process during the toddler and preschool years. Care-givers can provide many opportunities for children to use language. How can care-givers encourage children to represent their experiences through language?

courage representation. These activities are also meaningful in that they provide children with experiences at a concrete level.

Third, the Language Experience Approach (LEA) helps children express their ideas and allows them to see their thoughts transformed into words and sentences. In the LEA, children tell about their experiences in their own words and the care-giver or teacher uses pictures, words, and sentences to record their thoughts. This is an excellent way to promote symbolic representation and the writing and reading processes.

Care-givers should note that preoperational children benefit most from nonabstract experiences because they are still perceptually bound. Their experiences therefore should be concrete and have concrete referents, as the suggestions in the previous two paragraphs indicate.

Many kinds of social interactions are necessary to help children *decenter*, or develop out of their egocentrism. Preschoolers, and all children for that matter, need many experiences with a wide range of people including other children and adults. In this way they learn that others have opinions and thoughts different from their own.

In one preschool, one of the ways the staff provides children with opportunities to interact with other adults is through an intergenerational program. Once a month, all children ages two to five take the city bus and visit the Jewish Home for the Aged. There, in addition to learning concepts of empathy, caring, and sharing, they also have other adults to help them learn that not everyone has the same opinions they have.

LANGUAGE DEVELOPMENT

Piaget's View

Piaget's theory of cognitive development is based in part on the premise that intellectual development is a prerequisite for language development.

Piaget is quite specific and emphatic about this: "Articulate language makes its appearance, after a phase of spontaneous vocalization . . . at the end of the sensorimotor period with what have been called 'one-word sentences.'"[7] Language literally springs forth from cognitive development. For Piaget, then, the question of whether language or intelligence comes first is answered in favor of intelligence: "Language is a product of intelligence rather than intelligence being a product of language."[8]

Vygotsky's View

As you might expect, not everyone agrees with the view that language development is dependent on intellectual development. In particular, the Russian psychologist Lev S. Vygotsky (1896–1934) believed almost the opposite, that communication is the origin of mind. Vygotsky's opinion was that thinking and language develop in two parallel but unrelated "streams." At about two, or the end of the sensorimotor stage, these streams converge and become interdependent. Children become more aware of what words stand for and language *assists* intellectual development. According to Vygotsky,

> at a certain moment at about the age of two the curves of development of thought and speech, till then separate, meet and join to initiate a new form of behavior. . . . This critical instant, when speech begins to serve intellect, and thoughts begin to be spoken, is indicated by two unmistakable objective symptoms: (1) the child's sudden, active curiosity about words, his question about every new things, "What is this?" and (2) the resulting rapid, saccadic increases in his vocabulary.[9]

Contrasting views about language development are reflected in the different views of cognitive development. In Chapter 2, we discussed other theories of language development, principally the "nativists," who believe language is innate and "unfolds" in response to maturation. According to Piaget, children use language to represent already acquired sensorimotor schemes. Children have thoughts about objects before they can name them. In this sense, language development "follows" intellectual development.

The Sequence of Language Development

Regardless of the theory of language development we chose to adopt as our own, the fact remains that children develop language in predictable sequences, and they don't wait for us to tell them what theory to follow in their language development. They are very pragmatic and develop language regardless of our beliefs.

Language development during the second year — the toddler year — progresses in the sequence and at the rate depicted in Table 3-5.

TABLE 3-5

The Sequence of Language Development During the Second Year (Toddler Stage)

Age (months)	Language Milestone
10	Babbling — "Da-da"/"Ma-ma"
11	One word
12	Two words
14	Three words
15	Four to six words
15	Immature jargoning
18	Seven to twenty words
18	Mature jargoning
18	Says name of one body part
21	Says names of three body parts
21	Two-word combination
23	Names five body parts
24	Fifty words
24	Two-word sentences (nouns, or pronoun inappropriately, and verb)
24	Pronouns (*I, me, you*, etc., inappropriately)

Source: Arnold J. Capute and Pasquale J. Accardo, "Linguistic and Auditory Milestones During the First Two Years of Life: A Language Inventory for the Practitioner," *Clinical Pediatrics* 17 (November 1978): 847–853.

First Words. Although the process of language development begins at the moment of birth, parents usually don't think of language as beginning until children say their first word. "At about a year children produce their first understandable words, often reduplicated syllables like mama, dada, or papa, or single consonant-vowel syllables like da for dog or ba for baby. For some children babbling ceases when the first words appear, but other children continue to produce long babbled sentences even when their intelligible vocabulary grows."[10]

The first words of children are just that, first words. What are these first words? Children talk about people — dada, papa, mama, mummie, and baby (referring to themselves); animals — dog, cat, kitty; vehicles — car, truck, boat, train; toys — ball, block, book, doll; food — juice, milk, cookie, bread, drink; body parts — eye, nose, mouth, ear; clothing and household articles — hat, shoe, spoon, clock; greeting terms — hi, bye, night-night; and a few words for actions — up, no more, off.[11] Interestingly enough, the first words of children today are remarkably similar to those of children fifty years ago.[12]

Holophrasic Speech. Children are remarkable communicators without words. If they are fortunate and have attentive parents and care-givers, they are skilled communicators, using gestures, facial expressions, sound intonations, pointing, and reaching to make their desires known and get what they want. Pointing at an object and saying, "uh-uh-uh" is the same as saying, "I want the rattle" or "Help me get the rattle." Usually caregivers will respond by saying, "Do you want the rattle? I'll get it for you. Here it is!" One of the attributes of an attentive care-giver is the ability to read children's signs and signals, anticipating their desires even though no words are spoken.

The ability to communicate progresses from "sign language" and sounds to the use of single words. Toddlers are skilled at using single words to name objects, to let others know what they want, and to express emotions. One word, in essence, does the work of a whole sentence. These single-word sentences are called *holophrases*.

The one-word sentences children use are primarily *referential* (used primarily to label objects, such as "doll"), or *expressive* (communicating personal desires or levels of social interaction, such as "bye-bye" and "kiss"). The extent to which children use these two functions of language depends in large measure on the care-giver, as the de Villiers have pointed out:

> The referral-expressive dimension is clearly a continuum, and most children have both types of words in their early vocabulary, but the classification reflects the predominate use to which the child put language in the early one-word stage. To some extent the child's early use of language reflects his mother's verbal style. Mothers who spend most of their time pointing out objects and their properties tend to have referential children; mothers who use language mainly to direct their child's behavior tend to have expressive children.[13]

Symbolic Representation. Two significant developmental events occur at about the age of two. First is the development of symbolic representation. Representation occurs when something — a mental image, a word — is used to stand for something else not present. A toy may stand for a tricycle, a baby doll may represent a real person. Words become signifiers of things — ball, block, blanket.

This ability frees children from the here and now, from acting on concrete objects present only in the immediate environment. It enables their thoughts to range over the full span of time — past and present — and permits them to remember and project thoughts into the future. "Things no longer need to be present for the child to act on them. In this sense, the ability to represent eventually liberates the child from the immediate present. He can imagine things that are both spatially and temporally separate from himself. It may therefore be said that the use of mental representation permits the child to transcend the constraints of space and time."[14]

The use of mental symbols also enables the child to participate in two processes that are characteristic of the early years, symbolic play and the beginning of the use of words and sentences to express meanings and make references. Piaget refers to the use of symbolic representation as the *semiotic* function.

Vocabulary Development. The second significant achievement that occurs at about two is the development of a fifty-word vocabulary and the use of two-word sentences. This vocabulary development and the ability to combine words mark the beginning of rapid language development.

Telegraphic Speech. You have undoubtedly heard a toddler say something like "Go out" in response to a suggestion such as "Let's go outside." Perhaps you've said "Is your juice all gone?" and the toddler responded "Juice gone." These two-word sentences are called *telegraphic speech*. They are the same kind of sentences you would use if you wrote a telegram. The sentences are primarily made up of nouns and verbs. Generally, they do not have prepositions, articles, conjunctions, and auxiliary verbs.

"Motherese." Many recent research studies have demonstrated that mothers and other care-givers talk to infants and toddlers differently than adults talk to each other. This distinctive way of adapting everyday speech to young children is called *motherese*.[15] Characteristics of motherese include the following:

1. The sentences are short, averaging just over four words per sentence with babies. As children become older, the length of sentences mothers use also becomes longer. Mothers' conversations with their children are short and sweet.
2. The sentences are highly intelligible. When talking to their children, mothers tend not to slur or mumble their words. This may be because mothers speak slower to their children.
3. The sentences are "unswervingly well formed," that is, they are grammatical sentences.
4. The sentences are mainly imperatives and questions, such as "Give Mommie the ball" and "Do you want more juice?" Since mothers can't exchange a great deal of information with their children, their utterances are such that they direct their children's actions.
5. Mothers use *deictic* sentences in which referents ("here," "that," "there") are used to stand for objects or people: "Here's your bottle." "That's your baby doll." "There's your doggie."
6. Mothers *expand* or provide an adult version of their children's communication. When a child points at a baby doll on a chair, the mother may respond by saying, "Yes, the baby doll is on the table."
7. Mother's sentences involve repetitions. "The ball, bring Mommie the ball. Yes, go get the ball — the ball — go get the ball."

Grammatical Morphemes. There is more to learning language than learning words. There is also the matter of learning grammar. Grammar is the way we change the meanings of sentences and place events and action in time: past, present, and future tense. Grammatical morphemes are the principal means for changing the meanings of sentences. A *morpheme* is the smallest unit of meaning it is possible to have in a language. A morpheme can be a word, such as "no," or an element of a word, such as "ed." A morpheme that can stand alone, such as "child," is a *free morpheme*. A morpheme that cannot stand alone is a *bound morpheme*. "Kicked" consists of the free morpheme "kick" and the bound morpheme "ed." Morphological rules include the rules governing tenses, plurals, and possessives.

The order in which children learn grammatical morphemes is well documented. The pattern of mastery is orderly and consistent. The first morpheme to be mastered is the present progressive (I drink*ing*), followed by prepositions (*in* and *on*), plural (two doll*s*), past irregular (toy *fell*), possessive (Sally*'s* doll), uncontractible verb (there it *is*), articles (*a* block, *the* doll), past regular (Eve stopp*ed*), third-person regular (he run*s*), uncontractible auxiliary (I *am* going), contractible verb (*that's* a doll), and contractible auxiliary (*I'm* going).[16]

Negatives. If you took a vote on the toddler's favorite word, "no" would win hands down. When children begin to use negatives, they simply add "no" to the beginning of a word or sentence, e.g., "no milk." As their sentences become longer, they still put "no" first, e.g., "no put coat on." Later, they place negatives appropriately between subject and verb, e.g., "I no want juice."

Lois Bloom, a child language development researcher, found that when children move beyond the use of the one-word expression "no," the expression of negation progresses through a series of meanings. The first meaning conveys nonexistence, such as "no juice" and "no hat," meaning that the juice is all gone and the hat isn't present. The next level of negation is for the rejection of something. "No go out" is the rejection of the offer to go outside. Next, the use of "no" progresses to the denial of something the child believes to be untrue. If offered a carrot stick under the pretense it is candy, the child will reply, "No candy."[17]

By the end of the preschool years, children have developed and mastered most language patterns. Language development continues through the adolescent years, mainly as a process of refining and extending previously learned language patterns. The basis for language development is the early years and no amount of later remedial training can make up for development that should have occurred during this sensitive period for language learning.

Implications for care-givers. Care-givers must attune themselves to children's developing language style and abilities. As children develop in their ability to use language, care-givers can "mirror" that language back, adapting their way of talking to children in accordance with their growing use of language. Communicating with children provides a rich linguistic environment for children to learn language. Language that is short, direct, and grammatically correct supports children's efforts at language development. The care-giver's expanding what the child says is also helpful.

P. S. Dale, a researcher of children's language, says that "the child can

Children can talk about what they know. Care-givers should provide many experiences for children about which they can talk.

talk about only what he knows."[18] Care-givers need to provide children with a wide range of experiences so they can build a knowledge base. Walks, encounters with other children and adults, field trips, and vicarious experiences through reading and film all provide children with things to talk about. The other half of the equation, of course, is that children need care-givers who will talk with them and provide opportunities for conversation. Having an opportunity to talk is as important as having something to talk about.

Children's first words are the names of things. Parents and care-givers can teach children the names of things directly ("This is a ball") or indirectly ("Tell me what this is"). They can label, putting the name of the object on the object: "chair." They can use the names of things in their conversation with children, "This is a shoe, let's put your shoe on." The important thing to remember is that children need to know the names of things if they are going to refer to them and talk about them.

Since children's first words are words for things, and since Piaget believes children need a mental representation of an object to match a name to it, it makes sense to give children experiences with real objects to lay the foundation for knowing their names. Experiences with balls, dogs, pots, dolls, and other everyday items will provide the basis for developing mental representations to which names can then be attached. On the other hand, a child whose environment lacks opportunities for experiences with real objects will have fewer mental representations and consequently a more limited vocabulary of the names of things.

Given the biological propensity for language development and the tremendous ability of children to learn language on their own even under the most difficult circumstances, there may be a tendency for parents and care-givers to treat language development with benign neglect and not do much to assist children with language acquisition. This approach is unfortunate and does a great disservice to children. The ability of children to teach themselves language flourishes best in a cooperative and supportive environment for language development.

Success in school is marked by how well children know and use language. Children who know the names of things, who can express themselves well, who can talk to the teacher, who understand the language of schooling, are children who, for the most part, will do well in school and life.

Language allows humans to do what no other creatures of creation can do. The abilities to express emotions, recall past experiences, ask questions, make thoughts known, and intimately share hopes and dreams with others are all unique capacities rendered possible by language. Language development affects future learning and life success. People are frequently judged by the sophistication of their language and the impressions their language conveys to others. Language helps define and express the humanness of humans. It is the responsibility of parents, care-givers, and teachers to help children develop this most remarkable of human abilities so they can express their humanness throughout their lives.

PSYCHOSOCIAL DEVELOPMENT

Erikson and Psychosocial Development

In Chapter 2, we began a discussion of Erik Erikson's theory of psychosocial development and its implications for infants. Erikson believes psychosocial development results from the interaction between maturational processes such as biological needs and the social forces encountered in everyday living. Socialization provides the context for conflict and crisis resolution during eight developmental stages that occur throughout life. Social and emotional maturity develop as a result of children's abilities to resolve conflicts at each stage. Interactions of children's needs and drives with the environment and care-giver demands (or lack of them) shape and to a large degree determine personalities. Societal demands help shape and form lives.

Stage 1 — Oral-Sensory (Trust vs. Mistrust). Stage 1 begins at birth and ends at eighteen months to two years. The primary psychosocial conflict during this stage is the development of trust or mistrust as a result of interactions with care-givers. The very young develop a sense of trust in people and the perception that the world is a good place to be as a result of consistency, continuity, and sameness of care. Children need adults whom they can trust as consistent sources of care.

Stage 2 — Muscular-Anal (Autonomy vs. Shame). This stage begins at eighteen to twenty-four months and continues until age three. During this stage, toddlers and preschoolers develop feelings of autonomy or shame. Toddlers develop a sense of autonomy by controlling their physical behavior. Autonomy is not a sudden occurrence. Achievement of autonomy is a developmental process that occurs across the life span. A toddler may be autonomous one day and very dependent the next. A child may demonstrate more autonomy in one setting than in another and at one task or another. Care-givers can assess each child's developmental level of autonomy and determine how to help enhance that growth. Barry may need more of the care-giver's time and personal attention to encourage him to do things for himself, whereas Beth may need only occasional help such as a few timely suggestions and supervision from a distance.

Developmental milestones. Major maturational milestones achieved during this stage are walking and control of elimination. These developmental processes provide the context in which children develop feelings of shame or autonomy.

Walking. As anyone who has provided care for toddlers knows, they like to get into everything and do everything for themselves. They have a basic need to do and to be involved. Parents and care-givers sometimes respond to this natural state by being restrictive, punitive, and overprotective. They try to impose their wills on toddlers. Such care-giver behaviors are antithetical to the development of autonomy. Common sense dictates that toddlers should not be allowed to do everything they want to do. But care-givers need to accommodate their views of acceptable behavior to the needs of the very young in order to meet toddlers' needs for autonomy.

Toddlers want and need to explore their environment and to test the limits of their physical abilities. They should be given the opportunity. Shame and a sense of doubt result from not being allowed to deal effectively with the world.

Toilet Training. The second milestone of this stage is toilet training. This time of life can be difficult and has the potential for creating anxiety in care-givers and parents. Care-givers need to avoid shaming children ("Mindy's been toilet trained for two months and she's younger than you." "When are you going to learn to go in the toilet like a big boy?"). Training toddlers when they are ready and in nonpunitive ways helps them develop feelings that they have control over their own behavior.

Sigmund Freud (see Chapter 1) believed that when parents are too strict, overdemanding, and punitive in the process of toilet training, children develop "anal" personalities. Adult manifestations of an anal personality, according to Freud, include an overemphasis on neatness, punctuality, and cleanliness.

Stage 3 — Locomotor-Genital (Initiative vs. Guilt). This stage is marked by an increasing desire for independence and control over behavior. If given the opportunity, preschoolers will move further away from care-givers in terms both of distance and of the nature of the activities in which they are involved. They continually strive to meet their own needs and are characterized by an "I-want-to-do-it-for-myself" attitude.

Children's attempts to develop autonomy and initiative often meet with punishment. Punishment, especially when it is harsh and unreasonable, results in feelings of guilt. The child feels that what was attempted should not have been tried and tends to reduce further attempts at initiative. (See Chapter 7 for an extended discussion of how to guide children's behavior without trauma or tears.)

Implications for care-givers. First, working with other care-givers, parents need to develop plans and arrangements for providing continuity, consistency, and sameness in child-rearing patterns. Parents who give their children over to the care of others need to communicate their desires for child rearing to assure that there is a match between what they want and what others are able and willing to do. On the other hand, surrogate care-givers may need to help parents articulate what they believe constitute appropriate child-rearing practices. In any event, a high degree of continuity in beliefs and practices needs to exist between parents and others to assure the continuity and consistency that will promote basic trust.

More parents must be willing to seek out acceptable sources of child care that are congruent with their parenting styles, rather than leaving their children in homes and centers where there is a mismatch between what they believe constitutes quality child care and what is being offered. Understandably, this is easier said than done. Also at issue is the unavailability of quality child care to those parents who must work. At stake, however, is the issue of how best to provide for the needs of children.

Second, Erikson's beliefs about developing basic trust, autonomy and initiative make a great deal of sense. Erikson's ideas are positive in nature and stress the good things that occur as a result of the relationships and interactions between care-givers and children. Building basic trust, autonomy, and initiative in others is a marvelous way to help individual children and affect future generations as well. When viewed in this way, care-giving is seen as an honorable profession, a task to be enjoyed rather than a sentence to be endured.

Third, parents need to balance their desire for perfection and obedience with toddlers' and preschoolers' needs for doing things on their own and accomplishing tasks even though they are not done in accordance with adult standards. Adults should compliment children for their efforts rather

Young children need opportunities to accomplish things and experience success. Care-givers must provide settings in which children can do things without fear of criticism. How does success contribute to a child's self-image?

than criticize them because the product is not completely finished or is done without the precision they would like. Preschoolers are interested in initiating and accomplishing. During this stage of their lives they are not ready to have their accomplishments judged by adult standards. Doing the task brings success. Success leads to self-confidence, which leads to initiative. These are the ingredients that will enable children as adolescents and adults to achieve well by adult standards. (In Chapter 1, in the Park Road program vignette, teacher Joann Anderson relates how she lets toddler Kathryn put on her own shoes even if they are wrong in order to help her fulfill her need for autonomy.)

Fourth, toddlers and preschoolers need opportunities to explore, achieve, go places, and meet people. Overprotection and undue restriction lead to shame and uncertainty. A lesson all care-givers have to learn, albeit a difficult one, is how to let go of their children while they simultaneously provide support and protection.

(Again, recall how the staff at Park Road took toddlers out into the community to learn and do. Such experiences provide the context for developing autonomy.)

Fifth, care-givers should do nothing for toddlers and preschoolers that they can do for themselves. As Maria Montessori said, "This is our mission: to cast a ray of light and pass on."[19] Efforts at helping children should be directed toward teaching them the skills they need to be independent of adults. Helping the very young become independent also includes helping them set and accomplish achievable goals. Appropriate expectations for the age and the maturity of particular children help assure that what they are asked to do is reasonable for them.

Sixth, how much and for what to punish is a problem faced by all care-givers. Excessive or punitive punishment stifles attempts at initiative. Guidance and participation in activities with the very young offer a reasonable solution to the punishment dilemma.

Developing routines with children helps them learn what to expect and what behavioral standards are associated with the routine. The toddler's natural desire to do everything, for example, can be channeled into the routine of helping prepare for snack time and clean-up. The care-giver establishes the routine expectation that children, not other care-givers, will put out napkins and cups, pour the beverage, and serve the snack. He or she makes snack time a routine by always having children be the main participants — for example, by making sure cups and pitchers are child-size. Such opportunities for involvement not only control behavior, but also provide for feelings of accomplishment, autonomy, and self-worth.

CHILD-REARING PRACTICES
AND PSYCHOSOCIAL DEVELOPMENT

Parents are the primary determiners of children's environments in the early years, and they are the persons with whom children have their major social encounters. Consequently, how parents rear their children influences psychosocial development. A word of caution is in order.

Parent-child interactions are not the only determiners of behavior and personality. Children themselves play a role in personality development. In Chapter 2 we discussed temperament. A child's temperament influences how a parent responds to that child. A parent who by nature is placid and calm may have difficulty dealing with a "difficult," hard-to-manage baby. Parent-child interactions are bidirectional; that is, parents are influenced by their children and children are influenced by their parents. The sum of this interaction may be greater than the influence of one of the interactions by itself. A mother whose baby constantly reminds her of the husband who abandoned her may have difficulty showing warmth and affection.

Public policy may also influence child rearing. A mother who has to stay home another year with her child because the state raised the admittance age to kindergarten may resent what she considers a wasted year in her life. This resentment can spill over to the child.

Lack of specific parenting skills and information can influence how parents treat their children as well. Parents may not know what to do or how to do it. The point is this: parents influence children, but many things influence parents in their behavior toward children, and quite often, parents have little control over these influences. Parents may take credit and blame for how their children "turn out," but it is unfair to say that parents are totally responsible.

Two developmental psychologists, Eleanor Maccoby and John Martin,

FIGURE 3-4
Classification of Parenting Patterns

	ACCEPTINGNESS	
	Parent is accepting, responsive; relationship is child-centered.	Parent is rejecting, unresponsive; relationship is parent-centered.
Parent is demanding and controlling.	1. Authoritative Characterized by reciprocal relations; high in bidirectional communication.	2. Authoritarian Characterized by emphasis on parent's assertion of authority over child.
Parent is undemanding, makes few attempts to control.	3. Permissive Characterized by parental indulgence of child's desires.	4. Indifferent Characterized by parental neglect of child; parent tends to neglect child and avoid involvement.

DEMANDINGNESS

Source: Adapted from Eleanor E. Maccoby and John A. Martin, "Socialization in the Context of the Family: Parent-Child Interaction," in *Socialization, Personality, and Social Development,* ed. E. Mavis Hetherington, vol. IV of *Handbook of Child Psychology,* 4th ed., ed. Paul H. Mussen (New York: John Wiley, 1983), 39.

reviewed the literature relating to parenting styles and developed a matrix of parental characteristics as depicted in Figure 3-4.

As the figure indicates, four characteristic parenting styles — authoritative, authoritarian, permissive, and indifferent — are demonstrated by parents in their day-to-day interactions with their children. These classifications are useful to characterize parenting styles. Some parent's parenting practices may fit neatly into one of the four categories, but other parents may have styles that overlap. Similarly, some parents may change their styles from time to time, exhibiting some or all of the listed characteristics. What is important for psychosocial development is the consistent style used by parents across developmental time. The day-to-day demands of being a parent call for many kinds of responses. There are times when an authoritarian parent could be classified as an indulgent-permissive parent. These permissive times depend on circumstances and result from conscious decisions, usually involving the child and his or her mother.

Authoritative Parenting

Being an authoritative parent means being involved in the right way. Baumrind provides us with a comprehensive portrait of authoritative parents. They expect mature behavior from children, set clear standards, enforce rules, encourage children to be independent and to express themselves as individuals, communicate well with their children, encourage children to express their points of view, and recognize their parental rights and the rights of their children.[20]

What kind of children does authoritative parenting produce? According to Baumrind, such children are more competent, independent, self-reliant, self-controlled, content, friendly, and cooperative. This array of positive attributes makes the children of authoritative parents sound almost too good to be true. They are the type of children most parents want. As with many things, being an authoritative parent is easier said than done. Many parents lack the knowledge and skills necessary to be authoritative. Unfortunately, some parents persist in their beliefs that either the permissive or authoritarian styles are best. Care-givers and programs can help parents by conducting parenting programs that help them

1. Develop an understanding of the basic needs of children, how to meet these needs, and how meeting needs influences children's behavior.
2. Identify and clarify their parenting goals and the behavior expectations they have for their children. It is surprising how many parents don't know what they believe as parents, what behaviors they want their children to demonstrate, and what expectations they have for their children. Furthermore, many parents don't agree with each other about how to rear their children. Conflicts in parenting styles can also exist in extended families, step-families, and blended families, which result in confusion for parents and children.
3. Use techniques of positive reinforcement to achieve their goals of authoritative parenting.

Authoritarian Parenting

Maccoby and Martin describe the authoritarian style of parenting this way:

> In the authoritarian pattern, parents' demands on their children are not balanced by their acceptance of demands from their children. Although it is understood that children have needs that parents are obligated to fulfill, power-assertive parents place strict limits on allowable expression of these needs by children. Children are expected to inhibit their begging and demanding, and in extreme cases they may not even speak before being spoken to. Parents' demands take the form of edicts. Rules are not discussed in advance or arrived at by any consensus or bargaining process. Parents attach strong value to the maintenance of their authority, and suppress any efforts their children make to challenge it. When children deviate from parental requirements, fairly severe punishment (often physical) is likely to be employed.[21]

The important issue in a discussion of parenting styles is the ultimate effect they have on children and psychosocial development. Maccoby and Martin summarize the relation of authoritarian parenting styles to children's personality characteristics this way:

> Children of authoritarian parents tend to lack social competence with peers: They tend to withdraw, not to take social initiative, to lack spontaneity. Although they do not behave differently from children on contrived measures of resistance to temptation, on projective tests and parents' reports, they do show lesser evidence of "conscience" and are more likely to have an external, rather than internal, moral orientation in discussing what is "right" behavior in situations of moral conflict. In boys, there is evidence that motivation for intellectual performance is low. Several studies link authoritarian parenting with low self-esteem and external locus of control.[22]

Many parents believe reality is the opposite of what research data depict as reality. The folklore of childhoods remembered is full of accounts of parents being "taken out behind the woodshed" as children. Many parents believe that controlling children with a "firm hand" lays the foundation for right behavior. Parents believe that "to spare the rod is to spoil the child." In the case of child-rearing practices, however, a heavy hand and always having to do it the parent's way appears to be an undesirable approach and not in the best interests of children.

Permissive Parenting

It might be better to refer to this parenting style as "indulgent" parenting — the meaning of the term "permissive" is often elusive. One person's concept of permissiveness may differ from another person's.

Maccoby and Martin say that permissive parenting consists of a cluster of behaviors, including

1. The ideological belief that it is "right" for children to display their feelings and emotions. This belief, however, can lead to frustration with children's behavior and can result in harsh punishment.
2. Inattention.
3. Indifference.
4. Nonintervention in children's affairs because of tiredness, depression, or preoccupation.

What are the consequences of permissive parenting? Diana Baumrind, a researcher and psychologist, provides us with a picture of the consequences of failing to be actively involved in parental responsibilities. She found that children of permissive parents are immature and their behavior is characterized by a lack of impulse control, self-reliance, independence, and social responsibility.[23,24]

The consequences of permissive parenting suggest that parents must actively participate in the process of parenting. But isn't the authoritarian parent actively involved in parenting? Of course. But the key is to be involved in the right way.

Indifferent-Uninvolved Parenting

Maccoby and Martin characterize uninvolved parents as wanting to keep their children at a distance. Such parents "orient their behavior primarily toward the avoidance of inconvenience. Thus they will respond to immediate demands from the children in such a way as to terminate them."[25] The extreme result of uninvolved parenting is psychological detachment from children and disinterest in them. Another consequence is neglect, which is a component of abuse. On the other hand, involvement is an elusive characteristic. How much involvement is too much or too little? The amount of involvement parents have in children's lives is a function of where they are in their growth and development as parents. The author, for example, is constantly involved in his children's lives, but there are times when he exerts more or less guidance, depending on the needs of each child. The point is that involvement in children's lives is essential, but too much involvement may be just as bad as too little.

PEER RELATIONSHIPS

Most mothers want their children to play with other children in order to socialize. In fact, over 50 percent of babies between the ages of six and twelve months have contact with other babies.[26] The large number of children in child-care centers accounts for some of the social contact between infants. In child-care centers, however, "contacts with adults are seven times as frequent as contacts with other babies. Clearly when competition exists for the infant's attention from adults and toys, peer socialization is not extensive."[27] These social contacts are not characterized by a high degree of social skill, because babies simply don't have the skills necessary for sustained social interaction.

By the second year, infants' and toddlers' social interactions are more frequent. Between children who are acquainted with each other, the encounters may be sustained. During the second year of life, however, "there is no evidence that children are extensively sought out as social objects nor that they serve necessary or unique functions in socialization."[28]

During the preschool years, children continue to "spend considerable amounts of time by themselves or in noninteractive contact with other children."[29] Preschool children do, however, spend more time in peer interaction and learn more sophisticated social skills than do toddlers. The play group, play environment, and processes of play provide opportunities for children to engage in social interactions. (For a comprehensive discussion of play, see Chapter 5.)

Peer relations in the early years are important. But given the ability of children to be in a group yet apart from the group, and given the solitary nature of many of their activities even in the presence of others, it can be seen that parents and care-givers, not peers, are the primary influence on children's personality development.

THE DEVELOPMENT OF SELF-AWARENESS

Included in psychosocial development is the process of the development of self-awareness. Piaget believes that "a baby has no sense of self at all."[30] If this is so, how do we come to know who we are? Child development researchers provide us with some interesting answers.

Developmental psychologists see each individual as two persons. One is the *existential self* — the self as subject — and the other the *categorical self* — the self as object. This idea of two selves in one is known as the *duality of self* concept.

The self as subject is the self that is distinct from others and from the world. This is the self that thinks, remembers, and perceives. As researchers Michael Lewis and Jeanne Brooks-Gunn point out,

> The basic notion of existence separate from other (both animate and inanimate) develops as the infant differentiates self from other persons. The first social distinction probably involves the mother or caregiver. . . . This primitive self develops from birth and therefore exists in some form in the early months. In fact, 3- and 4-month old infants are able to differentiate between mother and female stranger, as measured by a variety of infant responses. . . . It is not unreasonable to assume that the self-other differentiation also occurs by this time.[31]

According to Lewis and Brooks-Gunn, the development of awareness of self as subject occurs primarily through (1) the infant's actions, (2) social interactions, and (3) the development of object permanence.[32]

The infant's own movements and actions provide a basis for the development of self-awareness. For example, the infant learns that he — not others — has control over his body. Waving, kicking, grasping, and reaching, he learns that he causes his bodily actions and that he is therefore separate from others.

Social interactions provided by care-givers also help young children differentiate themselves from others. When a care-giver responds to a child's actions — crying, smiling, cooing, attempting to talk, walk, etc. — the child is in a sense controlling his environment in that he (as opposed to others) is causing events to happen. The child's sense of his instrumental role in social interactions promotes self-other differentiation and con- tributes to the development of self-awareness.

The development of object and person permanence — the recognition that persons and objects exist even when a child cannot see them — also plays a role in the development of self-awareness. The ability to under- stand that one is distinct from objects and people in the environment is a necessary requisite for self-awareness. Lewis and Brooks-Gunn believe that "the early differentiation of self and other should take place at the same time the child is differentiating its mother from others and is acquir- ing object permanence."[33] (See also our previous discussion of the devel- opment of object permanence on pages 101–105.)

The categorical self — the self as object — is the other part of the dual self. This self consists of attitudes, abilities, and values; taken as a whole, it constitutes what we refer to as our self-concept. Developmentally, we are concerned with how children define themselves in relation to the ex- ternal world. During the course of human development, our self-concept undergoes many changes based on developmental processes and social in- teractions. It is important for care-givers to provide children with oppor- tunities and feedback that promote a positive self-concept.

One of the interesting ways researchers use to study the development of self-awareness is through visual recognition. Table 3-6 outlines the se- quence of acquisition of self based on children's ability to recognize them- selves. Notice in particular that at fifteen to eighteen months, the child "sees image and touches rouge on nose." Mothers participating in the study were given cloths that had red rouge on them and were told to wipe their children's noses so they were noticeably red. If a child touched her nose when she saw herself in a mirror, this was a good indicator that she recognized *she* was the child in the mirror and therefore that she had de- veloped self-awareness.

Keep in mind that although we discuss the self as a duality, we should not think of children as having two selves. A child is an individual person, both separate and distinct from others and possessing a self-concept con- sisting of who he believes he is.

Implications for care-givers. The knowledge that developing children pos- sess about themselves is a function of social interaction. Since most signif- icant social interactions in the early years occur between child and care- giver, the care-giver must provide care that is warm, consistent, caring, and responsive to the infant. For the development of self-concept, feed- back to children communicates that they are worthy, important, compe- tent, and good.

Information about the categorical self can be provided by feedback that promotes a positive self-concept ("Great, Maria! You are really learning to crawl nicely!"). There should be no feedback that promotes a negative self-

TABLE 3-6

The Emergence of Self

Age (months)	Behaviors	Interpretation
Emergence of Self as Subject — as Active, Independent, Causal Agent		
5–8	Interest in mirror image; regards, approaches, touches, smiles, vocalizes. Does not differentially respond to self vs. other in mirror, videotape, or pictorial representation.	No evidence that self is perceived as a causal agent independent of others. No featural differentiation between self and other.
9–12	Understands nature of reflective surface: contingency play, imitation, rhythmic movements, bouncing, waving; can locate objects in space, attached to body.	Active agent in space emerges, awareness of cause-effect relationship between own body movements and moving visual image.
12–15	Uses mirror to locate people or objects in space. Reaches toward person, not image, and reaches toward object not attached to body. Distinguishes between own movement and movement of others on videotape.	Distinguishes self from others. Appreciates self as an active, independent person separate from others, who can also cause their own movements in space.
Emergence of Self as an Object of One's Knowledge		
15–18	In mirror and videotape, demonstrates mark-directed behavior, sees image and touches rouge on nose. Points to self. Distinguishes between self and other in pictorial representation and videotape.	Featural recognition of self; has internal schema for own face that can be compared to external visual image.
18–24	Verbal labeling: infant can state name, attach appropriate personal pronoun to own image in mirror. Can distinguish self from same-gender infant in pictures and can label self.	Appreciation that one has unique featural attributes that can be verbally labeled as the self.

Source: Susan Harter, "Developmental Perspectives on the Self-System," in *Socialization, Personality, and Social Development*, ed. E. Mavis Hetherington, vol. IV of *Handbook of Child Psychology*, 4th ed., ed. Paul H. Mussen (New York: John Wiley, 1983), 283.

Care-givers who are warm, consistent, caring and responsive help children learn that they are important, competent, and good. What can care-givers do to assure that they help children develop good self-images?

concept ("I don't know what is wrong with you. You're the only child in the center who hasn't learned to crawl yet!").

Care-givers should organize the environment so children can receive feedback about both selves. Many child-care programs use mirrors for learning purposes. Some are placed in a vertical position so standing children can see themselves. Mirrors are also placed horizontally at floor level so infants can see their images. The purpose of these mirrors is to provide the child with feedback about the self as subject (for example, facial features, actions, and movements).

Another environmental feature that can strengthen self-concepts is the interactive setting in which care-givers and materials are responsive to the children. Care-givers, for example, can assist children with the mastery of the environment and the use of materials. This can be accomplished by putting materials where children at all ages have access to them. Materials can be provided that allow children to develop competence. For the toddler, one might provide push-pull toys, climbing apparatus, and discovery toys.

SEX-ROLE DEVELOPMENT

Gender is a factor involved in psychosocial development and knowledge of the objective self. Children identify themselves as belonging to a particular gender and subsequently acquire sex-role behaviors. Sex-role behavior consists of the behaviors, activities, attitudes, and values related to being male or female. Three processes are used to explain sex-role development.

Biology

Biological factors are used to explain gender development in a number of ways. First is the anatomical differences between male and female. Freudian psychoanalytic theory places heavy emphasis on the effects of the discovery of anatomical sexual differences on the psychosocial development of children. According to this theory, a boy's discovery of his penis at the end of the first year (or earlier) leads to self-exploration and accompanying pleasurable sensations. During the second and third years, boys experience a castration anxiety based on their fear of losing their penis. This anxiety is resolved through identification with the father or a father figure and through the continued pleasure they find in their bodies.

According to psychoanalytic theory, the task of accepting gender is more difficult for girls. Their discovery that they don't have a penis results in penis envy, which causes anger, anxiety, and defiance. This anxiety is resolved through identification with the mother or a mother figure and feelings of competency and accomplishment.

Erik Erikson, extending psychoanalytic theory, believes that male and female behavior can be explained on the basis of anatomical differences. Erikson says that because of anatomy, males are more intrusive and aggressive. Females are more inclusive and passive.[34]

Psychoanalytic explanations of sex-role development have come under attack in the last decade on the grounds that the theory fails to fully explain male or female sex-role identity and behavior.

Socialization

Another theory of sex-role development is based on environmental and social interactions. This theory holds that children's sex role development results from environmental reinforcement — children are socialized into sex roles. Parents treat boys as boys and girls as girls. In a study of opposite-sex twins, Lewis and Brooks-Gunn found that sex-role-appropriate behavior was reinforced as early as one year of age.[35]

The Role of Parents.   Parents play an important part in the sex-role development of their children. Children identify with their parents and the behaviors they model. Through example, then, parents influence what their children will be like.

Androgyny

There is currently increasing interest in the concept of *androgyny*, the realization that beneficial male and female characteristics can and should exist in the same person. Rather than possessing sharply polarized male or female characteristics, the androgynous person blends characteristics. Whether male or female, such a person can be both assertive and nurturing when considered within the framework of traditional gender roles.

Efforts to promote androgynous personalities meet resistance from those who hold stereotypical views of sex roles. In a recent study of sex-role attitudes of father-son pairs, psychologist Catherine Emihovich and her colleagues found that men held "very traditional sex role expectations for themselves and their sons."[36] Researcher Marie Richmond-Abbott, in a study of single-parent families headed by women, found that 90 percent of the time, the mothers gave their children sex neutral toys or toys traditionally associated with the child's gender. The same pattern held true with household chores: boys were more likely to do "male" chores and girls were more likely to do "female" chores.[37]

Implications for care-givers. Care-givers need to encourage cross-sex behaviors in girls and boys so that the positive characteristic of being male and female are experienced and incorporated into their developing behavioral systems. Boys need to receive and learn how to offer warmth and nurturance. Girls need opportunities for competitiveness and assertiveness. Rigidly defined sex roles limit children's opportunities to become all they are capable of becoming.

All who care for children must be involved in the elimination of stereotypical sex-role behavior. Specific information and ideas for providing nonsexist care and programs are provided in Chapter 6.

SUMMARY

During the toddler and preschool years, the very young become independent, self-directing, perplexing individuals. They learn how to talk and think. During these stages of development, some of life's most remarkable changes occur in a very short time. Two developmental accomplishments during this period of life stand out from all the others because of their significance. One is cognitive development and the other physical and behavioral independence. The cognitive development of children enables them to use symbolic representation — the transformation of physical objects and events into mental symbols. Cognitive development and independence are intertwined. Physical and behavioral independence enables children to develop cognitively. Cognitive development fuels toddlers' and preschoolers' needs for exploration and independence.

Although the toddler and preschool years have historically been depicted as difficult and stressful for care-givers, they are now being recognized as of critical importance in children's present and future development. Part of the early childhood profession's responsibility is to work with vigor, persistence, and dedication to eradicate from the public's thinking the beliefs that the twos are terrible, the threes are trying, and the fours are fearsome. The other part of the challenge is for the profession to dedicate itself to provide the support care-givers need in their efforts to nurture toddlers and preschoolers in the most positive and least punitive ways in their developmental journey so they can truly benefit from these marvelous years.

PROGRAM VIGNETTE

RIDES: Florida International University and AMI-Parkway Regional Medical Center
Miami, Florida

The Educational Research Center for Child Development at Florida International University and the AMI-Parkway Regional Medical Center in Miami, Florida, conduct a cooperative, transdisciplinary parent-child enrichment program known as RIDES (Resources For Infant Development, Education, and Stimulation). RIDES is a twelve-week program for parents and their one- to two-year-old children. RIDES activities are conducted two times a week for an hour and fifteen minutes. RIDES is designed to achieve the following objectives:

- Give parents the opportunity to actively participate in their children's education and development.
- Make learning and parenting activities enjoyable and meaningful.
- Help parents be better parents through child growth and development information.
- Provide an environment in which parents and their children can become involved in research projects designed to determine the effectiveness of learning materials and activities.
- Develop a transdisciplinary model for working with normal young children and their parents.
- Develop an interdisciplinary model through the cooperative efforts of a university child-development research center and a community health facility.

The RIDES team consists of the following members: an education specialist (who is the team leader), a recreation specialist, a nutritionist, an occupational therapist, a registered nurse, and a speech and language therapist.

RIDES is organized around twelve themes or topics designed to increase parents' understanding of their children's development and provide meaningful parent-child activities in each area. These twelve themes are introduced over a twelve-week period, as follows:

Week 1. Developmental screening using the Denver Developmental Screening Test (DDST).

Session 1. The Denver Developmental Screening Test is individually administered to screen for potential developmental problems and establish guidelines for facilitating children's individual learning and development.

Session 2. The RIDES staff discusses with parents the results of the DDST. Suggestions are made on an individual basis, and where appropriate, parents are referred to services at AMI and in the community.

Week 2. Motor development — fine and gross motor.

Session 1. The occupational therapist of the RIDES team focuses on children's posture, reflex integration, and motor development.

Session 2. The RIDES education specialist conducts fine and gross motor activities with the children. Some of these activities include rolling and catching balls, balloon play, and painting with water (conducted as an outside activity).

In addition, the specialist shows parents how to conduct activities at home. To facilitate learning at home, parents are given "task cards," which state objectives and activities for facilitating learning and development.

Week 3. Health and safety.

Session 1. CPR, Heimlich maneuver, and first aid for infants and small children are demonstrated by the registered nurse. The nurse also discusses safety and accident prevention in the home. Topics covered include what to do if there is a fire in the home ("Stop, drop, and roll") and how to store medicines and cleaning materials away from children.

Session 2. This session provides parent and child activities, with an emphasis on learning health and safety skills. The primary activity is medical play utilizing clothing associated with the health professions (masks, gowns, and hats), medical equipment (stethoscope, medical bag), and props such as baby dolls.

Week 4. Toys that teach.

Session 1. The education specialist demonstrates toys and other learning materials that promote fine motor, gross motor, cognitive, and social skills.

Session 2. A variety of different toys and materials are displayed for parent-child interaction and teacher discussion. Parents and their young children select a toy and the parent tells why they selected it and how they can use it to promote learning.

Week 5. Creative movement.

Session 1. The focus in this session is on children's movement as a form of communication. The importance of nonverbal communication is stressed, and parents are shown how to "read" their children's nonverbal communication.

Session 2. Children and their parents are involved in different forms of music and movement activities. Commercial records designed to promote body awareness, creative activity, and creative play acting are used, as are other activities, such as sand painting, which integrates movement and sensory experiences.

Week 6. Learning readiness.

Session 1. This session is devoted to a demonstration of how visual, auditory, vocabulary, and language skills work together to form the foundation for learning readiness.

Session 2. Parents and children play with texture books and "feel boxes," string large macaroni, and play with play dough while the education specialist explains the role of manipulative skills, eye-hand coordination, and sensory integration in learning.

Week 7. Nutrition in the early years.

Session 1. The RIDES team dietitian provides guidelines for planning well-balanced diets and offers tips for feeding young children.

Session 2. The dietitian conducts activities involving "healthy" foods. Children wash fruits and vegetables and help prepare a healthy snack.

Week 8. Hygiene and grooming.

Session 1. The occupational therapist of the RIDES team discusses the development of hygiene and grooming skills and how they influence self-image and healthy living. Practical advice is also given about what grooming products and health aids are most appropriate for young children.

Session 2. This session is devoted to grooming and hygiene activities involving washing (how to use soap, wash cloth, and towel), tooth brushing, and comb and hair brush.

Week 9. Dressing.

Session 1. The occupational therapist models dressing techniques and skills. The therapist also demonstrates developmental sequences involved in dressing.

Session 2. Children and parents participate in games and activities related to dressing. Dolls and flannel figures are utilized.

Week 10. Language development.

Session 1. The certified speech therapist and language specialist discusses speech and language development, emphasizing developing communication skills and parent-child communication.

Session 2. Parents and children play language games and perform reading activities. The emphasis is on how to talk to children, questioning techniques, and shared communication.

Week 11. Life with infants and toddlers.

Session 1. The education specialist discusses the importance of routines and expectations in developing basic trust. Ten tips for positive parenting are discussed, and examples and illustrations are provided.

Session 2. Parents and children act out daily routines such as bathing and going to sleep. Songs, games, and other activities are taught for developing the routines of waking up, washing, eating, brushing teeth, "helping" with home activities, and going to bed.

Week 12. Concept review and graduation.

Session 1. The education specialist reviews concepts from previous sessions. The emphasis is on having parents share what activities they found most helpful and how they benefited from the program.

Session 2. A "graduation ceremony" is held in which children and parents participate in games and other activities designed to reinforce skills and activities learned throughout the RIDES program. A clown (one of the program staff) distributes awards, certificates of accomplishment, and packets of learning materials.

Parents are very positive about RIDES and find the program meaningful and worthwhile. According to Nancy Rich, parent of fifteen-month-old Mandy, "RIDES teaches parents many new skills and provides opportunities for interaction between my daughter and me in ways that I might not have thought about before. I also see the reasons for doing and not doing many things I might have just taken for granted."

Faith Powers, mother of one-year-old Chayce, believes it is important for children and parents to have a program in which they are able to share and benefit from a positive, pressure-free approach to learning. As she says, "I want my daughter to have an 'educational experience' and I want to learn more about child rearing and parenting. A program such as RIDES focuses on more than the traditional three Rs to learning and provides me with many experts from different fields to talk to and learn from. The task cards are very helpful because they not only provide me with great ideas for activities at home, but they are also constant reminders to me that I can do many different activities in many different ways to help Chayce learn."

The unique features of RIDES include the following:

1. The transdisciplinary model provides a team approach to the education and development of normal young children. The transdisciplinary model is quite common in the education of special-needs children (see Chapter

9), but more early childhood programs are discovering the benefits of such a model for normal children.

2. Early developmental and education screening identifies developmental delays prior to the "normal" educational process. This early identification encourages early prevention and remediation.

3. The collaboration of a university and a major medical program provides an opportunity for early educators and health professionals to interact and develop a program for educating and developing the very young.

4. RIDES helps parents recognize the importance of early learning. By providing a rationale for early learning and activities that promote it, parents are more likely to be aware of and sensitive to the need to include learning activities as part of children's daily living.

5. The program challenges educational and medical staff to share their knowledge through activities. It is one thing to *tell* parents what they should do, but quite another to develop an activity-based program that helps them *know* and *see* what to do.

ENRICHMENT THROUGH ACTIVITIES

1. Interview parents about when and how they toilet trained their children. Also ask pediatricians, child-care workers, and nurses how they tell parents to toilet train.
    a) How do parents' and professionals' ideas differ?
    b) What did parents say they would do differently (or did do differently in the case of a second child) the next time they toilet trained a child?

2. Talk to children ages twelve, fifteen, eighteen, twenty-one, twenty-four, twenty-seven, and thirty months. Record the words they know. What are the differences in the number and kinds of words they know? How do you explain these differences? What implications does your information have for parenting and child care?

3. Read and review an article on children's language development. Summarize the main ideas, findings, and conclusions. What was the article's main idea?
    a) How would you apply the article to teaching and child care?
    b) How does the article agree or disagree with information presented in this chapter?

4. Maria Montessori believed that one of the purposes of education was to help children become independent of adults.
    a) Do you agree that independence is a major goal of education?
    b) List some specific things parents and care-givers can do to encourage the development of independence in children.

5. Personality consists of an individual's enduring qualities and typical ways of reacting to persons and situations.
    a) Observe two preschool children and list some of their personal qualities and the ways they react to people and situations. How are the children's personalities similar and different?

b) In what ways do parents and care-givers help determine children's personalities?

c) What other factors, including parenting practices, influence personality development?

6. Toddlers' drive for autonomy assures that they will test boundaries in exploring their environment. This constant testing of the limits — the limits of parent's patience, the limits of what they can get into, the limits of always wanting to do things their way — can be frustrating to them and their care-givers.

a) What can parents do to make life easier for themselves and their children during this trying child-rearing time?

b) How can child-care and preschool teachers work with parents to help them with their toddlers?

7. Based on families you know or have come in contact with, give specific examples of the four categories of parenting styles presented in this chapter.

8. Freudian theory suggests that sex-role development occurs through identification.

a) In what ways can children learn sex roles through identification?

b) What implications does single parenting have for the development of sex roles through identification?

9. Identify specific behavioral characteristics that indicate the toddler's emerging independence.

10. Interview parents, teachers, and child-care providers of children ages three, four, and five. Ask them to identify characteristics typical of children at each age level.

a) How do these age groups resemble and differ from each other?

b) In what ways do you agree or disagree with these behavioral descriptions?

11. Learning to walk is a skill that changes the toddler's life in many important ways.

a) What effect does learning to walk have on toddlers?

b) What effect does toddlers' learning to walk have on parents and care-givers?

c) Visit the home of some friends or relatives. What specific suggestion would you make to them for "child-proofing" their home?

12. In what ways can the self-concepts of care-givers affect the self-concepts of children? Give specific examples.

13. Mike Kinard is four years old and has the language skills of a three-year-old. He has difficulty communicating with his care-givers and peers. Mike's parents were invited to the preschool for a conference. Mike's mother came to the conference and brought Mike with her. During the conference, Mike's mother held him on her lap, "pampered" him, and talked to him using baby talk.

a) What might be some reasons for Mike's language delay?

b) What are some things Mike's mother can do to assist with his language development?

c) What can the staff members do to help Mike and his mother?

14. Describe different ways care-givers communicate with the very young. Do these ways of communicating change depending on such variables as culture of child or care-giver, the child's state of health, and the objectives of the program?

ENRICHMENT THROUGH READING

Ausberger, Carolyn, et al. *Learning to Talk Is Child's Play.* Tucson, Ariz.: Communication Skill Builders, 1982.

The authors have developed a method of language development called *responsive language teaching.* Its primary ingredients are the care-giver's openness to what the child is trying to say and the ability to provide the language the child needs to hear. As the authors state, "The key to helping children develop language skills lies in understanding that normal children are experts in learning language. Given the opportunity to experience the world and to have a caring, perceptive adult respond, children are capable of guiding that adult into helping them. The adult's job is to be the child's assistant. The adult who is effective at teaching language is one who can observe a child and provide words that go with the child's actions, interests, and perceptions." This is an excellent book that shows how to be a child's language-learning assistant.

Cazden, Courtney B., ed. *Language in Early Childhood Education.* rev. ed. Washington, D.C.: National Association for the Education of Young Children, 1981.

Early childhood teachers want to know how to develop an effective program of language development. This book helps with that process by providing practical ideas and suggestions. The most useful topics are those dealing with developing a total language curriculum, bilingual education, and the integration of language and reading. The book is practitioner-oriented and easy to read.

Hass, Carolyn Buhai. *Look at Me: Activities for Babies and Toddlers.* Glencoe, Ill.: CBH Publishing, 1985.

As the title suggests, this is a book full of easy-to-use activities. There are chapters entitled Toys To Make, Learning Games, Indoor/Outdoor Fun, Books and Reading, Positive Self-Image, Imaginative Play, Arts and Crafts, and Easy and Nutritious Recipes, among many others. Care-givers can adapt the ideas presented to make them developmentally appropriate to the children they care for. If you are looking for an activities resource book, this is it.

Heath, Shirley Brice. *Ways with Words.* Cambridge, England: Cambridge University Press, 1983.

In the prologue to her book, Professor Heath states, "In the late 1960's, school desegregation in the southern United States became a legislative mandate and a fact of daily life. Academic questions about how children talk when they come to school and what educators should know and do about oral and written language were echoed in practical pleas of teachers who asked: 'What do I do in my classroom on Monday morning?'" To help teachers answer this question, Heath studied how two culturally different communities in the Piedmont Carolinas learned to use language in their homes and communities. The result is a fascinating account of children's ways with words, which will enable teachers to be better teachers of language learning.

Lief, Nina R., and Fahs, Mary Ellen. *The Second Year of Life: A Guide for Parenting.* New York: Dodd, Mead and Company, 1984.

This is a very practical book designed to give care-givers month-by-month help in rearing children. Each chapter begins with a section on developmental highlights. A unique feature of this book is that it utilizes the actual conversations and questions of parents as a basis for discussions about how to rear and care for the two-year-old. This book contains much useful information.

Karnes, Merle B. *You and Your Small Wonder: Activities for Parents and Toddlers on the Go.* Circle Pines, Minn.: American Guidance Service, 1982.

The author provides 156 activities to help care-givers help children develop during the toddler months. The activities cover physical, emotional, and intellectual growth as well as language development in children between eighteen and thirty-six months. In addition to the activities, which are practical and easy to implement, there is valuable information on health, safety, and child development. This is an excellent resource for parents and other care-givers.

White, Burton L. *The First Three Years of Life: The Revised Edition.* Englewood Cliffs, N.J.: Prentice-Hall, 1985.

White is convinced that parents and care-givers should focus most of their attention on the first three years of life. He has written a readable, practical, commonsense approach to the development of children. Dr. White takes the reader step by step through all stages of development during the first three years and provides an in-depth discussion of topics of concern to care-givers for each stage. This book should be required reading for all care-givers.

NOTES

1. Carol A. Kavanagh and Leonard Banco, "The Infant Walker: A Previously Unrecognized Health Hazard," *American Journal of Diseases of Childhood* 138 (March 1982): 206.
2. Langdon G. Longstreth, "Human Handedness: More Evidence for Genetic Involvement," *The Journal of Genetic Psychology* 137 (December 1980): 275–283.
3. Caroline B. Sinclair, *Movement of the Young Child: Ages Two to Six* (Columbus, Ohio: Charles E. Merrill, 1973), 3.
4. T. Berry Brazelton, *Toddlers and Parents: A Declaration of Independence* (New York: Delacorte, 1974).
5. Benjamin Spock and Michael Rothenberg, *Dr. Spock's Baby and Child Care* (New York: E. P. Dutton, 1985).
6. Jean Piaget, *The Origins of Intelligence in Children*, trans. Margaret Cook (New York: International Universities Press, 1952), 269.
7. Jean Piaget and Barbel Inhelder, *The Psychology of the Child* 85. Translated from the French by Helen Weaver. Copyright © 1966 by Presses Universitaires de France Paris. Copyright © 1969 by Basic Books Inc. Reprinted by permission of the publisher.
8. Jean Piaget, "Schemes of Action and Language," in *Language and Learning: The Debate Between Jean Piaget and Noam Chomsky*, ed. Massimo Piattelli-Palmarini (Cambridge, Mass.: Harvard University Press, 1980), 167.
9. L. Vygotsky, *Thought and Language*, ed. and trans. Eugenia Hanfmann and Gertrude Vakar (Cambridge, Mass.: MIT Press, 1962), 43.
10. Peter A. de Villiers and Jill G. de Villiers, *Early Language* (Cambridge, Mass.: Harvard University Press and William Collins Sons, Ltd., 1979), 19–20.
11. Eve V. Clark, "Meanings and Concepts," in *Cognitive Development*, ed. J. H.

Flavell and E. M. Markman, vol. III of *Handbook of Child Psychology*, 4th ed., ed. Paul H. Mussen (New York: John Wiley, 1983), 798.

12. Clark, "Meanings," 798.
13. de Villiers and de Villiers, *Early Language*, 39.
14. Herbert Ginsburg and Sylvia Opper, *Piaget's Theory of Intellectual Development* (Englewood Cliffs, N.J.: Prentice-Hall, 1979), 78.
15. Elissa L. Newport et al., "Mother, I'd Rather Do It Myself: Some Effects and Non-Effects of Maternal Speech Style," in *Talking to Children: Language Input and Acquisition*, ed. Catherine E. Snow and Charles A. Ferguson (Cambridge, England: Cambridge University Press), 112–129.
16. Roger Brown, *A First Language* (Cambridge, Mass.: Harvard University Press, 1973), 281.
17. Lois Bloom, *Language Development: Form and Function in Emerging Grammars* (Cambridge, Mass.: MIT Press, 1970).
18. P. S. Dale, *Language Development*, 2nd ed. (New York: Holt, Rinehart and Winston, 1976), 157.
19. Maria Montessori, *The Discovery of the Child* (Notre Dame, Ind.: Fides Publishers, 1967), 117.
20. Diana Baumrind, "Current Patterns of Parental Authority," *Developmental Psychology Monograph*, 1971, No. 4, Part 2.
21. Eleanor E. Maccoby and John A. Martin, "Socialization in the Context of the Family: Parent-Child Interaction," in *Socialization, Personality, and Social Development*, ed. E. Mavis Hetherington, vol. IV of *Handbook of Child Psychology*, 4th ed., ed. Paul H. Mussen (New York: John Wiley, 1983), 39.
22. Maccoby and Martin, "Socialization," 43–44.
23. Diana Baumrind, "Child Care Practices Anteceding 3 Patterns of Preschool Behavior," *Genetic Psychology Monographs*, 1967, 43–88.
24. Baumrind, "Current Patterns," No. 4, Part 2.
25. Maccoby and Martin, "Socialization," 49.
26. Willard W. Hartup, "Peer Relations," in *Socialization, Personality, and Social Development*, ed. E. Mavis Hetherington, vol. IV of *Handbook of Child Psychology*, 4th ed., ed. Paul H. Mussen (New York: John Wiley, 1983), 113.
27. Hartup, "Peer Relations," 115.
28. Hartup, "Peer Relations," 115.
29. Hartup, "Peer Relations," 117.
30. Jean Piaget, "The First Year of Life of the Child" (1927), in *The Essential Piaget*, ed. and trans. H. E. Gruber and J. J. Voneche (New York: Basic Books, 1982), 200.
31. Michael Lewis and Jeanne Brooks-Gunn, *Social Cognition and the Acquisition of Self* (New York: Plenum Press, 1979), 9.
32. Lewis and Brooks-Gunn, *Social Cognition*, 9–10.
33. Lewis and Brooks-Gunn, *Social Cognition*, 10.
34. Erik H. Erikson, *Identity: Youth and Crisis* (New York: Norton, 1969).
35. Lewis and Brooks-Gunn, *Social Cognition*, 268.
36. Catherine Emihovich et al., "Sex Role Expectation Changes by Fathers for Their Sons," *Sex Roles* 11 (November 1984): 861–868.
37. Marie Richmond-Abbot, "Sex Role Attitudes and Children in Divorced, Single Parent Families," *Journal of Divorce* 8 (Fall 1984): 61–81.

Chapter 4

How Do the Young Children We Care For Learn?

Questions to Guide Your Reading and Study

- What are the major theories that explain how young children learn?
- Why is it important for care-givers to know about how young children learn?
- How do theories help explain how young children play?
- How does play contribute to and promote learning?
- How and why is play important in the lives of the very young?
- What are Piaget's stages of children's play?
- How does Mildred Parten classify children's play?
- What are the purposes of block, water, dramatic, and medical play?
- What are the roles and responsibilities of care-givers in promoting play?
- What are the characteristics of effective play environments and playgrounds?
- What are major issues associated with learning through play?

INTRODUCTION

Care-giver Tasks

In their development as professionals, teachers and care-givers have to grapple with a theory about how children learn. Trying to determine how children learn is a never-ending process, one that involves three steps. Teachers and care-givers must:

1. Formulate a theory about how children learn. Beliefs about how children learn influence how professionals teach and care for children. How professionals care for and teach children influences how and what children learn.
2. Base teaching and care-giving behaviors on a theory about how children learn. Realistically, teachers and care-givers seldom adopt one pure theory of learning (if indeed there is a pure theory); rather, they select from several theories ideas they like and agree with. This is an *eclectic* approach to care-giving. It works well, especially for those who can explain what ideas from different theories they use and why.
3. Consider new information and change old ideas. Across the life span of their work with children, parents, teachers, and care-givers need to challenge their own beliefs, and when appropriate, incorporate others' ideas and research findings. All who want the best for children do not let their beliefs about what is "right" stand in the way of discovering new truths to help them achieve that goal.

MATURATION AND LEARNING

In Chapters 2 and 3 you read about the physical growth and development of the very young. Physical growth is regulated by genetic factors working through biological processes. The result is *maturation*. From the moment of conception, the regulating genetic code determines biological development across the life span. This code governs the development of bones, tissues, and muscles that enables children to look like humans, to grow in height and weight, to walk, and to speak. This genetic code also governs the process by which children develop through childhood, adolescence, adulthood, and old age. In sum, maturation is the process of changing growth patterns that begin at conception and end at death.

Much of maturation is orderly and predictable. We have seen evidence of this orderliness in the developmental schedules of Arnold Gesell and in the stages of language development. We rely on data to understand the characteristics of normal growth and development and to be alert to children who do not meet or approximate these patterns.

Learning, on the other hand, is the process by which individuals change as the result of experiences. You have undoubtedly heard the saying that people learn by their experiences, and this is true. Many varied experiences from the social, physical, ecological, and emotional environments influence and promote learning.

Experiences influence development. Lack of learning experiences retarded and otherwise negatively influenced the language growth of Genie (Chapter 2). Experiences that influence the processes of learning and maturation are entwined and interrelated. These two interactive processes determine what children will be like, and helping determine what children will be like is the essence of parenting, teaching, and care-giving.

THEORIES ABOUT HOW CHILDREN LEARN

Learning Through Unfolding

Friedrich Froebel was the historical popularizer of learning through unfolding, the concept that inner forces — maturation — determine the rate and time at which learning occurs. Children learn when the time is right for learning. This is the foundation of the concept of readiness.

Froebel likened the growth of a child to the growth of a plant. Caregivers nurture children much as gardeners care for tender plants. At the very heart of Froebel's concept of unfolding was his belief that education — whatever is done for children — should be in harmony with God and nature. Education should promote harmonious living in relation to the spiritual and natural world. It is in the context of such a harmonious relationship that children unfold to their true potential. This fundamental belief, that children are children of God and should be treated accordingly, underlies not just Froebel's theory, but the theories of other great educators as well.

Froebel had several things in mind when he gave his "school" the name "kindergarten." First, he believed that development proceeds best through unfolding, not through molding or forcing. In the *Education of Man*, he says, "We grant time and space to young plants and animals because we know that, in accordance with laws that live in them, they will develop properly and grow well; young animals and plants are given rest, and arbitrary interference with their growth is avoided, because it is known that the opposite practice would disturb their pure unfolding and sound development; but the young human being is looked upon as a piece of wax, a lump of clay, which man can mold into what he pleases."[1] To Froebel, nothing was more obnoxious and wrong than forceful and artificial educational practice.

Second, Froebel didn't want his educational process to be conceived of as a traditional school. For Froebel, traditional schools were used to force children to learn in unnatural, artificial ways.

Third, the principle of not forcing children to learn implies that each child will be treated individually. Children, Froebel believed, should not be taught and reared as though they were alike, nor should they be forced to be alike.

Arnold Gesell and his followers (see Chapter 1) are the modern popularizers of the theory of unfolding. The unfolding theory of development has not enjoyed much favor of late, particularly because of the dominance of the back-to-basics movement and the emphasis on early cognitive learning. The advocates of unfolding, however, are persistent in their beliefs, and in the United States today there is a decided reawakening of interest in unfolding. This renewed interest is due largely to the feeling on the part of many educators that children are being hurried and forced to grow up too fast. This hurrying not only deprives children of their childhood, it forces learning on them before they are ready.

Learning Through the Senses

The belief that children learn primarily through their senses is another popular view about how children learn. John Locke (1632–1704), an English medical doctor and philosopher, helped develop and popularize the idea of *environmentalism* — the belief that the environment, not innate ideas, determines what a child will be. Locke likened the human mind at birth to a blank tablet and maintained that experiences are the foundation of all knowledge. Given this basic assumption, experiences determine the nature of children, who are literally the sum total of their experiences.

Locke and others who were influenced by him, particularly Maria Montessori (see Chapter 6), believed that the best way to make children sensitive and receptive to their experiences was through sensory training. This belief that sensory knowledge of the world is the basis of learning is known as *empiricism*. An empiricist approach accounts for the heavy emphasis in many contemporary early childhood programs on sensory training and the use of materials and equipment designed primarily to train the senses.[2]

There are several assumptions associated with the empiricist view of learning. First, the child is viewed as a *receiver* of sensory information from the environment. There is no need for the child to restructure knowledge intellectually. She learns through stimulus properties — size, shape, color, and so on — what the world is like.

Second, the teacher's role is to provide sensory experiences in order to help children refine their powers of sensory perception. What is important is how well the child develops her senses and uses them rather than how she intellectually restructures what she takes in through her senses.

There are two major difficulties with empiricism. The first of these is the restriction of the concept of learning to knowledge gained through the senses. If a child can learn only by seeing, touching, feeling, smelling, hearing, and tasting, this makes for a limited view of reality. In your own life, think what a day would be like if you limited the way you could learn to only sensory impressions! The world of things and objects would be available to you, but not the world of thoughts and ideas. Ideas and thoughts are not subject to seeing, touching, and tasting!

Second, empiricism rules out or severely de-emphasizes the *child's* intellectual or cognitive role in learning. In the empiricist view, the child merely takes in sensory data and has little if any role in restructuring or interpreting that data. Likewise, the teacher's role is limited to providing children with sensory experiences, with minimal emphasis on having those experiences make sense to the child. The teacher sees her performance as sufficient as long as she has provided sensory experiences. Sensory experiences become ends unto themselves rather than foundations for cognitive thoughts and ideas.

Behaviorism: Learning Through Stimulus and Response

The learning theories based on the ideas of Froebel, Gesell, Montessori, and Piaget all have a decided maturational or biological theme. Their stage theories are based on the assumption that there are underlying structural components in development that follow a timetable for emergence. Learning is, in part, a result of maturation.

In the behaviorist view, the emphasis is not on biology or a series of age-bound stages, but on how development results from learning. Learning occurs as a result of children's interaction with the environment and the reinforcement or reward systems of that environment. Changes don't depend on age. B. F. Skinner (b. 1904), generally considered the modern popularizer of behaviorism, sees development as a continuous, incremental sequence of specific conditioned acts. Given such a point of view, there are endless possibilities for parents and care-givers to shape and control development. (See Chapter 1, especially the quotation by J. B. Watson on page 00.)

Ivan Pavlov (1849–1936), the Russian physiologist and Nobel laureate, laid the foundation for behaviorism with his demonstration of *classical conditioning*. Pavlov took an *unconditioned response*, in this case, salivation in a dog, and made it a *conditioned response*. Pavlov conditioned the salivary response by providing meat simultaneously with the ringing of a bell. After several occurrences in which the dog was presented with both meat and a ringing bell, Pavlov could merely ring a bell and the dog would salivate. Salivating, which had been an unconditioned response, became a conditioned response because every time Pavlov rang a bell, the dog salivated.

In addition to classical conditioning, there is also *operant conditioning*. Operant conditioning is based on the *law of effect*, which states that a behavior can be strengthened or weakened by its effects. Behaviors that bring pleasure and satisfaction are more likely to be repeated — and therefore learned — than are other behaviors. The *imperial law of effect* states that the consequences of a particular behavior determine whether or not the behavior will be repeated. A child who cries and is immediately given a cookie will probably learn to use crying to get cookies.

Social Learning Theory

A group of behaviorists known as social learning theorists emphasize the role of social interactions in the process of learning. A leading proponent of social learning theory is Albert Bandura (b. 1925). He and other social learning theorists believe learning occurs through modeling, observation, vicarious experiences, and self-regulation or internal mediating processes. Concerning modeling, Bandura says, "Learning would be exceedingly laborious, not to mention hazardous, if people had to rely solely on the effects of their own actions to inform them what to do. Fortunately, most human behavior is learned observationally through modeling: from observing others, one forms an idea of how new behaviors are performed, and on later occasions this coded information serves as a guide for action."[3]

There are four processes or steps involved in modeling: attention to people, remembering the observed behavior, reproduction of what was observed, and adjusting the modeled behavior in response to feedback.

The biggest difference between the perspectives of regular behaviorists and social learning theorists concerns the self-regulation process. According to the behaviorist viewpoint, a stimulus automatically produces a response in a child, as shown in Figure 4-1. According to social learning theorists, however, behavior resulting from a stimulus is mediated by the child. The child's response is a product of the child's past experiences, cognitive level of functioning, and the value of the stimulus for the child. The process of development, then, is a reciprocal one, as shown in Figure 4-2.

The behaviorist theory has a wide following, particularly in applied areas such as teaching. Many teachers have been trained in the use of "behavior modification techniques" and use them in discipline and to manage behavior (see Chapter 7). Critics of behaviorism believe its rationale is too "economical" to adequately explain the full range of human learning, which they believe involves more than stimuli and responses. Furthermore, much of the experimental data that supports behaviorism was gath-

Stimulus———→Response in Child   **FIGURE 4-1**
Regular Behaviorist Theory

Stimulus→Child Processes Stimulus———→Response in Child   **FIGURE 4-2**
Social Learning Theory

ered from animal experiments. Critics contend that learning in animals is different from learning in humans.

Piaget and Constructivism

Two leading Piaget scholars, Constance Kamii and Rheta Devries, point out that Piaget's theory of *constructivism* states that each child constructs his physical and logical-mathematical knowledge through his own actions on objects.[4] As Kamii explains, "Constructivism refers to the fact that knowledge is built by an active child from the inside rather than being transmitted from the outside through the senses."[5] The Piagetian view of how children learn, then, is the opposite of the Montessori view of how children learn.

The constructivist process "is defined in terms of the individual's organizing, structuring, and restructuring of experience — an ongoing life-long process — in accordance with existing schemes of thought. In turn, these schemes become modified and enriched in the course of interaction with the physical and social world."[6] Experiences provide a basis for constructing schemes. As a result of experiences and interactions with care-givers, children modify and restructure their schemes or mental images of the world. A child modifies her mental idea of cats, for example, from one that originally included all four-legged creatures she encountered on her daily walk with her care-giver to one that includes only small, furry four-legged animals. Eventually, she will restructure her scheme of *cat* to ex-

Children's knowledge of the physical world is built through active involvement. Each child must have opportunities to develop new schemes through assimilation and accommodation. What knowledge about the physical world is this child learning through his play?

clude squirrels and include only those animals society has come to agree are cats.

According to the constructivist theory, there are essentially three sources of knowledge for the child: the child herself, objects, and people. The child develops new schemes through assimilation and accommodation with the physical world — objects — and with the social world. It is primarily through people that the child gains knowledge of elements of the social world such as customs, manners, and how to behave in certain situations.

LEARNING THROUGH PLAY

Modern learning theorists, including Piaget, incorporate in their theories of learning a fundamental principle advocated by Froebel: that children as developing organisms are unities and develop — unfold — through creative self-initiated activity. Froebel believed this creative activity is enhanced by interaction with other children. Since children are, at least in part, the products of creative activity, what they become is a product of what they do. Through activity organisms realize their potential and become unified wholes. *Play* is the word most frequently used to identify this activity.

This belief in the active child developing in accordance with stages of development is like the recurring theme of a symphony. It emerges every so often to remind us what education is all about. Froebel advocated it, Montessori believed it, Piaget adopted it, and teachers everywhere embrace it as a truth of teaching and learning. It is like an eternal truth that is part of educational practice. The perplexing problem that has plagued and challenged educators is how to operationalize into the reality of everyday home and classroom practice the belief that learning does indeed occur through play.

A corollary of the belief that children develop through active play is that they must have access to the materials and equipment of play as well as the time, place, and opportunity for play.

What Is Play?

Robert H. White believes play is a response to and a result of effectance motivation, the inner motivation that "represents what the neuromuscular system wants to do when it is otherwise unoccupied or is gently stimulated by the environment." Through play

> the child appears to be occupied with the agreeable task of developing an effective familiarity with his environment. This involves discovering the effects he can have on the environment and the effects the environment will have on him. To the extent that these results are preserved by learning, they build on

an increased competence in dealing with the environment. The child's play can thus be viewed as serious business, though to him it is merely something that is interesting and fun to do.[7]

Play as Self-Motivated Activity and Learning. So much has been said about play, it seems as though the more we say about it, the less we are really sure what it is. One thing most people are sure of, however, is that children learn through play. *Play* can be defined, then, as a self-motivated activity through which learning occurs. Children do not have to be told to play except in instances where they are restricted from engaging in self-initiated play. This restriction can be physical or emotional. Children who are undernourished may not have the energy to engage in play. Children reared in a restrictive environment may not have toys or materials to play with. Children whose psychological needs for love and caring have not been met may not want to or be able to express an interest in the environment or toys. The infant who is socially insecure may not be able to make excursions into the play environment.

Other attempts to define play involve comparing work and play. Play is frequently called children's work. Friedrich Froebel started us thinking about this relationship. Froebel believed that it is possible to help children transfer the happiness, joy, and pleasure of play to the world of adult work. Froebel reasoned that by doing this, adults would find more satisfaction and fulfillment in their daily lives.

The comparison of work and play frequently confuses the issue and makes us think of the two as synonymous. When this occurs, adults force on children's play the many connotations they associate with their work, namely that it is difficult and highly structured. When adults associate work with play, they tend to want to structure and control it. Children's play is not work in the adult sense of the word. Play is children's work in the sense that they are involved in activities in which they use their time, energy, and past experiences to develop talents and skills.

Another concept of play suggests that it is not goal-directed, but this is untrue. All play is goal-directed in some way, even when children play "for the fun of it." Claiming that when a child, parent, or teacher attaches a goal to play it ceases to be play is an artificial and unnecessary restriction. One of the problems the proponents of play have in defending it from its detractors is distinctions of this sort. A major problem with some play-oriented curricula for the very young is that they are not goal-directed.

Reasons Children Play

Why do children play? There are many theories that try to address this question. One is the *excess energy* theory, which holds that children play to release excess energy. Many teachers view play in this way. Undoubtedly, physical activity through play does give children an opportunity to release energy, and releasing energy is important. Every child needs and enjoys a change of pace. But there is more to play than releasing energy, as you will discover shortly.

Another theory holds that children play in order to learn adult roles and occupations. Certainly dramatic play provides opportunities for children to try out adult roles. William T. Harris, an early supporter of public kindergartens in the United States, believed that children's play activities — for example, block building, construction activities, and housekeeping — could have implications for children's involvement in adult roles and occupations.

Benefits of Play

Whatever the theory, children play in order to learn. Play provides many opportunities for children to develop physically, socially, and intellectually.

Physical Development. Play activity is important for physical development. Without the opportunity to exercise and strengthen muscles, tissues, and bones, children would not gain the strength they need to participate in play and life activities. Play helps children discover how their bodies function and how they can be used in learning.

Play helps in the development of large muscles as children run, walk, climb, dig, and throw. Small muscles are developed as children grasp toys, pick up blocks, and use crayons and paint brushes. Children learn independence through buttoning, zipping, and tying.

Social Skills. Children learn social skills as they interact with others during play. Experiences in social relationships give them confidence to relate to a wider range of children and adults. Play helps children learn that not all people think and believe as they do. These encounters help children decenter from their egocentrism and give them new information and views to assimilate and accommodate.

Although the social benefits of play are the ones usually cited by its supporters, play is also an excellent way to integrate into children's lives the academic areas of science, mathematics, and language development. Children learn about color, shape, and size through play. They learn the concepts of "under," "over," and "through" by playing with objects that they push under bridges, over roads and through tunnels. Play provides opportunities for making decisions about what to play with, how to play, who to play with, and how to use the materials and objects of play.

Through play, children learn how to relate to others and the feelings others have. They become more civilized in managing their confrontations and conflicts with their peers and hence grow in maturity. Play offers opportunities to try out different roles, express feelings in a nonthreatening setting, and consider the roles of others.

Risk Taking. Play provides a secure (although not always safe) context in which children can take risks, including physical risks such as climbing higher and attempting activities not previously tried, and emotional risks such as sharing feelings with others and learning firsthand how words, thoughts, and actions affect others.

Attitudes Toward Play. Lifetime attitudes toward play are developed in early childhood. Children learn motoric skills that become the foundation for adult play. Good experiences with play in the early years helps children understand that play can be restful, therapeutic, and fulfilling. On the other hand, if children are taught that play is work, that play is something that happens only after work is done, or that play occurs only on special occasions, then they can develop negative attitudes toward play that will carry over to adulthood.

Many people, although they recognize that children play and concede that there is a relationship between play and learning, do not fully respect the role of play in learning.

Piaget and Stages of Play

There are many ways to classify play. The important thing to remember about play is that it is not one-dimensional; there are many different kinds of play, which can occur in many settings and involve many different materials.

Piaget describes four stages of play through which children progress as they develop, including functional play, symbolic play, playing games with rules, and constructive play.

Functional Play. Functional play, the only play that occurs during the sensorimotor period, is based on and occurs in response to muscular activities and the need to be active. Functional play is characterized by repetitions, manipulations, and self-imitation. Piaget described functional play (which he also called *practice play* and *exercise play*) this way: "The child sooner or later (often even during the learning period) grasps for the pleasure of grasping, swings [a suspended object] for the sake of swinging, etc. In a word, he repeats his behaviour not in any further effort to learn or to investigate, but for the mere joy of mastering it and of showing off to himself his own power of subduing reality."[8]

Repetition of language is common at this level. Functional play allows children to practice and learn physical capabilities while exploring their immediate environments. Very young children are especially fond of repeating movements for the pleasure of it. They engage in sensory impressions for the joy of experiencing the functioning of their bodies.

Symbolic Play. The second stage is symbolic play, what Piaget also refers to as the "let's pretend" stage of play. During this stage, children freely

Symbolic play, or pretend play, provides children with opportunities to display their creative and physical abilities. Sand becomes a pie, ready for baking. What are some concepts and skills that children learn through symbolic play?

display their creative and physical abilities and social awareness in a number of ways. A child's pretending to be something else, such as an animal, is an example of symbolic play. Symbolic play also occurs when children pretend that one object is another — that a building block is a car, for example. Symbolic play may also entail pretending to be another person — a mommy, daddy, or care-giver. As toddlers and preschoolers grow older, their symbolic play becomes more elaborate and involved.

Games with Rules. The third stage of play, games with rules, begins around the ages of seven or eight. During this stage, children learn to play within rules and limits and adjust their behavior accordingly. During this stage, children can make and follow social agreements. Games with rules are very common in middle childhood and adulthood.

Constructive Play. A fourth stage of play, constructive play, develops from symbolic play and represents children's adaptations to problems and their creative acts. Constructive play is characterized by children being involved in play activities in order to construct their knowledge of the world. They first manipulate play materials and then use these materials to create and build things (a sand castle, a block building, a grocery store) and to experiment with the ways things go together.

George Forman and Fleet Hill, at the School for Constructive Play at the University of Massachusetts, developed a system of constructive play. They describe it this way:

Constructive play is a preliminary stage in the development of skill, and skill is preliminary to creativity. Play that does not increase skill may be pleasurable in a narrow sense but is not what we would call constructive. Constructive play, by definition, builds on itself to increase the competence of the child. This competence, in turn, increases the child's pleasure by making even more creative acts possible. The cycle repeats itself, with the new creative acts becoming yet another form of play at a higher level of understanding until they are mastered. Development, as Piaget phrases it, is a spiral of knowledge moving upward through alternating play and skill.

Another characteristic of constructive play central to Piaget's theory of development is that the player herself must do the constructing. Meaningful learning is more likely when the child herself invents the alternative ways of doing something. In fact, if the child is only imitating alternatives modeled by a teacher or parent, we do not call it play; it becomes drill.[9]

Social Play

In 1932, Mildred Parten observed children at play in social settings. She classified social play into six developmental stages. Keep in mind three things about Parten's work. First, it is a description of children's play in social contexts, that is, in the presence of other children. Second, although Parten's research was conducted in 1932, her findings have been substantiated by others, so her findings are still valid today. Third, you will sometimes hear others talk of Parten's stages of play as though all play were social, but this is not so. Certain types of play are not social. As our discussion of Piaget's stages of play demonstrated, although a child may play in social contexts — with other children — it is inaccurate to think of all play as social. Parten's stages of play are outlined in Table 4-1.

Social play provides the basis for developing relationships and friendships with others. As Felicisima Serafica points out,

> It is interesting to note that [Parten's] classic description of play is as much a characterization of age-related changes in the frequency and nature of peer interaction as it is of play activities. Essentially, children progress from a passive but interested stance toward their peers, as evidenced by being an onlooker or engaging in solitary independent play, to a more active interest and involvement with peers reflected in associative play and organized, supplementary, or cooperative play.[10]

THE MATERIALS OF PLAY

Toys

When we think of children's play, we almost automatically think of toys, the primary materials of play. This perception is justified; children between the ages of nine and eighteen months, for example, spend about 46 percent

TABLE 4-1

Mildred Parten's Developmental Stages of Social Play

Stage	Age (years)	Characteristics of Play
Unoccupied behavior	0–2	Children are not playing, but are engaged in "unoccupied behavior," e.g., looking around the room and following adults.
Onlooker behavior	2 and older	Children spend their time watching others play. They may verbally interact with others but do not engage in play with them.
Solitary play	2½ and older	Child engages in play by himself. He plays with his toys or materials on his own. His play is not dependent on or involved with the play of others.
Parallel play	2½–3½ and older	Child plays near other children. Child may choose a toy, material or activity that brings him alongside others or others alongside him. He is still involved in his own play, however.
Associative play	3½–4½ and older	The child plays with others in a group. Children may exchange materials. Although children are playing together, there is no intended purpose of the play. Children are involved in interpersonal relations during play. Children at a water table frequently exhibit this kind of play.
Cooperative play	4½ and older	The child plays in and with a group that has some intended purpose or goal, e.g., building a fort, making a sand sculpture, playing a game, or dramatizing (such as playing house).

Source: Mildred Parten, "Social Play Among Preschool Children," *Journal of Abnormal and Social Psychology* 27 (1932): 243–269.

of their time looking at and playing with objects.[11] Johnson & Johnson, a leading developer and manufacturer of children's toys, shows that children use and are interested in toys in the ways indicated in Figure 4-3.

Criteria for Toy Selection

Given the large role toys have in children's play, it makes sense to have a set of criteria for their selection and use by young children.

FIGURE 4-3
Children's Use of Toys

How objects are used follows predictable patterns. Data from both natural settings and laboratory research suggest that an infant is interested in objects with respect to:

- Their physical characteristics.
- Their separate parts, and relationships between these parts.
- The way they "work."
- The opportunities they present for practicing emerging skills.
- Their use as tools to accomplish tasks.
- Their use to facilitate self-discovery.
- Their use to facilitate social interaction.
- Their use to facilitate the growth of thought and understanding.
- Their use to achieve mastery.
- Their use as symbolic elements in fantasy play.

Source: Johnson & Johnson Child Development Products Professional Brochure and Catalogue (Skillman, N.J.: Johnson & Johnson, 1981), 2.

Safety. Safety is the first consideration in selecting any toy. Of special concern are pieces that can be removed, chewed, inhaled, or swallowed. Examine all moving parts to make sure they can't be removed. Avoid toys with sharp points or edges. Inspect toys to make sure they are not flammable or toxic. Especially with babies and infants, watch for eyes, ribbons, bells, and shoes that can be removed or chewed off. When it comes to eyes and other decorations, those that are stitched on are the best. When selecting any play material, remember that all infants explore with their mouths and all toddlers explore with their hands.

Durability. A toy should last a reasonable time and should be able to stand the use it will receive from many children in a child-care center or preschool program.

Cleanability. A toy must be able to withstand being cleaned, washed, and sanitized. This is particularly true of soft toys that are used by babies and infants.

Child Appeal. Toys must appeal to children. Some factors to consider in this regard are color and colorfulness, ability to be mouthed, moving parts, ability to make noise, and variety of textures.

Real Life Appeal. As first-time parents of infants and toddlers soon learn, the best toys, and those that children often prefer, are found in kitchens. Pots, pans, plastic measuring cups, plastic bowls and cups, pie pans, and wooden spoons all provide excellent opportunities for children to stack, nest, bang, and imitate.

Age Appropriateness. Toys need to be matched to the ages and developmental abilities of children. Toy manufacturers frequently provide age-appropriateness labels, although age labeling is not required by law. One of the best reasons for following the age recommendations of manufacturers is safety. A toy may have small parts that could be dangerous for a child younger than the stated age level. Federal safety standards require that toys for children under three be made without small parts. Following the age recommendations listed by manufacturers, however, is no substitute for the thoughtful selection of toys by parents and care-givers. Care-givers should not rely solely on manufacturers' recommendations to make their toy selections. Likewise, the very young cannot be expected to read and follow manufacturers' recommendations, so parents and care-givers must take into consideration the habits and abilities of children when giving them toys.

Crib toys. Toys for infants should be colorful and easily activated. Crib mobiles, pictures, mirrors, crib play gyms, clutch balls, soft toy animals, rattles (watch out for the cheap kind), and materials that provide visual stimulation are all good toys. Remember, however, that toys don't replace the attentive care-giver. Nurturing, not a toy, is the most important ingredient in the child–care-giver relationship. Toys should not be used as an excuse to keep infants in their cribs. Also, make sure infants get a chance to change positions in their cribs. They should not spend all their time on their backs just because they have crib mobiles to look at or toys in their cribs.

An interesting sidelight is worthy of mention. Friedrich Froebel emphasized that babies should not be left in their cribs without toys. He recommended that care-givers suspend a live bird in a cage over the crib within the baby's vision. Practical care-givers accepted his idea, but substituted a colorful paper bird instead.

Toddler toys. As toddlers learn to walk, they like toys to hold on to, push, and pull. Since toddlers don't spend all their time walking, other toys such as puzzle toys, toys that have parts that disappear (shape mailboxes, pound-a-pegs), and nesting toys provide interest and stimulation. Pretend play is encouraged through the use of dolls and play furniture. Blocks — small wooden ones as well as the large cardboard kind — are also popular with this age group. In addition, toddlers enjoy larger toys such as dump trucks and toys they can straddle and ride.

Preschool toys. Preschoolers like to participate in dramatic play, so dolls, puppets, and clothing that facilitate this play should be provided. Preschoolers like involvement in the creative arts, so materials that involve them in coloring, painting, making music (rhythm band instruments), and dancing and singing (phonographs, records) are all appropriate.

The larger wheeled toys such as tricycles and wagons help in large muscle development. Children at this age can and should participate in the care of their environment. Consequently, the equipment used to keep the environment clean, such as vacuum cleaners (children like to use all kinds — canister, upright, and the new hand-held Dust Busters), brooms, dustpans, mops, and buckets also becomes a source of play for children. Manipulatives like Tinker Toys and Legos are favorites of preschoolers, too.

Don't overlook "modern" toys such as computers, which teach numbers, the alphabet, and nursery rhymes. Videocassettes that teach sizes and shapes and computer programs that teach counting are also good.

Learning and Creativity. Toys should have the capacity to challenge children's imaginations and let them take more from their interaction with the toy than they brought to it.

Play occupies a vital place in the lives of children. Toys help facilitate children's play and in many ways make it more meaningful, enjoyable, and rewarding. More important, toys — physical objects — are a major source of children's knowledge of the physical world. Toy selection demands the same thoughtfulness and wise decision making that any prudent care-giver would bring to any other important child-related decision.

CARE-GIVER ROLES IN FACILITATING PLAY

Care-givers have more of a responsibility toward children's play than merely to let children play. The following are some of these responsibilities:

1. Observe children in their play to determine how they are playing, what toys and materials they are playing with, and their level of development. Information gathered from observation can be used to plan for play activities.
2. Expand children's play by preparing the environment, adding props, describing for and with them what they are doing, and asking open-ended questions. The teacher and care-giver are not *passive* onlookers during children's play. Teachers should not assume that children's playtime is a time to catch up on paper work or planning. Quite the contrary. During children's play, the teacher should be active as an observer, note-taker, facilitator, and participant.
3. Allow children to discover concepts and ideas on their own. Avoid telling, showing, and overexplaining. Above all, let children be independent in what they do.
4. Encourage child-directed and child-selected play. Avoid interrupting child-directed play in order to involve children in care-giver–initiated and -directed play. If care-givers believe that children learn through active play, then they should have the opportunity to be involved in this kind of play rather than adult-directed play. Through observation and planning, care-givers can use the incidental play of children to teach concepts.
5. Let children know and see that you are interested in what they do.

Teachers and care-givers can use their own parallel play to show interest, involve children in discussion, extend and clarify ideas, and provide props and materials. Care-givers should avoid dominating children's play activities, however.

6. Provide an appropriate physical and emotional environment for play. The physical environment includes such things as toys, equipment, and the arrangement of the environment such that it supports play. Avoid putting out so many materials or toys that infants and toddlers become overwhelmed and confused. One of the mistakes care-givers sometimes make in their desire to give children choices is to give them too many.

   The emotional or affective environment of play includes such things as accepting children's play, not dominating or dictating children's play, and avoiding needless adult conversation and interruptions.

7. Plan for children's play. Teachers' plans for play can include the following:

   a) Goals, objectives, and activities that specify the what, how, and when of children's play. These learning objectives can and should be held in abeyance until the teacher sees what goals children establish for themselves.

   b) How the play environment will be organized to support play and help promote learning objectives care-givers have for children.

   c) Materials to be added or changed. Specifications about how the environment will be prepared so children have choices, special play experiences, and a wide range of play activities.

   d) Provisions for the time and place for play. Play time needs to be scheduled; it should not just be something that is done when there is nothing else to do.

   e) Opportunities for the children to be actively involved. There should be enough materials and play centers so children don't have to wait to play. Also, toddler and preschool play should include the opportunity to participate in small groups rather than have everyone participate in one large group. This encourages social interaction as well as unhurried interactions with materials.

The teacher's plan for play is implemented as opportunities arise. The what, how, and when of the plan are determined by following the children's lead. Admittedly, this is easier said than done and takes skill and practice.

The kind of program a teacher plans and implements for children influences children's play behavior. James E. Johnson and his colleagues found that children enrolled in a formal preschool that emphasized Piagetian concepts of logical development engaged in more constructive play than children enrolled in a discovery-based preschool program. Children in the discovery program, on the other hand, exhibited more functional play.[12]

Water play provides many opportunities for children to learn concepts and develop language and social skills. How can care-givers provide children with opportunities for water play?

WATER PLAY

Children like to play with water. Water play provides many opportunities for children to learn concepts, develop oral language, develop and practice social skills, practice and perfect fine-motor coordination necessary for pre-writing and reading, and increase their attention spans. Water play is a natural medium and setting that can be utilized to promote the skills associated with learning how to learn.

Equipment for Water Play

The physical equipment for water play can range from the commercial varieties to the homemade kind. Which is used depends upon the teacher's preference and ingenuity and the amount of money available to a program. The commercial varieties of water tables, which also can be used for sand (rice, wheat, barley, birdseed, oatmeal, etc.), can be rather expensive but have the advantages of being sturdy and specifically built for water play.

Lack of a commercial water table should not prevent any teacher from having children participate in water play. Plastic pans filled with water and placed on plastic sheets on the floor or a low table offer a suitable but slightly messier alternative. A parent volunteer can build a table with two-inch-by-two-inch boards around the edges so pans of water won't fall off. Indeed, some of the better water play situations I have observed have been with tables that creative teachers designed and built with the help of parents.

Materials and Activities for Water Play

The materials care-givers use in a water play area are limited only by their imaginations. Some of the essentials include

1. Plastic aprons for children to wear while involved in water play.
2. An extra set of dry clothing, including extra shoes and socks. These are not always necessary, especially when children are taught to manage well while playing at the water table.
3. A variety of water play materials, including funnels, small containers of various sizes and shapes, pitchers, egg beaters, objects that float and sink, plastic detergent bottles, measuring cups, dish pans, small buckets, and plastic tubing.
4. Sponges, mops, buckets, and soft cloths for clean-up.
5. Dry media materials such as rice, beans, etc. Many of the same containers used for water play are also appropriate for use with a dry mix.
6. Materials used with teachers' direct supervision, such as liquid detergent for making bubbles, straws for blowing, and food coloring for colored bubbles.

Activities associated with water play help children learn about such things as measuring, pouring, classifying, caring for the environment through clean-up, experimenting, and identifying.

Implications for care-givers. Care-givers must supervise water play areas in a number of ways in order to assure that the experience is satisfactory for all concerned. Some things that need to be attended to are

1. Cleaning. Water in a water play table can get dirty very quickly, depending on the climate and the activities used at the table. In one program, when the water needs to be changed and the table cleaned, the teacher introduces an activity involving soap suds. In this way, a double purpose is served. Not only do children play, experiment, and create with soap bubbles, they also clean the water table. The children empty the water in a bucket that the teacher dumps, and they clean the table and the materials. In this way, they participate in washing activities as well as taking the responsibility of caring for their own environment.

2. Hygiene and health. Teachers must monitor the water table so that young children don't drink the water. In the beginning stages of water play, children have to be taught not to drink the water while they are playing with it. This is especially true when they are using straws.

3. Proper use. Children need to be taught how to use and care for the water play area. Some care-givers don't allow children the opportunity to play with water because they are afraid they will make a mess. Better by far to show children the proper use of materials than to deny them opportunities to learn.

Water play offers many rewards for teachers and children. It is a medium that many children are familiar and comfortable with as a result of baths and water play at home. It offers a natural and relaxing way to have children learn many concepts and skills while having fun.

BLOCK PLAY

Block play is one of the most popular kinds of children's play. Blocks are one of the chief manipulative materials used in early childhood programs. Friedrich Froebel, founder of the kindergarten, developed materials for children, some of which consisted of maple wood blocks. There are many kinds of blocks: wooden unit blocks, hollow blocks, cardboard blocks, and table blocks made of wood or plastic.

Caroline Pratt (1867–1950) developed the unit block, the most commonly used block in early childhood programs. The basic unit block is five-and-a-half inches long, two-and-three-quarters inches wide, and one-and-three-eights inches high. All other sizes of unit blocks are in exact proportion to the basic block. The double block, for example, is exactly as big as two unit blocks. There are about twenty-five shapes and sizes of unit blocks.

Purposes of Block Play

Block play serves a number of purposes. First, it is a means for creative expression and the development of creativity. Children enjoy building what they consider aesthetically pleasing structures. Many of these structures are props in their imaginative, creative, and dramatic play — the castle, the fort, the spaceship — that support the process of learning through play.

Second, block play is a means of learning many concepts related to school readiness. These concepts include color, size, shape, classification, seriation, equivalency, recognition of likenesses and differences, planning for an activity, measurement, balance, spatial relations, volume, and area.

Third, block play is a context for developing feelings of self-worth and social competence. Block play gives children a sense of accomplishment as they engage in and complete various projects. A great deal of satisfaction as well as feelings of competence come from planning for, undertaking, and completing a block construction project. Indeed, there is hardly any learning in any of the three domains — cognitive, affective, and psychomotor — that the proponents of block play have not identified as benefiting from playing with blocks.

Stages of Block Building

Harriet Johnson (1867–1934), a famous nursery school teacher and advocate of learning with blocks, identified seven stages of block use through which children pass as they play with blocks.

Stage 1. Blocks are carried around and not used for construction.

Stage 2. Building begins. Children make mostly rows (horizontal) or columns (vertical). Block building in this stage is characterized by much repetition.

Stage 3. Bridging. Two blocks with a space between them are bridged by a third block.

Stage 4. Enclosures. Blocks are placed so that they enclose a space.

Stage 5. Decorative patterns. Buildings with decorative patterns are built.

Stage 6. Naming of structures. Children build and name structures for use in dramatic play.

Stage 7. Reproduction of actual structures. Children use these structures in dramatic play.[13]

DRAMATIC PLAY

Dramatic play (also called *symbolic play*) occurs when children use symbolic representations (blocks for food and a box for a stove, for example) and imitate roles they have seen or heard (mommy and daddy, teacher and care-giver, baby sister or brother, for example). Thus, dramatic play is symbolic, representational, and imitative. When two or more children engage in such play, it is called *sociodramatic play.* Dramatic play gives children the opportunity, the freedom, and the emotional safety to try out new roles and skills, to master skills, to express feelings (both positive and negative), to release tensions, to consider the feelings and behaviors of others, to develop emerging language skills, to learn different customs and habits from others, and to be creative and develop new friendships. Through dramatic play, children endeavor to symbolize life as they see it.

Smilansky's View of Dramatic Play

Sara Smilansky, a noted play researcher, believes that sociodramatic play develops three main areas in children: creativity, intellectual growth, and social skills. Specifically, Smilansky believes that by participating in sociodramatic play, children learn to gather scattered experiences and create new combinations; to draw on their experiences and knowledge; to discern and enact the central characteristics of a particular role; to concentrate around a central theme; to control themselves in terms of their evolving sense of order and in relation to the play context; to be flexible in their approach to various situations; to set their own standards for their actions; to experience the feelings of being creators; to cooperate and experience social interaction; to observe reality with a view toward future utilization of these observations; to acquire new concepts; to develop toward more advanced stages of abstract thought; and to generalize vicariously from the experiences and knowledge of other children.[14]

The essentials for dramatic play are an opportunity to engage in it and supportive props such as a dress-up and house-keeping center with materials such as a stove, refrigerator, and table and chairs. Expensive, elaborate materials are not as important as an area and concrete materials for dramatic play. For children's activities to be considered dramatic play, they must use symbolic representations, pretending, for example, that a blanket is a tablecloth or a cape.

Implications for care-givers. Important care-giver roles in facilitating dramatic play include the following:

1. Provide children with experiences — actual, through field trips and classroom activities, and vicarious, through stories — so they have a background to draw on and use in their play.
2. Provide the setting and materials for dramatic play.
3. Plan a schedule that includes time for dramatic play.
4. Observe, and when appropriate, participate in dramatic play as a means of gaining insight into children's behavior. Observation of children's dramatic play is also an excellent way to determine how children play and what types of play they prefer. Observation gives the teacher insights into the individuality of play styles, play interests, individual abilities, and the play settings children prefer.
5. Maintain an environment that is conducive to dramatic play. You might provide space so several or many children can play at one time, or provide different centers — house-keeping, dress-up, grocery store, medical office — and enough appropriate theme-related materials to support play.
6. Manage children's behavior so that all have an opportunity to play and those who become overzealous in their play are guided in new directions.
7. Extend, enrich, and encourage the dimensions of dramatic play. Teachers can increase the use of language and social interactions or change the type of play, perhaps from parallel to associative play. If children are interested in grocery store play, for example, the teacher can read stories related to shopping, take children on a trip to a grocery store, provide play money, have children collect materials for use in their store, and help children set up a check-out counter with a cash register.
8. Make sure that materials and props are nonsexist and culturally relevant.
9. Accept children's dramatic play. Recently, in one center, Bobby engaged in parent play as the mother. Suddenly he picked the baby out of the crib, shook her, and said, "If you don't stop your crying, I'm going to beat your ass." Bobby was working out aggressive feelings. It

would have been very easy for the teacher to reprimand Bobby for his behavior and language. Instead, she quietly noted his behavior and realized that the play setting was helping him deal with feelings toward the child-rearing process.

MEDICAL PLAY

Medical play is the symbolic reproduction of the procedures necessary for medical treatment. Many hospitals and other health-care agencies hire *Child Life Specialists,* who work with children and parents in a *Child Life Program* of medical play and education. Medical play is used to reduce anxiety and stress in children and parents; help children distinguish between fact and fantasy; prepare children for future hospitalization; respond to children's interests and concerns; provide information about medical procedures and health care; supplement physical treatment with emotional treatment; assist parents in the bonding process; and help parents provide better postoperative care. In many ways, medical play has a decided therapeutic purpose.

"My goal is to help make the hospital experience a positive one," explains Letitia Cason, Child Life Specialist with Baptist Hospital in Miami, Florida. "I also like to think of myself as an advocate for children." Cason uses play to educate children about their illnesses and medical care. "Play is an opportunity for children to express their fears and misconceptions and for me to communicate a clear understanding of what is going on with their conditions. Play also promotes a sense of mastery and allows children to be decision-makers. For example, playing doctor with a doll allows a child patient to assume the active role of giving and performing tests and treatments on someone else rather than remaining passive. This kind of play increases self-esteem by allowing children to make choices and decisions."

Hospitals also help prepare children for future hospitalizations by conducting tours, which help them become familiar with the medical facility. These tours often include an opportunity for medical play. Although many hospitals conduct such tours for children — usually those over the age of four — there is not universal agreement that such tours are helpful. Some professionals question whether or not such familiarization might not do more harm than good by unnecessarily creating anxiety in children prior to their hospital stay.

In medical play, the materials needed usually include miniature hospital and medical supplies, miniature furniture, real medical equipment such as stethoscopes and surgical masks, medical clothing such as gowns and hats, and puppets.

Medical play is conducted by having children take care of dolls using play medical equipment as well as real equipment. It is important for children to have the opportunity to use real equipment on dolls as a means of becoming familiar with equipment such as intravenous bottles and tubes. Children should also have an opportunity to practice medical procedures, such as listening to heartbeats with other children.

OUTDOOR PLAY AND PLAYGROUNDS

Outdoor play is viewed as an integral part of programs for young children. The places where outdoor play occurs can range from rooftops in the inner city to suburban tree houses, from vacant fields to architecturally designed playscapes with all the latest equipment. In one preschool, part of the children's play area is a third-floor breezeway with Astroturf and play equipment.

Outdoor areas should be safe for children to play. Usually, states and municipalities have regulations requiring that playgrounds be fenced, have a source of drinking water, have a minimum number of square feet of play space for each child, and have equipment that is in good repair and safe.

Outdoor play areas should also provide opportunities for children to learn concepts, develop skills and social relationships, engage in creative activities, and enjoy themselves through play activities. Penny Lovell and Thelma Harms developed a playground improvement rating scale that provides many insights into how to enhance outdoor play (Figure 4-4).

Outdoor play can provide children with many opportunities to learn important concepts, skills, and social relationships and to engage in creative activities. What can care-givers do to facilitate such learning?

FIGURE 4-4
Playground Improvement Rating Scale

Program _____

Number of Children _____   Date _____

Ages of Children _____   Rater _____

Number of Staff _____

Score each item: **3** — outdoor play area meets this goal very well
2 — outdoor play area needs to be improved to meet this goal
1 — little or no evidence that outdoor play area meets this goal

(Examples of items to look for are listed in parentheses.)

ACTIVITIES AND EQUIPMENT
Range of Activities
_____ 1. The equipment provides appropriate and stimulating levels of difficulty for all the age groups served (infants, toddlers, preschool children, school-age children).
_____ 2. A variety of equipment is provided to stimulate different types of physical activity (balls, balance beams, wheel toys, swings, climbing equipment, jump ropes, ladders, planks).
_____ 3. Some of the equipment and materials invite cooperative play (outdoor blocks, rocking boat, dramatic play props).
_____ 4. Creative materials are readily available for children (clay, carpentry, paints, water, sand).
_____ 5. Some of the equipment is flexible so that it can be combined in different ways by the children, with adult help if necessary (planks, climbing boxes, ladders).
_____ 6. The climbing equipment incorporates a variety of spatial relationships (through tunnels, up or down ramps, over or under platforms).
_____ 7. There is a suitable place for gardening (window box, tubs with soil, garden plot).
_____ 8. There are enough options for the children to choose from without unreasonable competition or waiting.

SAFETY AND HEALTH
_____ 9. The equipment is substantially constructed (anchored climbing structures and swing frames).
_____ 10. Cushioning is provided under swings and climbing apparatus (loose sand or tanbark at least one foot deep within a containing edgeboard, rubber padding).
_____ 11. Swing seats are made of pliable material.
_____ 12. Swings are separated from areas where children run or ride wheel toys.
_____ 13. Protective railings prevent children from falling from high equipment.
_____ 14. Equipment is well maintained (no protruding nails, splinters, flaking paint, broken parts, frayed ropes).
_____ 15. The play area is routinely checked and maintained (trash picked up, grass mowed, good drainage).
_____ 16. The health hazards from animal contamination are minimized (sand box covers, fences, children wash hands after playing outdoors).

ORGANIZATION OF PLAY AREA
_____ 17. The play area is well defined (fence that cannot be climbed).
_____ 18. There are clear pathways and enough space between areas so that traffic flows well and equipment does not obstruct the movement of children.
_____ 19. Space and equipment are organized so that children are readily visible and easily supervised by teachers.

FIGURE 4-4 (*continued*)

_____ 20. Different types of activity areas are separated (tricycle paths separate from swings, sand box separate from climbing area)

_____ 21. Open space is available for active play.

_____ 22. Some space encourages quiet, thoughtful play (grassy area near trees, sandbox away from traffic).

_____ 23. Blocks and props can be set up outdoors for dramatic play.

_____ 24. Art activities can be set up outdoors.

_____ 25. The area is easily accessible from the classroom.

_____ 26. The area is readily accessible to the restrooms.

_____ 27. A drinking fountain is available.

_____ 28. Accessible and sufficient storage is provided.

_____ 29. A portion of the play area is covered for use in wet weather.

_____ 30. An adequate area is sunny in cold weather.

_____ 31. An adequate area of shade is provided in hot weather.

VARIETY OF PLAY SURFACES

_____ 32. A hard surface is available to ride wheel toys, play group games, or dance.

_____ 33. Soil, sand, and water are available for digging and mud play.

_____ 34. A grassy or carpeted area is provided.

_____ 35. Good drainage keeps all surfaces usable.

SURROUNDING ENVIRONMENT

_____ 36. The fence creates an effective screen for the playground by blocking out unpleasant or by admitting pleasant aspects of the surrounding environment. It protects children from intrusion by passers-by.

_____ 37. The setting visible from the play area is pleasant.

_____ 38. The location is relatively quiet (little noise from railroads, traffic, factories).

SUPERVISION AND USE OF PLAY AREA

_____ 39. A sufficient number of adults supervise the children during outdoor play.

_____ 40. Responsibility for specific areas is assigned to staff to assure that the entire playground is well supervised.

_____ 41. Teachers focus their attention on and interact with the children to enhance learning and maintain safety (adults do not talk together at length or sit passively when supervising children).

_____ 42. Children are guided to use the equipment appropriately (climb on ladders instead of tables).

_____ 43. The daily schedule includes morning and afternoon active play periods for all age groups, either outdoors or in suitably equipped indoor areas.

_____ 44. The schedule for use of the play area minimizes overlap of the age groups to avoid conflicts, overcrowding, and undue competition for materials.

_____ 45. Special activities are planned for and set up in the outdoor area daily (games, painting).

_____ 46. Teachers add to or rearrange large equipment at least every six months (spools, crates, tunnels).

_____ 47. Teachers encourage and assist children in rearranging small flexible equipment (ladders, planks, boxes).

_____ 48. Most of the children are constructively involved with the equipment and activities in the playground.

_____ 49. Children help clean up the area and put away equipment.

_____ **Total score**

Source: Penny Lovell and Thelma Horms, "How Can Playgrounds Be Improved? A Rating Scale," *Young Children* 40 (March 1985): 7–8.

PLAY AND TELEVISION

Television is a passive medium and does not require any participation from children. Neither does television provide the concrete experiences children need for developing concepts and skills. When children spend long hours watching television, they are not involved in the play they need for learning. What many parents and educators object to most about television is the violence it models for children. Many television cartoons involve pratfalls and slapstick, and resolutions are based on violence. Violence as a behavioral model is not what young children need since they may resort to hitting, biting, or kicking as a means of dealing with frustration. They need models that show them how to solve problems through acceptable and peaceful means rather than through violence.

ISSUES IN PLAY

In these conservative, back-to-basics times, when the educational emphasis is on the direct teaching and learning of basic skills in preschools, the advocates of learning through play find themselves exceedingly hard pressed to justify and defend their belief that play promotes learning. Part of the difficulty of such justification comes from issues associated with play-based programs and play curricula. Some of these issues are

1. Care-givers' inability to demonstrate to the satisfaction of parents — and the general public — precisely how skills and learning develop through play. This issue is related to professionals' abilities to be clear in their own minds about *how* play promotes learning and the skills children learn as a result. Merely saying "I believe learning occurs through play" does not go far enough to explain to the inquisitive and demanding parent the what and how of play.
2. The second issue is related to the first: what and how much learning occurs through play. This issue is related to planning and care-givers' abilities to skillfully help children learn through play.
3. The third issue is related to the second, and deals with whether or not care-givers who leave children to their own devices for "free play" can be assured that learning will occur. The outcome depends on a number of factors. The first is the skill of the care-giver in planning for play and in helping children learn through their activities. Allowing children to play with blocks is no guarantee that they will learn classification, seriation, and numeration. A curriculum that only uses free play does not guarantee that learning will occur.
   A second factor involved is the children. Some children, because of previous experiences and the nature of their home lives, learn better through play than other children. Not all children will learn equally well through play. Not all kinds, amounts, and proportions of play are

suitable for all children. Play needs to be individualized for children just like any other activity.

4. The fourth issue relates to care-givers and the profession. A system based on play is not always neat and clear-cut. It is not always possible to show a direct relationship between what care-givers plan and what children learn. Some care-givers are better at achieving this match than others. Similarly, not all care-givers are emotionally or professionally suited to making the adjustments needed to fit learning goals to children's play.

SUMMARY

How do children learn? In many ways, as we have discussed. Play, however, is the primary activity through which children learn in the early years. It is through play that the very young develop the skills and concepts that form the basis for all their learning throughout life. Understood in this way, then, play is too important in the lives of children for teachers, parents, and care-givers to take it lightly or treat it as being of little consequence in the process of learning. Play plays a major role in the game of life and needs to be provided for and encouraged. Above all, children need time, space, environments, and care-givers who are willing to allow them to learn through play. As NAEYC's "Position Statements on Developmentally Appropriate Practice in Early Childhood Programs" so eloquently points out,

> Children's play is a primary vehicle for and indicator of their mental growth. Play enables children to progress along the developmental sequence from the sensorimotor intelligence of infancy to preoperational thought in the preschool years to the concrete operational thinking exhibited by primary children. In addition to its role in cognitive development, play also serves important functions in children's physical, emotional, and social development. Therefore, child-initiated, child-directed, teacher-supported play is an essential component of developmentally appropriate practices.[15]

PROGRAM VIGNETTE

Turtle Walk Toy-Lending Library
Fort Lauderdale, Florida

Cindy Genovese, a former child-care center director, never dreamed she would be a truck driver. "My friends couldn't believe it when I told them I quit my job and was going to drive a truck." Driving a silver library van with a big green turtle painted on each side is a part of the job Cindy relishes as director of the

Broward County Turtle Walk Toy Library in Fort Lauderdale, Florida. "I jumped at the chance to direct the toy-lending library," says Cindy. "Through Turtle Walk, I'm influencing more children and families than I would if I were only at one center."

Two days a week — Tuesdays and Thursdays — Cindy rolls with her cargo of toys, books, tapes, and other learning materials to Broward County Library branches and child-care centers. "I really look forward to the days I drive the library van into the community. It is very rewarding to watch parents and children develop and change as a result of coming to the toy library," says Cindy. "Parents are the key to children's education. Toy-lending libraries are based in part on the assumption that parents can provide significant educational experiences for their preschool children. This makes my work all the more meaningful."

Cindy's enthusiasm for lending toys to children and parents is contagious. Reza Yamanni, age two, can't wait for Cindy to come each week so he can have his hand stamped with the turtle logo and talk with her about the toys he wants to borrow. His mother, Lee, thinks the program is great. "It's part of Reza's life to see Cindy. He likes her and it's a good introduction for him about what a teacher is like. It's good for me too, since I get to talk to Cindy about certain toys and how I can use them with Reza at home. I wish every parent could have the opportunity to visit the mobile library as I do."

Cindy tries to be as helpful as she can about making suggestions for new materials. "Borrowing toys is popular with parents because they know we have selected toys with an educational purpose in mind. We offer toys that promote skills that children need to learn. Part of my job is to help children and parents make appropriate selections. Some parents use toys and learning materials to help their children achieve their readiness levels. Other parents select materials below the readiness level of their children because they don't know what they can do. The other day a mother brought her six-month-old baby and asked for a rattle. I gave her a rattle but also helped her select some crib toys and other materials. Some parents are used to saying to their children 'go and play.' I try to get them to say 'come and let's play' so they can really see what their children can do."

Parents select toys from the Turtle Walk Van for various reasons. Sue Morford has a Down's syndrome child. She chooses toys and materials that will stimulate him to talk, move, and be more involved. Some parents select a toy because they would like to use it to play with their child. Other parents see the library as a means to use materials they otherwise couldn't afford to buy. Then there are the parents who don't have room in their apartments for a toy such as a wagon but can make do for a week or two.

At each stop, the scene is the same — a group of parents and children anxiously waiting for "the turtle toy truck." Cindy parks, opens the van, and admits the first group. Because of space limitations, only about two parents and four children can use the van at one time. When she finishes helping parents on the van she tells the other parents about upcoming events sponsored by the library — story hours and used toy drives, for example — and

Programs such as Turtle Walk provide children and their parents access to learning materials they might not otherwise have. Here, Cindy Genovese helps two children make appropriate toy selections.

shares information about new toys in the van. "I also get a chance to talk with first-time parents," says Cindy. "Some of them are really unsure about what they should be doing with their children. For some parents, Turtle Walk really fills the void caused by a lack of parenting information."

The Turtle Walk van is well stocked with learning materials designed to appeal to children from birth to age five. These include small toys (blocks, crib toys, nesting toys), transportation toys (tricycles and wagons), games, puzzles, books for children and parents, dramatic play props (one set contains doctors' and nurses' clothing and equipment), records, filmstrips, cassette tapes, rhythm band instruments, flash cards, and art materials. Cindy doesn't stock certain kinds of toys, such as stuffed animals (because of the possibility of spreading germs) and guns (which encourage violence).

Before parents borrow materials, they sign a form saying they will return the materials clean and in good condition. Toys can be borrowed for twenty-eight days.

According to Cindy, children borrow toys for a number of reasons. Cindy Smith selects a toy she played with before. Taneka Jones wants a toy she saw on television. Josh Jacobson always selects a toy he doesn't have at home, and Samantha Gill chooses a toy because she "likes" it. Whatever the reason, Cindy is glad to have them visit her library.

About 70 percent of the over two thousand toys available in the program were donated. "Every year we do a Christmas toy drive and we get a good response," says Cindy. "Toys that we can't use we donate to child-care centers. Our toy drive encourages parents and children to give to a program that has helped them. A lot of the children who borrow materials donate toys to us. Children really learn a sense of community by donating to a program they use." Other Turtle Walk materials are purchased or made by volunteers.

Parents are not the only ones who borrow materials. Grandparents, child-care workers, librarians, baby sitters, college students, and workers at agencies that serve the handicapped are among the other borrowers. Anyone with a library card can borrow from Turtle Walk. In addition to making stops at library branches, Cindy stops at child-care centers, other child-serving agencies, and community centers.

Toy-lending libraries in the United States are not new. The first one began in Los Angeles, California, in 1935. Their number is growing as they become more popular with children and parents. The address of the USA Toy Library Association, an organization of toy-lending libraries with over 350 members, is 1800 Pickwick Ave., Glenview, Ill. 60025.

Lekotek is a toy-lending library program that began in Sweden. This Scandinavian model is designed exclusively for handicapped children and their families and is staffed by professionally trained personnel who combine toy-lending libraries with parental guidance and assessment of children's needs. This model is also becoming more popular in the United States.

Although the majority of toy libraries are sponsored by agencies such as libraries (the Broward County Library sponsors Turtle Walk), other toy libraries are operated by individuals. Some are nonprofit and some are for profit. These libraries are usually supported by membership fees.

Lee Remington, the mother of three-year-old Carol, is very emphatic about why she comes to Turtle Walk. "There is an educational value associated with Turtle Walk. The library provides a variety of educational playthings, many I would never know about if we didn't have Cindy and her turtle van. We also get to meet different people and that is important. Since we have been using the materials from the toy library, there is a different kind of interaction between Carol and me. We make a point of playing together with the things we borrow."

Cindy believes toy libraries build strong supportive relationships between agencies and parents. "Toy libraries are good ways for children to explore new materials and for them to experience success through activities provided by toys and parents. For parents, we have done a lot to involve them with their children, help them learn about child development, and learn criteria for toy selection and appropriate ways to use readiness materials.

"I think the two most important values of Turtle Walk are that it legitimizes the role of play in learning and it provides toys and learning to any child, regardless of socioeconomic background."

ENRICHMENT THROUGH ACTIVITIES

1. Visit various child-care and preschool programs. Observe the children in dramatic play. Tell what you think were the strengths and weaknesses of each program. What suggestions would you make in each program for improvement? Give your reasons for each suggestion.

2. Teachers have to be able to tell parents why dramatic play is important, how it benefits children, and what learning results. Write a speech titled "The Importance of Dramatic Play" that you would give to a parents' group.

3. Review the requirements for an outdoor play facility in your state or municipality.

4. You have been asked to plan the development of a forty-five-by-fifty-foot outdoor playground. Tell what equipment you want and where you would place it. Tell why you made the decisions you did.

5. When many parents send their children to child care or a preschool, they expect them to learn. How would you respond if a parent said to you that she thought children really didn't learn much by playing all the time?

6. You have been given five hundred dollars to purchase toys for a toy-lending library to serve children between the ages of one month and five years. Select toys appropriate for all age groups and tell why you selected each. Include the cost of each toy. Do not exceed the allocated money.

7. Develop a list of toys and classify them according to how they would promote specific learning in the physical, social, emotional, and cognitive domains.

8. How important is an outdoor play area for a preschool program? What can children learn outdoors?

9. In a group discussion, consider each of the following statements:
   a) Boys shouldn't be encouraged to play in a house-keeping area.
   b) It is better to have many toys that are less expensive than to have a few toys that are expensive.
   c) Real learning occurs only when teachers tell children what to do.

10. Which theory of learning presented in this chapter do you agree with the most? Tell how you think children learn. Support your ideas with material presented in this chapter.

11. Observe children's play to find evidence of the different stages of social play as described by Mildred Parten.

12. Visit hospitals and medical centers that conduct programs of play therapy and medical play. How are these programs conducted? What are the benefits to children and parents? Tell what you think are the pros and cons of each program. Would you let your child participate in such a program? Why? Why not?

13. Angelia Martin is terrified by the way her husband Achilles plays with their infant son, Albert. Achilles tosses Albert high in the air and catches him at the last second before he would hit the floor. He is very rough and loud with Albert, often mimicking characters from the TV shows they watch together. When Angelia says anything to Achilles about his rough play with Albert, he retorts that she is just jealous of their time together and that she is trying to interfere with the bond he is building with his son.
   a) What different points of view are present in the tension between Angelia and Achilles?
   b) Is there potential for Albert being hurt in any way in his play with his father?
   c) What advice do you have for Angelia and Achilles?

14. The five care-givers of the toddler program at Mount Zion Child Care Center always differ in their objectives of how to promote children's learning. Two care-givers are in favor of teacher-directed activities and three are in favor of learning through play.
   a) Is either group of care-givers wrong?

b) How can the care-givers reconcile their differences?
15. Write your personal philosophy of how children learn through play.
16. Gather daily schedules from child-care and preschool programs. What amount of time is devoted to play? Is too much or too little time devoted to play? Is it clear from the schedules what learning results from play?
17. Develop a starter list of toys that would be appropriate to give to new parents.
18. List and describe activity centers that can be included in outdoor play areas.
19. Is outdoor storage an important consideration when designing an outdoor play area? Why? Why not?
20. Develop a plan for a block area in a preschool program. Tell what blocks you would buy and how you would store them. Include a weekly lesson plan for how children would use the block center.
21. What learning centers would you include in a toddler child-care room? Justify your decisions.

ENRICHMENT THROUGH READING

Bjorn, Eva Noren. *The Impossible Playground: A Trilogy of Play.* Vol. 1, *Why* West Point, N.Y.: Leisure Press, 1982.
   This is a summary of a study of children's play activity at twenty-seven playgrounds in Sweden. The author conducted the study at the request of the Swedish Council for Children's Play in order to determine how playgrounds are used by children. From this data, some conclusions are drawn through words and pictures about how play equipment stimulates and inhibits children's play. This volume, like the others in the trilogy, is very practical and useful. It gives the reader an idea about how advanced the Swedish government, the only national government that has a Council on Play, is in its approach to providing for the total development of children.

Creative Associates. *Blocks: A Creative Curriculum for Early Childhood.* Washington, D.C.: Creative Associates, 1979.
   This book is a practical manual for anyone who wants to do more with blocks. Chapter 1 introduces the reader to blocks and some of the practical considerations in their use. Chapter 2 is a discussion of the play environment and blocks. Chapter 3 outlines the teacher's role in the block corner, and Chapter 4 deals with blocks and dramatic play. Opportunities for mathematics learning through block play are presented in Chapter 6.

Goldberg, Sally. *Teaching with Toys.* Ann Arbor, Mich.: University of Michigan Press, 1981.
   This book is a compilation of educational games and toys to make and use at home with children from birth to age three. All the toys and games are designed to support development in young children by promoting specific skills relating to self-awareness, color and shape recognition, reading, numbers, and letters. Each game and activity has an objective, description, a list of materials needed, and directions for construction and use.

Goldberg, Sally. *Growing with Games.* Ann Arbor, Mich.: University of Michigan Press, 1985.

    This is a companion book to *Teaching with Toys.* All the games and activities, which can be constructed from easily accessible household items, are designed to foster growth and development in children ages three to six.

Hirsch, Elizabeth S., ed. *The Block Book.* Washington, D.C.: National Association for the Education of Young Children, 1974.

    Almost all you want and need to know about the history of blocks and how to use them is contained in this informative compilation of chapters by experts in the field. This book tells and shows through drawings and pictures how to teach skills and concepts from all the content areas. Chapters are devoted to science, mathematics, social studies, and dramatic play. In addition, practical considerations relating to how to buy, store, and manage the environment for block play are included.

Hogan, Paul. *The Nuts and Bolts of Playground Construction: A Trilogy of Play.* Vol. 3, *How.* West Point, N.Y.: Leisure Press, 1982.

    As the title implies, this third volume in the *Trilogy of Play* is devoted to showing the reader how to construct playgrounds and playground equipment. There are several emphases in the book. The first is that responsibility can be fostered in children by involving them (and their parents and the community) in the design and construction of the play environment. Second, self-designed and -built playgrounds using available materials such as old tires are far superior to commercial playground equipment. Many excellent photographs and designs from playgrounds around the world are included.

Kamii, Constance, and DeVries, Rheta. *Physical Knowledge in Preschool Education: Implications of Piaget's Theory.* Englewood Cliffs, N.J.: Prentice-Hall, 1978.

    The authors show preschool teachers how Piaget's theory can be used in practical ways in the area of physical knowledge. The activities presented are designed to help teachers involve children in acting on objects in order to observe their reactions and support their efforts at constructing their knowledge in ways that are natural extensions of the knowledge they already have. As the authors point out, "All babies and young children are naturally interested in examining objects, acting on them, and observing the objects' reactions." Of particular interest are two chapters on water play. The authors specifically address the issue of how teachers can improve water play by providing better materials and interacting more effectively with children.

Mason, John. *The Environment of Play: A Trilogy of Play.* Vol. 2, *Where.* West Point, N.Y.: Leisure Press, 1982.

    This second volume in *A Trilogy of Play* examines in detail the environmental features and criteria necessary for outdoor play. The author provides many practical ideas, suggestions, and illustrative pictures. The book is a valuable source that provides information about how to plan for outdoor play, how to design a playground, safety considerations, and the role of the environment in outdoor play. There is a very interesting section devoted to horticulture, which provides advice about how to grow plants and landscape. Part three is devoted to play in back yards, children's farms, gardens, and environmental trails. Very informative for anyone who wants to improve the quality of children's outdoor play.

NOTES

1. Friedrich Wilhelm August Froebel, *The Education of Man* (Clifton, N.J.: August M. Kelly Publishers, 1974), 8.
2. Maria Montessori, *The Absorbent Mind,* trans. Claude A. Claremont (New York: Holt, Rinehart and Winston, 1967), 25.
3. Albert Bandura, *Social Learning Theory* (Englewood Cliffs, N.J.: Prentice-Hall, 1977), 22.
4. Constance Kamii and Rheta DeVries, *Physical Knowledge in Preschool Education: Implications of Piaget's Theory* (Englewood Cliffs, N.J.: Prentice-Hall, 1978), 21.
5. Constance Kamii, "Application of Piaget's Theory to Education: The Preoperational Level," in *New Directions in Piagetian Theory and Practice,* ed. Irving E. Siegal et al. (Hillsdale, N.J.: Lawrence Erlbaum Associates, 1981), 5.
6. David M. Brodzinsky et al., "New Directions in Piagetian Theory and Research: An Integrative Perspective," in *New Directions in Piagetian Theory and Practice,* ed. Irving E. Siegal et al. (Hillsdale, N.J.: Lawrence Erlbaum Associates, 1981), 5.
7. Robert H. White, "Motivation Reconsidered: The Concept of Competence," *Psychological Review* 66 (1959): 321.
8. Jean Piaget, *Play, Dreams and Imitation in Childhood* (London: Routledge and Kegan Paul, 1967), 162.
9. George E. Forman and Fleet Hill, *Constructive Play: Applying Piaget in the Preschool* (Monterey, Calif.: Brooks/Cole, 1980), 2.
10. Felicisima C. Serafica, "Friendship Patterns and the Preschool Child," paper presented at a conference, Play and the Preschool Child, Ohio State University, Columbus, Ohio, November 1979, 19–20.
11. K. Alison Clarke-Stewart, "Interactions Between Mothers and Young Children: Characteristics and Consequences," *Monographs of the Society for Research in Child Development* 38 (1973): 1–109.
12. James E. Johnson, Joan Ershler, and Colleen Bell, "Play Behavior in a Discovery-based and a Formal-education Preschool Program," *Child Development* 51 (1980): 271–274.
13. Harriet M. Johnson, "The Art of Block Building," in *The Block Book* ed. Elizabeth S. Hirsch (Washington, D.C.: National Association for the Education of Young Children, 1984, revised edition), 15–49.
14. Sara Smilansky, *The Effects of Sociodramatic Play on Disadvantaged Preschool Children* (New York: John Wiley, 1968), 12–15.
15. National Association for the Education of Young Children, "NAEYC Position Statements on Developmentally Appropriate Practice in Early Childhood Programs," *Young Children* 41 (September 1986): 6.

Chapter 5

Programs for the Education and Development of the Children We Care For

---

Questions to Guide Your Reading and Study

- What are the distinguishing characteristics of nursery schools, laboratory schools, parent cooperatives, church-related programs, Head Start, and child-care programs?
- How are programs for the very young similar to and different from each other?
- How is center-based child care similar to and different from family child care?
- What are the major sources of funding for child-care programs?
- What are the major roles of quality care-givers?
- What are the characteristics of quality care-givers?
- What are the characteristics of quality programs for the very young?
- How can care-givers provide for the safety of the very young?
- Why is the nanny movement growing in popularity?
- What are critical issues facing care-givers and programs for the very young?

INTRODUCTION

To understand the contemporary nature of programs for very young children, it is necessary to understand how they are similar and how they differ. Although we can say that programs for the very young are alike in many ways, the same programs are also diverse in many ways. A common goal of all programs is to provide quality services, yet how they achieve this broad goal depends on the nature of the children served and the reasons the services are provided.

Although at first it may seem as though program diversity is undesirable, this is not so. Diversity is a unique characteristic of programs for young children in the United States, a characteristic that distinguishes them from programs for young children in other countries. Diversity provides for rich program services, creates an atmosphere in which new ideas can be tried, and gives parents a wide choice of programs for their children. How dull — let alone undemocratic — it would be if there were only one kind of program for the very young! The various types of programs available are described in Table 5-1.

PRESCHOOL PROGRAMS

Preschools are educational programs for three- to five-year-old children prior to their entrance into kindergarten. Preschools provide a full range of services, with an emphasis on *educational* experiences. Preschools come in many different formats, depending on their purposes, the children served, and the funding agencies. Preschools are both public and private and are operated by many different agencies.

The Nursery School

Nursery schools are the most popular preschool programs. They are places where children are actively engaged in learning. The nursery school began in London in 1914 when Margaret and Rachel McMillan started an open-air nursery that emphasized health care and healthy living. Because the early emphasis in such programs was on health care, they were given the name *nursery,* which is derived from "nurse." The McMillan sisters emphasized activities that nurtured children's development through play rather than through the teaching of academic subjects. For this reason, nursery schools have traditionally been viewed as places where children can learn without the pressure of being specifically taught reading, writing, and arithmetic.

In 1919, in the United States, Harriet Johnson started the Nursery School of the Bureau of Educational Experiments. The Bureau, founded in 1916, was an organization devoted to the study of children and educational practice. The Bureau would later become the Bank Street College of Education. The Nursery School enrolled children from fourteen months to three years; the activities were based on active experimentation through play. The teacher's role, according to Ms. Johnson, was to facilitate: "Our task is that of making sure that the children have access to suitable materials, of protecting them from encroachments and of assuring them safety in their early adventuring."[1]

Teachers, especially those who work with young children, are frequently asked about the purposes of the programs they operate. Harriet Johnson answered the question this way:

> My conclusion is that [young children] are leading productive lives. They are learning to live happily away from intimate contact with the family whose concerns are most emotionally bound up with theirs; they are establishing control over their own bodies so that they approach the physical environment with readiness and confidence; they are learning to route themselves through a day with the least possible amount of direction and dictation; they are establishing interests which they can explore independently; and they are learning to share the life of a social group, to modify their demands upon the world in relation to their fellows, and to appreciate the compensations as well as the restrictions that social living implies with the result that their emotional lives are functioning on a normal level.[2]

If all early childhood programs could say they were achieving these goals, there would be progress indeed.

Harriet Johnson's nursery school was in the same building as Caroline Pratt's famous City and Country School (also known as the Play School), which enrolled children from ages three to eleven. Caroline Pratt is noted as a developer of nursery school practices and materials (unit blocks), as a promoter of learning through play, and as a leader in the child-study movement.

Abigail Elliot, another nursery-school pioneer, studied for six months with the McMillan sisters and started the Ruggles Street Nursery School in Boston in 1922. Also in 1922, Edna White opened a nursery school at the Merrill Palmer School of Motherhood and Home Training in Detroit. This is now the Merrill Palmer Institute.

Most nursery school programs are characterized by a concern for the total needs of children, with an emphasis on learning through play. Many nursery schools operate a half-day program, but as the need for child-care services increases, many nursery schools are operating full-day programs to meet parents' needs and children's needs for learning in a play environment. Some nursery schools give parents the choice of a whole- or half-day program.

The daily schedule of Pat Vicenzi's classroom at the Plymouth Children's Center in Milwaukee is illustrative of the programs in many nursery schools (Figure 5-1).

TABLE 5-1

Programs for Infants, Toddlers, and Preschoolers

Program	Children Served	Age (years)	Purposes	Program of Services	How Supported
Nursery schools	All, but mainly middle class	2–5	Develop whole child, with emphasis on social and emotional development	Play-oriented	Parent tuition
Laboratory schools.	Children in a university community. Most laboratory schools try to have a balance of cultural backgrounds and socioeconomic classes; no longer just for children of faculty	Varies. Some configurations are: 3–5, Pre-K–6 grades, Pre-K–K–12 grades	Provide model programs and teacher training. Try new methods, materials. Provide for research, disseminate information	Academic	State, university
Parent cooperative preschools	Children of participating parents	2–5	Provide for whole child. Emphasis on social and emotional development	Play-oriented	Parent tuition and services
Head Start	Children from low socioeconomic levels and their families	2–5	Give children a "head start" on learning.	Comprehensive: academic, social, parent involvement, health	Federal subsidies, local funds, and in-kind services
Church-supported or -related	Members of the church and church community	2–5	Provide for whole child with emphasis on spiritual development. Community outreach	Play-oriented academic and religious development	Church congregation and parent tuition

Child-care homes and centers	All	6 weeks and up. Includes programs for children before and after school.	Provide comprehensive education and development for all children	Physical care: emphasis is now on comprehensive care; increasing attention to cognitive development	Federal Government: Title XX, food program, parent fees
Parent and infant participation programs such as Gymboree	Mainly middle class	1–5	Give children a place to play and interact with other children; provide parent information	Play, with emphasis on large motor skills	Parent fees
For-profit child care and preschools	All, but mainly for parents who can afford tuition	6 weeks through preschool	Provide parents with good programs; give parents alternative programs to choose from; make a profit for owners and shareholders	Comprehensive care, play, academic	Parent tuition
Preschools for four-year-olds operated by public schools	For all children in the District of Columbia and New York City; in some states, such as Texas and Florida, only for the disadvantaged	4	Develop readiness for basic skills and schooling	Academic	Taxes and special state allocations

FIGURE 5-1
The Rose Room: Daily Schedule

A.M.

7:30–9:30	Children arriving
	Free choice activities
	Quiet place open
	Art experiences
9:50–10:00	Allow time for finishing up activities
	Clean-up
10:00–10:15	Snack time
10:15–11:00 (approx.)	Group time; stories, songs, movement, yoga, cooperation games, special unit activities
11:00–11:30 (approx.)	Gym or outdoor play, walks
11:30–12:00	Quiet activities
	Gather for lunch, wash hands
12:00–12:30	Lunch

P.M.

12:30–12:50	Brush teeth
	Quiet activities, stories, music
1:00–3:15	Naptime: as children awaken, the same kinds of activities are available as in the morning
	(2:00–3:00 — Rose Room staff member is in the nap room)
3:15–3:30	Finish-up time — Clean-up
3:30–3:45	Snack
3:45–4:00	Group time
4:00–4:30	Gym or outdoor play
4:30–5:30	Quiet activities in the classroom
5:30	Center closes

This schedule remains flexible but provides a consistent structure for each day.

Laboratory Schools

College and university laboratory schools are model programs dedicated to research, teacher training, and promoting exemplary educational practices. University laboratory schools are viewed as places that support the development and dissemination of new ideas.

In 1921, Patty Smith Hill started a progressive laboratory nursery school at Columbia Teachers College in New York. In 1926, Ms. Hill founded the National Committee on Nursery Schools. Today, this group is the National Association for the Education of Young Children (NAEYC), which has a membership of over fifty thousand early-childhood professionals.

Many laboratory schools have programs from preschool through the elementary grades. Some also have high-school programs. Some university laboratory schools have programs for children from eighteen months to five years.

Parent Cooperative Preschools

Parent cooperative preschools are organized and operated by parents. The fact that parents have a role in operating the programs distinguishes them from programs where parents are not involved in program operation. A basic goal of cooperative preschools is to educate parents as well as children.

Many cooperative preschools operate play-based programs, and as a group they are responsible for helping maintain an emphasis on learning through play. The educational thrust of the various programs varies because the goals are determined by the parents who operate the program. Likewise, the ages of children attending the specific programs vary according to the philosophies and needs of the parents. Generally, however, the preschools enroll children between the ages of two and five.

Parent Cooperative Preschools International was founded in 1960 as an organization for persons interested in exchanging information on preschool education.

Church-Related Programs

Churches and synagogues throughout the United States operate preschool and child-care programs. Because of their Saturday or Sunday programs,

Programs for young children should provide quality services that enable children to experience a wide range of activities. What concepts can this young child learn from art activities?

many have the space, facilities, and equipment that make them ideal for weekday programs. Churches conduct weekday programs in response to the needs of their members and to provide an outreach to the community. As a result, they meet community needs for preschool child care and preschool education and at the same time use otherwise idle facilities. In addition, many denominations have a long history of providing people with the option of choosing either a religious or secular education.

One popular service provided by churches is "mother's day out," which is designed to provide parents — usually mothers — with a few hours a week away from their children. Mother's day out, then, is a support service to parents through which churches provide quality child-care and preschool programs to children. Churches also see mother's day out as a means of inviting families into the total church program. Most programs operate one day a week from 9:00 A.M. to 3:00 P.M.

The curricula of religious preschool programs are similar in many respects to those found in secular programs, with the exception that they provide for spiritual development through moral and religious education and activities. Churches that operate preschool and child-care programs see themselves as conducting quality programs based on spiritual values, with provision for community outreach to parents with children.

THE MONTESSORI SYSTEM

Maria Montessori (1870–1952) developed one of the most widely known programs for teaching young children. She spent her life developing her system, which has influenced virtually all early childhood programs. In many respects, Montessori was ahead of her time. She "discovered" and articulated learning and teaching concepts many early childhood educators today take for granted. These include the concepts of "sensitive periods" for learning; the importance of activity in learning; and the role children play in their own education. Montessori was indeed a pioneer in taking philosophical thoughts and putting them into a practical educational system.

Most professionals and parents who visit a good Montessori program come away impressed by what they observed. What impresses them the most are the orderliness and arrangement of the environment; the learning materials; the respectful way teachers treat children and the children treat each other; the way children are independently involved and engaged in learning activities; and the tranquil serenity of the learning environment. As one impressed parent commented, "I almost wish I were a child so I could attend a Montessori program."

The best-known portion of Montessori's system is for children between three and five. Lately, given all the interest in infant and toddler programs, applications of her methods for this age group are gaining more popularity in the United States.

Origin of the Montessori System

Montessori began her career as the first woman physician in Italy. Following this achievement, she turned her attention to finding an educational solution to mental retardation. While working with mentally retarded children, she developed materials and activities that enabled many of them to read and write, educational accomplishments that were unheard of at that time, in the early 1900s. Montessori, however, had a larger vision in mind. As she said, "While everyone was admiring the progress made by my defective charges, I was trying to discover the reasons which could have reduced the happy, healthy pupils of the ordinary schools to such a low state that in the intelligence test they were on a level with my own unfortunate pupils."[3]

The opportunity to perfect her methods and apply them to normal children came in 1906 when she was invited to organize educational programs for the Roman Association for Good Building to benefit children living in tenement housing. Her first school was called the *Casa dei Bambini* or *Children's House,* a name still used by many Montessori programs.

Basic Features of the Montessori System

A number of features and beliefs set the Montessori system apart from other programs. It is not that other programs don't accept these basic principles; many do. But they are important aspects of the Montessori system, and are well integrated into the program practiced by her followers.

Sensory Materials. Since Montessori believed that children learn through the senses, she developed a set of materials designed to train the senses and facilitate learning. The sensory materials make children more aware of the capacity of their bodies to receive, interpret, and make use of stimuli. Montessori sensory materials are listed in Figure 5-2.

Respect for Children. Montessori believed respect for children as individuals is an essential foundation of all education. This respect is manifested in several ways. First, all children are treated with dignity and respect as worthy children of God. Like the famous French philosopher and educator before her, Jean Jacques Rousseau (1712–1778), Montessori believed that children are born with an essential nature that is good, not bad. Consequently, Montessori children's houses are places where children are treated in mannerly, humane ways.

Second, each child is given an individualized program. What is more of a sign of respect than to teach each child according to his or her own needs and developmental level? Also, Montessori thought that to treat children as adults is a sign of disrespect, and she repeatedly cautioned educators against regarding children as miniature adults.

Sensitive Periods. Montessori believed there are genetically programed *sensitive periods* in children's lives during which they are more capable of

FIGURE 5-2
Montessori Sensory Materials

1. Pink tower — (visual discrimination of dimension). Ten wood cubes of the same shape and texture, all pink, the largest of which is ten centimeters cubed. Each succeeding block is one centimeter smaller. The child builds a tower beginning with the largest block.
2. Brown stairs — (visual discrimination of width and height). Ten blocks of wood, all brown, differing in height and width. The child arranges the blocks next to each other from thickest to thinnest so the blocks resemble a staircase.
3. Red rods — (visual discrimination of length). Ten rod-shaped pieces of wood, all red, of identical size but differing in lengths from ten centimeters to one meter. The child arranges the rods next to each other from largest to smallest.
4. Cylinder blocks — (visual discrimination of size). Four individual wood blocks, which have holes of various sizes. One block deals with height, one with diameter, and two with the relationship of both variables. The child removes the cylinders in random order, then matches each cylinder to the correct hole.
5. Smelling jars — (discrimination involving the olfactory sense). Two identical sets of white, opaque glass jars with removable tops through which the child cannot see but through which odors can pass. The teacher places various substances, such as herbs, in the jars, and the child matches the jars according to the smell of the substance in the jars.
6. Baric tablets — (discrimination of weight). Sets of rectangular pieces of wood which vary according to weight. There are three sets, light, medium, and heavy in weight, which the child matches according to the weight of the tablets.
7. Color tablets — (discrimination of color and education of the chromatic sense). Two identical sets of small, rectangular pieces of wood are used for matching color or shading.
8. Sound boxes — (auditory discrimination). Two identical sets of cylinders are filled with various materials such as salt and rice. The child matches the cylinders according to the sound the materials make.
9. Tonal bells — (sound and pitch). Two sets of eight bells, which are alike in shape and size but differ in color. One set is white, the other brown. The child matches the bells according to the tone they make.
10. Cloth swatches — (sense of touch). The child identifies two identical swatches of cloth according to touch. This activity is performed first without a blindfold, but is later accomplished using a blindfold.
11. Temperature jugs or thermic bottles — (thermic sense and the ability to distinguish between temperatures). Small metal jugs are filled with water of varying temperatures. The child matches jugs of the same temperature.

Source: George S. Morrison, *Early Childhood Education Today,* 4th ed. (Columbus, Ohio: Charles E. Merrill, 1988).

learning certain tasks. She felt that children's lives were a succession of these sensitive periods. A critical teacher role is to observe when these periods occur and, when they do, provide an environment that supports learning. She believed that "childhood passes from conquest to conquest in a constant rhythm that constitutes its joy and happiness."[4]

The Absorbent Mind. In Chapter 4, we discussed Montessori's theory of learning in some detail. One of the features of this theory is that children's absorbent minds literally act as sponges and absorb sensory information from the environment. From birth to three years, the *unconscious absorbent mind* develops the senses used for seeing, hearing, tasting, smelling, and touching. From three to six years, the *conscious absorbent mind* selects sensory impressions from the environment and further develops the senses. The child refines what he or she knows. Prior to three, for example, the child sees and absorbs colors without making any distinctions among them. After three, he or she develops the ability through the conscious absorbent mind to distinguish, match, and grade colors.

The Prepared Environment. Montessori believed that adults do not — should not — mold children. Rather, children themselves are responsible for their own learning. She believed that when children are actively involved in a prepared environment, with the freedom to choose, they educate themselves. This ability to self-educate is known as *auto-education.*

The key to auto-education is a *prepared environment* where children can do things for themselves and become independent of adults. In this sense, a prepared environment can be any place — home or child-care center, for example — as long as it provides materials for learning and the freedom to learn.

Criticism of the Montessori System

As with most things, there are a number of criticisms of the Montessori system of education. Some of these criticisms are discussed here.

1. *Education comes from things — objects — not people.* The teacher's role in a Montessori program is different from that of teachers in other programs. The Montessori teacher prepares the environment and the child learns by interacting with materials. Montessori materials are designed to meet children's developmental needs and are a key to the Montessori program. These materials make Montessori programs unique. The reality of life in a Montessori program, however, is that children can and do learn from teachers as well as materials.

2. *Learning is too impersonal.* This criticism is related to the first. Because children are interacting with learning materials and working independently, the predominant methods of learning are not through peer and group interaction. The emphasis is on the children educating themselves, not being educated by others. Again, the reality of most Montessori classrooms is that there is ample opportunity for social interaction.

3. *Montessori emphasizes the cognitive at the expense of the social and emotional.* Montessori programs are cognitive-based and are designed to be so. The Montessori system assumes that it is not others — teachers or other children — who teach children, but children themselves. Therefore the emphasis is on learning through materials, not learning through others.

Caveat Emptor (Let the Buyer Beware)

Several Montessori organizations set standards for Montessori programs, including the American Montessori Society (AMS) (150 Fifth Avenue, New York, N.Y. 10011) and the Association Montessori Internationale (AMI) (780 West End Avenue, New York, N.Y. 10025). Nevertheless, no "truth in advertising" policy applies to Montessori programs. Some programs that call themselves Montessori bear little or no resemblance to a good Montessori program. At a minimum, parents should visit the program before enrolling their children to determine, first, if the school is associated with the AMS or AMI. Although affiliation with either of these two organizations does not necessarily indicate that a program is of high quality, the better programs will be affiliated. Second, care-givers should determine if the staff has Montessori training.

HEAD START

Head Start has had more influence on early childhood programs than any other single program or agency. Head Start began in the summer of 1965 as a program to help disadvantaged children who would enter first grade. As the program has matured, it has developed year-round programs for children ages two to five.

In its beginning, Head Start was based on the socialization models of many nursery schools. Over the years, however, Head Start programs have developed curricular models designed to meet the needs of the particular children being served. As a result, Head Start has been a leader in providing *comprehensive* programs that are developmentally and educationally appropriate for young children from low-income families.

Head Start Objectives

Head Start's national program serves as a guide to the operation of all local programs. Within the national guidelines, however, each local program is free to implement a program that best meets the needs of its children and families. Head Start components include education, parent involvement, health services (including psychological services, nutrition, and mental health), social services, and career development for staff, parents, and administration.

Each program area has objectives that program developers follow. The educational objectives are:

1. To provide children with a learning environment and the varied experiences that will help them develop socially, intellectually, physically, and emotionally in a manner appropriate to their age and stage of development toward the overall goal of social competence.

2. To integrate the educational aspects of the various Head Start components in the daily program of activities.
3. To involve parents in the educational activities of the program to enhance their role as the principal influence on their child's education and development.
4. To help parents increase their knowledge, understanding, skills, and experience in child growth and development.
5. To identify and reinforce experiences that occur in the home that parents can utilize as educational activities for their children.[5]

Although Head Start developers, program directors, and staff have been somewhat beleaguered in their continued defense of their program from its multitude of critics, parents have always enthusiastically supported its efforts and results. A growing body of evidence also supports the ability of Head Start and other early intervention programs to make a difference. One of these, the Lazar study, found that early education programs significantly reduced the number of children assigned to special education, significantly reduced the number of children retained in a grade, and significantly increased children's scores on fourth-grade mathematics achievement tests. There was also a suggestive trend toward increased scores on fourth-grade reading tests. In addition, low-income children who attended preschools surpassed their controls on the Stanford-Binet IQ test for up to three years after the program ended, and children who attended preschool were more likely than control children to cite achievement as a reason for being proud of themselves.[6]

For the 1986 fiscal year, the national Head Start budget was $1,075,059,000. There were 1,305 local Head Start programs, which served 452,080 children between the ages of two and six. This was about one-sixth of the children eligible for services.[7]

CHILD-CARE PROGRAMS

Over the past decade, there has been a growing realization that the care of infants and toddlers should entail more than just baby-sitting. Just as caregivers have recognized that older children need individualized programs, they are recognizing that infants and toddlers also need individualized attention. Along with this recognition has come the realization that people who care for infants and toddlers need special training.

Historical Background

As long as there have been children, there has been a need to provide care for them. Child care has traditionally connoted the physical care of children, and many programs have emphasized as their primary goals the physical health and well-being of children. For many years, *day care* was a popular term for the physical care of children. Much of this kind of care was similar to baby-sitting. Today, the preferred terminology is *child care,* which when used by professionals means the *comprehensive* care of children covering all the areas of development: the intellectual, social and emotional, and physical.

Although there has always been a need for child care, the ways society responds to child-care needs depend on the social and economic conditions of the times. The roots of child care in the United States and other countries are firmly planted in the concept of need. Frequently, child care is viewed as a service to be provided only to families who cannot provide care independently, not as a service available to all families regardless of need. The first child-care programs in the United States were associated with charity and charitable organizations. In 1854, New York Hospital opened a nursery for children of the poor. Many child-care programs were operated in settlement houses. Unfortunately, to this day, the "need" stigma is still placed on child-care programs and services.

Programs for the care of children have also been used to provide for the welfare of children and their parents as a means of promoting the general welfare of a country and its citizens. In 1907, Maria Montessori started her program in Rome to provide for the educational and health needs of children from slum neighborhoods. In 1914, the McMillan sisters started their nursery schools in London as a means of providing better health care for children from slum neighborhoods.

In 1933, during the Great Depression, the Federal Relief Emergency Administration established nursery schools to provide work for the unemployed and care for the nation's needy children. In 1940, Congress passed the Lanham Act, which provided funds for the establishment of child-care centers to care for children while their mothers worked. One of the best known of these centers was operated at the Kaiser Shipyards in Portland, Oregon.

In 1965, the Economic Opportunity Act funded the Head Start program, which was designed to provide services to the nation's socially and economically deprived children. Although there was and still is a social welfare philosophy associated with Head Start, this program more than any other has educated the public and the early childhood profession about the need for comprehensive care and education for young children. Head Start has helped make child care respectable, although it still has the image problem of being only for children of the poor and disadvantaged.

Sources of Child-Care Funding

The sources of child-care funding are many and varied. Particular sources often depend on the purpose of the child care. The most common sources of child-care funding are:

1. *Parents.* Parents who pay all or part of child-care fees are the chief financial supporters of child care. Because working parents often pay for their own child care, there is a tendency on the part of parents and the profession to keep the cost of child care low. This results in poorly paid — and some would say minimally qualified — staff and adds to the image of child care as a poor profession. Unfortunately, some parents select child care on the basis of how little it costs, not on the basis of quality.

2. *State Agencies.* Agencies such as offices of health and human services provide support for child care. State programs may operate their own programs or purchase "slots" in programs operated by other agencies. Often, these slots are reserved for parents who participate in job training or are seeking employment. Sometimes, state agencies use slots when a child or parent will benefit from child-care placement.

3. *The Federal Government.* One of the largest supporters of child care is the federal government. The government supports child care in four ways. One is through state agencies. Title XX of the Social Security Act provides monies to states in the form of "block grants." These monies are used to provide certain groups and classes of parents and children with child care. Some eligibility criteria under Title XX are that the parent be receiving aid to families with dependent children; that the parent be receiving a social security payment supplement; that the gross income of the parent be below an eligibility level established by the state; or that a parent belong to a group such as migrant farm workers that is considered automatically eligible for child-care services. In 1985, monies for child care under Title XX programs amounted to about 700 million dollars.

A second source of federal support for child care is the United States Department of Agriculture Child Care Food Program. The USDA provides monies and commodities to child-care centers and homes to support their nutritional programs. Children twelve years old and younger are eligible. In 1986, the USDA provided approximately 483 million dollars of support through the food program.

A third source of federal support for child care is child-care tax credits. Since 1975, parents have been able to itemize the cost of child care as a deduction against their federal income taxes. Currently, the amount that can be deducted is based on a sliding scale. Beginning at $10,000 dollars of annual income, 30 percent of the cost of child care can be deducted. As income increases, the percentage decreases until it reaches 20 percent. The maximum amount a family can deduct is twenty-four hundred dollars for one child and forty-eight hundred dollars for two children. In 1983, the amount of the deductions for child care amounted to 2.1 billion dollars.

A fourth source of federal support to child care is employer support or employer sponsorship. The federal tax code provides employers with certain tax breaks or benefits for providing child care for their employees.

4. *Private and Charitable Organizations.* Agencies such as the YMCA, YWCA, YMHA, YWHA, United Way, and Easter Seal Society support child-care programs and child-care staff training.

5. *Religious Organizations.* Many churches and synagogues provide child care at lower rates than their members would pay on the open market. In effect, these agencies subsidize the cost of child care.

6. *Employers.* As an employee benefit, many employers provide free or reduced-cost child-care services on their own premises or through the purchase of slots from other agencies.

What Is Child Care?

Bettye Caldwell, a leader in efforts to provide children with quality care, defines professional child care as "a *comprehensive* service to children and families which functions as a subsystem of the child-rearing system and which *supplements* the care children receive from their families. Professional child care is not a substitute or a competitor for parental care. To some extent, professional child care represents a version of the extended family which has adapted to the social realities of the modern world."[8]

Types of Child-Care Programs

Family Child Care. Family child care (or family day care, as it is popularly known) is the most widely used form of child care. Parents want their children cared for in a home setting. Family child care may be provided by unlicensed and unregulated homes, licensed and regulated homes, and homes that are licensed, regulated, and sponsored by a social service agency.

The definitions of and requirements for family child care vary from state to state. In Pennsylvania, for example, the definition of family day care is "any premise other than the child's own home operated for profit or not profit, in which child day care is provided at any one time to four, five, or six children, who are not relatives of the care-giver."[9]

The range of child-care services provided in family homes includes care for infants, toddlers, and preschoolers, plus after-school care for school-age children.

Good family child care is much more than baby-sitting. But what constitutes good family child care? This depends to a large extent on parents' needs and desires. There are a number of characteristics and qualities, however, that should be present in a home.

Licensed facility. The fact that a home is licensed does not guarantee that it will provide quality care, but it does signify that the care-giver has met certain standards and that the home has been inspected. With the current epidemic of child abuse, many states have legislation requiring background checks for care providers as a prerequisite for licensing. In addition, licensed facilities meet state and municipal minimum standards for space, equipment, and safety.

Any facility should be clean and bright. If the parent wouldn't want to spend eight or nine hours there, neither would the child.

Care-giver training. Care-givers may say they love children, but love is not enough. Training increases the probability that the care will be of high quality. As researcher Steven Fosburg says in *Family Day Care in the United States: Summary of Findings,* "the effects of training are strong and positive."[10] Such training may be sponsored by an agency or acquired independently. It is critical for professionals to engage in such self-development.

Daily activities. Daily activities should include more than supervised recreation. Home-care providers can and should engage children in cognitive activities such as language development and fine motor activities. Many of these activities can be incorporated into the routines of daily living and housekeeping. A care provider should have and follow a daily schedule that includes a variety of activities.

Personal qualities and characteristics. Parents have to ask themselves if a home care-giver is the kind of person they really want to leave their children with. If the care-giver is immature and little more than a child herself, for example, then regardless of the pressure for child care, parents should look elsewhere.

Family child care will continue to be the primary type of care for children. Early childhood professionals need to do all they can to help increase the quality and availability of this preferred and important service.

Center-Based Child Care. When child care is provided in a center setting, the environment is decidedly different from that of a family home or family child care. Usually, center settings have larger, open spaces, more children and adults, and an institutional atmosphere. Because of the lack of adequate home-based child-care programs, center child care offers the best alternative to meeting the child-care needs of parents.

The fact that child care is center based does not mean the setting or the care has to be institutionalized and routinely impersonal. Because they provide child care in center settings, care-givers must make every effort to ensure that the setting and care are warm, personalized, and developmentally appropriate.

Center-based care provides many challenges for child care that other kinds of programs may not. There are more children in a center program; children are in the company of more children their own age; depending on state child–care-giver staffing ratios, one adult may be providing care for up to six infants; parents may not have the opportunity to match their parenting philosophies to those who care for their children; and the needs of the center may take precedence over those of parents and children.

Critical Roles of Care-givers

Care-givers, not the building, make a child-care center more than just an institution. It is therefore important to examine some of the critical care-giver roles that are essential for quality care.

Meet Children's Needs. Care-givers must meet the physical, emotional, and cognitive needs of children. At one time, the emphasis in child care centered on providing for physical needs. Some care-givers thought that meeting physical needs promptly and efficiently constituted quality care. Now there is an equal emphasis on meeting children's total needs: physical, cognitive, social, and emotional. The foundation for development is laid in the early years and children need and deserve care-givers who can meet all their basic needs in many ways. Care-givers are children's surrogate parents, and they are the ones who have to physically and emotionally nourish children in their care.

Implications for care-givers. In the context of daily acts of providing for the physical needs of children, care-givers must also meet their emotional needs. Diapering, for example, is a custodial need that can be used to meet emotional needs. Care-givers must be consistent in their care-giving habits. They must try to express an even, warm, happy nature with children all the time. Children need the security and confidence that come from knowing that they can depend on having the same kind of care day in and day out. They don't need care-givers who have wide swings of mood from day to day. Meeting the emotional needs of children is one of the most important roles of the care-giver.

Care-givers make a child-care program more than just an institution. They must provide for the physical, cognitive, and socioemotional needs of children. How is this care-giver demonstrating that she accepts and respects this child?

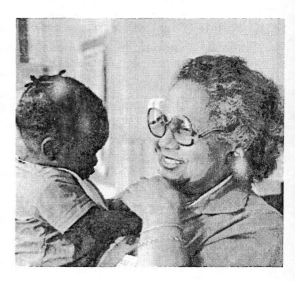

FIGURE 5-3
Action Plan

DEVELOPMENTAL AREA: PERCEPTUAL/MENTAL
AGE GROUP: SIX WEEKS–THREE MONTHS

Activity:	Mobile — from all sides
Purpose:	To encourage the baby to turn his head and to increase the number of things he can see.
Materials:	Merry-go-round mobile or other mobile.
Position of the Baby:	In the crib.
Procedure:	Let baby watch a mobile. Hang a merry-go-round mobile over the baby's crib. Place it on one side for a few days and then change it to the other side. When you feel that the baby can focus on the mobile for a few moments, place a mobile on each side of the crib. After a while the baby will learn to shift his gaze from one mobile to the other.
Activity:	Bright Colors at Feeding Time
Purpose:	To increase the baby's focused attention.
Materials:	Bright colored towel.
Position of the Baby:	In your arms.
Procedure:	Use a bright towel at feeding. Place a brightly colored towel or receiving blanket over your shoulder while feeding the baby.
Activity:	Crib Positions
Purpose:	To increase the time the baby spends exploring his surroundings with his eyes.
Materials:	Crib.
Position of the Baby:	In the crib or in an infant seat.
Procedure:	Change position of the crib when you feel the baby has explored with his eyes everything he can see from the old position. Move crib to different positions in the room. This gives the baby a change of scenery. Or let him sit in a carry-all for part of the day. He will enjoy seeing things from a different point of view.

Source: Used with permission of Kinder-Care Learning Centers, Inc., 2400 Presidents Drive, Montgomery, AL 36116.

As a care-giver, you can provide opportunities for children's cognitive development. Speak often to children. Talk with them about what you and they are doing. Play music for them while they are being diapered and are playing. Be a good language model for children. Use a pleasant tone of voice to talk to children.

Accept and respect young children for who and what they are. All

FIGURE 5-4
Infant Daily Activity Record

Child's Name _____ Date _____

Special Instructions (please initial) _____

_____

_____

ACTIVITIES _____

_____

_____

FOOD	Time	Food	Amount	NAP(S)		
BREAKFAST				Time		Length
	___	___	___	___		___
	___	___	___			
	___	___	___	OUTSIDE PLAY		
LUNCH						
Vegetable	___	___	___	Time		Length
Fruit	___	___	___			
Meat	___	___	___	___		___
JUICE				MEDICATION		
				Time	Amount	Administered By
	___	___	___			
	___	___	___	___	___	___
MILK						
	___	___	___			
	___	___	___			
	___	___	___			

children have individual needs. Although it is true that varied needs can be provided for within the larger context of care-giving, it is also true that individual children have individual needs that must be taken into account.

Care-givers must admire young children's growing abilities and their striving for independence. They must avoid emotionally and physically rejecting children's independence. One way to do this is to share leadership and task roles with them.

Plan for Care-giving

Care-givers must plan for activities and events in their programs. They need to plan for how they will encourage children's mental and physical

FIGURE 5-4 (continued)

DIAPER CHECKS

Code

		AM							PM			

A = Arrival at Center
D = Dry
W = Wet
B = BM
S = Sleeping whole hour

6	7	8	9	10	11	12	1	2	3	4	5	6
—	—	—	—	—	—	—	—	—	—	—	—	—

COMMENTS, ACHIEVEMENTS, UNUSUAL BEHAVIOR, ETC. _____

_____

_____

_____

Caregiver _____ Hours _____

_____ Hours _____

Source: Used with permission of Kinder-Care Learning Centers, Inc., 2400 Presidents Drive, Montgomery, AL 36116.

development. When care-givers don't plan what they will do with children, children's lives lack order and consistency. Planning helps provide clarity, consistency, and direction.

Implications for care-givers. Care-givers can develop activity plans similar to those shown in Figures 5-3 and 5-4. Figure 5-3 is a completed activity plan and Figure 5-4 shows a suggested activity planning guide. At the very least, an activity plan should be written weekly for each group of children in the program. Plans should not be written for more than two weeks at a time. In an activity plan, care-givers can specify what kind of materials they and children will use and how they will use them, in the crib and out of the crib.

Planning should take into consideration play areas for each group — noncrawling, crawling, and walking. Specify how these areas will be furnished and what opportunities will be provided in each center. When babies are awake, they need to be out of their cribs as much as possible. Plans can include out-of-crib activities.

Plans should also include outside activities. Children should not spend all their days inside a center or home.

Plan for infants, toddlers, and preschoolers to do things at their physical and developmental levels. Infants can crawl to mirrors placed at floor level. Objects such as beach balls and toys tied to a hula-hoop can be hung from the ceiling so they are at the eye level of infants. Household items such as pots and pans and Tupperware containers make good toys. Also, care-givers can make many children's play items, such as balls of colored yarn (which, incidentally, were one of Froebel's toys for children).

Qualities and Characteristics of Care-givers

The qualities and characteristics of care-givers are as important as their roles, if not more so.

Nurturing. According to Alice Honig, a noted professor of child development, "The high quality infant care-giver is a special kind of nurturing person, with keen observation skills. Flexible, creative, comforting — she or he has a calm style that radiates secure commitment to an infant's well-being, even when the infant seems overwhelmed by colic or other upsets."[11]

Professional Development. Quality care-givers are people who are interested in their professional growth. They want to do what is right for children and make efforts to get the professional training and education they need to be effective care-givers.

Knowledge of Growth and Development. Quality care-givers know child growth and development. They also know the children they care for so they can provide care that is appropriate for each child's developmental level. Care providers and educators believe that one of the care-giver's most important qualities is the ability to provide for children's growth and development.[12]

Personal Health and Grooming. Quality care-givers care about themselves. This caring is reflected in part in their neatness, cleanliness, and personal grooming. Caring about oneself is also reflected in good physical and mental health. Providing care for children requires stamina and patience. Children deserve care-givers who take care of themselves so they can give their best to those entrusted to their care.

Interpersonal Relationships. Quality care-givers care about the children and their parents. They accept and respect the backgrounds and cultures of children and parents. They use their knowledge of children's cultures to enhance the program by providing culturally relevant nutritional and educational activities.

Quality care-givers do their best to get along with parents and other staff members. They are empathetic and helping and work cooperatively for the good of all.

CHARACTERISTICS OF QUALITY PROGRAMS FOR YOUNG CHILDREN

It is easy for parents who must work to leave their children in programs they demand little of. The necessity of working and the urgency of finding infant care (a service that is in high demand but short supply) sometimes makes parents willing to take what they can get, and what they can get is not always the best. What qualities and characteristics set apart the good from the unacceptable? The following are benchmarks that should set the standards for quality care.

Quality Care-givers

Within the criteria previously outlined for good care-givers, programs should make every effort to hire care-givers with the appropriate professional and personal qualities.

Stable Staff

Staff stability means that young children will have continuity in their care over a period of time — usually a year. As Alice Honing states, "Continuity permits a baby to relax into the certainty of a sustained relationship she or he can count on."[13]

Professional Staff-Child Ratios

Programs should have a care-giver–child ratio that permits individualized attention and promotes physical, social, and intellectual development and good mental health. Mandated ratios vary from state to state and municipality to municipality. Staff-child ratios as a function of group size, as recommended by the National Academy of Early Childhood Programs, are given in Table 5-2.

These ratio guidelines indicate that for infants, the highest acceptable ratio is one care-giver per four infants, which is lower than the standards established in many states. In many states, the care-giver–child ratios exceed those recommended for other age groups as well. There may be a tendency to think that if state standards for care-giver–child ratios are met, then a program is providing quality care. This is not necessarily so. High ratios exist for a number of reasons, the primary one being that they keep costs lower. High ratios, however, are not in the best interests of children. Low ratios do not necessarily mean that high-quality care is provided, but they make quality care more likely.

TABLE 5-2

Staff-Child Ratios and Group Size

Age of Children*	Group Size									
	6	8	10	12	14	16	18	20	22	24
0–12 months	1.3	1.4								
12–24 months	1.3	1.4	1.5	1.4						
24–36 months		1.4	1.5	1.6†						
2- and 3-year-olds			1.5	1.6	1.7†					
3-year-olds					1.7	1.8	1.9	1.10†		
4-year-olds						1.8	1.9	1.10†		
4- and 5-year-olds						1.8	1.9	1.10†		
5-year-olds						1.8	1.9	1.10		
6- to 8-year-olds								1.10	1.11	1.12

*Multi-age grouping is both permissible and desirable. When no infants are included, the staff-child ratio and group size requirements shall be based on the age of the majority of the children in the group. When infants are included, ratios and group size for infants must be maintained.

†Smaller group sizes and lower staff-child ratios are optimal. Larger group sizes and higher staff-child ratios are acceptable only in cases where staff are highly qualified.

Source: National Association for the Education of Young Children, *Accreditation Criteria and Procedures of the National Academy of Early Childhood Programs* (Washington, D.C.: National Association for the Education of Young Children, 1984), 24.

Responsive Environment

An environment that is sensitive to the unique needs and temperaments of children is considered a responsive environment. It is one thing to have a program that meets the needs of the "average" child. It is another thing to have care-givers and an environment that meets the needs of *all* children.

Developmental Program

An essential for any quality program is a written, development-based curriculum for meeting children's needs. The curriculum should specify objectives and activities for children of all ages. These activities should stimulate infants, allow for the growing independence of toddlers, and address the prereading and language needs of four- and five-year-old children.

The National Association for the Education of Young Children (NAEYC) has developed guidelines for developmentally appropriate practice to guide care-givers in their selection of curricula, practices, and activities. These guidelines include the following principles:

1. Developmentally appropriate curriculum provides for all areas of a child's development: physical, emotional, social, and cognitive through an integrated approach.

2. Appropriate curriculum planning is based on teachers' observations and recordings of each child's special interests and developmental progress.

3. Curriculum planning emphasizes learning as an interactive process. Teachers prepare the environment for children to learn through active exploration and interaction with adults, other children, and materials.

4. Learning activities and materials should be concrete, real, and relevant to the lives of young children.

5. Programs provide for a wider range of developmental interests and abilities than the chronological age range of the group would suggest. Adults are prepared to meet the needs of children who exhibit unusual interests and skills outside the normal developmental range.

6. Teachers provide a variety of activities and materials; teachers increase the difficulty, complexity, and challenge of an activity as children are involved with it and as children develop understanding and skills.

7. Adults provide opportunities for children to choose from among a variety of activities, materials, and equipment; and time to explore through active involvement. Adults facilitate children's engagement with materials and activities and extend the child's learning by asking questions or making suggestions that stimulate children's thinking.

8. Multicultural and nonsexist experiences, materials, and equipment should be provided for children of all ages.

9. Adults provide a balance of rest and active movement for children throughout the program day.

10. Outdoor experiences should be provided for children of all ages.[14]

Parent Involvement

Every program benefits from parent involvement. Involving parents helps ensure that programs will be sensitive and responsive to parent's needs and concerns. Chapter 9 provides detailed information for conducting such programs.

Staff Development

A program of staff development helps all care-givers and support staff acquire the knowledge and skills necessary for quality care-giving.

QUALITY AND PROFESSIONAL ORGANIZATIONS

Many professional organizations advocate on behalf of children and their families. This may entail taking positions about what constitutes quality in programs. One organization that takes such positions is the Southern Association on Children Under Six. The board of directors of this organization believes that quality child care meets the following needs of young children:

- Children need to feel that the situation is a safe and comfortable place for them to be.
- Children need to learn to feel good about themselves.
- Children need to be fully employed in activities that are meaningful to them and that support them in their full-time quest to learn.
- Children need to develop the ability to live comfortably with other children and adults.
- Children need to have their physical development supported and be helped to learn health, nutrition, and safety practices.
- Children in care need to feel that there is consistency in their lives and a shared concern about them among the important people in their lives — their parents and their care-givers.[15]

SAFETY IN CENTER PROGRAMS

Providing a safe environment is one of the most important functions provided by center staff members. Care-givers should take a number of safety precautions in every program.

1. Provide constant and alert supervision for all children at all times. This constant supervision function does not mean that infants are kept in their cribs all the time or that they are not allowed to do anything. Quite the contrary. Infants should be involved in a full range of activities. But they must be supervised in the process. There is no substitute for good supervision. As experienced care-givers know, an infant can twist and turn and roll off a diapering counter in the blink of an eye.

   Toddlers also have a way of disappearing in the twinkling of an eye. They, too, need constant supervision, but not a rigid kind that prohibits their being involved in a full range of activities. The best kind of supervision occurs when the care-giver is involved with children as a participant, guide, and observer. A care-giver's full attention should be on the children cared for, not on other staff members.

2. Arrange the environment so it promotes safety and supervision. A low barrier or fence around a toddler play area allows freedom of exploration, for example, but it also sets a limit on unrestricted exploration.

3. Provide for the proper storage of all materials. This is essential. In particular, hazardous materials need special storage areas. They should be in separate areas away from the children, in locked cupboards or high enough that they cannot be reached by toddlers even if they pull a chair over to the storage area and climb.

   All other materials should be appropriately stored and shelved. The Montessorians say that everything should be in its place and there should be a place for everything. Children need access to learning materials. Children need an environment that is rich in learning materials. But keeping materials picked up and stored, helping children pick up and store materials, and teaching children to put materials away when they are done with them keep the environment orderly and reduce the possibility of accidents.

4. Identify all exits with signs. This identification is usually a state or local requirement as part of licensing standards.

5. Place emergency cribs near the exits of the infant area so they are readily available during an emergency. All emergency exists and passages should be free from obstructions.

6. Establish and post procedures for dealing with emergencies. These procedures should cover what to do with children in an emergency and include emergency phone numbers. Develop procedures for all emergencies that are likely to be encountered in a particular geographic area. In addition to fire, procedures for tornados, hurricanes, and earthquakes may be necessary, depending on geographic location.

7. Each child should have a permanent folder that contains information about what to do in an emergency. At a minimum, it should include telephone numbers, people to contact, names of doctors, and authorization to provide emergency care.

8. Practice emergency procedures. Awareness of emergency procedures is not the same as knowing what to do in an emergency.

9. Establish and follow procedures for disinfecting and cleaning toys. Safety in any program includes maintaining a healthy environment. All toys and materials should be disinfected at least once a day. Toys that are mouthed should be cleaned after each child. Some programs use a bucket with water and bleach in which toys are placed after each use. Dolls and other toys such as puppets should be washed each day.

10. Keep materials and equipment in good repair. If materials cannot be repaired, they should be discarded.

11. All electrical outlets should be covered and electrical cords should be out of children's reach.

12. Any spilled water or liquid on the floor should be wiped up immediately.

THE NANNY: ONE-ON-ONE CHILD CARE

Nannies are popular. They are the latest rage among upwardly mobile working couples who can afford them. As more and more women enter the work place, they are looking for alternative child-care arrangements for their children. The use of a nanny (female) or manny (male) is one of these arrangements.

Nanny training is the latest frontier in efforts to satisfy parents' needs for quality child rearing. The American Council of Nanny Schools is one of the agencies trying to upgrade the image of nannies from glorified baby-sitters to highly skilled care-givers and teachers. An increasing number of four- and two-year colleges are offering one- and two-year nanny training programs. In 1986, according to the American Council of Nanny Schools, there were seventeen nanny training schools in operation. These are two-year training programs that provide curricula in child development, infant care, nutrition, grooming, manners, and family management. Indeed, this curriculum and training is what separates nannies from *au pair* ("working in tandem") workers, European (or, increasingly, South American) baby-sitters, house-keepers, and mothers' helpers.

The living arrangements and child-care circumstances of nannies are almost too diverse to generalize about, except in the broadest of terms. Some live and work twenty-four hours a day with their charges and have weekends off, whereas others work an eight-hour-day and have their own living arrangements. Some limit their responsibilities to child care, whereas others teach the children, do light housework, and prepare meals.

For their devotion and services to the child and family, a nanny can receive, in addition to a salary, a paid vacation, vacation days, medical benefits, overtime pay, and use of the family car.

Parents want nannies for several reasons. First, they are a constant presence in a child's life. Second, they are reliable and available since many live with the family. Nannies are a solution to the lack of quality child care. Third, nannies meet upwardly mobile families' desire to have more than just child care for their children.

Debbie Anderson, Nanny

Debbie Anderson, age twenty-two, has a B.S. in elementary education with a minor in special education. She is a nanny and tutor to Jenny, three, and Marie, four. Debbie decided she wanted to do something other than teach in a public school. She looked for and quickly found a job as a nanny with a family in Southern California. "They are wonderful people. They treat me as part of the family, are always ready to listen, and are open to any suggestions about the children's care and education."

Debbie's responsibilities begin after breakfast. She helps the children get dressed and ready for the day. The morning from ten to twelve is devoted to "learning time" when Debbie involves the children in language development and small-motor, creative, and other learning activities. "I love teaching the children this way," says Debbie. "They not only learn a lot but they like it too. There is no pressure and I can do a lot of things without the feeling that I have to. It is really individualized and self-paced learning at its best."

"I use life experiences such as lunch and dinner preparation to teach too. The girls help set the table, pour juice, and do anything they can to be helpful. I don't have to make dinner, but it is something I want to do. Many evenings the parents can't be home in time to have dinner with the children because of their work schedules, so I don't mind doing it. It is just a natural part of family living."

"We also do a lot of outdoor activities such as going for walks into the community and the parks. I'm also teaching the girls how to swim. Once a month, their mother and I take them to someplace special such as Disneyland, Knotts Berry Farm, a museum, zoo, or nature walk."

"After dinner and baths, I'm done for the day and can do whatever I want. I also have two days a week off, which are usually the weekends. I have a separate apartment in the home so I'm able to have some privacy. For me, it is an ideal living and working arrangement."

Debbie is paid $150.00 a week and receives a furnished room and board. She gets medical insurance, the use of a car, and an annual bonus, and she goes with the family when they travel. "I don't know how long I will be a nanny," says Debbie, "but as long as I enjoy it and the girls and family benefit, I want to continue."

ISSUES IN THE CARE OF CHILDREN

Early childhood professionals and professional care-givers face a number of issues that are neither easily addressed nor likely to disappear in the foreseeable future.

Should Women Work?

Should women work or stay at home with their children? Many parents, especially mothers, feel guilty about leaving their children with a sitter or in child care. Some mothers, when they have to share their children with a second care-giver, feel sad and have a sense of loss. There is a growing tension between the advocates of working parents and those who feel that a parent's place — usually the mother's — is in the home with her children. Some, such as pediatrician and author T. Berry Brazelton, think that women can handle two roles at one time and that it is time for our country to recognize this fact as a national trend.[16]

Others, such as author and parent Deborah Fallows, who gave up a career to raise her family, says that children are treated with benign neglect in child-care programs and that children bear the brunt of being left in the care of others.[17] Burton White, a noted researcher and author, agrees with Fallows and believes that full-time out-of-home care for children under the age of three is not in the best interest of children.[18]

The issue is not whether or not parents should work, but what kind of care children should receive, regardless of who is providing it. Questions of whether a parent should or shouldn't work depend on a number of

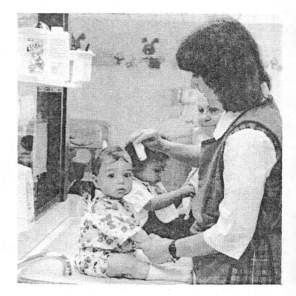

What kind of care do children receive in their parents' absence? Here a care-giver makes sure that one of "her babies" looks nice. How else can care-givers provide individual attention to babies?

critical factors. First, the nature and kind of care the child receives in the parent's absence is of crucial importance. There is bad care, custodial care, and good care. Parents who work should make every effort to find and use good care.

Second are parents' attitudes toward work and child rearing. Some parents want to work more than they want to rear their children. Some parents cannot provide the emotional and social interchanges that are the basis of effective care. These parents would probably be happier working while entrusting their children to quality child care.

The available evidence does not support the conclusion that parents' working *per se* is bad for children. As researchers Jay Belsky and Laurence Steinberg point out,

> With regard to children's intellectual development, the available evidence indicates, in general, that day care has neither beneficial nor deleterious effects. For children growing up in high-risk environments, however, experience in center-based care does appear to attenuate the declines in IQ frequently observed in youngsters from economically disadvantaged backgrounds. With regard to emotional development, the weight of evidence indicates that day care is not disruptive of the child's emotional bond with his mother, even when day care is initiated in the first year of life. In addition, there is no indication that exposure to day care decreases the child's preference for his mother in comparison with an alternative familiar care-giver. Finally, with respect to social development, the existing data indicate that day-care-reared children, when compared with age-mates reared at home, interact more with peers in both positive and negative ways.[19]

In a review of research on the effects of child care, John and Jean Pardeck came to similar conclusions. Among children from advantaged backgrounds, studies have found no differences in intellectual development between home-reared children and those experiencing day care. Among high-risk children, day care appears to have a positive impact on intellectual development. With a few exceptions, studies have not found major differences in mother-child attachment between children reared at home and those reared in day care. Day care does appear to influence children's social development. Compared to home-reared children, children experiencing day care seem to be more peer-oriented and less likely to interact with adults.[20]

Other Issues

Child Care and Societal Purposes. Questions about the impact of group child care on the goals and purposes of American society must be raised. Traditionally, American society is based on the ideals of individuality and freedom. Does group child care promote these ideals, or does it promote group living and group behavior at the expense of the individual? Group child care seems to best suit the societal objectives of socialist countries. The role of group care in perpetuating democratic ideals is indeed an issue that needs to be considered.

The Cost of Child Care. At the heart of many child-care issues is the issue of cost. Many parents feel that the cost of quality care is beyond their ability to pay. Child-care workers feel that they are underpaid and that their low wages subsidize low-cost child care. Given the current federal attitude toward service programs, it is doubtful that professionals can look to the federal government to increase its support of child-care programs. In fact, the federal government's support will probably decrease.

The question arises, then, of who will support quality child care. There is no final or perfect answer. The reality is that parents, especially those who can afford it, will have to pay more and that child care will continue to be underpaid, as the teaching profession is in general.

The Image of Child-Care Workers. As a group, child-care workers are underpaid. They are dissatisfied with their compensation and working conditions.[21] Given the historic poor pay of child-care workers and the increased demand for child care, one of the challenges facing the profession is how to increase monetary benefits to child-care workers. Ways also must be found to upgrade working conditions.

Achieving these goals may not be easy. Most child-care workers are not members of organizations designed to advocate on their behalf. Perhaps what is needed is a national organization that will exclusively represent the child-care profession in its quest for higher pay and status.

Need for Continuing Research. More research on the benefits and effects of child care is needed. Early childhood educators cannot assume that what they have been doing is benign to children. The profession must keep pressing for answers about the influences of child care in general and different kinds of child care in particular.

Training for Child-Care Providers. Increasingly, care-givers realize their need for ongoing training. There is a special need for training for those who provide care for infants and toddlers. Some states have mandated specific training for child-care workers in the areas of child development, nutrition, and child abuse. These efforts, while noteworthy, don't begin to meet the ongoing training needs of all those who work with the young.

Vulnerability of Child Care to Political and Social Changes. Increasingly, programs for the very young seem to be vulnerable to state and federal budget cuts as well as politicians' views of who should and shouldn't be receiving services. Early childhood professionals must work in a concerted manner to raise the public's as well as politicians' consciousness about the ongoing need for good programs for all children and parents, not just for particular groups or under particular circumstances.

The Role of Employers. Further efforts must be made by employers not only to provide child care for their employees, but also to adopt policies that allow parents to select other child-care alternatives. Some of these are flexible work hours, enabling both parents to work and still care for their children, or in any case to leave them in child-care programs less often; job sharing, enabling parents to work part-time and be with their children more; and working at home (especially with the use of computers), enabling parents to be at home with their children.

There are many kinds of programs for providing for the developmental and educational needs of the very young. Although different approaches to providing child care exist, all must be judged by their ability to provide the best care for the clients they serve.

SUMMARY

There are many different early childhood programs for educating and enhancing the development of young children. Although most have their distinctive goals and features, they also frequently share common traits. In selecting a particular model on which they will base their own program, care-givers should keep in mind these two points:

1. The care-giver must be comfortable with and should therefore be able to publicly support the basic premises on which the program is based. If there is little or no congruency between what the care-giver believes

and the philosophy of a particular program, more often than not the care-giver will be unhappy and the children will receive lower-quality care than they are entitled to.

2. The program model should serve the needs of children and families. Changing life-styles, family patterns, and social, economic, and political conditions all greatly influence how one answers the question of what kind of care is best for children. As needs change, therefore, the response of care programs must also change. While certain basic tenets of early childhood care, such as promoting learning through play, remain constant, other ways of meeting children's needs have to keep up with society's and parents' changed attitudes. Programs that fail to adjust to changed attitudes regarding children with special needs, women, and children's rights are out of step with reality.

There are many ways to achieve the desired goal of providing the best for young children. It is unlikely and indeed probably undesirable that there will be agreement on one "best" method. What is important is that within the care program selected care-givers provide developmentally appropriate experiences as advocated by NAEYC.

PROGRAM VIGNETTE

Robin's Infant Nest Nursery
Detroit, Michigan

Robin's Infant Nest Nursery is a storefront child-care program located on a bustling inner-city thoroughfare in metropolitan Detroit. At first glance, prospective parents may think they have the wrong address. How could an infant-care program be situated in a nondescript building between an insurance office and a speedy copying service? Only the brightly lettered sign with an infant in a nest assures the parent that this is the right place.

Crossing the threshold brings a revelation. As the door swings shut, the cacophony of street sounds recedes, the bleakness of urban life fades, and a different world is revealed. It is a child's world of bright colors. Curtains and pictures are hung on walls to provide a home-like atmosphere. The latest in equipment and materials is provided. Soft music is playing, and the immaculately dressed care-givers are smiling.

Welcome to the world of infants as created by Lois Madison, a woman who has one goal in life: to provide the best infant care program possible. Lois is a bright, articulate advocate of quality infant care who devotes her talents, energies, and money to carrying out her calling in life.

"I received the call from God in March of 1976 to open up an infant nursery and to provide quality infant care. I was astounded but aesthetically happy as

I pursued my calling of providing this very necessary service to the parents of the Detroit area. I discussed this calling with my family, some close friends, and my pastor because I knew I would need their support in carrying out this very important project. I started my research by pursuing those tasks that would enable me to open Robin's Infant Nest. I studied the child-care guidelines established by the state of Michigan and the city of Detroit, and the other requirements such as zoning, fire and safety, and architectural design. I worked closely with a staff person from the Michigan Department of Social Services, who advised and supported me in my undertaking. I worked for two years getting everything as I wanted it before I opened the program."

The result is a private, for-profit infant program licensed by the state of Michigan and designed specifically for infants between the ages of six weeks and fifteen to eighteen months. "You have to be dedicated to this age," Lois explains. "I've designed this facility specifically to meet the needs of infants, and it is the only age group I provide care for. The beginning of life, the first year, this is the important part of life. The beginning of life is the beginning of God's creation. Therefore, infants should not be shortchanged. This is why everything here is engineered and designed for quality infant care."

The physical facility is bright, airy, and visually pleasing. The storefront windows bathe the interior in natural light. The large open area is decorated like a home and the atmosphere is relaxing and pleasant. Curtains placed on the walls in strategic locations resemble windows and enhance the home-like quality of the environment. Dressers, stands, rocking chairs, and cribs are placed to create the appearance of "rooms." The staff tries to approximate the personal care and attention children would receive at home.

The environment is clean, sterile, and safe. Lois and her staff stress cleanliness. Care-givers wash their hands with Derma Scrub before and after each diaper change. Disposable plastic gloves are used for all diaper changes involving feces. Disposable towel wipes are used at diaper changes instead of individual washcloths. Plastic cups and spoons are used for solid foods and discarded after use. These procedures may increase program cost, but "if you're going to have quality care," Lois says, "then everything has to be quality. The few cents it costs to do things the right way pay off in the long run."

Cleanliness is not necessarily a criterion for uniqueness. All of us have been in places that were sterile but that we didn't want to spend any more time in than we had to. Sometimes programs are germ-free but sterile in other ways too. They lack individual attention and a stimulating program. Not at Robin's Nest. The program offers a wide range of toys and materials used by the attentive staff to provide stimulation and encourage cognitive growth and physical development.

Robin's Hollow is a special area where infants creep, crawl, and play with developmentally appropriate materials. It is separated from the rest of the facility by a two-foot-high wood-paneled barrier. This is an infant's world of tactile toys, busy boxes, building blocks, and bouncing balls. Care-givers follow an activity lesson plan to provide sensory, perceptual, social, and language activities for each infant.

A number of qualities and features make Robin's Infant Nest unique. First and foremost is Lois Madison. She has developed what corporate planners call a "strategic vision" of quality infant care. This vision is lacking in many programs, which have not developed a philosophy and program goals. Lois is "called" to provide quality infant care. Often, the absence of this conviction is what separates outstanding programs from average ones.

Second, Robin's Infant Nest Nursery is a place that emphasizes a nurturing child-care environment. Lois puts it this way: "People say they work in or operate a program because they love children. I provide infant care because infants are my love. Nurturing is my business, not money. I nurture through love. Our primary role is to provide children the nurture they need, just as though they were in their own homes. We hug and hold children close. We make feeding a pleasant experience, we talk *to* the babies, not *at* them, we keep the infants and the environment clean, and when appropriate, we provide stimulating sensory and cognitive activities. Since we have babies in our care forty to forty-five hours a week, we get to know them real well as individuals and provide for their physical, social, and emotional needs as individuals."

Third, as mentioned earlier, the program only serves infants from about six weeks to fifteen to eighteen months. Not very many programs serve only this age group. This enables Robin's Nest to focus exclusively on the needs of one group and provide specialized services. The environment is designed for infant care and to meet all the needs of infants. The staff is hired for their personal qualities and abilities to care for this age group.

Fourth, Lois Madison receives no "outside" funding or assistance for Robin's Nest. This means she must rely solely on tuition to operate the program. Part of Lois's philosophy is that people will pay for quality and she relies on quality to attract young professional parents to her program. One parent remarked, "The program is not mediocre, and therefore it's not cheap. I don't have a mediocre child and I don't want mediocre care. The tuition of seventy-five dollars a week may seem expensive to some parents, but not when your baby is involved."

Convenience and quality are two criteria parents look for in child-care programs. They get these and much more at Lois Madison's Robin's Infant Nest Nursery.

ENRICHMENT THROUGH ACTIVITIES

1. The care-givers of Wee Care child-care program believe the parents are becoming too demanding. At the last parent meeting, Shirley Zimmerman, a parent spokesperson, read a list of "demands" the parents were making to the care-

givers. These demands included demand feeding of infants instead of scheduled feeding and the center furnishing all supplies — including toys and diapers — without increasing fees.

   a) How would you respond to the parents' demands?

   b) What could be done to prevent such a confrontation?

2. Happy Days Child Care Center administration and staff felt that given the high demand for infant care, it was time for them to open an infant program.

   a) Make a list of things that the administration and staff should do prior to opening an infant program.

   b) What characteristics should be required of the infant care-givers?

3. During the planning of the Happy Days infant care program, the administration discovered that approximately half the current employees — ten in all — had children under two years of age and that they anticipated enrolling them in the program.

   a) What are the advantages and disadvantages of employees enrolling their children in the program?

   b) Should a care-giver provide care for his or her own child?

4. Jennifer Gordon wants to visit at least six family day-care homes in her search for the right one for her daughter. She believes that if she has a set of criteria to use while visiting the homes, she will be able to make a wise decision.

   a) Develop a checklist that will help Jennifer in her search. Assign each criterion a numerical value of one to ten so the checklist yields a total point value.

   b) Tell why you gave some criteria higher point values than others.

5. Develop a list of infant needs. Place these needs in one of three categories: physical, social-emotional, or cognitive.

   a) Tell which needs you think are more important than others.

   b) Select two needs from each category and develop a set of activities and toys that care-givers can use to help meet these needs.

6. List the pros and cons of having children under six months cared for in a center setting.

7. Robert and Silvia Abru are having an argument over child care for their son Hector, aged nine months. Robert thinks the convenience of having child care close to their home so they can quickly pick up Hector should be their number-one priority. Silvia thinks that the kind of care Hector receives should guide their decision. What suggestions do you have for Robert and Silvia?

8. At the open house of Country Day Preschool, many parents inquired about when their children would be learning to read and write. Some parents complained that they felt their efforts to teach their children to read at home were not being followed up at the preschool.

   a) What skills should receive priority in a preschool program?

   b) What is the difference between teaching preschoolers to read and guiding them to read through experiences?

   c) What are some things preschool teachers can discuss with parents about reading and their preschooler?

   d) Identify at least five games that can help preschoolers learn to read.

   e) Develop objectives and activities for a parent workshop about what parents can do to promote reading readiness at home.

9. Two-year-old Teresa Martinez has started to cry whenever her mother brings her to Tiny Tot child-care center. Her mother claims Teresa is not being cared for properly at the center. Now when Teresa begins to cry when brought to the center, her mother won't leave her and instead takes her to work with her or drops her off at a friend's house.
   a) Why is Teresa acting the way she is?
   b) What advice can you give Teresa's mother?
10. Develop a list of ten things care-givers can do to promote language and communication development in infants.
11. List the pros and cons of child care in a home and in a center.
12. Develop a position statement about your preferences for at-home or center child care.
13. Some critics of child care believe that child care destroys families and encourage people to go on or remain on welfare. Do you support such a view? Why? Why not?
14. In the Armbruster household, the job of taking care of newborn Jessica belongs to her mother, Amy. Her husband, Larry, thinks that taking care of children is "women's work" and refuses to care for Jessica in any way except to occasionally hold her.
   a) What advice would you give to Amy? To Larry?
   b) What is the source of beliefs such as Larry's?
   c) Develop a plan to help parents participate in shared parenting.
15. How do child-care programs directly influence child growth and development? Give specific examples.
16. List what you believe to be the pros and cons of child care for infants.
17. Interview parents to determine their reasons for sending their children to preschool or child care. Compare and contrast their reasons. Are there differences between working and nonworking mothers? What other differences, if any, are there in their reasons?
18. Observe a Montessori preschool program.
   a) What features did you like about the program?
   b) What features did you disagree with?
   c) Would you send your child to a Montessori preschool? Why? Why not?

ENRICHMENT THROUGH READING

American Academy of Pediatrics. *Tips on Selecting the Right Day Care Facility.* Elk Grove Village, Ill.: American Academy of Pediatrics, 1985.
   This useful pamphlet provides ten guidelines to follow in selecting quality child care. This would be an ideal resource to distribute at parent meetings and seminars. The guidelines cover the nature of child-care workers, kinds of activities, cleanliness, and health services, among other subjects.

Biber, Barbara. *Early Education and Psychological Development.* New Haven, Conn.: Yale University Press, 1984.

Barbara Biber is one of the leading proponents of the developmental-interaction approach to early childhood education. This is basically a "whole child" approach that advocates conducting a program that encourages children to exercise control over their learning, a program in which teachers serve as guides for interactions between students and staff. This work provides valuable insight into the development of this child-centered approach at Bank Street College, where Biber has been for over half a century.

Burud, Sandra L.; Aschbacher, Pamela R.; and McCroskey, Jacquelyn. *Employer-Supported Child Care: Investing in Human Resources.* Dover, Mass.: Auburn House, 1984.

The authors have done a fine job of providing all the information employers need to establish child-care programs that will benefit themselves and their employees. The information included is based on data provided by over four hundred employer-supported programs. Included are many useful charts and forms.

Burtt, Kent Garland. *Smart Times: A Parent's Guide to Quality Time with Preschoolers.* New York: Harper and Row, 1984.

One of the most-used buzz words in education today is "quality time." Parents and early childhood educators are always searching for ways to put the quality into quality time. Here is some help to achieve that goal. This book contains over two hundred activities designed for quality time. Activities are classified into twenty-three categories, from "Kitchen Companions" to "Skills for Writers-To-Be."

Comfort, Randy Lee, and Williams, Constance D. *The Child Care Catalog.* Littleton, Colo.: Libraries Unlimited, 1985.

This "catalog" is an excellent resource guide. It includes extensive bibliographies, descriptions of unique programs, names and addresses of people and agencies, and many questions to guide the reader's quest for answers about child care. This is also a valuable research tool for anyone who wants a quick overview of the field of child care. This book is a top candidate for inclusion in a parents' resource library.

Gorder, Cheryl. *Home Schools: An Alternative.* Columbus, Ohio: Blue Bird Press, 1985.

Gorder wants parents to realize that they have a choice about where and how their children are educated. Through her book she seeks to empower parents so they can make choices on the basis of what they believe about their life-styles, values, and priorities. In making choices about their children's education, she wants parents to be aware of and consider the option of home schooling. This book provides a rationale and much of the guidance necessary to help parents who might want to consider home schooling as an alternative to the public schools. This book should be read by all preschool and early childhood teachers for the perspective it provides on why parents want home schooling and the obstacles they encounter.

Johnson, Eric W. *Raising Children to Achieve.* New York: Walker and Company, 1984.

Johnson believes the secret to success and achievement is the motivation to achieve. In this book he provides specific steps for parents to follow in instilling achievement motivation in their children and themselves. This advice will particularly appeal to people who are involved in the home education movement.

Lurie, Robert, and Neugebauer, Roger. *Caring for Infants and Toddlers: What Works, What Doesn't.* Vol. 2. Redmond, Wash.: Child Care Information Exchange, 1982.

> Some of the outstanding authorities in the child-care field, such as Bettye Caldwell and Alice Honing, have contributed material to this excellent resource on infant and toddler care. The individual readings resulted from the third annual conference on infant and toddler care sponsored by the Summit Child Care Center in Summit, New Jersey. Topics include issues, curriculum, discipline, health, parents, the environment, staff, administration, and resources.

National Association for the Education of Young Children. *How to Choose a Good Early Childhood Program.* Washington, D.C.: National Association for the Education of Young Children, 1984.

> This information pamphlet, by the largest early childhood professional organization, provides sound advice to anyone thinking about enrolling a child in an early childhood program. These ideas about what parents are to look for can also be used by a staff to ascertain if they are providing a good program.

Oryx Press. *Directory of Child Care Centers.* Vol. 1, *Northeast.* Phoenix, Ariz.: Oryx Press, 1986.

> Volume 1 in this series lists child-care services in the Northeast: Connecticut, Delaware, Kentucky, Maine, Maryland, Massachusetts, New Hampshire, New Jersey, New York, Pennsylvania, Rhode Island, Vermont, Virginia, West Virginia, and Washington, D.C. Other volumes in the series list services for North Central, Western, and Southern states. There are over twelve thousand entries in the first volume, which gives the name of the center, address and telephone number, contact person, capacity, and ages served. This series provides a valuable service to parents who move to a new city and desperately seek child-care services.

Resources for Family Development. *How to Jump into Child Care Head First and Land with Your Feet Firmly on the Ground.* Livermore, Calif.: Resources for Family Development, 1985.

> An excellent, practical, easy-to-read and easy-to-understand guide for developing a child-care program. Squarely addresses the business and quality issues. Topics include licensing, landlord-tenant relationships, administration and staffing, programming, health and safety, parent involvement, management, community awareness, and special services.

Rice, Robin D. *The American Nanny.* Washington, D.C.: TAN Press, 1985.

> A comprehensive guide to finding, assessing, living with, and becoming today's highest quality child-care provider.

Siegal-Gorelick, Bryna. *The Working Parents' Guide to Child Care: How to Find the Best Care for Your Child.* Boston: Little, Brown, 1983.

> This is a very interesting and valuable addition to the literature for parents on how to select child care. Three chapters are especially noteworthy. Chapter 1 is devoted to care-givers and day-care environments; Chapter 5 advises parents on how to assess day-care programs; and Chapter 7 deals with how parents can help themselves and their children adjust to child care. This book can be read quickly and is worth the time.

Thomas, Carol H., ed. *Current Issues in Day Care: Readings and Resources.* Phoenix, Ariz.: Oryx Press, 1986.

This is a collection of nineteen articles that address important issues and concerns of parents and care-givers. It also serves as a guide to the selection and evaluation of child-care programs. In addition, there is information relating to employer-sponsored child care, trends, and environmental and health concerns.

NOTES

1. Harriet M. Johnson, *Children in "The Nursery School"* (New York: Agathon Press, 1972), 10.
2. Johnson, *Children*, 314-315.
3. Maria Montessori, *The Discovery of the Child*, trans. M. J. Costello (Notre Dame, Ind.: Fides Publishers, 1967), 28.
4. Maria Montessori, *The Secret of Childhood*, trans. M. J. Costello (Notre Dame, Ind.: Fides Publishers, 1966), 49.
5. U.S. Department of Health, Education, and Welfare, Office of Child Development, "Head Start Performance Standards," *Head Start Policy Manual*, OCD Notice N-30-36414 (Washington, D.C.: Government Printing Office, July, 1975), 8–9.
6. Irving Lazar et al., "Lasting Effects After Preschool," report of the Consortium for Longitudinal Studies, Administration for Children, Youth, and Families, Office of Human Development Services DHEW No. (OHDS) 79-30179 (Washington, D.C.: Government Printing Office, September 1979).
7. U.S. Department of Health and Human Services, Administration for Children, Youth, and Families, Office of Human Development Services, Project Head Start, "Statistical Fact Sheet" (Washington, D.C.: Government Printing Office, December 1985).
8. Bettye M. Caldwell, "What Is Quality Child Care?" *Young Children* 39 (March 1984): 4.
9. Pennsylvania Department of Public Welfare, Bureau of Child and Youth Development, "Regulations for Family Day Care Homes" (June 1981), 7.
10. Steven Fosburg, *Family Day Care in the United States: Summary of Findings*, U.S. Department of Health and Human Services, DHHS Publication No. (OHDS) 80-30282 (Washington, D.C.: Government Printing Office, September 1981), 90.
11. Alice S. Honig, "High Quality Infant/Toddler Care," *Young Children* 40 (November 1985): 40.
12. Nancy A. Busch-Rossnagel and Barbara Mead Worman, "A Comparison of Educators' and Providers' Rankings of the Important Competencies for Day Care Professionals," *Child Care Quarterly* 14 (Spring 1985): 59.
13. Honig, "High Quality," 41.
14. National Association for the Education of Young Children, "Position Statement on Developmentally Appropriate Practice in Early Childhood Programs Serving Children from Birth Through Age 8," *Young Children* 41 (September 1986): 4–29.
15. Southern Association on Children Under Six, *Position Statement on Quality Child Care* (Little Rock, Ark.: SACUS, 1986).

16. T. Berry Brazelton, *Working and Caring* (Reading, Mass.: Addison-Wesley, 1986).
17. Deborah Fallows, *A Mother's Work* (Boston, Mass.: Houghton Mifflin, 1986).
18. Burton White, *The First Three Years of Life* (Englewood Cliffs, N.J.: Prentice-Hall, 1986).
19. Jay Belsky and Laurence D. Steinberg, "The Effects of Day Care," in *In the Beginning: Readings on Infancy*, ed. Jay Belsky (New York: Columbia University Press, 1982), 255.
20. John T. Pardeck and Jean A. Pardeck, "The Impact of Day Care on the Pre-school Child: Research Findings and Implications," *International Social Work* 28 (Summer 1985): 40–48.
21. Willa Pettygrove et al., "Beyond Baby-sitting: Changing the Treatment and Image of Child Care-givers," *Young Children* 39 (July 1984): 14–21.

Chapter 6

Methods for the Education and Development of the Children We Care For

Questions to Guide Your Reading and Study

- Why is it important for care-givers to plan for what they and children will do?
- How does task analysis contribute to young children's learning?
- How can care-givers use modeling to help young children learn?
- What is discovery learning and how can young children learn through discovery?
- How can care-givers use questions to help young children learn?
- What are the roles of care-givers in the use of direct teaching?
- How can care-givers arrange environments to promote education and development?
- How can care-givers use interest centers to promote learning?
- Why are routines important in programs for the very young?
- What routines are important in the care of young children and how can care-givers establish and maintain these routines?

INTRODUCTION

People have always cared for children in one way or another; the idea of caring for children is not new. What is new today is the different emphasis and meaning caring has for parents, care-givers, and the early childhood profession. In years gone by, when people spoke of caring for the very young, the emphasis was on physical care. Today, with more children than ever before being cared for away from their homes by people other than their parents, professionals and parents are increasingly concerned about the nature of children's care. They recognize that physical care, while important, is not by itself sufficient to meet the totality of young children's physical, emotional, social, and cognitive needs. This dramatic shift in emphasis away from *primarily* providing physical care to providing young children comprehensive quality care and developmentally appropriate education is one of the major differences between caring for children today and caring for them a decade ago.

PLANNING FOR EFFECTIVE EDUCATION AND DEVELOPMENT

Care-givers must not be satisfied to allow children to do nothing all day or to let them do only what they want to do. Staff members must plan how they and children will spend their time. The daily schedule from the Infant-Toddler Program at the University of Arkansas at Fayetteville shows how a program can be planned to promote optimum child development (Figure 6-1).

In addition to planning daily schedules for the program, care-givers must plan for activities within the daily schedule. These plans can be written on a daily or weekly basis and developed from existing curriculum materials. The important thing is that care-givers have plans to guide them in their interactions with young children. Refer back to Chapter 5 for more information on planning.

METHODS FOR EDUCATING AND DEVELOPING THE VERY YOUNG

Care-givers and teachers of the very young have a number of methods to choose from in selecting strategies for teaching young children. The options presented here are not "pure" in the sense that each has none of the features of the others. On the contrary, teaching methods frequently overlap, and strategies used in one method can be and are used in another. Methods alone do not make a quality program. As with most processes surrounding the teaching and learning processes, an enthusiastic, caring well-trained staff is as important, if not more so, than the methods used.

FIGURE 6-1
Infant-Toddler Schedule from University of Arkansas at Fayetteville

INFANT SCHEDULE

7:45–8:15	Greeting, health check, free play
8:15–8:45	Free play, diaper check, individual activities
8:45–9:15	Breakfast
9:15–10:30	Morning naps, art, outdoor play, discovery, diaper check
10:30–10:45	Diaper check, transition (music)
10:45–11:10	Lunch
11:10–11:30	Transition (free play)
11:30–12:30	Diaper check, porch play, individual activities
12:30–2:45	Diaper check, naps, free play or porch play, diaper check
2:45–3:10	Snack
3:10–3:25	Language activity
3:25–4:30	Diaper check, outdoor play

TODDLER SCHEDULE

7:45–8:50	Greeting, health check, learning center activities, diaper check
8:50–9:00	Clean-up, transition, handwashing
9:00–9:30	Breakfast
9:30–10:40	Outdoor play, art, diaper check
10:40–10:55	Music
10:55–11:00	Transition, handwashing
11:00–11:30	Lunch
11:30–12:20	Porch play, diaper check, toothbrushing
12:20–12:30	Language activity
12:30–2:45	Naps, diaper check, porch play
2:45–2:55	Group activity
2:55–3:00	Transition, handwashing
3:00–3:20	Snack
3:20–4:30	Outdoor play, diaper check, art

Source: Courtesy of Sue Martin and Deborah Stogsdill, University of Arkansas, Fayetteville.

Task Analysis

The field of special education contributes greatly to the early childhood educator's understanding of how to teach young children, especially those who are developmentally delayed.

Task analysis is a method for examining the component skills of a task and the behavioral requirements necessary to perform each task so the target or terminal skill is achieved. Essentially, teachers ask themselves,

FIGURE 6-2
Specification and Utilization of En Route Behavior

GOAL: To teach children to cut with scissors.

TERMINAL OBJECTIVE: Given blunt-tip scissors, a piece of paper on which are drawn a 3-inch straight line, a 3-inch curved line, a 3-inch diameter circle, and the directions to cut on the line and cut out the circle, the children will cut as directed, staying within ¼ inch of the line. They will complete the total task within 5 minutes.

EN ROUTE BEHAVIOR (least to most skilled): Prerequisite skills: pincer grasp, holding paper between fingers.
1. Given tongs (similar to those used in cooking), 5 cotton balls, and a 4-inch bowl, a child will allow the teacher to place his or her thumb through one finger hole, the forefinger on the outside of the bar, and the remaining fingers into the other hole. With the teacher's help, child will open and close the tongs on a cotton ball, lift it to the bowl, and release it into the bowl. Criterion includes keeping fingers in the correct position and accepting teacher's help.
2. Given the same circumstances as above, the child will perform the same action without teacher's physical help but with encouragement and any needed reminders.
3. Given the above materials, a child will (a) maintain correct finger positions, (b) lift cotton balls with tongs and drop them into the bowl, (c) drop no more than one cotton ball outside the bowl, and (d) complete the task within 2 minutes.
4. Given strips of construction paper 1 inch wide and 11 inches long, and blunt-tip scissors, the child will snip the strip of paper into at least 10 pieces within 5 minutes.
5. Given strips of construction paper 1 inch wide and 11 inches long with heavy black lines at 1-inch intervals, and blunt-tip scissors, the child will snip within ¼ inch of the line, cutting with one snip for each line through the paper.
6. Given strips of construction paper 3 inches wide and 11 inches long, and heavy black lines at 1-inch intervals, using blunt-tip scissors the child will make 3 cuts on each line within ¼ inch of the line, severing each piece within 10 minutes.
7. Given a piece of construction paper or paper of similar weight on which are drawn a 3-inch straight line, a 3-inch curved line, and a 3-inch (diameter) circle, using blunt-tip scissors the child will cut on the straight line and the curved line and cut out the circle, staying within ¼ inch of the lines, within 10 minutes.
8. Same as terminal objective.

Adaptations for children with physical handicaps include a squeeze scissors instead of traditional scissors. For some children scissors with four finger holes may be useful because they allow the teacher to cut with the child. Visually impaired children should be provided buff-colored paper with a heavy brown line for necessary contrast.

Source: Ruth E. Cook and Virginia B. Armbruster, *Adapting Early Childhood Curricula* (St. Louis: C.V. Mosby Company, © 1983), 100. Copyright 1985 Merrill Publishing Company, Columbus, Ohio. Reprinted by permission of Merrill Publishing Company.

"What is a child to learn and how is she to learn it?" The answers comprise a task analysis. In the example in Figure 6-2, the goal, learning how to cut with scissors, is identified and the *en route behaviors* — the behaviors necessary to achieve that goal — are listed in a hierarchy from the least skilled behaviors to the most skilled.

The advantages of employing task analysis as a teaching method are several. First, it enables care-givers and teachers to understand that some tasks cannot and should not be taught in their entirety in one lesson and that skills consist of many subskills that contribute to the terminal behavior. Frequently, teachers hand children scissors and paper and assume they can cut. If they can't, little is done except repeated attempts with the same strategy. Using the task analysis approach, a child is empowered with the appropriate sequence of skills resulting in the terminal behavior.

Second, teaching with task analysis makes failure almost impossible, because a child masters skills a step at a time in sequence, resulting in success. One skill builds on another until the target or terminal goal is mastered.

Task analysis is based on behaviorist ideas. Providing children with tasks they can achieve by breaking skills into achievable components is consistent with the behaviorist view that learning small components of a skill is one way to provide immediate feedback.

There are several problems associated with task analysis, however. First, it can be a formidable task to specify all the subskills that constitute a major goal. A practical solution is to use existing task analyses such as the one shown in Figure 6-2.

Second, it would require a staggering amount of work to do a task analysis of all the skills, cognitive and psychomotor, that children need to know. One solution to this dilemma is to provide an environment that enables children to intuitively learn many concepts and skills without having to be taught them directly. Then a task analysis approach can be used on those a child has difficulty learning and that are critical for future success, such as the motor skill of learning to cut.

Task analysis, however, does provide teachers and care-givers with a sensible, practical, easy-to-use way to promote success among children, particularly in areas where a structured approach is needed.

Modeling

Modeling as a teaching technique is the demonstration of behaviors for others to learn through imitation. Modeling also occurs when a child imitates the behavior of another. Notice that the definition of modeling implies intention. This is because we expect care-givers to *intend* to have children model and learn certain behaviors. Children don't distinguish between intended and unintended modeling, however. Children learn desirable as well as undesirable behavior from others, even those who are not aware that they are acting as models. Many parents have learned to their regret that children will imitate their bad habits!

In Chapter 4, we discussed social learning theory. You should review that section for the theoretical basis for modeling.

Implications for care-givers. One of care-givers' critical roles is to model desired behavior to assure that proper behaviors are imitated. This can be facilitated in a number of ways.

Teachers can do many things to help children learn, such as modeling, showing, and helping. Why is it important for teachers to be involved — but not intrusive — in children's learning?

1. Specify and plan for desired behaviors. Care-givers must understand in their own minds that they want children to put toys away when they are finished with them. This may sound trite in the telling, but unless care-givers know what they want children to do and model that behavior, it is not likely to happen.

2. Specify the desired behavior to children by telling and showing. Although telling is not teaching, telling and reminding are adjuncts to modeling and good teaching.

3. Arrange the environment so it supports imitation of the behavior. If care-givers want children to put materials back in their original condition and return them to shelves when they are done, they must have an environment that supports these behaviors. Some ways care-givers can structure the environment to support the behavior of putting back materials are

   a) Use materials that are easy to put back in their original condition.

   b) Provide storage containers for materials such as beads.

   c) Make shelves easily accessible to children.

   d) Have storage places for individual materials identified with pictures, painted outlines, and color codes to signify where materials belong.

   These procedures make it easier for children to model the desired behavior of putting away.

4. Model the desired behavior. This means that, especially in the begin-

ning, the care-giver puts toys away, helps put toys away, and shows children how to put toys away.

5. Model the desired behaviors with children. Modeling frequently includes physically showing the children what they are to do. Having children learn how to put on a coat, for example, includes showing them how to put it on as a means of modeling.

6. Reinforce modeled behavior. Praise children who are performing the desired behavior *as well as* those who are trying. Be precise and specific about praising the modeled and imitated behavior. Keep in mind that *efforts* at performing, especially in the initial learning stages, are just as important as performing successfully. A care-giver might say, "Susan, you put the toys on the shelf just as we are supposed to" or "John, you did a good job, you really are learning to put the toys on the shelf."

7. Group children who can model the desired behavior with those whom you want to imitate the behavior. Children are more apt to model the behavior of someone they like. Thus, pairing a child who does not have the behavior with a child he or she likes who has learned the behavior is an effective way of teaching a specific skill.

One of the reasons for mainstreaming handicapped with nonhandicapped children is to enable the handicapped to imitate normal behavior (see Chapter 8). Similarly, one of the reasons for integrating normal children in handicapped programs is to enable the handicapped to observe normal behavior.

Modeling Prosocial Behavior. Children can model and help each other learn *prosocial* or helping behavior. As James Bryan, a researcher of prosocial behavior, points out, "The evidence is abundant that children will imitate the helping activities of models whether those models are alive and present or televised and absent. The list of responses shown to be affected by observing models is almost endless, and it is not surprising that helping actions can also be added to the list."[1]

The Peer Group and Modeling. Children entering child-care programs and preschools are sometimes having their first experience being part of a group. Many children have little experience with peer groups and have not learned the behaviors necessary for successful group living. The peer group provides children with opportunities to observe and model behaviors important for successful group living, such as sharing, taking turns, cooperating, following directions, conforming to requests, doing one's share, managing conflicts, and engaging in acceptable competitive behavior. It is important for care-givers to see that these behaviors are modeled and modeled well.

Implications for care-givers. Care-givers' roles in social learning are not passive. In addition to modeling appropriate social behaviors, they must also nurture and call attention to positive social relationships. Care-givers provide opportunities for children to share, form friendships, be cooperative (two children pass out the napkins at snack instead of one), use language instead of hitting as a means of resolving conflicts, and use language to express feelings, both positive and negative. The social environment care-givers establish is just as important as the physical environment.

The peer group setting also offers care-givers unique opportunities to model and have children observe prosocial behaviors such as giving and receiving affection and praise.

Discovery Learning

Care-givers provide many opportunities for children to discover and learn for themselves. In this sense, "learning through discovery" is really a misnomer, for if care-givers relied solely on children discovering everything they needed to know, they might not learn much. Left to their own devices, children could also learn the opposite of what care-givers want them to learn.

Discovery learning occurs when children learn concepts and skills through their own physical and mental activity from the learning opportunities provided for them. Children are the agents of their own learning in discovery learning. Teachers and care-givers are the secondary agents and promote mental activity by asking questions and eliciting responses from children.

Discovery learning is intuitively selected as the teaching strategy of choice by many child-care and preschool programs. Discovery learning has been advocated by Froebel, Montessori, Piaget, and the supporters of open education. In child-care programs and preschools, discovery learning occurs primarily through play and includes many of the materials and learning centers discussed in Chapter 4.

Discovery learning periods can be used as the only method of implementing the curriculum, or they can be used to complement, enrich, and extend concepts and skills taught in teacher-directed activities. The curriculum of discovery learning can include self-help skills such as health care, personal hygiene, and eating habits. The teacher, for example, can set up the house-keeping area with dolls, water, soap, washcloths, and towels. While children bathe and wash dolls, she can talk about, question, and explain how to wash and the importance of washing. She can also answer children's questions.

Implications for care-givers. By planning, care-givers can ensure that learning occurs through discovery. The bases for this planning are the goals of a particular program and the curriculum designed to implement those goals. An objective of most child-care programs, for example, is to help children learn self-help skills. The curriculum specifies what self-help skills will be promoted and what materials and activities are necessary to achieve these objectives. Care-givers' lesson plans specify what will be done each day to involve children in specific discovery learning activities.

Discovery learning opportunities are provided for all children. They are individualized and include all areas of development — physical, cognitive, social, and emotional. In this sense, discovery learning is child-centered, not teacher- or subject-centered.

Although blocks of time are devoted to discovery learning, which is most often thought to fall under the heading of free play, discovery learning is not and should not be limited to play times. It should take place all day. A teacher may plan for the discovery of color concepts during the discovery period, but learning about colors should not be limited to that time. Questions about the colors of foods at lunch and colors of children's clothing, for example, could be used to integrate discovery learning into the whole curriculum.

Care-givers provide the environment and learning materials for children to discover. This includes providing materials that will encourage and promote the discovery of intended learnings. Changing materials as needed to support discovery learning is also a prerequisite. Children cannot discover all they need to know from a limited set of materials that remain the same throughout the program year.

Care-givers verbally interact with children with comments and questions, examples and explanations. Discovery learning is supported by asking the right questions and offering summaries and comments to guide children's thinking so they discover concepts. Without such verbal interaction, it might be that little discovery learning would occur.

Good questioning strategies are an integral part of any kind of teaching strategy. Through questions, care-givers encourage children to think, develop language skills, make decisions, and learn concepts. Care-givers might ask the following questions:

- Snack time: Do you want peanut butter on your cracker?
- Art: What color do you want to paint your house?
- Housekeeping: How long does your baby sleep?
- Block: What kind of blocks do you need to build the bridge?
- Water: Why do we wear aprons when we play at the water table?
- Cooking: Why do we have to mix everything together?
- Language: What's the best thing you like about your new toy?

Discovery learning and the traditional play-oriented preschool curriculum are quite in harmony with Piagetian theory of intellectual development. Opportunities to interact with rich resources of materials, both physical and human, in a semistructured environment provide an ideal context for the development of general cognitive structures and mental schemes that will contribute to children's later learning and performance in school settings. Thus, such a program anticipates many of the cognitive schemes children need and provides the environment in which children intuitively learn.

Direct Teaching

In *direct teaching*, the care-giver is directly involved in managing children's learning activities. The care-giver plans for learning outcomes and specifies what activities the children will participate in. The care-giver informs children ahead of time what they will do; specifies the nature of the learning outcomes and product; has the material prepared ahead of time and ready for children's use in the activity; directs the children's involvement in the activity; manages children's behavior; shapes the final product; and evaluates the final product as well as the children's performances.

In direct instruction, the care-giver, not the children, selects the learning activity. The care-giver is also in direct control of the learning activity. Direct instruction is widely used as a teaching strategy and is one many care-givers feel comfortable with, primarily because they were taught and trained with this method.

There are many instances when direct instruction is the most effective instructional strategy. In a cooking activity, for example, direct instruction would be the strategy of preference. The care-giver writes the plan for the cooking activity, states the learning outcomes and the materials needed, and decides how the activity will be conducted. The care-giver arranges for the cooking activity and specifies what children will do and how they will do it. There are many opportunities in a cooking activity for many kinds of learning. For example, children might be taught concepts (ingredients are combined to form a product) and motor skills (measuring, pouring, and mixing).

ARRANGING THE ENVIRONMENT FOR EFFECTIVE LEARNING AND DEVELOPMENT

The environment in which the very young spend most of their day should be child-centered, attractive, safe, well lighted, aesthetically pleasing, clean, and nurturing. Ideally, it should be designed and arranged to approximate a home-like atmosphere. In the program described in the vignette at the end of Chapter 5, Lois Madison at Robin's Infant Nest decorated her storefront center to resemble a home by painting windows with outdoor scenes on the wall. She hung curtains on the "windows" to add to the effect. Chests of drawers, rocking chairs for adults and children, pictures on the walls at the children's eye level, and pleasing pastel colors helped make the center a home away from home.

Thelma Harms and Richard Clifford of the Frank Porter Graham Child Development Center at the University of North Carolina, Chapel Hill, de-

FIGURE 6-3
Components of Early Childhood Environments

Personal Care Routines of Children
All routines associated with the comfort, health, and well-being of the children — for example, diapering, rest, and meals.

Furnishings and Display for Children
Making available, taking care of, arranging, and using regularly with children the furniture, storage shelves, and display space necessary to provide personal care and an educational program.

Language-Reasoning Experiences
Use of materials, activities, and teaching interactions to help children learn to communicate in words and to use relationships basic to thought, such as size relationships, cause and effect, steps in a sequence, and time relationships.

Fine and Gross Motor Activities
Fine motor activities exercise the fine or small muscles, such as the muscles of the hand used in drawing, cutting with scissors, or picking up a small object. Since the coordination of the eye and the hand is usually needed for fine motor work, these activities are sometimes called perceptual fine motor activities.

Gross motor activities exercise the gross or larger muscles, such as the muscles of the legs used in climbing and running or the muscles of the arms used in swinging.

Creative Activities
Activities and materials, such as those used in art, block building, and dramatic play, are flexible, open-ended, do not have one right answer, and allow for a wide variety of constructive uses. Creative activities reflect the abilities and interests of children. (This section is omitted for rooms used exclusively for infants under nine months of age.)

Social Development
Guiding the children's development of a good image of themselves and others and of helping others; helping them to establish interaction skills.

Adult Needs
Providing space and equipment for the key adults in the early childhood setting — the teachers and parents. Staff members have both personal comfort needs and professional needs for meeting their requirements in the teaching role. Parents have personal needs for reassurance and inclusion as well as information and skill-development needs to help them in their parenting role.

Source: Thelma Harms and Richard M. Clifford, *Early Childhood Environment Rating Scale* (New York: Teachers College Press, © 1980 by Teachers College, Columbia University.), 9-37. All rights reserved. Reprinted by permission of the publisher.

veloped an Early Childhood Environment Rating Scale. This is an informative instrument early childhood professionals can use to self-evaluate their early childhood setting. The authors use a broader definition of environment than is customary. Their scale includes the following seven areas: personal care routines of children, furnishings and display for children, language-reasoning experiences, fine and gross motor activities, creative activities, social development, and adult needs.[2] Figure 6-3 provides a more detailed explanation of the environmental areas.

Children learn many concepts and skills by having opportunities to be actively involved. What skills is this child learning?

Interest Centers

Interest centers (also called "learning centers" in kindergarten and the primary grades) offer an effective way to arrange the environment so the very young have the freedom within structure that they need to play and learn.

Learning centers are appropriate for all ages of children, from infants to preschoolers to primary children. There may be a tendency to think that infants and toddlers cannot benefit from interest centers, but they can.

Some centers and family day-care homes may have limited space for interest centers. With such constraints, only several centers need be set up at a time. Centers can be rotated every few days. In one center where both space and storage are a problem, creative staff members have "containerized" their learning centers in boxes. Each day, with the children's help, they unpack two interest centers. The children play with the contents, and when they are finished they pack everything back into the boxes. The staff creatively designed about two dozen interest-center boxes.

Some interest centers popular with the very young and with caregivers are described in the next few pages.

Dramatic Play Center. The dramatic play area offers children the opportunity to engage in play — any kind from parallel to cooperative. It also, gives children opportunities to develop language and social relationships.

Boys and girls should be encouraged to engage in dramatic play. Materials and props should be nonsexist and multicultural. Some suggestions for dramatic play interest centers are

1. Medical center. Supply nurse and doctor clothing such as hats, gloves, gowns, and masks. Props could include a stethoscope, a medical bag, and dolls.
2. Housekeeping. Supply child-size table and chairs, sink, stove, refrigerator, mirror (hung at child height), doll furniture (such as high chair and crib) cupboard, and dresser. Props could include baby dolls representative of different ethnic groups and cultures; kitchen utensils and dishes; food containers such as cereal boxes; and household items such as brooms, mops, and dustpans.
3. Dress-up clothing. A wide variety of dress-up clothing can be provided in the house keeping area, or a separate dress-up center can be maintained. This area can include male and female clothing such as hats, coats, dresses, shoes, purses, and scarves. Props can include mirrors, both wall-mounted and hand-held. Mirrors are an excellent way to promote expression and language development. (See also the use of mirrors in the section on development of self in Chapter 3.) The dress-up center can also double as a community-helpers center in which clothing, blocks, pictures, and posters add to the center's purpose.

Discovery Center. Discovery centers offer the very young opportunities to explore interesting materials. Discovery center activities can include a large tray with three bowls of cooked spaghetti, each colored a different color — perhaps green, red, and yellow — or a wash basin filled with rolled oats, plus a scoop and measuring cups. The water play table can also be used for dry materials.

Water play is an excellent way for children to sensually explore and learn. The very young are fascinated by and love to play with bubbles. Opportunities can be provided by using mild liquid detergent or baby shampoo. Children seem to gain a sense of power by being able to dip and blow bubbles. See also the section on water play in Chapter 4 for additional suggestions concerning water play materials and activities.

Fine Motor or Manipulative Center. A manipulative center is a must in all infant and toddler programs. Materials to include in this center are puzzles with different numbers of pieces and complexity to meet the developmental needs of all children in the program; pop beads; nesting cups and materials; shape boards; magnetic designs; and small blocks such as legos.

Storage is a key factor in the manipulative center. Materials need to be stored on shelves that are easily accessible to children. Transparent plastic storage trays are ideal for providing a convenient method of storage that enables children to clearly see materials and carry them from the storage area to the activity area, be it table or floor.

Gross Motor Center. Young children like to be actively and physically involved in activities. Therefore, a gross motor center, either indoors or out (preferably both), is a necessity. This area can include wheel toys such as tricycles and wagons, climbing apparatus, and slides.

Language Development Center. Since language development is one of the critical development tasks of the very young, it makes sense to have an interest center devoted to this skill. This center should be furnished so it invites children to come and be involved.

The language development center can also serve as a relaxation and comfort center. This is a "soft" area in which children may relax and be comforted. It can also be used as a story area where children "read," are read to, and are engaged in conversation. Furnishings such as carpets, cushions, and child- and adult-size rocking chairs can help make it a most inviting place.

This center can have a wide variety of books that encourage children to want to read and be read to. The books should be the ones children like. Their preferences can be ascertained by letting children have experiences with a wide variety of books. They should be displayed so children have freedom of access and selection. All reading materials selected for use with children should be nonsexist and free of cultural bias. They should cover a wide range of topics and cultures.

Children- and staff-made "books" are materials of high interest and are excellent ways to actively involve children in reading. Photo albums with children's, parents', and care-givers' pictures can be used as first reading books and conversation starters.

Story telling and finger plays are ideal ways to involve children in language activities. Props such as hand puppets are ideal resources, especially for telling stories.

Art Center. Art activities provide opportunities for creative expression and sensory exploration and promote language, social, and aesthetic development. As much as practical, art activities should always allow free expression by children.

The art center should be located near water to facilitate clean-up. If the art area is carpeted, a large plastic sheet placed on the floor prior to the art activity will make clean-up easier. Parents should know that their children will participate in art activities so they do not overdress them with clothes that can be ruined by paint or glue.

With infants, many art activities can take place in highchairs. Finger painting with pudding and Ivory flakes on wax paper and coloring with large pieces of paper and big pieces of chalk offer infants opportunities to participate in art.

Children can paint and print with different objects, such as wheeled toys that leave painted tracks, potato blocks, and string. Sand painting, in

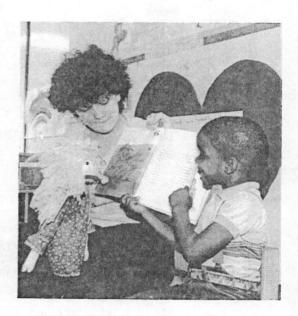

Storytelling is an ideal way to involve children in experiences that promote language development. How is this teacher promoting language development?

which the care-giver puts glue on paper and infants shake sand on the glue using salt shakers, is also popular.

Infants and toddlers can participate in a wide variety of activities. They should be supervised so they do not harm themselves or others with scissors and paint brushes.

Mirrors should also be included in the art center. Children can paint on mirrors with finger paint and soap flakes; the mirrors can be cleaned easily afterwards.

Block Center. As discussed in Chapter 4, blocks can be used in a variety of ways to promote learning.

Many other interest centers can be included in early childhood programs. These include music centers, nature centers, and animal centers. Indeed, the kinds of centers care-givers choose to use are limited only by their imaginations and children's interests. Well-designed interest centers furnished with a rich variety of materials give children opportunities to overtly manipulate materials that can help them in the development of thinking skills.

ESTABLISHING AND MANAGING ROUTINES

The routines of coming to and leaving a program, eating, napping, diapering, and the transitions from these routines to other activities help determine the success and quality of programs. How care-givers manage these routines sets the tone for the happiness of children, staff, and parents.

Types of Transitions

Signals. The effectiveness of the transition from one activity to another frequently determines the success of both activities. Care-givers have developed a number of *signals* or prearranged signs for beginning and ending activities as a means of helping children make transitions. Some care-givers turn the lights on and off, others ring a bell, some sing a song.

Direct Participation and Telling. Many care-givers tell children when it is time to clean up, go to the bathroom, get ready for lunch, and leave the center. This arrangement works best because the care-giver is part of the process and can be directly involved in the activities. The younger the children, the more help they need in making transitions until they become part of the routine.

Several points are imperative, however. First, all children need to participate in the transitions, regardless of how young they are. Learning to help themselves and others do things is crucial to independence and autonomy. Second, routines for activities and transitions must be consistent over time so children can be familiar with how each functions.

Stories and Finger Plays. Storytelling, story reading, and finger plays provide ideal ways for care-givers to help children make transitions from one activity to another. Story time is naturally relaxing and quieting, so it makes a good transition from interest center activities and discovery activities to other quieter, calmer activities. Thus, stories can be used to make the transition to nap time or from a discovery activity to hand washing before lunch time. Also, stories and quiet finger plays are ideal for use when some children have finished an activity (for example, hand washing) and are waiting for other children to finish.

Routines

Arrival and Departure. Effective routines of arrival and departure are critical for the emotional well-being of children and parents. When children are happy, parents are more at ease and more confident in the program.

The child and parent should be greeted on arrival by a staff member. With infants and toddlers, the primary care-giver should do the greeting. This greeting by the same person every day adds to the child's developing sense of trust. The child comes to know that he or she can depend on being met by the same person every day.

Some care-givers tend to become preoccupied with children who have already arrived and become involved in the ongoing process of providing care. As a result, they tend to neglect the routine of arrival. This is a mistake. Infants and toddlers especially need consistency to build basic trust that comes from knowing that their care-giver will be there every day to greet them. During arrival, parents and care-givers share much important

Arrival and departure are important times for care-givers to share with parents important information about their children. Care-givers should make a routine of greeting and talking with parents at these times. What important information can care-givers provide parents?

information about the child, such as, health status, emotional state, what was eaten for breakfast, and medication.

Children's arrivals can be personalized in many ways. One program takes a picture of each child with the parents. On arrival, children and parents find their picture and place it in the "present" box. When they leave, they place their picture in the "home" box.

How routines are handled depends on a number of factors: staff and program beliefs, licensing regulations, parental input, and program resources. Figure 6-4 describes how routines are handled in the Day Care Center at the University of Wisconsin, Milwaukee.

SUMMARY

Care-givers are the persons responsible for facilitating and fostering the education and development of young children. Faced with a myriad of procedures and activities to select from, the process of making wise selections is critical. In this decision-making process, care-givers must keep children as the focus of their deliberations. Care-givers must observe and study children and keep children's and families' best interests, not their own, in the forefront of their thinking. They must constantly be willing to learn how individual children grow and develop. Then they are able with reasonable confidence to make decisions about how to best select procedures and activities that will support children's learning and development. As a result, care-givers can also say with reasonable confidence, "I did my best." And this is what children deserve.

FIGURE 6-4
Routines of the Day Care Center University of Wisconsin at Milwaukee

ARRIVAL
Greet parents and children individually by name. Greet children with hugs by one or more staff and other children, all of whom are incorporated into play by a staff person.

As parents sign in, encourage them and the children to greet other children and staff.

Arrival provides the opportunity to share in written or verbal communications regarding a child's specific needs for the day and what has happened since the staff has seen the child last. This may entail such matters as signs of teething, sleep patterns, illness, changes in home life, Aunt Maude visiting, or that the child went to the show last night.

Toddlers are encouraged to bring their lunches to the refrigerator.

Each child has an assigned cubby or locker with space for diapers, change of clothing, art work, outer wear, and posted communications from the room and Center.

Parent and Child's First Day
Verify nap information and food concerns. Introduce parents and children to the room. Orient them to the location of information regarding activities, naps, lunch, diapers, and snacks.

Assign cubby.

Answer any questions or concerns.

Let parents know they may call back to check on how their child is doing and adjusting.

Additional written information is made available in a newsletter explaining the room, weekly themes, daily schedule, etc.

EATING
Record everything infants eat in a day, including ounces of juice and formula, and feed them on their own schedules.

Rocking chairs, couches, and nap rooms provide warm, comfortable areas for parents to nurse.

Children provide their own lunches, but the program provides milk or juice.

Labeled name cards are placed by each child's lunch for easier access and visibility in giving lunches.

Assist children by (1) helping unpack their lunches; (2) warming up food as necessary; (3) providing child-size portions; and (4) offering them a variety of selections from their lunches.

Offer child-size utensils.

High chairs available in infant rooms.

Child-size chairs and tables.

Adults sit with children and encourage them to try all food groups. Care-givers use appropriate conversation and promote appropriate behavior, e.g., milk is for drinking, chairs are for sitting.

Toddlers are encouraged to bring their cup to the sink when they are through.

The program provides the snacks. Care-givers have a small group of children help prepare snacks.

Appropriate portions are offered to encourage safe, healthy eating habits (small size and high nutrition).

Provide alternate snacks for those who need them, such as juice instead of milk for a child with a milk allergy or nonhoneyed grahams for children under a year, etc.

FIGURE 6-4 (*continued*)

DIAPERING
Diapers are checked once an hour. Diapering is seen as a time to have special, individual time with the child.

Sing songs, perform finger plays.

The environment is decorated to spark conversation between adults and children.

Washcloths are used in lieu of expensive disposable wipes that contain alcohol and perfumes that can be an irritant. Washcloths are sterilized after each use.

REST AND SLEEP
Sheets are removed and laundered each day between each use (sterilized). This may be a part of opening and closing or nap procedures, according to room staffing and space requirements.

Nap rooms are located adjoining the playroom and children nap individually in a darkened room.

Rocking chairs are used as appropriate.

Cribs, cots, and mattresses are used. Children nap according to their own needs.

Nap rooms are monitored by staff electronically.

The nap room is decorated with stars, night scenes, and mobiles. Care-givers sing songs to children.

Cribs or cots are numbered or charted so that children consistently nap in the same area.

Source: Special thanks to Pam Boulton and the staff of the Day Care Center of the University of Wisconsin at Milwaukee for providing this information on their routines.

Diapering is more than just a job that needs to be done. It provides opportunities for care-givers to interact with children, promoting cognitive and language development. What specific activities can care-givers do with children during diapering?

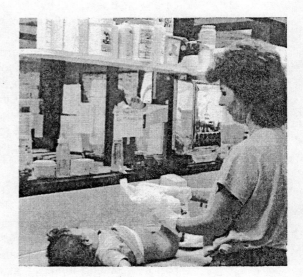

Whatever the methods used, the following guidelines can be helpful as you plan for your involvement with the very young.

- Want the best and be the best for children.
- Plan what you and children will do in order to educate and develop children to their fullest capabilities.
- Allow children to participate in a wide variety of structured and unstructured activities inside and outside the program.
- Provide for individual, small-group, and large-group activities.
- Base program activities on the developmental needs of children while providing for individual needs and differences.
- Establish and maintain routines and transitions that provide children with the security they need.

PROGRAM VIGNETTE

The Four-Year-Old Program at the Victory School
Milwaukee, Wisconsin

All Milwaukee public elementary schools have noncompulsory four-year-old programs. Since more parents want their children to attend than there is space available, admission is by lottery. Parents apply in the spring of the school year and children are randomly selected for participation. Children who don't "win" the lottery are placed on a waiting list. Kindergarten classes are taught in the mornings and the four-year-old programs are conducted in the afternoons.

The four-year-old program at Victory Elementary School begins at 11:45 A.M. It is taught by Chris Holicek, who also teaches a morning kindergarten program. One hallmark of Chris's four-year-old program — as well as her kindergarten program — is an integrated discovery approach to teaching and learning. In an integrated curriculum, children's interests and activities, not subject matter, are the basis for the program. Activities and involvements are used as the basis for learning skills and concepts.

The first-time visitor to Chris's four-year-old program at Victory School is immediately impressed by the wide variety of children's art and "writing" prominently displayed around the room, by the discovery learning centers, and by the children's independence. It is no accident that these features — art, language, discovery learning, and independence — are impressive parts of Chris's program, since she believes that children learn best when they are busily involved in direct experiences and "hands on" activities designed to promote active learning.

"Art is a key component of my program and art activities are part of our daily routine," explains Chris. "I believe art is a basic component of an early childhood program and that used effectively, it develops individuality, imagination, aesthetic appreciation, hand-eye coordination, and creativity and provides children concrete ways to respond to their environment. Art can also be used to promote and develop language skills. When children draw about their experiences, I label objects and write what they say about their pictures. [See Figures 6-5 and 6-6.] In this way, I use art to integrate language skills. Labeling children's drawings helps them understand that writing and words have meaning in their daily lives."

Chris also places a heavy emphasis on language arts skills and provides ample time for children's independent explorations in reading and writing. As Chris explains, "At the writing center, children are free to explore with paper, various writing instruments, commercial dictionaries, class-made dictionaries, and also to "read" children's writing from previous years. When I introduce the center in September, the children are somewhat leery about "writing," but by November, many children choose the writing center first during their self-choice time."

Chris's efforts at involving children in writing are not limited to the writing center. Children keep spiral notebooks in which they dictate stories, thoughts, answers to questions posed by Chris, and accounts of their many field trips. Children take their notebooks home at the end of the year.

Reading is a key element of Chris's language arts program. She reads to the children each day from a wide variety of fiction, nonfiction, and poetry. She reads and rereads — with much student participation — the children's favor-

When Do I Cry? Why?

FIGURE 6-5
Child's Art and Dictated Story

I cry because I fall sometimes. I fell off my bike at grandma and grandpa's house. I fell going up the step - I didn't remember there was a step!

What I Do At Home

I was playing outside and Joe was. We played basketball and football. We played games with grandma and grandpa. We played different cards. Grandma brought me something that grows in cold water— not dirty water— clean water— as big as they come! It's a monster! Some are dinosaurs.

FIGURE 6-6
Child's Art and Dictated Story

ites and uses many patterned stories, such as *The Three Billy Goats Gruff.* The children love to repeat words and phrases and act out story themes.

Since Chris believes so strongly in discovery learning, she utilizes many discovery learning centers. She describes these centers as "exciting places where children can learn by discovery and experimentation." Chris also feels that children learn better when they initiate their own learning and are free to discover. Some of the centers the children like most are (1) the measuring center. This is a variation on the sand table. Chris uses many dry materials such as corn meal, beans, and rice with containers of various sizes and shapes. (2) the nut and bolt center. Here children learn to match nuts and bolts of all sizes. (3) the button center. At this center, children match, sort, create sets, duplicate sets, and make designs with the wide array of buttons Chris, children, and parents have accumulated over the years.

In her integrated discovery approach to learning, Chris uses units of study based on themes. An ongoing theme used throughout the year is "I'm Me, I'm Special." Chris places a great deal of emphasis on helping children develop a positive self-image. As she explains it, "I utilize child-centered activities to foster a joy of learning. I work hard at providing a positive atmosphere which encourages self-expression." As part of this theme, children draw a monthly self-portrait, which they keep in a booklet throughout the year. Also, during

At Victory School, Chris Holicek uses many learning centers to actively involve children. These children wear Puritan hats they made themselves to celebrate Thanksgiving. What can children learn from such involvement?

the year, all children have their own "special week." During their special week, children bring in pets, toys, pictures, and whatever else they want to share about themselves. One child brought in his grandparents to talk to his classmates about camping!

The program's unique feature is its integrated, discovery-based curriculum. Chris believes in and implements an integrated discovery approach for a number of reasons. "First, I can provide the children with a wide variety of activities. Young children learn by being active in their environment. Active involvement is a natural motivator and helps children be enthusiastic about their learning. It is almost as though children are learning and are not aware of it.

"Second, an integrated discovery-based program provides children with choices of activities, learning centers, and things to do. When children make choices about what they will do and how they will learn, then they are becoming autonomous as well as learning how to learn on their own.

"Third, integrating helps me address children's individual rates of learning as well as their different learning styles. Some people think that simply because children are young they all learn in the same manner. My children are at different stages in their abilities to do activities and complete tasks, so I make sure I have activities appropriate to their learning levels.

"Fourth, through integration, I can incorporate concepts related to science, social studies, language arts, and math in all we do without teaching them as 'special' subjects."

Chris believes that planning is a key to conducting a good integrated discovery curriculum. "I feel good teaching and learning result from careful planning and foresight," she says. "I plan activities and develop discovery centers in advance, but flexibility is important too. I follow the children's interests and also try to capitalize on those "teachable moments" that continually occur in a child-centered program."

Chris recognizes the importance of parent involvement and provides many opportunities for parents to participate. Chris sends home monthly newsletters and activity guides. Food for class activities and special events is provided by parents. Parent volunteers help on a daily basis, assisting with art projects, discovery centers, and language arts activities. Chris also involves parents in gathering materials for the discovery centers and art projects. "We make use of many second-hand and recycled materials. It is surprising the things parents bring in for us to use that normally might be thrown out!"

ENRICHMENT THROUGH ACTIVITIES

1. Observe in infant, toddler, and preschool programs to determine how care-givers promote the education and development of the very young. How are the methods used similar to or different from those discussed in this chapter?
   a) What evidence of planning by care-givers did you find in your program visits?
   b) If you were a care-giver in the programs you observed, what methods would you use to educate and develop children?
2. Select two interest centers discussed in this chapter. Develop learning objectives for infants and toddlers. What materials will you need for each center?
   a) Contact an infant or toddler program and ask permission to use your interest centers with children. Report your experiences to your classmates.
   b) What would you change in your interest centers as a result of using them with children? Why?
3. Why are routines important in the lives of children?
   a) A parent comes to you and asks for advice on establishing and maintaining routines in the home. What is your response?
   b) Should routines always be maintained? Are there times and conditions when breaking routines is appropriate? If so, when? How?
4. Give specific examples from your life and experience with young children that indicate that young children model behaviors of others.
5. List five key behaviors you think should be modeled for infants, toddlers, and preschoolers. Tell how you would ensure that children would have opportunities to observe these behaviors.
6. Which method of teaching and learning presented in this chapter do you like best? Why?
7. Use the Environmental Rating Scale to informally analyze an infant or toddler program.

a) What problems did you encounter in the use of this scale?

b) What did the data from the scale reveal?

c) How would you use your data to improve a program?

8. Interview child-care workers and preschool teachers to determine the skills and behaviors they think are important for school readiness. How does the data you collected match your views about school readiness?

9. While observing in the Tiny Tot child-care program, you notice there is a great deal of confusion at arrival time in the mornings. In particular, a number of infants cry when their mothers leave, and the care-givers seem inattentive to the parents. What kinds of arrival routines would you recommend to eliminate these two problems?

10. Critique the routines for arrival, eating, napping, and diapering presented in this chapter. What features do you like most about the routines? How would you improve them?

ENRICHMENT THROUGH READING

Ames, Louise Bates, and Chase, Joan Ames. *Don't Push Your Preschooler.* New York: Harper and Row, 1973.

As the title implies, this book is devoted to telling parents about the dangers of pushing their children too soon, too far, and too fast. The authors point out that children learn to do a great many things without adult interference. They advise parents to relax and enjoy with their children the years before school. Relaxing does not mean doing nothing. The authors provide many useful suggestions to parents for helping their children become ready for school and life. This is another good book that explains the practical application of the maturation approach to development.

Brown, Janet F., ed. *Curriculum Planning for Young Children.* Washington, D.C.: National Association for the Education of Young Children, 1982.

This is a collection of articles from *Young Children,* the journal of the National Association for the Education of Young Children. These articles help early childhood educators keep up with research and apply the implications of this research to everyday practice. Topics included are play, communication, exploring the world, and integrating the arts. A final section deals with techniques for implementing an effective curriculum.

Dittmann, Laura L., ed. *The Infants We Care For.* Washington, D.C.: National Association for the Education of Young Children, 1984.

The authors of the individual chapters have identified the complexities and factors that should be kept in mind whenever and wherever babies are being cared for. Members of the NAEYC Commission on the Care and Education of Infants in 1969 identified three goals for the care of infants: development of a healthy body, development of an active mind, and development of wholesome feelings. This book raises questions and issues relating to these goals so that care-givers can develop the best possible programs.

Houle, Georgia Bradley. *Learning Centers for Young Children.* West Greenwich, R.I.: Tot-Lot Child Care Products, 1984.

>Ms. Houle presents a wide variety of usable, practical learning centers for use with young children. Each one is teacher-created and tested by the author. All utilize existing classroom materials and props, so the old argument, "I can't afford the materials," won't work in this case. Each center description is accompanied by a drawing of the center. The author's ideas concerning the educational values of the center and materials are also included. An excellent resource and learning tool.

Leavitt, Robin Lynn, and Eheart, Brenda Krause. *Toddler Day Care: A Guide to Responsive Caregiving.* Lexington, Mass.: D.C. Heath, 1985.

>This book provides useful information on toddler care from two practitioners who operate the Developmental Child Care Program at the University of Illinois at Urbana-Champaign. The chapters cover topics from play to assessment and are practical and developmentally based. The strengths of this text are twofold. First, it focuses exclusively on toddler care and education, an area that is in need of sound information based on theory and practice. Second, it is easy to read and understand. These are two qualities that should appeal to many child-care workers.

Mahoney, Ellen, and Wilcox, Leah. *Ready, Set, Read: Best Books to Prepare Preschoolers.* Metuchen, N.J.: Scarecrow Press, 1985.

>Based on the principles that readers are made, not born, and that parents are children's first and most important teachers, the authors provide practical and realistic ideas for laying the foundation for reading. This book gives parents — and others — help in selecting the best in literature and art to share with children. Many suggestions are provided for how to read aloud and how to promote in children listening skills, art appreciation, and the desire to participate in the reading process. Two aspects of this book particularly recommend it. First, it is organized according to developmental levels, beginning with the infant. Second, in addition to providing many practical resources, it also provides insight into language development. The authors accomplish all of this in an easy-to-read, informative style.

White, Burton L. *A Parent's Guide to The First Three Years.* Englewood Cliffs, N.J.: Prentice-Hall, 1980.

>White has created quite a bit of controversy with his ideas about what constitutes optimum care for children in the first years of life. Essentially, he believes that parents should provide care for children in their homes. As he states, "Put bluntly, after more than twenty years of research on how children develop well, I would not think of putting a child of my own into any substitute-care program on a full-time basis, especially a center-based program." His critics charge that White fails to take into account the economic and political realities of the times and that he presents a narrow solution to the child-care needs of parents. This book outlines White's ideas in detail. If early childhood educators want to know about one side of a big issue in child care, this book is must reading.

Zigler, Edward F., and Gordon, Edmund W., eds. *Day Care: Scientific and Social Policy Issues,* Boston, Mass.: Auburn House, 1982.

>This is an excellent examination of the majority of issues facing day care. The

primary issues of child care, however, are two: What constitutes quality care? How should it be delivered? These articles examine the body of child-care research in relation to past federal and social policies. The results are recommendations for current and future policy decisions. This is must reading for child-care administrators and policy planners.

NOTES

1. James H. Bryan, "Prosocial Behavior," in *Psychological Processes in Early Education,* ed. Harry L. Hom, Jr., and Paul A. Robinson (New York: Academic Press, 1977), 241.
2. Thelma Harms and Richard M. Clifford, *Early Childhood Environment Rating Scale* (New York: Teachers College Press, 1980).

Chapter 7

Guiding the Behavior of the Children We Care For

Questions to Guide Your Reading and Study

- How does behavior guidance differ from discipline and punishment?
- What is self-regulation and how can care-givers facilitate its development?
- How should the developmental characteristics of the very young influence how care-givers guide their behavior?
- What are the important concepts associated with the behaviorist approach to behavior guidance?
- How do natural and logical consequences influence techniques of behavior guidance?
- Why is it important for young children to learn conflict resolution skills?
- How can care-givers use the guidelines presented in this chapter to guide children's behavior?
- What problems and issues are associated with the use of physical punishment?

INTRODUCTION

Many people feel that children don't "behave" as well as they did in previous generations. It is not uncommon to hear people complain about how today's children are decidedly undisciplined and ill-behaved. The perceived breakdown in discipline and behavioral standards is attributed most often to the breakup of the traditional nuclear family, the absence of teaching about moral values, and a permissive society.

Children's behavior is usually a high-priority discussion topic among parents, care-givers and early childhood teachers. The public's and the profession's interest in children's behavior is certainly justified. How children behave — or don't behave — influences the attitudes of parents, helps set the tone and quality of family life, determines care-givers' attitudes toward their jobs, and affects how well children will be cared for and helped. Given the influences that children's behaviors have on people and programs, it is natural for care-givers to want to know how to guide children so they become autonomous, helping, and caring. Perceptive care-givers know that they are rearing, caring for, and teaching the generations of the future. The effective guidance of children's behavior extends beyond the here and now of a particular moment. How care-givers guide children today helps determine how children will act tomorrow and the tomorrow after that. By guiding children's behavior and by helping children learn to guide their own behavior, care-givers do indeed influence eternity.

GUIDING THE BEHAVIOR OF INFANTS, TODDLERS, AND PRESCHOOLERS

Discipline and Punishment

In the seventeenth Gallup poll of the public's attitudes toward the public schools, respondents identified discipline as the most important problem facing the schools.[1] Care-givers are constantly faced with the task of developing readiness for the basic skills and at the same time developing children's autonomy, self-direction, and self-control.

Topics such as discipline, behavior management, and guiding behavior generally generate a great deal of discussion. Probably no subject creates as much interest at a parents' meeting as the topic of how to discipline without difficulty, spanking, or spoiling.

Discipline for many care-givers is their response to children's misbehavior because they did not "follow rules." Parents, especially, view discipline as bringing children into compliance with adult rules through the use of punishment.[2] Consequently, discipline and punishment are frequently seen as complementary, if not identical, processes.

Punishment also implies the use of physical force, through which a child suffers physically, emotionally, or both. Punishment generally provides no clear direction for children; it only indicates what they are *not* to do. Punishment neither helps children learn new behaviors nor develops their capacity for self-discipline.

Behavior Management

Behavior management is a term used to describe the application of behaviorist theories to help children learn new behaviors and discontinue misbehavior. The behaviorist ideas of positive reinforcement for good behavior and negative reinforcement for misbehavior can play a major role in guiding children's behavior. Sometimes, however, behavior management can have a negative connotation that implies that children are being manipulated. When care-givers consider the management of children's behavior, there may be a tendency to force adult will on children, to treat them as passive, compliant individuals acted on by adults.

Behavior Guidance

Behavior guidance, on the other hand, conveys the concept that children can be reared and taught to behave responsibily and appropriately through a process of adult-child interaction based on respect and knowledge of chil-

Guidance of children's behavior should be based on respect for children and the belief that they can learn to be responsible for themselves. How can care-givers help children be responsible?

dren. The ultimate goal of behavior guidance is responsible children who are capable of managing and controlling their own behavior. Self-discipline is a self-regulating process and should develop from within the child rather than be imposed from the outside by fear of punishment. The goal of behavior guidance is assisting children in their development of self-regulation.

Self-Regulation

Claire B. Kopp summarizes the definition of self-regulation this way: "Self-regulation has been variously defined as the ability to comply with a request, to initiate and cease activities according to situational demands, to modulate the intensity, frequency, and duration of verbal and motor acts in social and educational settings, to postpone acting upon a desired object or goal, and to generate socially approved behavior in the absence of external monitors."[3]

Self-regulation is a lifelong goal, not necessarily something that is achieved in the early years in the twinkling of an eye. A person is always in the process of becoming more self-regulated and refining his or her skills in self-regulation.

The stages of development of self-regulation in the early years are outlined in Table 7-1. The table also illustrates the behavioral features of each stage as well as care-giver behaviors that promote development of self-regulation.

GUIDANCE AND CHILDREN'S BEHAVIORAL CHARACTERISTICS

Care-givers must know children well in order to guide their behavior and development. When care-givers know and understand children's behavior, they are more likely to expect and accept age-appropriate behaviors rather than behaviors far above what children are able to do. Care-givers can become frustrated and expect too much or too little of the very young when they are unfamiliar with age-appropriate behavior.

Some behavioral characteristics of the very young that have implications for behavior guidance are described in the following paragraphs.

1. *Children want and need to be independent.* Children want to do things for and by themselves. When care-givers understand and support children's efforts at independence, everyone is happier. Children should be allowed to do things for themselves as long as their behavior does not endanger them or others. Children do not need care-givers who interfere and control; rather, they need care-givers who assist *if needed.*

As children grow, their quest for independence is verbally expressed by their protests of "no." This and other signs of autonomy are natural and to be expected. Care-givers should not overreact and punish children be-

TABLE 7-1

The Development of Self-Regulation

Phases in the Development of Self-Regulation	Age	Features	Care-giver Roles
Neurophysiological modulation	Birth to 2 or 3 months	Development of clearly defined periods of wakefulness; development of schemes to self-soothe, e.g., nonnutritive sucking.	Provide interactions and opportunities for stimulation; provide routines of eating and sleeping.
Sensorimotor modulation	3 months to 1 year	Ability to engage in sensorimotor acts and change an act in response to events. Modulations help infants become aware of their *own* actions in holding, reaching, and playing. When infants differentiate their own actions from those of others, the potential for self-regulation emerges.	Provide care-giver–infant interactions; provide activities for the infant.
Control	1 year to 18 months	Shows awareness of social and task demands defined by care-giver. Can initiate, maintain, modulate, or cease physical acts, communication, and emotional signals.	Provide interactive patterns of communication and interaction. Provide opportunities for toddlers to notice the effects of their actions. Call attention to expectations. Channel the toddler into desired activities.
Self-control	2 years or older	Compliance and emergent abilities to delay an act or request and to behave according to care-giver and social expectations in the absence of external monitors.	Continue to provide and call attention to expectations. Avoid "controlling" toddlers' behaviors. Avoid being critical of behaviors.
Self-regulation	3 years or older	Growing ability to adapt and regulate behavior to set behavioral demands.	Continue to provide and call attention to expectations. Encourage independence, provide verbal interaction, and give reasons for behavior.

Source: Adapted from Claire B. Kopp, "Antecedents of Self-Regulation: A Developmental Perspective," *Developmental Psychology,* 18 (March 1982): 200. Reprinted by permission of the American Psychological Association.

Guiding the behavior of infants and toddlers includes giving them the freedom they need in an environment where they can actively explore. How can such an environment promote a child's growing autonomy?

cause of this negativism. Instead, when the "no" doesn't matter, ignore it. When a child must do something — put on his coat, for example — the care-giver can help him do it despite his protests.

2. *Because of their growing independence, children want to do things for themselves.* As a result, they frequently spill and break things. This is normal behavior. The best way to deal with such situations is to dress children in washable clothing; make clean-up a pleasant, happy experience; and give children materials that can withstand constant experimenting.

3. *When infants become toddlers they are actively mobile.* This means toddlers can and do get into many things. As indicated elsewhere, the best way to guide this behavior is to give them the freedom they need in a child-proof environment. Care-givers can cause needless stress in themselves and children when they try to unrealistically constrain and restrain children's growing autonomy. Also, as Kopp points out,

> It is likely that care-giver sensitivity to a child's preferred style of interacting with the world of objects and people is a crucial facilitator or deterrent to growth of control. Given a child with very high energy levels and great enthusiasm for movement, the fact that care-givers repeatedly call attention to expectations for acceptable forms of child behavior should be helpful. Similarly,

verbal communications that specify acts for the child to do or that focus child activity into specific channels of play should also foster control.[4]

4. *Young children learn by doing.* Adults frequently try to guide children's behavior with explanations. Children should be given explanations of why their behavior is unacceptable or why they have to do something. Young children, however, have a limited ability to comprehend adult explanations, especially before they learn language. Care-givers should keep their explanations short and concise as they guide children through a behavior. Rather than ask, "Do you want to wash your hands?" say "Let's wash our hands before we eat. We don't want to eat with dirty hands."

Providing reasons for behaviors is important, and children's abilities to understand these reasons increase with development. As Table 7-1 shows, with the beginning of the stage of self-regulation, care-givers should communicate reasons and expectations.

Sometimes care-givers use language in abusive ways to control children's behavior. Abusive language of any kind has no place in child guidance as it models the wrong behavior and demeans both the user and the hearer.

Because of children's limited language ability, care-givers must be alert to their behavior and signals so they can anticipate their needs. Part of being a sensitive and responsive care-giver is learning how to interpret young children's needs and wants.

5. *Children do not think like adults.* They are egocentric and believe they are the center of the world. Children develop a sense of right and wrong, good and bad, through experiences and maturation. Children, then, act the way they do not out of any sense of inherent badness but because they have not learned how to behave.

Care-givers' moods, temperament, and level of patience are factors in guiding children's behavior. A care-giver who is warm, nurturing, and patient will be more effective in interacting with children than one who is cold, impatient, and demanding.

APPROACHES TO GUIDING BEHAVIOR

There are a number of different approaches to child guidance. The behaviorist view is discussed first.

Behaviorism

The behavior modification approach of B. F. Skinner and his followers is a frequently used, although not always well understood, method for guiding children's behavior. The basic assumption of behaviorism is that behavior is shaped by consequences. Children do what brings them pleasure and avoid what brings them pain. Basically, the two most frequently used means of shaping children's behavior are reinforcement of appropriate behavior and ignoring undesirable behavior. These strategies work well when used in the right way in the right circumstances. Some guidelines for using behavioral techniques are:

1. *Reinforce or reward children for desirable behaviors.* Children like to be reinforced for what they have done well. A care-giver might say "Great, Craig, you are doing a good job of passing out the napkins" or "Here, Karen, you earned a happy-face sticker for helping John log in on the computer." Reinforcers can be social, such as praise, gestures, or facial expressions; activities, such as caring for the pets, playing at the water table, or engaging in art activities; or tangibles, such as food. Reinforcers that have proven effective in early childhood programs are spending time with the care-giver in an activity, going for a walk, and reading stories together.

A word of caution about food. Many early childhood educators and nutritionists believe it is unwise to use food as a reinforcer with children since many of the foods used as reinforcers are sweet. Consequently, children may be taught to crave sweets, resulting in poor nutritional habits.

Also, food should never be withheld from children as a means of punishment. When this is done, children may later use food to make up for the lack of certain accomplishments or to satisfy themselves when they are frustrated.

2. *Reinforcers work best when they immediately follow the desired behavior.* The very young lack the ability to wait hours and days for rewards. As children grow and develop, they gradually learn to delay gratification, but in the early years they live in the world of the immediate present.

3. *Consistently reward a desired behavior.* Care-givers cannot keep changing their minds about what they will or won't reinforce. In the beginning stages of developing behavior, frequent reinforcement — i.e., every time the behavior occurs — works best.

4. *Ignoring is often appropriate to extinguish undesirable behavior.* When a behavior is ignored, it is not reinforced and should eventually stop. Ignoring as a strategy, however, is not always appropriate. Aggressive behavior cannot be ignored. If a child is biting another child, the two children must be separated. After the separation, the child that did the biting should be ignored while the child who was bitten is attended to. Aggressive behavior may only get worse if it is ignored.

Care-givers who rely on ignoring as their primary strategy for dealing with behavior problems actually encourage misbehavior because they believe that ignoring cures all misbehavior. There is a difference between making a conscious decision to ignore a behavior as part of an overall plan and merely using ignoring as a habitual response to all misbehavior.

5. *Cue desired behavior.* Cuing is a process of alerting children to expected behavior. Children may be so engrossed in an activity that they are

Encouraging children to give and to share with others are good ways to promote positive interpersonal behaviors. What can teachers do to help children develop skills necessary for getting along with others?

unaware of the need to begin something else, such as cleaning up. Cuing children by singing "The Clean-up Song" would alert them and put them on task.

6. *Reinforce the behavior of one child as a way of calling the desired behavior to the attention of another child.* If Marcia and Tiffany are playing at the water table and Marcia is playing without splashing and Tiffany is not, praise Marcia for her behavior and ask Tiffany if she, too, can play without splashing.

Praise children when they do part of a behavior. Allison, who has poor eating habits, should be praised for eating some of her lunch.

7. *Use "time out" when it is appropriate to children's developmental levels.* *Time out* is the removal of a child from an activity because she has done something wrong. Presumably, the time out gives her an opportunity to think about her misbehavior. After a set amount of time or when the child says she can behave, she is allowed to return to the activity. This strategy is inappropriate for the developmental levels of infants and toddlers but can be used effectively with preschoolers. "Timing out" infants or toddlers doesn't give them the guidance or help they need to develop desired behaviors.

Beginning when the child is about thirty-six months old, care-givers should explain to child why he has been removed and what would be a better way to act. Not getting to play on the playground because he pushed may be just what a child needs to learn how to regulate his behavior.

Behaviorists believe children learn by interaction on and within their environments. Building behavior is a process of teaching right behavior from the beginning and, when necessary, reteaching to replace undesired behavior. Children learn what care-givers reinforce.

Natural and Logical Consequences as a Method of Guiding Behavior

Some parents and early childhood educators believe children can and should learn from the consequences of their behavior. This is in keeping with the behaviorist view of rewards and punishment. This theory maintains that the consequences — the feedback from behavior — determine how and if a child continues to engage in that behavior. Consequences teach children that all behavior has a reaction of some kind — pleasant or unpleasant. Good behavior brings desirable consequences and misbehavior brings undesirable consequences.

Some consequences occur as a natural result of a child's behavior, hence the name *natural consequences*. When a child does not put on his gloves before going outside in freezing weather, the consequence is cold hands. It is to be hoped that he won't forget his gloves again.

Natural consequences as a way of promoting desired behavior are useful up to a point. Care-givers have to take into consideration the age and developmental level of the children as well as the appropriateness of the consequence. Keeping a toddler in wet training pants all day as a natural consequence of having an accident borders on cruelty. Furthermore, it is doubtful that the consequence would be anything but anguish and emotional distress.

Similarly, to permit a child to eat all the cookies he wants with the belief that the natural consequence will be an upset stomach is not acting in the best interests of the child or as a responsible care-giver. Neither is it the best way to teach a child good nutritional habits.

Logical consequences are those that are *arranged* by care-givers. When children pour their juice at snack time and spill it, for example, they clean it up. Logical consequences are not and should not be punitive. In this instance, cleaning up spilled juice helps children be self-directed in their behavior.

Conflict Management and Resolution

Quite often, conflicts result from children's interactions with others. Increasingly, early childhood educators are advocating teaching children ways to manage and resolve their own conflicts.

The rationales for teaching conflict resolution strategies are several. First, it makes sense to give children the skills they need to handle and resolve their own conflicts. Second, teaching conflict resolution skills to children will enable them to use these same skills as adults. Third, the peaceful resolution of interpersonal conflicts contributes, in the long run, to world peace. In this sense, peace curricula and attempts to teach children concepts of peace begin with harmony in the child-care and preschool classroom families. When care-givers involve children in efforts to resolve interpersonal behavior problems peacefully, they intuitively learn that peace begins with them.

Strategies used to teach and model conflict resolution include:

1. *Talk it over.* Children can learn that talking about a problem often leads to a resolution. In addition, by talking about a problem, they learn there are always two sides to an argument. Talking also helps children think about other ways to solve problems.

2. *Model resolutions.* Care-givers can model resolutions for children. "Erica, please don't knock over Shantrell's building because she worked hard to build it." "Barry, what is another way (instead of hitting) you can tell Pam that she is sitting in your chair?"

3. *Teach children to say "I'm sorry."* Saying "I'm sorry" is one way to heal and resolve conflicts. It can be a useful step toward good behavior. Piaget maintained that prior to the stage of concrete operations (before the age of seven), young children do not have the cognitive maturity to take another's point of view. Since they cannot "decenter," it is difficult for them to know how others feel and therefore to be sorry for something. Thus, the very young are not cognitively able to learn to say "I'm sorry" and really mean it. Care-givers claim that children sometimes say "I'm sorry" just to get out of trouble without having any real conviction that they indeed are sorry. Nevertheless, children need to be reared in an environment where they see and experience others being sorry for their inappropriate actions toward others.

4. *Do something else.* Teach children to get involved in another activity. Children can learn that they don't always have to play with a toy someone else is playing with. They can get involved in another activity with a different toy. They can do something else now and play with the toy later. Chances are, however, that by getting involved in another activity they will forget about the toy they were ready to fight for.

5. *Take turns.* Taking turns is a good way for children to learn that they can't always be first, always have their own way, or always do the prized activity. Taking turns brings equality and fairness to interpersonal relations.

6. *Share.* Sharing is a good behavior to promote in any setting. Children have to be taught how to share and how to behave when others do not share. Children can be helped to select another toy rather than hitting or grabbing. Again, keep in mind that during the early years children are egocentric and acts of sharing are likely to be motivated by expectations of a reward or approval such as being thought a "good" boy or girl.

Also, it doesn't make sense for a care-giver to insist that a two-year-old share his toy when he does not want to. Children learn to share by participating in acts of sharing. A two-year-old can go get a toy to give to another child. A three-year-old can give napkins to everyone at the table.

What interpersonal skills can children learn by working with and helping others?

7. *Ignore others' behavior.* Children can be taught to ignore rudeness and misbehavior in others. This is a very effective strategy. At ages four and five, name calling becomes very popular, and ignoring the name caller is a way to help the "wounded" child.

8. *Walk away.* All children can be taught and shown that walking away from a situation is a good way to handle it.

9. *Wait a while.* This strategy, combined with others such as doing something else and walking away, lessens tensions and reduces the likelihood of a confrontation.

PRINCIPLES FOR GUIDING CHILDREN'S BEHAVIOR

Care-givers and Their Behavior

Care-givers can help children develop appropriate behavior in many ways.

1. *Be knowledgeable.* Know what behaviors are normal at what ages and base your guidance accordingly. Expecting a two-year-old to share is a bit unrealistic, for example. Table 7-2 outlines the normal behaviors accompanying social development in the first five years.

2. *Be an authoritative care-giver.* In Chapter 3, we identified four different parenting styles. These parenting styles can also be applied to care-

TABLE 7-2

Behavioral Indicators of Social Development, Birth to Age Five

Behavior Item	Age Expected
	(weeks)
Responds to smiling and talking	6
Knows mother	12
Shows marked interest in father	14
Is sober with strangers	16
Withdraws from strangers	32
Responds to "bye-bye"	40
Responds to inhibitory words	52
Plays pat-a-cake	52
Waves "bye-bye"	52
	(months)
Is no longer shy toward strangers	15
Enjoys imitation of adult activities (smoking, etc.)	15
Is interested in and treats another child like an object rather than a person	18
Plays alone	18
Brings things (slippers, etc.) to adult (father)	18
Shows beginning of concept of private ownership	21
Wishes to participate in household activities	21
Has much interest in and watches other children	24
Begins parallel play	24
Is dependent and passive in relation to adults	24
Is shy toward strangers	24
Is not sociable; lacks social interest	27
Is ritualistic in behavior	30
Is imperious, domineering	30
Begins to resist adult influence; wants to be independent	30
Is self-assertive, difficult to handle	30
Is in conflict with children of own age	30
Refuses to share toys; ignores requests	30
	(years)
Begins to accept suggestions	3
Has "we" feeling with mother	3
Likes to relive babyhood	3
Is independent of mother at nursery school	3
Tends to establish social contacts with adults	3
Shows imitative, "me, too" tendency	3

(continued)

TABLE 7-2 (*continued*)

Behavior Item	Age Expected (years)
Begins strong friendships with peer associates, with discrimination against others in group	3½
Is assertive, boastful	4
Has definite preference for peer mates	4
Tries to gain attention; shows off	4
Tends to be obedient, cooperative; desires to please	5
Seeks approval; avoids disapproval of adults	5
Shows preference for children of own age	5
Shows protective, mothering attitude toward younger sibling	5

Source: Adapted from Joanne Hendrick, *The Whole Child* (St. Louis: Times Mirror/Mosby College Publishing, 1980), 210–211.

giving. Translating what we know about parenting styles to care-givers, the "ideal" care-giver style is authoritative. An authoritative care-giver sets clear standards, encourages children to be independent, communicates well with children, encourages children to express themselves, and is warm and supportive. The authoritative teacher balances the needs and rights of children with those of care-givers and programs.

An authoritative care-giver acts with authority. Care-givers are the authority in the home, child-care center, and classroom. This authority should not be usurped by a three-year-old. When a mother chronically brings her three-year-old daughter late to preschool and explains it away by saying "We're late today because Jennifer didn't feel like getting up," then Jennifer, not her mother, is in control. Such relinquishing of control and role reversals can become a routine to the point that children determine how care-givers behave.

3. *Be willing to change ideas and expectations about what is appropriate for young children.* Care-givers must change their ideas about what constitutes good care based on what is best for children. Placing infants in their cribs and expecting them to remain quiet all day is an unreasonable expectation. Expecting a toddler to be content in a playpen all day is also unreasonable. Setting ten toddlers at a table and expecting them to be quiet and busily involved is unreasonable. A care-giver who thinks that eighteen-month-old children should be "disciplined" in their behavior and always do what she tells them to do needs to change her expectations.

A care-giver who fails to consider children's needs, who has unreasonable expectations, and whose behavior is demanding and controlling would be classified as *authoritarian*.

4. *Be sensible.* Only intervene when necessary. Care-givers must be sensible about children's behavior and their own. Many observed behaviors don't need a response. When two young children are playing and one takes the other's toy, there is probably no need to make a fuss about it. Many interactions and "behavior problems" solve themselves when care-givers don't interfere.

5. *Plan for what children will do.* Planning helps identify and clarify expectations, organizes the day, and leads to care-giver confidence about activities and interactions with children. Children regulate their behavior better in the presence of confident care-givers than in the presence of those who lack self-confidence.

6. *Be positive about personal behavior.* Have a good opinion of yourself and a positive outlook on life. A negative outlook on life leads to negativism with children, which leads to behavior problems.

7. *Be positive about children's behavior.* Do everything in a positive manner. Instead of saying "Don't do that" or "Don't run in here," say "Sally, remember our rule about walking in the classroom."

   Being positive about a behavior can be combined with making choices. If Bret is throwing blocks in the block corner, the care-giver can say, "Bret, blocks are for building, not for throwing. If you want to throw, then you can use the bean bags and throw them at the clown face. What do you want to do, build with the blocks or use the bean bags to throw?"

8. *Model appropriate behavior.* Young children learn by precept and example. Care-givers must model behaviors they want children to demonstrate. Role playing to show children how to act is a wonderful way to build appropriate behavior.

   Many routines at home and center are established and maintained through participation. When care-givers help and show children how to clean up and put things away, they are modeling the behavior they wish to develop and maintain. Children can help others ("Sue, will you please hold the door open for Joe") and at the same time, model their behavior for other children.

   In the modeling process, don't forget manners. Not all parents teach children to say "please" and "thank-you." Also, if care-givers have certain terms and greetings they want children to use they should model this behavior. Saying "good morning" to children as they enter the program models polite behavior for them, and is also a method of greeting.

   Many words and explanations have meaning for children only when they are accompanied by modeling or showing. Telling Jane to put her arm in the sleeve of her coat is more effective when she is shown how to put on her coat concurrently with being told how to do it.

Remember that children may see as appropriate any behavior care-givers model for them. If a care-giver is "bossy," she can't expect the children to be warm and cooperative with each other.

9. *Make the activities and program appealing to children.* A good way to avoid behavior problems is to keep children busy, happy, and involved in activities they find interesting. Children need opportunities to experiment. Young children need time to be involved in activities without being rushed. They also need equipment and materials that they can experiment with to find out how things work.

10. *Communicate with parents.* Parents and care-givers need to share beliefs about child rearing. Parents need to know what a program can or cannot do for and with their children. It is also important that behaviors expected at home and in the program be complementary. Many behavior problems in the home and child-care setting can be avoided when parents and care-givers agree on expectations and acceptable behavior.

11. *Communicate with children.* Remind children of limits, expectations, and behavior rules. Also, tell children when they have followed the rules and met expectations.

12. *Be willing to modify the environment to help children meet behavior expectations.* Parents in particular need to understand that from the time children can crawl they are territorial animals. This means that things that interfere with their territory should — within reason — be put away.

13. *Respect children as persons.* Care-givers and parents can and do wield a lot of power in children's lives. This power should not be abused, nor should children be the victims of adult intimidation. Truly respecting children means accepting them for what and who they are. Respect for children also means not towering over them. Getting down at the children's level by kneeling or sitting on the floor makes it easier to communicate with them and to make them feel secure.

Care-givers and Children's Behavior

1. *Let children be active.* Children learn through activity, so they should have opportunities to be active. Trying to keep children inactive is a source of many behavior problems. Play and involvement in interest centers are excellent ways to provide for children's intrinsic need for activity.

Often-overlooked sources of active involvement in homes and pre-schools are responsibilities related to maintaining the environment. At home children can help make beds, wash clothes, dust, and clean up after dinner. Children can also help maintain the child-care and pre-school environments. Such responsibilities help children be active in controlled ways, give them feelings of accomplishment, and enable them to contribute to family and group living.

If infants and toddlers are to be involved in responsibilities, care-givers cannot expect perfection. If they help bake, cake mix may get spilled. So be it. That is a small price for having autonomous children.

2. *Establish reasonable limits for children and help them live within these limits.* Care-givers have to establish limits pertaining to what is unacceptable behavior. Setting limits is important for a number of reasons:

   a) Limits help care-givers clarify in their minds what they believe is unacceptable behavior. When care-givers don't set limits, they are frequently inconsistent in what they will allow. This leads to insecurity and behavior problems in children because they don't fully understand what to do. Also, when care-givers don't set limits they accept almost any behavior and then complain because children don't behave. Parents, for example, can decide that every time their child gets in the car the child has to buckle up in his car seat. This is both an expectation and limit. The limit is that the child cannot do what he wants to in the car.

      The limits established should not interfere with children's development. Setting a limit that a toddler cannot explore is inappropriate for the child's developmental needs. On the other hand, there can and should be limits to how and where the toddler can explore.

   b) Limits make care giving easier because care-givers and children know what the limits are. When limits are known, children don't always have to "test" to find out what those limits are, nor are they faced with surprises when their care-giver suddenly decides that their behavior wasn't acceptable. A child can act with confidence, knowing that the behavior is acceptable.

   c) Limits give children security. Children want and need limits. When they know what they can and can't do, they are happier and so is the care-giver.

   As children grow and mature, they will test limits. This is natural. It is also why it is important for care-givers to set limits and maintain them. As children grow and mature, however, limits need to be changed and adjusted to fit their developmental levels and life situations.

3. *Develop and establish reasonable expectations.* Limits relate to unacceptable behavior. Expectations relate to desired behavior. Parents have to decide what they want their children to be like. Care-givers and teachers have to decide what behavior they expect of children. Helping with household chores and going to bed at a regular time are reasonable parental expectations. Putting learning materials away and helping keep the classroom clean are reasonable teacher expectations.

Expectations are as important as limits, if not more so. Expectations are the guideposts children use in learning to direct their behavior. Children need guideposts to help them along life's way.

Expectations are important and take the place of rules. The fewer rules the better. Rules should not be unreasonable, solely for the convenience of adults. They should not interfere with children's need for developing independence. Rather, rules should be stated positively so children will know what is expected of them.

4. *Let children make choices.* Children like to have choices. Choices help children develop and become independent. Making choices develops confidence and self-discipline. Learning to make choices early in life lays the foundation for decision making later on in life.

Some guidelines that should be followed in giving children choices are:

a) Give children choices when there are valid choices to make. When it comes time to clean up the classroom, children shouldn't be given the choice of whether or not they want to participate. They can, however, choose between collecting the scissors or the crayons.

A note of caution is in order here. When care-givers involve children in cleaning up toys and learning materials at home or school, they must avoid discouraging children from playing with certain materials because they are too hard to pick up. A toy may have many pieces and children may consciously or unconsciously avoid it. In such a case, if care-givers believe the toy is worthwhile, then they can make a special effort to help children select it for use and help them put it away.

b) Sometimes children need help making choices. Rather than saying to a child, "What would you like to do today?" say "Sarah, you have a choice between working in the wood-working center or the computer center. Which would you like to do?"

c) Help children make choices for themselves. Say "Sarah, here are two new computer programs, why don't you tell me which one you like?"

d) Children can be given choices among those desired by the care-giver. Saying "Hillary, do you want to wear the green dress or the blue dress?" gives Hillary a choice without raising the issue of whether or not she is going to wear a dress.

e) When care-givers don't want children to make a decision, they shouldn't be given a choice.

5. *Minimize waiting.* Have materials prepared ahead of time so children can move from one activity to another. When children have to wait, problems arise because children want to be busy and involved.

6. *Make transitions from one activity to another as smooth as possible.* In one program, the teachers sing "It's Clean-up Time" as a signal for the transition from one activity to clean-up and then to another activity. This

process becomes such a routine that the children sing the song as they clean up.

7. *Provide appropriate reinforcement.* Children need to know when they have done something right. A care-giver could say, "Silvia, you are learning to put on your jacket very well all by yourself" or "Juan, thank you for putting all the puzzles away in their boxes. The shelves really look neat."

8. *Develop, establish, and maintain routines and transitions.* Routines are established and expected ways of doing things. Have a standard clean-up routine that is used every day, from the first day. This routine can involve such procedures as having children put away what they use; asking children at the end of an activity to check and see if there is anything that needs putting away; asking children to check for paper on the floor; and performing other tasks that make clean-up easier. Such regular procedures encourage children to have a clean classroom and support their involvement in the routines.

Children need and like routines. Just as limits help children feel secure, so do routines. And a secure child is usually a well-behaved child.

GUIDING TYPICAL PROBLEM BEHAVIORS

Whenever young children are involved in social interactions, especially as they are learning social behaviors and how to get along with others, problems such as biting, grabbing, hitting, and shoving are inevitable. The important thing for parents and care-givers to understand is that such behaviors are normal, especially until children have an opportunity to learn appropriate behavior.

Biting

Biting is the most frequently asked about and discussed misbehavior of young children. Biting is dangerous and should not be allowed. Furthermore, a child who is bitten should not be encouraged to bite the biter back. Nothing but trouble will result from such a suggestion.

Children bite for a number of reasons. First, they may need oral stimulation and gratification. A child who is biting can be given soft toys to chew and bite on as source of oral satisfaction. Second, children bite because they don't know — and have not learned — more appropriate ways of responding to a frustrating situation such as having their toy taken away.

When a child bites another, he should be immediately removed from the other child. The child who was bitten should be attended to. The biter should not be rewarded with extra attention, but should be told that he cannot bite others and must become involved in another activity.

When a child is a known biter, care-givers should be especially alert to situations in which the child does bite and avoid them by diverting the child to another activity or providing him with something to eat, chew, or suck.

Hitting

As they develop, children engage in unsocial acts because they don't know any other way to behave. It is the responsibility of care-givers to tell and show children how to behave. When hitting and grabbing occur, care-givers have to say, "No! We don't hit others to get our own way. Ask Josh if you can please have a turn sweeping the floor."

The best way to reduce instances of aggressive behavior is to have children busily involved in a variety of interesting activities. When children have plenty to do and are happy doing it, in an environment characterized by structured freedom, they are less likely to engage in aggressive behavior.

SHOULD CARE-GIVERS SPANK?

An age-old question is whether or not care-givers should spank as a means of guiding behavior. There is a decided difference of opinion. Many parents spank their children. They follow a "No!" with a slap on the hand or a spank on the bottom. This form of discipline can be an effective means of controlling a child's behavior when used in moderation immediately following the misbehavior. Yet what parents do with their child in the home is not acceptable for other care-givers outside the home, where spanking is considered an inappropriate form of guidance. This is even more true today than it was a decade ago, given the current interest in child abuse. In fact, in some places, such as the state of Florida, physical punishment in child-care programs is legislatively prohibited.

There are a number of problems with spanking and other forms of physical punishment. First, physical punishment is generally ineffective in building behavior in children. Physical punishment does not show children what to do or provide them with an alternative way of behaving.

Second, when adults use physical punishment, they are modeling physical aggression. The care-giver is in effect saying that it is permissable to use aggression in interpersonal relationships. Children who are spanked are more likely to use aggression with their peers.

Third, spanking and physical punishment increase the risk of physical injury to the child. Spanking can be an emotionally charged situation, and the spanker can become too aggressive, overdo the punishment, and hit the child in vulnerable places such as the face.

The best advice regarding physical punishment is to avoid using it and make every effort to use a nonviolent form of behavior guidance.

SUMMARY

In the long run, teachers, care-givers, and parents determine children's behavior. In guiding the behavior of children entrusted to their care, care-givers must select those procedures that are acceptable to their own philosophies and that meet the particular needs of children. Guiding children to help them develop their own internal system of behavior control benefits them more than a system that relies on external control and authoritarianism. Developing self-discipline among children should be a primary goal of all care-givers.

PROGRAM VIGNETTE

Plymouth Children's Center
Milwaukee, Wisconsin

At the Plymouth Children's Center in Milwaukee, Wisconsin, the emphasis is on providing a program in which children can develop socially, emotionally, and intellectually in their own way and at their own pace. All this occurs in a context of freedom of choice, play, and quiet calm. As Jacquelyn Larus Conway, director of Plymouth Center, points out, "Kids need to have the freedom to move around, make choices, and explore their environment. I don't believe that I should impose my views and structure on children. I can help them learn through *their* play activities. I worry that many of today's parents and teachers are overly concerned about hurrying their children. Children need their early childhood years to find out about themselves and their world. Here at Plymouth, we are dedicated to letting children find out about themselves through self-selected play activities, exploration, and discovery."

Thirty-nine children between the ages of two and five attend Plymouth. All children are casually dressed in pants, coveralls, and similar clothing so boys and girls can actively participate in all the activities. "The majority of children are here because their parents work," says Jacquelyn. "We provide child-care services for parents and educational programming for the children. So, our goals differ for each group. For the parents, we are open long enough to accommodate their working hours and we provide quality child care so they are able to go to work secure in the knowledge that their children are being well cared for in a safe and loving environment."

Many early-childhood educators believe that facilities for learning through play are essential to ensure high-quality programs. How can care-givers help ensure that children learn through play?

The children's program is built on the needs of children and the needs of society. "When you work with children, you work with basic values such as learning how to take care of themselves and their environment and how to care for and get along with others," says assistant director Patricia Vicenzi. "We have an open environment that is stimulating and encourages self-direction so children can learn to teach themselves. We help children realize that they can learn by being curious and by exploring. We also want them to see that learning is fun — not necessarily through games, but by being involved by doing.

"We also individualize activities with children because there is a big difference in how children learn. I have many different activities that match the learning needs of children. If I have a child who needs and wants to write, then I will provide her with the necessary materials. It is the same way with discipline. With some children, a short "time out" works best. With others, natural consequences work best. So, you use the information and knowledge you have for each child to help him become self-disciplined."

The staff spends a lot of time in planning for their play-based program, which is operated in an open setting. As Pat emphasizes, "Everything isn't totally spontaneous in our program, although to the casual observer, it may look as though it is. We put a lot of time into planning how we will build on the spontaneous interests of children. Also, because we know our children so well we can anticipate and develop activities around what we believe they are and will be interested in. However, we never force our preconceived interests on children."

The Plymouth Center staff pride themselves on their open-door policy and actively encourage parent involvement. They consider themselves to be a big family community and try to be responsive to parent needs. The parents of Plymouth Center support and appreciate the good things the staff does with their children.

One parent, Virginia Hayes, looked a long time before she found a child-care program that provided the right environment for her son, Caleb. "I work full time so I need child care that provides quality, stable care. I also want a program that promotes learning through play. The play approach at Plymouth was the key for me. Finding a program that provides quality care was a lot easier than finding a program that encourages learning through play. A lot of programs say they let children learn through play, but they really don't. Either they let children do whatever they want or they provide too much structure."

Virginia has definite beliefs about how children learn. "I like the philosophy that children learn through play. I don't really go for an academic approach. It isn't suitable for a preschooler. I think learning through play is best.

"I visited some programs where they had the children sitting at tables working with pencil and paper. I don't have objections to children drawing or learning to write letters and their names. I do feel, however, that workbooks or "kit" curriculums are generally unsuitable for preschoolers. In one program, I thought I was in a high school rather than in a child-care program! In other programs, they said they encouraged free play, but what this meant was they let the children do whatever they wanted to do without any teacher objectives or guidance. The noise was so bad, I couldn't stand it after five minutes. The kids were running around all over the place. It was total chaos. That kind of program would really stress kids out.

"I worked with Jacquelyn before she was the director of Plymouth Children's Center," Virginia continues. "Because I knew we have similar philosophies about children and play, I thought that Plymouth might be a good choice for Caleb. After visiting several times, I enrolled him. I was particularly impressed with the emphasis on play and parent involvement and the interaction between the children. There was little conflict and the children were encouraged to work things out between themselves and to talk with and listen to each other.

"I feel strongly that there is nothing more important that kids should be doing than playing. If you provide a good program, they will develop at the pace they are comfortable with. Caleb was an early talker. He said his first word at nine months. At fifteen months he knew seventy five words. But, he didn't crawl till nine months and didn't walk until sixteen-and-a-half months. This goes to prove that kids need an environment in which they can develop in all areas, not just the cognitive. A good play program gives them opportunities for a variety of experiences.

"I'm starting to worry about what will happen when it is time for Caleb to go to public school. The schools place too much emphasis on academics. This back-to-basics business has gone too far. I'm seriously thinking about finding a private school where the teachers are in charge of the curriculum and where they are not interested in pushing the kids along at the same pace regardless of how fast or slow a child is developing."

The staff and parents of Plymouth Center believe there are a number of characteristics that make it unique.

1. The curriculum encourages learning through play.
2. The program has a caring staff. One of the parents summed up the attitudes of parents toward the staff when she said, "The teachers are really intimate and caring. As a parent, you can really have an influence on the program and activities. They listen to what parents say and take their opinions into consideration."
3. Groups are small. The average size of each group of children is eighteen. With three staff members for each group — teacher, assistant teacher, and aide — children receive the individual attention they need.
4. The staff is of high quality. Jacquelyn Conway believes that a program not only has to hire good care-givers to begin with but that they must be paid a decent wage and benefit package that will act as an incentive for them to stay. "We all know that we did not dedicate our lives to children because we knew we would get rich," says Jacquelyn, "but earning a living wage need not be an unreasonable expectation for people who work with a nation's greatest wealth."
5. There is a family-like environment in which staff get to know children and their families. As assistant teacher Laure Johnikin says, "A key to teaching children is really getting to know them. When you do, then there are all kinds of ways you can help them learn what they need to know and what they want to learn. If one thing doesn't work you try something else."
6. The setting and atmosphere of the program are home-like. The physical appearance of Plymouth Center is reminiscent of a home setting. Housed in the education annex of Plymouth United Church of Christ, the wood floors, fireplaces, leaded glass windows, and brightly colored child-size furniture create an environment where children and staff are comfortable and relaxed and the children are free to learn according to their interests.

ENRICHMENT THROUGH ACTIVITIES

1. At the last staff meeting of the Happy Days Child Care Center, the care-givers expressed a need to develop a parents' handbook on discipline. They said they had been getting many questions from parents about discipline and that instead of repeating the same information over and over again they would write it in a handbook.
   a) Do you think a parents' discipline handbook is a good idea? Give the pros and cons of such a handbook.

    b) Develop the table of contents for this handbook.

    c) List ten ideas that should be included in the handbook.

    d) Would you include this tip in your handbook? "Remain calm and count to ten." Why? Why not?

2. List three ways that meeting the physical and emotional needs of the very young can prevent the development of behavior problems.

3. What do you believe are the three greatest influences on children's behavior? Tell specifically how these factors influence behavior.

4. List three positive and three negative behaviors you developed as a child by imitating behavior modeled by adults.

5. Observe in a child-care or preschool program. List the behaviors you believe children are learning from care-giver modeling.

6. Interview child-care and preschool teachers. Ask them to define and explain their philosophies of discipline.

7. Develop a set of limits you think are appropriate for infants, toddlers, and preschoolers in the home and in a center or preschool setting.

8. In hiring a baby-sitter for your six-month-old child, what qualities, characteristics, and skills would you look for? How would these differ if you were hiring a baby-sitter to take care of a two-year-old?

9. How would you handle each of the following:

    a) A two-year-old who aggressively bites others.

    b) A preschool boy who constantly wants to fight with others when he can't get his own way.

10. Fifteen-month-old Albert loves cookies. In fact, he eats one whenever he gets a chance. Yesterday he pulled a chair over to the counter and climbed up to get the cookie jar. In the process, he knocked the jar off the counter. It broke and the cookies spilled all over the floor. By the time his mother got to the kitchen, Albert was happily stuffing cookies in his mouth. Albert's mother grabbed him, shouted "No!" and gave him several hard smacks, which made him cry in a loud voice.

    a) Did Albert's mother do the right thing?

    b) What could Albert's mother have done differently?

    c) What are the consequences of hitting a child?

11. What advice would you give to parents who think their toddlers should develop exactly the way child development texts say they should?

12. Is it the responsibility of parents, care-givers, or both to teach young children right from wrong? Explain your answer.

13. Silvia and Harry Lincoln are having a great deal of difficulty rearing their four-year-old daughter Harriett. They have listed Harriett's bothersome behaviors and have come to you for help.

    a) She interrupts all the time when her parents talk to other adults.

    b) She has difficulty sharing with other children.

    c) She always wants her own way.

    d) She only eats what she wants to eat.

    e) "We can't take her to the grocery store anymore because she screams and cries if we don't buy all the things she wants — especially candy."

    What advice would you give them?

14. List at least five aggressive behaviors in young children and tell how you would:

a) Deal with them as a child care-giver.

b) Advise parents to deal with them in the home.

15. Develop a list of the ways care-givers can reward children for good behavior.

16. In what situations can praise be overdone as a reinforcer? What are the consequences of this?

ENRICHMENT THROUGH READING

Bisschop, Marijke, and Compernolle, Theo. *Your Child Can Do It Alone.* Englewood Cliffs, N.J.: Prentice-Hall, 1981.

This is a fascinating book. It provides twelve steps for helping care-givers build new behavior in their children. The authors' basic premise is that the more independent children are and the more they can do for themselves, the fewer problems they will cause for care-givers and themselves. Many drawings and illustrations show care-givers what to do and how to do it.

Bluestein, Jane, and Collins, Lynn. *Parents in a Pressure Cooker: A Guide to Responsible and Loving Parent/Child Relationships.* Albuquerque, N.M.: I.S.S. Publications, 1983.

The goal of this book is to help care-givers rear responsible children who are self-regulated rather than dependent on others for external control. One of the authors' premises is that to rear responsible children you have to begin with responsible adults, so there is a chapter devoted to modeling. Another useful chapter deals with expectations. There are many helpful illustrations and drawings to help explain the main ideas.

Canter, Lee, and Canter, Marlene. *Assertive Discipline: A Take-Charge Approach for Today's Educator.* Santa Monica, Calif.: Canter and Associates, 1986.

Lee Canter is the leading proponent of "assertive discipline." Based on the principles of assertiveness training, this approach encourages teachers and parents to take charge of the discipline process. Assertive discipline derives its popularity from the self-help movement of the 1970s and 1980s. It is supported by those who advocate that parents and teachers should assert their right to discipline.

Crary, Elizabeth. *Without Spanking or Spoiling: A Practical Approach to Toddler and Preschool Guidance.* Seattle, Wash.: Parenting Press, 1979.

This is a very popular book that combines many approaches and theories of child management. Relying mainly on behaviorist ideas, the author provides much useful information and a systematic approach to solving discipline problems. There are many useful charts, activities, and examples to help care-givers put into practice what they read.

Essa, Eva. *A Practical Guide to Solving Preschool Behavior Problems.* Albany, N.Y.: Delmar Publishers, 1983.

Based on the behaviorist approach to guiding behavior, this book provides many practical ideas for care-givers. Specific behavior problems such as hitting, biting, tantrums, and whining are addressed in separate chapters. One section is devoted to social behaviors such as nonparticipation in play and group activities. Just about every behavior problem that a care-giver needs information about is discussed in this comprehensive guide.

Fontenelle, Don H. *Understanding and Managing Overactive Children*. Englewood Cliffs, N.J.: Prentice-Hall, 1983.

    Care-givers always have questions about how to guide the behavior of the children they assess as overactive. Quite often, children who are labeled overactive are not, so the first two chapters give the reader insight into the nature and causes of overactivity. The section on general management techniques is a good general discussion of how to guide children's behavior. Other interesting chapters deal with the roles of diet and medication in guiding behavior.

NOTES

1. Alec M. Gallup, "The Seventeenth Annual Gallup Poll of the Public's Attitudes Toward the Public Schools," *Phi Delta Kappan* 67 (September 1985): 42.
2. G. S. Morrison, "Parents' Views of Discipline: Implications for Early Childhood Educators" (Paper delivered at the Conference of the Southern Association on Children Under Six, Charleston, South Carolina, March 8–12, 1983).
3. C. B. Kopp, "Antecedents of Self-Regulation: A Developmental Perspective," *Developmental Psychology* 18 (March 1982): 199–214.
4. Kopp, "Antecedents," 206.

Chapter 8

Meeting the Special Needs of the Children We Care For

Questions to Guide Your Reading and Study

- Why is there so much interest in young children with special needs?
- How does federal legislation promote the education and care of young children with special needs?
- How do individual education programs help young children learn?
- How does Head Start help young children with special needs?
- How can care-givers use formal and informal assessment to identify young children with special needs?
- What are the special needs of the very young?
- How can care-givers provide for the special needs of the very young?
- What are mainstreaming and integration and how do they help young handicapped children?
- How can care-givers meet the educational and developmental needs of young children from diverse ethnic backgrounds?
- How can care-givers meet the educational and developmental needs of young gifted children?
- What are the current issues and trends in the education and development of young children with special needs?

INTRODUCTION

All children have needs. Some children have special needs that other children do not have. These children require special types of care and attention from care-givers. Special needs children include the physically and mentally handicapped, the gifted, and children from minority cultures.

Today, it is not unusual to find very young children with special needs enrolled in child-care programs and preschools. This was not always so. As recently as ten years ago, it was not uncommon for special needs children to be routinely denied admission to regular early childhood programs. Happily, this state of affairs is changing and early childhood educators are recognizing the importance and appropriateness of enrolling children with special needs in child care and preschools. These efforts to integrate special needs children into regular programs are called *main streaming*. Mainstreaming entails educating and caring for special needs children and non-special needs children in the same environment. As a result of mainstreaming, children at earlier ages are being identified, diagnosed, and placed in either regular early childhood settings or in programs designed to meet their special needs.

There is still much to be done, however. Not everyone is willing to mainstream special needs children in regular settings; some are content to see them segregated in special programs. Efforts to provide the best for all children, regardless of their needs, will continue to require the untiring efforts of all care-givers.

All children have special needs. However, some children have needs that require special attention and services. All early-childhood programs should provide children with whatever services they need to help them realize their full potential. What special needs do all children have?

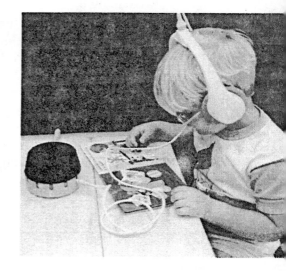

REDISCOVERING CHILDREN WITH SPECIAL NEEDS

There are several reasons for the enlightened view of mainstreaming special needs children in regular early childhood programs and for providing for the special needs of all children.

First, the rules of certain programs require the placement of handicapped children in regular classrooms. In 1972, Head Start regulations mandated that at least 10 percent of all the opportunities for enrollment in a Head Start program be made available to handicapped children. This helped set the stage for mainstreaming and encouraged early childhood educators to consider how to provide for the handicapped in regular programs.

Second, laws such as P.L. 94-142 require that where and when appropriate, the handicapped must be placed in what is known as the "least restrictive" environment. The *least restrictive environment* is the one in which children can benefit the most. This law and others are discussed in more detail later in the chapter.

Third, in the last ten years there has been a decided improvement in the attitude of the general public toward all children who have special needs. There is a greater willingness to understand and do something about the special needs of children. This has resulted in the provision of more educational resources for children and their parents.

Fourth, the growing interest in the very young that we discussed in Chapter 1 has created an interest in the special needs of the very young. Thus, there is increased recognition that the early years are important and that it is best to deal with special needs as early as possible. Waiting until children enter the public school system at ages five or six is much too late.

Legislation Supporting the Education of Special Needs Children

Public Law 94-142. P.L. 94-142 is also known as the Education for All Handicapped Children Act of 1975. Many professionals and parents of the handicapped consider this to be the most important law ever passed relating to the handicapped. The provisions of this law have had and will continue to have a sweeping influence on not only the handicapped, but normal children as well. P.L. 94-142:

1. Guarantees a free and appropriate public education for all handicapped children between the ages of three and twenty-one regardless of the nature and severity of their handicaps. The key here is that no children can be refused services. Prior to the passage of P.L. 94-142, school districts and other agencies that received federal funds quite commonly told parents that they could not help because of a child's handicapping condition. It was up to the parents, at their expense, to

try to find services in the private sector. There were two problems associated with this. First, too often the services were not available in the private sector, and second, the services, when available, were often beyond the financial means of the parents.

2. Provides an individualized and appropriate education to match the available services to the child's unique educational needs. The key word here is *individualized*. Every handicapped child must have a written, individualized educational program (IEP) (sometimes referred to as an individual program plan, IPP) designed to meet his or her particular needs. The IEP must include:

   a) A description of the child's current status and levels of performance in such areas as cognitive development, language development, social and emotional development, self-help skills, and motor functioning.

   b) A set of long-range (one year) goals for the child based on the previous description and diagnosis.

   c) A statement of short-term instructional objectives and the dates by which they will be achieved.

   d) A description of the special educational services and activities that will be provided along with the dates they will be delivered.

   e) A set of evaluative criteria for determining if the instructional objectives have been met.

   Parents and, where appropriate, children themselves must be involved in the development of the IEP. The parents must approve the IEP. Also, discussions about the child and the IEP, when the parent is present, must be in the parent's native language. *Staffings* are meetings to discuss information with parents about their child and to explain the development of the IEP and its provisions. (See the vignette of the Denver Cerebral Palsy program at the end of this chapter for an example of a staffing.)

3. Provides for nondiscriminatory testing, classification, and placement. All procedures used to assess, label, and classify the child must be free of bias and must be done with the parent's knowledge and consent.

4. Mandates that children shall be placed in the least restrictive environment. The least restrictive environment is the one in which the child will benefit most. For many handicapped children, this is the regular classroom. The emphasis in this regard is on normalcy — treating and educating the handicapped child in as normal a way and in as normal an environment as possible.

5. Provides for due process for each child and his or her family. Parents have the right to question and challenge private or public agency decisions concerning their child's handicapping condition. In addition, parents may be represented by legal counsel in such a challenge process.

6. Parent involvement is required in the development of educational policy for the handicapped and in implementing children's individual educational programs.

As far as the very young are concerned, the provisions of P.L. 94-142 often do not apply, for several reasons. First, the law does not apply to children from birth to age three. Second, a state is required to provide services to the handicapped in the three-to-five age range only if it provides services to the nonhandicapped. Many states only provide services to children at age five when they come to kindergarten. Some states don't provide kindergarten. This means that many handicapped preschool children must receive their services in private programs such as cerebral palsy programs or in federally supported programs such as Head Start.

An example of the diagnosis of a handicapped infant is shown in Figure 8-1 and the IEP for language development is shown in Figure 8-2.

The IEP does not need to be an elaborate document. *All* care-givers can provide an IEP for *all* children by identifying a child's special needs and specifying objectives stating what the child will learn during the time he or she is in the care of the care-giver. The ultimate purpose of the IEP is to meet a child's special needs and provide opportunities for success.

Public Law 90-538. In 1968, Congress passed P.L. 90-538, known as the Handicapped Children's Early Education Assistance Act. Also called the *First Chance Program* and *HCEEP,* the purpose of this legislation was to provide for the development of model demonstration programs to acquaint the community at large with the problems and potential of handicapped children. Currently there are First Chance programs or programs based on practices developed by First Chance in every state in the country. In 1974, an amendment to P.L. 90-583 provided support for individual state departments of education to develop comprehensive plans for the education of young handicapped children. Un Buen Comienzo, described later in this chapter, is an HCEEP program.

Public Law 93-644. In 1974, the Head Start program was amended by P.L. 93-644 to require that at least 10 percent of the enrollment opportunities in *each* program be made available to handicapped children. As a result, many preschool handicapped children have received services and an educational program that were previously unavailable to them.

Significant progress has been made in meeting the needs of handicapped children and their parents as a result of specific legislative acts. Practices called for in legislation are now accepted for the majority of handicapped children. In addition, there has been an increase in the number of state and private agency programs that provide services to young handicapped children.

FIGURE 8-1
Diagnosis of a Handicapped Infant

UPDATE

Team: Teacher/coordinator — Janet Speirer
Social Worker — Martha Rodgers
R.N. — Ginny Allen

Name _____ Ben _____   PT _____

Date of birth _____ May 8, 1984 _____   OT _____

Age _____ 11 months _____   Speech/language _____

Reassessment date __ April 1985 _____

Cognition

Ben is functioning at the 11-month level cognitively. He is very aware and interested in his environment, showing curiosity and persistence. He understands "no" and reacts. Also he responds to simple requests. He exhibits object permanence, drops objects systematically, demonstrates drinking from a cup, enjoys looking at pictures in books, removes a round piece from a formboard, and takes a ring stack apart.

Social-Emotional

Ben is a happy, good-natured baby who has appropriate social skills for his developmental level. He explores his environment, although his motor skills still limit him. He enjoys games and music and engages in simple imitative play.

Language

According to the HELP (an assessment instrument), Ben's expressive and receptive language skills are at the 11-month level with scatterings to 12 months. He is following normal language development at this time. His expressive language includes:

1. Babbles when left alone.
2. Waves bye-bye.
3. Says "Dada" and "Mama" nonspecifically.

Receptive skills include:

1. Imitates familiar then new gestures.
2. Responds to simple requests with gestures.
3. Listens to speech without being distracted by other sounds.

Although no delays are seen at this time an individual program plan will be written as Ben is at risk for future language delays because of his diagnosis of Down's syndrome.

Fine Motor

Ben has been reassessed in fine motor skills. According to the assessment he is functioning at 10 months with some emerging skills up to the 11-month-level, which is within normal limits of his appropriate developmental age. He uses radial grasp to obtain objects and rakes tiny objects. He reaches for the object with either hand with extended elbow and wrist. He releases the object voluntarily and he puts an object into a container with trial and error. He transfers the object from one hand to another. He bangs 2 objects held in his hands. He removes pegs from a pegboard and manipulates objects with an active wrist movement. He can supinate his forearm to beyond neutral. He appears to be taking a normal course in fine motor development at this time.

FIGURE 8-1 *(continued)*

Gross Motor

Ben is currently functioning at approximately 6 to 8 months with scattering to 11 months in gross motor skills. He continues to be very alert and eager to interact with others and with his environment. His muscle tone is less hypotonic and his trunk control is developing nicely. He rarely fixes in the neck region as was previously a problem, as his flexor control is becoming more refined. He does lack some shoulder stability and avoids standing upright as he is still insecure in this position. Ben can bear weight in good alignment when prone on extended arms or when he reaches or rolls over to play with toys. He is also starting to belly crawl with amphibian reciprocal movement of his legs but he is not yet assuming quadruped due to decreased shoulder stability, which is also delaying crawling. Ben is assuming sitting independently from side-lying on the R side with a good pattern and developing trunk rotation. He cannot yet sit up from the L side without assistance. In sitting Ben has proper alignment and good head and trunk control for independence indefinitely. Righting and balance reactions are developing appropriately, but with decreased quality on the L side. Protective extension reactions are present forward and laterally with some posterior responses emerging, but also decreased effectiveness on the L side. Ben is not yet pulling up to furniture, and standing is very primitive at this time. Ben also needs to learn to move out of sitting for more developmental sequencing.

FIGURE 8-2
United Cerebral Palsy Infant Development Program: Individual Program Plan

Name _____Ben_____

Date _____April 1985_____

Date of birth _____May 8, 1984_____

Present level _____11 months_____

Area of concern _____Speech/language_____

Goal
To maintain normal language development.

Objectives (by October 1985)

1. Ben will say "Dada" and "Mama" when referring to his parents, every day.
2. Ben will babble intricate inflection while at play.
3. Ben will use a 10–15-word sign vocabulary.
4. Ben will say no meaningfully 85 percent of the time.
5. Ben will vocalize wishes and needs at the table, naming desired items, at least once each day.
6. Ben will use his voice in conjunction with pointing.

Public Law 99-457. In 1986, at the end of the congressional session, Congress passed P.L. 99-457, a piece of landmark legislation relating to handicapped infants, toddlers, and preschoolers. P.L. 99-457 authorizes two new programs, the Federal Preschool Program and the Early Intervention Program.

The Federal Preschool Program extends the rights offered to the handicapped under P.L. 94-142 to handicapped children between the ages of three and five. By the 1990–1991 school year, states applying for P.L. 94-142 funds will have to prove that they are providing a free and appropriate public education to all handicapped children between the ages of three and five. Although the three-to-five age group was included in P.L. 94-142, the group often received no public school services under the law because states had the option of providing or not providing services to this age group.

P.L. 99-457 has a number of significant features. First, if states want federal monies under P.L. 94-142, beginning with the 1990–1991 school year they can no longer *choose* not to provide services for the three-to-five age group of handicapped children.

Second, the committee report accompanying the legislation recognizes that family services play a large role in the delivery of services to preschool handicapped children. Consequently, P.L. 99-457 provides that whenever appropriate and to the extent desired by parents, the preschooler's individualized IEP will include instructions for parents.

Third, the committee report also recognizes the desirability of offering a variety of program options in providing services to handicapped preschoolers. Such variations include part-day home-based programs and part- or full-day center-based programs.

The federal Early Intervention Program authorized by P.L. 99-457 establishes a state grant program for handicapped infants and toddlers from birth to two years. This program provides for early intervention services for all children from birth through two years who are developmentally delayed (what constitutes a developmental delay is determined by each state). A five-year implementation period is provided for in the law. During the fifth year of implementation, participating states must make early intervention services available to all handicapped infants and toddlers.

The early intervention services provided for under P.L. 99-457 include:

1. A multidisciplinary assessment and a written Individualized Family Services Plan (IFSP) developed by a multidisciplinary team and the parents. Services provided must meet developmental needs and can include special education, speech and language pathology and audiology, occupational therapy, physical therapy, psychological services, parent and family training and counseling services, transition services, medical diagnostic services, and health services.
2. An individualized family service plan. The IFSP must include:
   a) A statement of the child's present level of development.

b) A statement of the families' strengths and needs related to enhancing the child's development.

c) A statement of the major outcomes expected for the child and family.

d) A description of the criteria, procedures, and timing for determining progress.

e) A description of the specific early intervention services necessary to meet the unique needs of the child and family.

f) The projected dates for the initiation of the services.

g) The name of the case manager.

h) Procedures for making the transition from the early intervention program into the preschool program.

IDENTIFYING CHILDREN WITH SPECIAL NEEDS

The many methods for identifying the educational and behavioral performance of special needs children can be divided into two categories, *informal* and *formal*.

Informal Assessment

Informal assessment relies on two processes: (1) care-givers' observations of children's varying skills and behaviors, and (2) the assessment of children's work products.

Observation. One of the best ways to identify children with special needs is through observation. This approach is often overlooked. Observation enables care-givers to watch, listen to, and interact with children. It allows care-givers to gather data on children's behavior over a long period of time, under many different circumstances, and in many different emotional contexts. One observational method used to help identify children's special needs is the videotape. Videotapes permit care-givers to participate in an activity and later review children's responses and behaviors.

Another approach is the use of checklists and rating scales, which can help identify the behaviors and skills the observer is to observe. In this way they guide the observation and ensure that all who use a particular checklist will be following the same standard. Many care-givers, although they are well meaning, do not know what to observe or at what age a behavioral characteristic is appropriate. The checklist in Figure 8-3 provides examples of behaviors that care-givers can look for in infants from six months to one year old.

Another checklist is shown in Figure 8-4. It identifies behaviors care-givers can use if they suspect a child has a special need. The data provided by this checklist are very useful when referring children to a nurse, social

FIGURE 8-3
Infant Development Evaluation Sheet

Observer _____ Date _____ Time _____ Place _____

Infant's Name _____ Birth Date _____ Age _____

Average Age of Appearance	Behavior	Observed		Comments
		Yes	No	
Birth to Six Months				
GROSS MOTOR				
1 month	Moves head from side to side			
1 month	When lying down makes crawling movements			
1 month	Head held erect when held at shoulder for three seconds			
1 month	When cheek is rubbed turns to same side			
1½–2 months	Turns from side to back			
2–3 months	Held sitting, head is predominantly erect			
2–3 months	Prone, lifts head up			
2–4 months	Prone, lifts head and upper chest well up in midline using forearms as support, legs straight out with buttocks flat			
2½–3½ months	Rolls over			
3 months	Held standing, lifts foot			
5 months	Prone, holds arms extended			
5½ months	Reaches on same side as arm used			
5½–6 months	Stands holding on			
FINE MOTOR				
1 month	Regards bright object			
1 month	Turns eyes and head toward light			
1 month	When rattle placed in hand, drops immediately			
2 months	Holds rattle briefly			
2½ months	Will glance from one object to another			
3 months	Hands usually open			
3–4 months	Plays in simple way with rattle			
3–4 months	Inspects fingers			
3 months	Holds rattle actively			
3–4 months	Reaches for dangling ring			
3–4 months	Follows ball visually across table			
4 months	Carries object to mouth			
4–5 months	Recovers rattle from chest			
4–5 months	Holds two objects			
5 months	Transfers object from hand to hand			
5–6 months	Bangs in play			
5–6 months	Sits, looks for object			

Source: Rosalind Charlesworth, *Understanding Child Development, 2nd ed.* (Albany, NY: Delmar Publishers, © 1985), 88–90. Adapted from *Developmental Guidelines*, compiled by Sprugel and Goldberg under the direction of Merle B. Karnes.

FIGURE 8-3 *(continued)*

Average Age of Appearance	Behavior	Observed		Comments
		Yes	No	
Birth to Six Months				
COGNITIVE				
1 month	Responds to sounds			
1 month	Vocalizes (other than cry)			
1 month	Cries lustily when hungry or uncomfortable			
2 months	Smiles			
2–3 months	Laughs			
2 months	Visually recognizes mother			
2 months	Coos — single-vowel sounds			
3 months	Vocalizes when spoken to or pleased			
3–4 months	Shows preference for familiar persons			
4–5 months	Turns head to sound of bell			
4–6 months	Turns head to sound of rattle			
4 months	Increases activity at sight of toy			
4½–6 months	Fingers mirror image			
4½–5 months	Discriminates strangers			
5½–6 months	Plays peek-a-boo			
5½–6 months	Shows interest in sound production for pleasure and excitement			
Six Months to Twelve Months				
GROSS MOTOR				
6 months	Sits alone for 30 seconds			
6 months	Rolls from back to stomach			
6 months	Lifts legs to vertical and grasps foot			
6½ months	When on stomach, pivots 180 degrees in order to obtain toy which is kept just out of infant's reach			
6½–7 months	Sits: Briefly, leans forward on hands			
7 months	Lying on back, brings feet to mouth			
7½–8 months	Pulls self to stand			
8 months	Stands briefly with hands held			
9 months	Walks holding onto furniture			
9 months	Attempts to crawl on all fours			
9 months	Stands holding but cannot lower self			
9½–10 months	Sits steadily and indefinitely			
9½–11 months	Walks with both hands held			
9½–10 months	Stands momentarily			
10 months	Creeps			
11–11½ months	Stands alone well			
11–12 months	May walk alone			

FIGURE 8-3 *(continued)*

Average Age of Appearance	Behavior	Observed		Comments
		Yes	No	
Six Months to Twelve Months				
FINE MOTOR				
6 months	Secures cube on sight			
6 months	Follows adult's movements across the room			
6 months	Immediately fixates interesting small objects and stretches out to grasp them			
6 months	Retains rattle			
6½ months	Manipulates and examines an object			
6½ months	Can reach for, grab and retain rattle held in front of him			
7 months	Pulls string to obtain an object			
7½–8½ months	Grasps with thumb and finger			
8–9 months	Persists in reaching for toy out of reach on table			
8 months	Shows hand preference			
8–8½ months	Bangs spoon			
9 months	Searches in correct place for toys dropped within reach of hands			
9 months	May find toy hidden under cup			
10 months	Hits cup with spoon			
10 months	Crude release of object			
10½–11 months	Picks up raisin with thumb and forefinger pincer grasp			
11 months	Pushes car along			
11–12 months	Puts three or more objects in container			
COGNITIVE				
6 months	Spontaneous social vocal sounds			
6 months	Smiles and vocalizes at image in mirror			
7 months	Vocalizes for different syllables			
7½–8 months	Says "Da-Da" or equivalent			
8 months	Vocalizes single syllables such as *da, ka, ba*			
8½ months	Demands personal attention			
9 months	Vocalizes deliberately as means of interpersonal relationship			
9 months	Babbles tunefully, repeating syllables in strings ("mam-mam," "bibiba")			
9–9½ months	Clearly distinguishes strangers from familiars, and requires assurance before accepting their advances; clings to known adult and hides face			
9–10 months	Responds to name and to "no, no"			
10 months	Looks at pictures in book			
11 months	Says one word other than mama and dada — usually one syllable used to designate an object			
11 months	Will find hidden object			
12 months	May have two to eight words besides "mama" and "dada"			

FIGURE 8-3 *(continued)*

Average Age of Appearance	Behavior	Observed		Comments
		Yes	No	
Six Months to Twelve Months				
SELF-HELP				
6 months	Lifts cup			
8 months	Reaches for toys out of reach consistently			
9 months	Holds, bites, and chews biscuits			
9 months	Puts hands around bottle or cup when feeding			
9 months	Tries to grasp spoon when being fed			
9 months	Holds bottle to feed self			
11½–12 months	Is able to drink from cup when it is held though may spill			

worker, program administrator, specialist assigned to the program, or parent.

Work and Product Samples. Samples of children's work over time can provide care-givers with a descriptive and concrete record of how children accomplish tasks. Although the goal of early childhood programs should not be to produce products, the fact remains that the products children make in the course of their everyday activities at home and in a program can provide care-givers with clues about children's fine motor control, perception, attention span, and ability to complete tasks, all of which are indicators of school readiness and success. Teachers and care-givers need to understand that some behaviors children use in completing tasks may be labeled learning problems but actually have resulted from the child's not having been taught how to do a particular task.

Psychologist James Cornell, for example, studied mirror writing in young children.[1] Mirror writing is writing in reverse, or from right to left. When held to a mirror, the writing looks normal, hence the name. Cornell found that about half of the children printed their names in reverse during the learning-to-write process, but that mirror writing abruptly disappeared at about age five. Cornell maintains that when children persist in mirror writing, it is a problem of instruction, not a learning disability. Our experience is that when children are taught to write from left to right they will.

Formal Assessment

Formal assessment relies on the use of instruments developed by professionals and published by test publishers. Most of the tests available from test publishers are *standardized*. This means they have been given to a large

FIGURE 8-4
Referral Signals Checklist

	Sometimes	Yes	No
AUDITORY SIGNALS			
Observable Signs, Symptoms, or Complaints			
Fluid running from ears	[ ]	[ ]	[ ]
Frequent earaches	[ ]	[ ]	[ ]
Frequent colds or sore throats	[ ]	[ ]	[ ]
Recurring tonsillitis	[ ]	[ ]	[ ]
Breathes through mouth	[ ]	[ ]	[ ]
Complains of noises in head	[ ]	[ ]	[ ]
Voice too loud or too soft	[ ]	[ ]	[ ]
Delayed or abnormal speech, excessive articulation errors	[ ]	[ ]	[ ]
Seems to "hear what he wants to hear"	[ ]	[ ]	[ ]
Seems to be daydreaming	[ ]	[ ]	[ ]
Often looks puzzled, frowns, or strains when addressed	[ ]	[ ]	[ ]
Appears uninterested in things others find interesting	[ ]	[ ]	[ ]
Observable Behaviors			
Turns or cocks head to hear speaker	[ ]	[ ]	[ ]
Scans when called rather than turning to source	[ ]	[ ]	[ ]
Lack of "paying attention"	[ ]	[ ]	[ ]
Especially inattentive in large groups	[ ]	[ ]	[ ]
Extreme shyness in speaking	[ ]	[ ]	[ ]
Difficulty in following oral directions (and records)	[ ]	[ ]	[ ]
Acts out, appears stubborn, shy, or withdrawn	[ ]	[ ]	[ ]
Marked discrepancy between abilities in verbal and performance test items	[ ]	[ ]	[ ]
Watches classmates to see what they are doing before beginning to participate	[ ]	[ ]	[ ]
Often does not finish work	[ ]	[ ]	[ ]
Hears teacher only when he sees him or her	[ ]	[ ]	[ ]
Hears some days but not others	[ ]	[ ]	[ ]
Gives answers totally unrelated to question asked	[ ]	[ ]	[ ]
Frequently requests repetition or says "huh"	[ ]	[ ]	[ ]
VISUAL SIGNALS			
Observable Signs, Symptoms, or Complaints			
Red eyelids	[ ]	[ ]	[ ]
Pupils turn in, out, up, or down (perhaps independent of each other)	[ ]	[ ]	[ ]

Source: Ruth E. Cook and Virginia B. Armbruster, *Adapting Early Childhood Curricula* (St. Louis: C.V. Mosby Company, © 1983), 51–55. Copyright 1985 Merrill Publishing Company, Columbus, Ohio. Reprinted by permission of Merrill Publishing Company.

FIGURE 8-4 *(continued)*

	Sometimes	Yes	No
Watery eyes or discharges	[ ]	[ ]	[ ]
Crusts on lids or among the lashes	[ ]	[ ]	[ ]
Recurring styes or swollen lids	[ ]	[ ]	[ ]
Pupils of uneven size	[ ]	[ ]	[ ]
Excessive movement of pupils	[ ]	[ ]	[ ]
Drooping eyelids	[ ]	[ ]	[ ]
Excessive rubbing of eyes (seems to brush away blurs)	[ ]	[ ]	[ ]
Shutting or covering one eye	[ ]	[ ]	[ ]
Tracking or focusing difficulties	[ ]	[ ]	[ ]
Headaches or nausea after close work	[ ]	[ ]	[ ]
Tenses up during visual tasks	[ ]	[ ]	[ ]
Squints, blinks, frowns, and distorts face while doing close work	[ ]	[ ]	[ ]

Observable Behaviors

	Sometimes	Yes	No
Tilts head (possibly to use one eye) or thrusts forward	[ ]	[ ]	[ ]
Trys to avoid or complains about light	[ ]	[ ]	[ ]
Complains of pain or ache in eyes	[ ]	[ ]	[ ]
Holds objects close to face	[ ]	[ ]	[ ]
Complains of itchy, scratchy, or stinging eyes	[ ]	[ ]	[ ]
Avoids or is irritable when doing close work	[ ]	[ ]	[ ]
Moves head rather than eyes to look at object	[ ]	[ ]	[ ]
Tires easily after visual tasks	[ ]	[ ]	[ ]
Frequent confusion of similarly shaped letters, numbers, or designs	[ ]	[ ]	[ ]
Unusually clumsy or awkward, trips over small objects	[ ]	[ ]	[ ]
Poor eye-hand coordination	[ ]	[ ]	[ ]
Cannot follow a moving target held 10 to 12 inches in front of him	[ ]	[ ]	[ ]

HEALTH OR PHYSICAL SIGNALS

Observable Signs, Symptoms, or Complaints

	Sometimes	Yes	No
Flushes easily or has slightly bluish color to cheeks, lips, or fingertips	[ ]	[ ]	[ ]
Excessive low-grade fevers or colds	[ ]	[ ]	[ ]
Frequent dry coughs or complains of chest pains after physical exertion	[ ]	[ ]	[ ]
Unusually breathless after exercise	[ ]	[ ]	[ ]
Is extremely slow or sluggish	[ ]	[ ]	[ ]

FIGURE 8-4 *(continued)*

	Sometimes	Yes	No
Is abnormal in size	[ ]	[ ]	[ ]
Is excessively hungry or thirsty	[ ]	[ ]	[ ]
Complains of pains in arms, legs, or joints	[ ]	[ ]	[ ]
Has poor motor control or coordination	[ ]	[ ]	[ ]
Walks awkwardly or with a limp	[ ]	[ ]	[ ]
Shows signs of pain during exercise	[ ]	[ ]	[ ]
Moves in a jerky or shaky manner	[ ]	[ ]	[ ]
Walks on tiptoe, feet turn in	[ ]	[ ]	[ ]
Hives or rashes are evident	[ ]	[ ]	[ ]
Loses weight without dieting	[ ]	[ ]	[ ]
Appears to be easily fatigued	[ ]	[ ]	[ ]

Observable Behaviors

	Sometimes	Yes	No
Moves extremely slowly or in a sluggish manner	[ ]	[ ]	[ ]
Is excessively hungry or thirsty	[ ]	[ ]	[ ]
Complains of pains in arms, legs, or joints	[ ]	[ ]	[ ]
Is excessively restless or overactive	[ ]	[ ]	[ ]
Is extremely inactive, avoids physical exercise	[ ]	[ ]	[ ]
Faints easily	[ ]	[ ]	[ ]
Is extremely inattentive	[ ]	[ ]	[ ]
Is unable to chew and swallow well	[ ]	[ ]	[ ]
Exhibits difficulty with motor tasks, including balance	[ ]	[ ]	[ ]

LEARNING SIGNALS

Observable Signs, Symptoms, or Complaints

	Sometimes	Yes	No
Cries easily, is very easily frustrated	[ ]	[ ]	[ ]
Clumsy, awkward, visual motor difficulties (for example, unusual difficulty with coloring, puzzles, or cutting)	[ ]	[ ]	[ ]
Exhibits visual or auditory perceptual difficulties	[ ]	[ ]	[ ]
Appears easily disturbed by loud noises	[ ]	[ ]	[ ]
Often seems confused or unsure of self	[ ]	[ ]	[ ]

Observable Behaviors

	Sometimes	Yes	No
Works very slowly or rushes through everything	[ ]	[ ]	[ ]
Has difficulty working independently	[ ]	[ ]	[ ]
Is highly distractible, impulsive	[ ]	[ ]	[ ]
Extremely short attention span	[ ]	[ ]	[ ]
Unable to follow directions	[ ]	[ ]	[ ]
Excessively active or excessively inactive	[ ]	[ ]	[ ]
Perseverates (repeats activity over and over)	[ ]	[ ]	[ ]
Seems to catch on quickly in some areas but not in others	[ ]	[ ]	[ ]

FIGURE 8-4 *(continued)*

	Sometimes	Yes	No
Extremely inconsistent in performance	[ ]	[ ]	[ ]
Does not transfer what is learned in one area to another	[ ]	[ ]	[ ]
Actively resists change	[ ]	[ ]	[ ]
Constantly disrupts class	[ ]	[ ]	[ ]
Does not remember classroom routine, other memory problems	[ ]	[ ]	[ ]
Has difficulty making choices	[ ]	[ ]	[ ]
Lacks inventiveness, interests below age level	[ ]	[ ]	[ ]
Learns so very slowly that cannot participate well with others	[ ]	[ ]	[ ]

number of children under the same conditions, i.e., all children received the same instructions and had the same amount of time to complete the test.

Screening. Screening is generally recognized as the application of *quick* and *easily administered* tests to an apparently well population to differentiate between those who are at risk of having the condition being screened for. Screening is needed to identify previously undetected children who are in need of further diagnostic and treatment procedures.[2]

One of the most popular and widely used screening instruments is the Dial — R.[3] It is easily administered and takes only about twenty-five minutes for each child. The Dial — R has been normed for children between the ages of two and six, and there are separate norms for white and nonwhite populations. A *norm* is a sample of a large number of children's behavior — usually thousands — against which a particular behavior can be compared. A *norm-referenced test* is one in which a child's performance is compared to the performance of other children of the same chronological age. Many formal assessment tests are norm-referenced.

The areas that the Dial — R screens are

- *Motor* — catching, jumping, hopping and skipping, building, touching fingers, cutting, matching, copying, and writing one's name.
- *Concepts* — naming colors, identifying body parts, rote counting, meaningful counting, positioning, identifying concepts, naming letters, and sorting chips.
- *Language* — articulating, giving personal data, remembering, naming nouns, naming verbs, classifying foods, problem solving, and sentence length.

Ecological Assessments of Families and Children

This approach includes gathering information about a family, such as its social and economic status and its child-rearing strategies that influence development. Gathering data of this kind can often provide professionals with clues to children's behaviors. Although the environment children are reared in is not always predictive of their behavior, it certainly does influence it to the extent that it may be the source of a special need. In addition, the child's environment may be such that the parents are unaware either that the child has a need or that they can help meet that need. Also, some parents are the cause of the special needs of their children.

Cultural Differences and Assessment

One issue associated with the assessment of young children relates to cultural differences. Cultural differences in the population being screened often lead to the question of whether or not a test is "biased" against a particular cultural group because the test was normed on one cultural group and given to another. This necessitates the use of tests that have been standardized for the particular cultural population being screened. Dial — R, for example, has been normed on both white and nonwhite groups.

TYPES OF HANDICAPPING CONDITIONS

Definition of "Handicapped"

The generally accepted definition of handicapped is that given by the federal government: "The term 'handicapped children' means those children evaluated . . . as being mentally retarded, hard of hearing, deaf, speech-impaired, visually handicapped, seriously emotionally disturbed, orthopedically impaired, other health impaired, deaf-blind, multi-handicapped, or as having specific learning disabilities, who because of these impairments need special education and related services."[4]

Each of the terms used in this definition is defined in more detail in the *Federal Register.* Briefly, these are some of the types of handicaps you are likely to encounter in your work with infants, toddlers, and preschoolers.

- Mental retardation: subaverage intellectual functioning with deficits in adaptive behavior that adversely affects a child's educational performance.
- Hearing impairment: slightly to severely defective hearing that adversely affects a child's educational performance.
- Deafness: hearing impairment to the extent that the child is impaired

in processing linguistic information through hearing, with or without amplification.

- Speech impairment: disorders of expressive or receptive language, such as stuttering, chronic voice disorders, or serious articulation problems affecting social, emotional, and educational achievement.
- Visual handicap or impairment: disorders afflicting both partially seeing and blind children; any loss of visual function sufficient to restrict the learning process.
- Serious emotional disturbance: inability to learn that cannot be explained by intellectual, sensory, or health factors. Inability to build and maintain satisfactory interpersonal relationships. Dangerously aggressive toward others; self-destructive, severely withdrawn, and noncommunicative. Hyperactive to the extent that it affects adaptive behavior. Severely anxious, depressed, psychotic, or autistic.
- Orthopedic impairment: impairments caused by congenital defects, such as club foot, lack of a body member; impairment caused by a disease, such as polio; impairment resulting from another cause, such as an accident.
- Health impairment: illnesses of a chronic and prolonged nature such as epilepsy, hemophilia, asthma, cardiac conditions, severe allergies, blood disorders, diabetes, and neurological disorders.
- Learning disability: disorder in one or more of the basic psychological processes involved in understanding or using language, spoken or written, which may manifest itself in an imperfect ability to listen, think, speak, read, write, spell, or perform mathematical calculations.

The Learning Disabled

Probably no other term in the education of children with special needs has generated as much interest and controversy as *learning disabled*. This is a relatively new term and concept in education. It was coined by Samuel Kirk, a noted special educator.

There is probably not a care-giver who has not used the term or who thought that one or more of the children in her classroom or program was learning disabled. Although there are many definitions of "learning disabled," the one generally accepted is that adopted by the federal government in 1977. According to this definition, a learning disability is

a disorder in one or more of the basic psychological processes involved in understanding or in using language, spoken or written, which may manifest itself in an imperfect ability to listen, think, speak, read, write, spell, or to do mathematical calculations. The term includes such conditions as perceptual handicaps, brain injury, minimal brain dysfunction, dyslexia, and developmental aphasia. The term does not include children who have learning problems which are primarily the result of visual, hearing, or motor handicaps, or mental retardation, or of environmental, cultural or economic disadvantage.[5]

P.L. 94-142 uses the same basic definition of "learning disabled." This act also classifies as learning disabled children whose achievement is below the predicted level for their chronological age when this low level of achievement cannot be explained on the basis of a general disability.

The issue of whether or not a child is learning disabled prior to entering school is a significant one, for placement and funding are contingent on how children are classified. Since the "definitions" of "learning disabled" include the concept that learning disability is associated with the process of schooling, early childhood educators should be cautious in classifying children as learning disabled in the preschool years. As B. A. and J. M. Hare so wisely point out:

> During preschool years, when evidence of learning disabilities is generally clouded by unclear criteria and less than satisfactory measurement devices, a positive approach to preventing school failure is recommended. High priority probably should be given to curricula that include opportunities to learn to attend to critical aspects of the environment, organize information, develop systems to monitor and control one's behavior, and acquire the concepts of language necessary for school success.[6]

As a means of guiding our thinking about the learning disabled child, Kirk and Chalfant have developed a taxonomy of learning disabilities, as

FIGURE 8-5
Taxonomy of Learning Disabilities

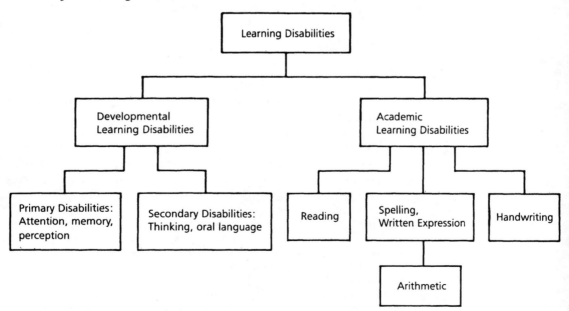

Source: Samuel Kirk and James C. Chalfant, *Academic and Developmental Learning Disabilities* (Denver: Love Publishing, 1984), 8.

TABLE 8-1

Factors Influencing Academic Underachievement

Extrinsic or Environmental Factors	Intrinsic Factors
Economic disadvantage	Mental retardation
Cultural disadvantage	Sensory handicaps
Lack of opportunity	Serious emotional disturbances
Inadequate instruction	Learning disabilities

Source: Samuel Kirk and James C. Chalfant, *Academic and Developmental Learning Disabilities* (Denver: Love Publishing, 1984), 7.

shown in Figure 8-5, and a list of factors influencing academic under-achievement, as shown in Table 8-1.

There are two special issues related to learning disabilities. First, no matter what children's special needs are, they should have the help they need to overcome the barriers to their achieving their potential. Second, there must be a greater effort to prevent problems of all kinds in children through better environmental conditions, better prenatal care, and enhanced parent-child interactions.

Care-givers need to be ever-vigilant to the characteristics of learning disabilities that may be present in young children from birth to age five. These are outlined in Table 8-2. When reviewing these characteristics, keep several things in mind. First, all children during normal growth and development may demonstrate some of these characteristics. What we need to watch for is the persistence of the characteristics over a period of months rather than days. (All children, for example, are hyperactive at one time or another in one setting or another).

Second, we need to be aware of the severity of the characteristics and their causes. Many preschool teachers, for example, say that children have short attention spans. This is a myth. The attention span is directly related to the child's interest in the activity and the training the child has had in attending to a particular task. Also, having a short attention span and being easily distracted are two different things, and they should not be confused in our teaching of young children.

PROGRAMS DESIGNED TO MEET THE SPECIAL NEEDS OF CHILDREN

Head Start

The federal legislation that funds Head Start mandates that at least 10 percent of enrollments in the program be made available to the handicapped. Head Start guidelines also allow 10 percent of the enrollment to be children from families above the income guidelines for admission to Head Start.

TABLE 8-2

Characteristics of Learning Disabilities and Their Observance in Children Before Age Five

Characteristic	Behavioral Description
Hyperactivity	Activity *beyond* the normal limits. This hyperactivity is usually evident from infancy.
Impulsivity	The child acts before he or she thinks.
Distractability	The child has difficulty attending to proper stimuli. Is easily distracted from a task. May not be able to attend to a task for more than a minute. This distractability is observable over time.
Perseveration	Carrying out an activity after it is no longer appropriate. Child may continue to keep running after others have stopped. May start to color grapes purple, but then continue on and color the whole page purple.
Difficulty with spatial relations	Inability to find way in familiar surroundings. Poor body image and difficulty reproducing shapes.
Poor listening ability	This does not include poor hearing; rather, it has to do with inattention and distractability. Child does not seem to register what is said to him.
Difficulty following oral directions	Associated with poor listening ability and lack of attention. The teacher gets the impression not only that the child doesn't hear, but that he or she won't follow directions. Associated with behavior problems.
Poor motor coordination	In the gross motor area, the child may fall down a lot, bump into things, and have difficulty balancing. In the fine motor area, may have difficulty holding pencils and crayons, copying shapes, and drawing.

Source: S. Kenneth Thurman and Anne H. Widerstorm, *Young Children with Special Needs: A Developmental and Ecological Approach* (Boston: Allyn and Bacon, 1985), 56–57.

These slots can also be used to enroll handicapped children. In effect, then, it is possible for 20 percent of the enrollment of a Head Start program to be handicapped children. Table 8-3 shows the types and number of children with handicapping conditions in Head Start programs.

TABLE 8-3

**Types of Handicapping Conditions of Children Professionally
Diagnosed as Handicapped in Head Start**

Handicapping Condition	Number of Children Diagnosed	Percentage of All Children Professionally Diagnosed as Handicapped
Speech impairment	33,460	60.9
Health impairment	6,121	11.2
Specific learning disability	3,242	5.9
Physical handicap (orthopedic)	3,161	5.8
Mental retardation	3,149	5.7
Serious emotional disturbance	2,487	4.5
Hearing impairment	1,701	3.1
Visual impairment	1,310	2.4
Deafness	153	0.3
Blindness	120	0.2
TOTAL	54,904	100.0

Source: "The Status of Handicapped Children in Head Start Programs," eleventh annual report of the U.S. Department of Health and Human Services to the Congress of the United States on services provided to handicapped children in Project Head Start (Washington, D.C.: U.S. Department of Health and Human Services, Head Start Bureau, 1985), 11.

Mainstreaming. Head Start is essentially a mainstreamed program, in which handicapped children are incorporated into the regular Head Start program as the least restrictive environment. As such, Head Start programs have been an example to private and public school programs in leading the way for educating special needs children within programs for average children.

Accessibility of Head Start Programs. Head Start programs serve the handicapped in all parts of the United States — in urban and suburban areas, on Indian reservations, in migrant camps — and in every conceivable kind of facility, including churches, storefronts, houses, and centers. Consequently, Head Start services are fairly accessible to those special needs children and their families who are eligible. Since Head Start reaches only about 18 percent of needy preschool children, however, there are many who need services but don't receive them.

Child Find

Child Find is mandated under the provisions of P.L. 94-142. The purpose of Child Find is to facilitate the identification of handicapped children.

Child Find — Denver, Colorado

Joncee Feakes is an educational evaluator with the Denver Public Schools Child Find Center. This program has as its major purposes:

- Locating, identifying, and evaluating handicapped children between birth and age twenty-one.
- Administering screening and assessment tests.
- Making recommendations about what educational and therapeutic services would best meet the special needs of the handicapped.
- Making referrals of handicapped children and their parents to appropriate agencies.
- Providing community awareness programs and in-services.

Joncee is a member of a full-time team of professionals that consists of a psychologist, an educator (Joncee), a speech therapist, a nurse, and a social worker. During 1985, the Denver Child Find Center identified, evaluated, and referred 875 children.

The Child Find Center identifies handicapped children in a number of ways. They receive some referrals from pediatricians, social workers, neighbors, and parents. Others result from their advertisements on radio, television, in newspapers, and on grocery bags. A third source of referrals is the annual city-wide kindergarten screening program conducted by the Denver public schools in the spring of each year for children entering kindergarten in the fall. Other referrals include those from preschool community agencies and from private schools.

In one instance, the program worked this way: in March, 1985, four-and-a-half-year-old Janice McCrary and her family moved to Denver from Michigan. Janice's mother, Mary, noticed that Janice's two-year-old sister Ellen was catching up developmentally and could do many of the things that Janice was able to do. "At first I didn't pay any attention to it," says Mary. "Like most parents I thought it was just a case of Ellen having a role model and that in time Janice would spurt ahead and that things would be all right. But it didn't work that way. It was almost to the point where Ellen was getting ahead of Janice. We got busy with the move and I kept putting things off, but right after we came to Denver, I took Janice to a pediatrician and she referred me to Child Find. This is how I met Joncee and we started to get the help we needed."

Joncee administered the DIAL — R to Janice, who scored below the developmental norms for her age on this screening test. The Child Find evaluation team then did a complete evaluation of Janice. They determined that she was below normal in cognitive development and was delayed in expressive and receptive language. The Child Find team then recommended the Educational Handicapped Program for Young Pupils (EHPYP), which is a half-day educational and therapeutic program for kindergarten-age children who are developmentally delayed and have two or more handicapping conditions. Since Denver has only a half-day kindergarten program, Janice was placed in the EHPYP program during the mornings and mainstreamed in a half-day kindergarten program in the afternoon.

The Denver Child Find program is very involved in helping handicapped children and parents make the transition from private and federal programs to the public school's half-day kindergarten program. As Joncee explains, "We in the Child Find Program are involved in many interagency contacts, and have developed a great many good working relationships. As a result, the transition from preschool to a mainstreamed kindergarten program is made easier for children and parents. I believe this is one of our most notable accomplishments."

The Handicapped Children's Early Education Program (HCEEP)

Special demonstration programs funded by the Handicapped Children's Early Education Program, one of the special education programs of the U.S. Department of Education, provide technical assistance and training to agencies and personnel serving young handicapped children and their

A nonrestrictive environment, such as a regular early-childhood program, is one in which children can learn and grow in as normal a manner as possible. What can teachers do to facilitate the placement of a special-needs child in a nonrestrictive environment?

families. Un Buen Comienzo, which you will read about later in the chapter, is an HCEEP program.

MAINSTREAMING CHILDREN

The concept of mainstreaming means that children with special needs will be placed in the least restrictive environment, where they are educated and cared for in as normal a manner as possible. *Normalcy* and *least restrictive* are the two key processes. The goal of all placements is to return children to a less restricted environment as soon as possible. Figure 8-6 outlines a continuum of services from the least restrictive to the most restrictive placement.

When handicapped children are mainstreamed in regular settings with children without handicaps, a number of factors must be taken into consideration, as the following account illustrates. The Match-Up Matrix described in the account is a planning guide to help care-givers match the environment to the needs of handicapped children.

Matching Children's Needs with Setting Resources*

Mainstreaming, as noted earlier, is the practice of bringing handicapped children into the "mainstream," a classroom with children who do not have special needs. This practice is growing, for several reasons. First, P.L. 94-142 specifies that the best setting for all children is the "least restrictive environment," the least specialized or the most "normal" setting, ideally a classroom among chronological age peers without special needs. Second, children may learn better from peers than from adults, particularly in social and language skills. Furthermore, children in different groups in mainstreamed classrooms help one another. Third, teachers, parents, and school staff gain a better understanding of handicapping conditions and the children who have them when mainstreaming is used. Parents of "normal" children can avoid the fear and ignorance they experienced with handicapped people by exposing their children early to those who are handicapped.

The placement of a handicapped child in a typical preschool classroom does not guarantee that his or her needs will be met. Decision-makers must recognize that in addition to placing a child in a quality program, each handicapped child's unique needs and strengths must be addressed. They must also realize that educational settings differ in their resources and limitations.

A good match of child needs and setting resources results in a successful placement, one in which all children learn, all staff cooperate, and

---

* This section was written by Mary Wilson, education director of the Orange County Cerebral Palsy Association, A. S. Deane Rehabilitation Center, Goshen, New York.

FIGURE 8-6
Continuum of Services: Least to Most Restrictive

1. Regular programs, with or without supportive services.
2. Regular programs plus supplementary instruction and support.
3. Part-time regular program and part-time special program.
4. Full-time special program placement.
5. Home-bound with home services.
6. Hospital, residential, or total care settings.

the program participants (parents, administrators, teachers, paraprofessionals, and specialists) are satisfied with the results. A mismatch can occur when program participants select a mainstreaming placement without examining the match between child needs and setting resources. This example illustrates how child needs can be matched to a specific setting through planning.

The Setting. Sunshine Preschool and Day Care Center has a "twos and threes" room of fifteen children. Mary Smith, the head teacher, is a college graduate with one year of experience as a certified early childhood teacher. She works with two paraprofessionals: Selma Brown, a grandmother who has worked with children in the day-care center for years, and Cathy Jones, nineteen, a high school graduate taking a year off before enrolling in a community college.

The fifteen children in the twos and threes room vary in skills and needs. Two-thirds of the group have been in child care or a preschool before, and six were in the same group last year with a different teacher. All the children have age-appropriate or better motor, language, cognitive, social, and self-help skills. Half the children are still in diapers.

The program begins at 9 A.M. and ends at 3 P.M. Some children of working parents participate in the center's "before and after" child-care program. The other children are brought to school and picked up by their parents. Lunch is provided by the center. The typical classroom day includes free play; large group circle time; a snack; a planned activity such as art, dramatic play, or a manipulative table task; an outdoor or gross motor activity; lunch; rest time; dressing and toileting times; and a story time.

The Child. Becky is three years old and has spina bifida, a birth defect. As a result, she lacks sensation and motor control below the waist. Becky does not stand or walk indepenently. She does crawl, pull herself into and out of small chairs, and sit independently. She lacks some fine motor coordination in comparison with other children her age, but can easily color with crayons, feed herself, and manipulate simple materials such as stacking blocks. Becky's language skills are above age level: she tells elaborate stories, and though shy at first, she quickly monopolizes a conversation with familiar adults. Becky's developmental assessment indicates no cognitive delays, though her lack of early motor experiences has somewhat affected her ability to discriminate spatial relations. Socially, Becky appears more comfortable with adults than with her peers. This is understandable given her ability to easily engage adults in conversation; young children often move away to do other things. Nevertheless, Becky is very interested and willing to interact with her peers — she merely lacks experience in doing so. With her motor handicap, Becky is unable to dress herself independently, nor can she control her bowel or bladder. With help to support herself, she can help remove or put on clothing. Becky may cry or withdraw from new situations, so she requires gentle encouragement. Like many with spina bifida, she has an internal shunt that prevents cerebral fluid from accumulating in the brain. This medical condition presents no danger to classroom participation and does not limit her in any way.

Becky's parents are very supportive of her early education. She has received physical therapy at home since nine months of age and has participated in play groups with neighborhood children for the past year. Her parents are particularly eager for Becky to be in a preschool with children who do not have special needs. They hope Becky will establish peer relationships with a variety of children and learn coping skills in a regular school setting as preparation for kindergarten.

The Match-up Matrix. The match-up matrix (Figure 8-7) is used to identify child needs (motor, language, cognitive, social, self-help, behavior, medical, and home) and setting resources (training, specialists, equipment and materials, appropriate peers, and aides and helpers). The question asked for each area formed by the matrix is this: Do child needs and setting resources match? If child needs can be met with current setting resources, a + is recorded. If setting resources do not yet meet child needs a − is recorded, and the resources needed to make the match are indicated. Some categories are not applicable to the "match-up" question and are indicated by "N.A." Action by staff members should be taken in any category (motor, self-help, etc.) where a match is lacking. The need for action is indicated by an asterisk (*) in the last column. These actions can be prioritized to indicate to all program participants which resources must be located first (*1, *2, etc.) to permit the "match" and, subsequently, the mainstreaming placement.

In the match-up matrix of Becky's needs and the resources of the twos and threes room, a match is seen in nearly every area. Nevertheless, a few actions are needed before the final placement decision should be made. The motor area is of greatest concern — training and equipment are needed. Though the peers in the twos and threes room are not Becky's motor peers, with adapted seating and mobility, they would be. The matrix indicates the staff need for medical information about spina bifida, especially about the shunt and how it functions. The team gave this second priority. Since self-help skills are an important part of an early childhood curriculum (e.g., snacking, toileting, dressing), the teachers wanted to de-

FIGURE 8-7
Match-up Matrix: Child Characteristics and Setting Resources

SETTING: TWOS AND THREES ROOM CHILD: Becky	TRAINING	SPECIALISTS	EQUIPMENT, MATERIALS	APPROPRIATE PEERS	AID, HELPERS	ACTION
MOTOR	− seating, mobility transfers	+ therapist from home	− wheelchair traffic in classroom	− not yet independent	+ mother volunteers	*1
LANGUAGE	+	N.A.	N.A.	+	N.A.	
COGNITIVE	+	N.A.	N.A.	+	N.A.	
SOCIAL	+	N.A.	N.A.	+	N.A.	
SELF-HELP	− dressing, toileting	+ therapist from home	− potty chair	+	+	*3
BEHAVIOR	+	N.A.	N.A.	+	N.A.	
MEDICAL	− information on shunt	+ doctor, parents, nurse, neurologist	N.A.	N.A.	N.A.	*2
HOME	+	N.A.	N.A.	N.A. only child	+ mother volunteers	*4

velop a plan for these activities with a motor specialist. The last action consisted of scheduling the parent as a classroom resource to facilitate the smooth transition of her child.

The decision: Becky is successfully enrolled in the twos and threes room of Sunshine Preschool and Day Care Center.

Mainstreaming, when realistically planned, can be a positive learning experience for all involved. The match-up matrix is a valuable planning tool that can be used to help make decisions about whether or not to mainstream a child in a classroom. Best of all, the matrix helps staff and parents make decisions on an individualized basis. The match-up matrix does not determine whether a particular program should have mainstreamed classrooms, nor does it determine which children will benefit from a mainstreamed classroom or what setting resources are absolutely necessary for successful mainstreaming of children with special needs. The match-up matrix does, however, organize the questions by which these important decisions can be made using the best approach possible: an individualized one.

Integration — Reverse Mainstreaming

Mainstreaming of another kind — *reverse mainstreaming* or *integration* — is growing in popularity. This is the opposite of the usual mainstreaming process. In a mainstreamed setting, normal children are the majority. Usually, two-thirds of the children are normal and one-third have special needs. Integration places nonhandicapped children in special education settings where handicapped children are the majority. Usually, two-thirds of the children have special needs and one-third of the children are normal.

There are a number of reasons for the growth of the integration movement.

1. It exposes handicapped children to nonhandicapped children.
2. "Normal" children can model normal behavior.
3. The social environment of the special setting is changed to include a range of children and behaviors.
4. Integration gives all children the opportunity to learn about individual differences.
5. Integration helps teachers maintain a perspective on normal development.
6. Inclusion of normal children provides natural helpers in the classroom.
7. Integration provides models for peer helping.

When integration occurs, we assume it is a positive experience for all. In a well-run program, handicapped children imitate and learn from normal children. The nonhandicapped have a better opportunity to learn skills such as turn-taking and independence. They also learn different kinds of behavior standards and different ways of completing tasks. Staff and parents are reminded that normal isn't perfect. The staff are also continually reminded of how young children behave. A normal three-year-old, for example, can show the staff how a three-year-old plays.

When considering integration there are a number of things to keep in mind:

1. The staff might need special training to help them teach special needs children.
2. The benefits of integration to children should be explained to the parents of both handicapped and nonhandicapped children.
3. The staff must ensure that the normal children receive the instruction they need to maintain normal development.
4. Staff must develop, explain, and maintain different rules for the two populations. A care-giver might explain, for example, "Johnny has to learn how to run, so he is allowed to run across the room. You already know how to run, so you can't run across the room."

5. An environment and materials that will support both groups must be established.
6. Nonhandicapped children of the same approximate age and developmental levels should be integrated with the handicapped.
7. Additional help may be needed, such as an aide or assistant.

ISSUES IN THE EDUCATION AND CARE OF SPECIAL NEEDS CHILDREN

Care-givers must consider a number of different issues in their work with handicapped children. They must ask such questions as how effective are current programs for meeting the needs of special needs children? What kinds of intervention programs work best? How should care-givers deliver an intervention program? Are intervention programs the best way to meet the needs of handicapped children, or would a family-based program drawing on the services of other agencies be better?

Care-givers and other professionals must know how to identify handicapped children and give them the services they need. If 50 percent of the women with children under six work, for example, then a significant number of children are being given care in family day-care settings or by babysitters. It is likely that a significant number of these children are handicapped in some way. Care-givers must ask how professionals can provide these children with the services they need.

Another issue is how professionals and parents can work together to prevent handicapping conditions. It is always better to prevent problems than to try and correct them after the fact. It is also more humane and dignified for the children and parents involved. One way to prevent handicapping conditions is to provide adequate income, housing, health care, and education for parents and children early in life. Proper health care and nutrition prior to and during pregnancy can prevent many pre- and postnatal diseases and disabilities. Another approach is to provide parenting education for all, before and after they become parents. This would give all parents the information and support they need to know what is best for them and their children. All children should be introduced to parenting skills beginning in the home and continuing in child care, preschool, and throughout grade school and high school. We need a fourth "R" — reading, 'riting, 'rithmetic, and *rearing*.

Finally, care-givers must learn how to avoid labeling unhandicapped children as handicapped in order to provide them with special education services. More regular education options to meet the requirements of children who are not handicapped are needed. The tendency has been to identify children as handicapped, and especially as learning disabled, in order to give them the help they need.

TRENDS IN MEETING THE SPECIAL NEEDS OF THE VERY YOUNG

Looking at the long-range future of meeting the special needs of the very young, a number of trends are apparent. First, the development of public school preschool programs for children with special needs should increase. There is growing recognition among public school educators that they have the funding base, material, and professional resources to provide for the needs of preschool handicapped children. This trend means that public schools will serve a broader range of children with special needs than they have in the past.

Second, the number of trained and certified personnel working with children with special needs must be increased. It is likely that more states will offer and require certification as a prerequisite for working with special needs children. Career opportunities for people desiring to work with special needs children will also increase.

Third, the use of an *interdisciplinary* approach to meeting the needs of special children should continue. Special education has probably been better than other disciplines in promoting a comprehensive approach to education.

Fourth, the integration of the nonhandicapped in special programs should continue. More parents of nonhandicapped children will recognize the benefits that accrue to all through integration.

Fifth, the training of early childhood educators, child-care workers, and parents in the skills they need to work with handicapped children will continue.

Finally, since family child care is the preferred type of care among all parents, there will be more emphasis on how to train family child-care providers in the skills they need to be intervention specialists with handicapped children in family day care.

Implications for care-givers

1. Accept all children and families regardless of their special needs. Care-giver acceptance is the first step in making children and parents feel wanted and secure in a program. Care-giver acceptance sets the tone and example for peer acceptance.
2. Include all children in all class activities. This involvement is based on the premise that activities and environments can be modified to permit participation by everyone.
3. Work with parents to help them and their children. (See Chapter 9 for specific suggestions for working with parents.)
4. Involve handicapped and nonhandicapped children in teams and groups to work together and help each other. Children learn from each other and from the earliest ages can and should be involved in situations where they can help and support each other.

5. Build positive, independent behavior in children. Children want to do things for themselves, and they learn by doing things for themselves. Care-givers must give handicapped children opportunities to do things for themselves by modifying the environment and learning activities.

   Positive behavior is built in part by care-givers' rewarding children for the good things they do. Don't be afraid to give genuine praise for good jobs and positive efforts.
6. Have goals and objectives for each child, based on developmental and behavioral abilities. This is the essence and purpose of the IEP. The IEP is an appropriate planning document for *all* children. Children need appropriate goals and activities adjusted to their abilities. Some children need more time than others to complete a task. Other children need learning activities divided into small learning tasks (see Chapter 6). Give children opportunities to practice what they are learning.
7. Use a variety of approaches to account for different learning styles in children. Use visual media such as big, bright pictures. Provide opportunities for children to do things with their hands, such as water play, toy dismantling, puzzles, cutting, and pasting. Repeat directions when necessary, have children repeat directions, and teach specific listening skills.

THE GIFTED

At two years of age, Lisa Cardinas could read such words as "refrigerator," "stove," and "television." At two-and-a-half, she could read whole sentences, and at three, she was reading books. She and her mother often go to the library and check out reading material. At her preschool, Lisa frequently reads stories to the other children during story hour.

Lisa's mother always suspected there was something special about Lisa. After consulting with the preschool administrator, she took Lisa to a local psychologist. The psychologist interviewed Lisa's parents and administered a series of tests. She identified Lisa as gifted and recommended several private schools that specialize in education for the gifted.

Lisa is a lucky child, for several reasons. First, she has a mother who can identify early signs of giftedness. Second, her parents are motivated to do something about her giftedness. Third, Lisa's giftedness is rather easy to identify.

"Gifted": A Definition

There are many forms of giftedness, but many gifted children are never identified. P.L. 97-35, the Education Consolidation and Improvement Act of 1981, identifies the gifted as "children who give evidence of high performance capability in areas such as intellectual, creative, artistic, leadership capacity, or specific academic fields, and who require services or activities not ordinarily provided by the school in order to fully develop such capabilities."[7]

Despite this "official" definition, there is not universal agreement about how to define the gifted, how to identify them, or whether they should receive special services. As is evident from the definition given, the abilities involved in being gifted and talented are not readily identified by existing testing instruments. The gifted and talented are usually identified through a series of tests and interviews with parents, teachers, and the child. Clearly, giftedness is much more than I.Q. It occurs among children from all social, economic and cultural groups.

There has been much more interest in identifying the handicapped than the gifted. This may be because it is easier to identify behavior and characteristics associated with being handicapped than those associated with being gifted. Also, as the definition implies when it refers to "services or activities not ordinarily provided by the schools," giftedness is frequently perceived as a characteristic identified when a child enters school.

Giftedness in the Very Young

The general belief is that the earlier giftedness is identified, the earlier caregivers can do something to promote it. A traditional method for identifying giftedness, the I.Q. test, does not work well with infants because intelligence in preverbal infants is not readily measured by traditional I.Q. tests.

Michael Lewis and Linda Michalson, professors at the Rutgers Medical School, believe there is a constellation of characteristics that identify young children who have the potential for being gifted.[8]

1. Cognitive abilities — curiosity, attention, and superior memory.
2. Language abilities — early use of sounds, first words, and speech.
3. Affective characteristics — pleasure in learning, positive self-concept, persistence, and task orientation.
4. Social knowledge and relationships — development of social knowledge (knowledge of others and their behaviors) and good socioemotional adjustment. (Young children who show signs of giftedness may have behavior problems, however).
5. Family interaction and environment — Parental responses that provide expriences, support, and encouragement for learning and independence.
6. Demographic variables — birth order may be a factor in giftedness, since mothers give first-born children more attention and stimulation.

Lewis and Michalson point out the developmental nature of giftedness and the importance of environmental interactions:

The development of giftedness, like all development, is a complex phenomenon, involving attributes of both child and the environment, and overlaid with

Early-childhood teachers should always be alert for signs of giftedness in young children. Once these children are identified, teachers should nurture and encourage that giftedness. What specific things can care-givers do to support the development of giftedness?

the possibility of a transformation of skills across age. One reason . . . for the difficulty in identifying gifted infants may be that the concept "gifted infant" is unwarranted; the reality may be that during infancy there is only a potential for giftedness that requires some "optimal" environment for development. In contrast to handicapping conditions, giftedness may not exist early in life, but emerge only as the product of an interaction between infants' genetic endowments and the environments in which they are raised.[9]

Implications for care-givers. Care-givers need to be alert to indicators of giftedness. The earliest sign is rapid development. Many gifted children do things earlier than their normal counterparts, and they are very alert and interested in almost everything. Other signs to look for are:

1. Early learning of any kind. This includes early reading, use of math skills, and talking. Many parents of the gifted report that their children learn to read by themselves at an early age.
2. Above-average curiosity. Gifted children are perpetually curious about, for example, how things work, fit together, or come apart.
3. Enhanced linguistic abilities, including an advanced vocabulary and a high frequency of questions.
4. Good memory skills. The gifted preschool child can remember many words, numbers, and signs.
5. Above average in physical development and health.
6. Ability to concentrate over long periods of time.
7. Independence. Gifted children are usually independent very early. They want to do things for themselves and, within reason and safety, should be allowed to do so.

There are a number of processes care-givers can promote in order to encourage children who may be gifted.

1. Provide opportunities for children to develop more advanced skills. A gifted preschooler may have no difficulty mastering skills taught in kindergarten and first grade. None of these activities should be done with any sense of hurrying or pushing the child. However, the gifted child may become easily bored by "normal" and "routine" activities.

   In preschool programs, the curriculum enrichment approach is the preferred method of providing for the gifted. In this way, the gifted remain with their age peers and learn and develop appropriate social skills. In addition, having the gifted and nongifted in the same classroom benefits all the children as a result of the enriched curriculum.

2. Enrichment provides opportunities for gifted children to have broader, more diverse kinds of experiences in areas related to a particular talent or ability. A three-year-old gifted in mathematics might count the money donated to the wishing well at a local shopping center. A gifted four-year-old could help other children — older and younger — learn computer skills.

3. Gifted children may need help in the areas in which they are not gifted. Four-year-old Lisa, for example, reads at a third-grade level but lacks interpersonal skills necessary for getting along with other children.

4. Provide an environment in which gifted children can use their talents and abilities. The primary factor in helping children develop their potential for giftedness is an interactive environment that supports the development of their abilities.

MULTICULTURAL EDUCATION

The United States has always benefited from the heritages and cultures of other countries. America prides itself on being a country where people from all backgrounds can find opportunity and acceptance. This is true today more than ever. In many cities — Los Angeles, Miami, San Antonio — the majority culture today was formerly a minority culture.

Some early childhood programs find they don't have a majority of children from any country. In one preschool program, there are children from Israel, Honduras, Nicaragua, Cuba, Puerto Rico, Argentina, Nigeria, Saudi Arabia, Columbia, Haiti, and the United States.

Children are influenced by and learn from the homes in which they live. These homes usually reflect the culture of the parents. Different cultures follow different customs regarding communication, interactions with others, and child rearing. For many parents and children, being assimilated into the American educational system is a difficult and sometimes unpleasant process. All care-givers and early childhood professionals must

Care-givers must accept and respect children from all cultures. How can care-givers promote multicultural education and understanding in their programs?

help parents and children make the transition to the educational and social processes of American culture.

Implications for care-givers. Care-givers must strive to create an environment and program in which children and parents will feel comfortable and accepted regardless of their cultural background. This can involve a number of attitudes and practices.

1. Accept all children and parents as unique individuals without regard to their culture. Each parent and child has something special to contribute to the program.
2. Promote the uniqueness of each child as a positive attribute.
3. Learn about the cultures of children entrusted to your care. Knowledge of these cultures can be used to help plan the curriculum and teaching activities. In one program, an ongoing curricular theme is "Around the World." Throughout the year, the children "visit" the cultures of every child. These visits cover authentic dress, foods (many of which the children help prepare), customs, music, toys, games, books, and special days. All cognitive, behavioral, social, and psychomotor skills are integrated into this thematic approach.

   Finding out about the customs and practices of others also helps care-givers avoid "cultural mistakes" such as one care-giver made when he first taught Vietnamese preschoolers. He invited them to the "circle time" activity by beckoning with his index finger. Fortunately, he had a Vietnamese parent as an aide, who told him about his cultural faux pas. Beckoning with the index finger is a gesture the Vietnamese use when they want dogs, not children, to come to them.

4. Exhibit an accepting and respectful attitude toward all cultures and people.
5. Work with parents to orient them to customs and practices in the United States and in the program. Many American practices are strange to others and can conflict with their beliefs. Many South American Hispanics, for example, have beliefs about early autonomy and independence that conflict with traditional American ideas. Some Hispanic parents still have children on bottles at age four, and some Hispanic children are still being fed by parents or a nurse at age five.
6. Every effort should be made to communicate with parents in their native language, especially when they have a limited knowledge of English. Bilingual staff and parents can be enlisted to help parents learn about the program in their own language.
7. Share your own heritage with children and other staff members.
8. Identify and use in your program such ethnic resources as parents, community residents, and foreign consuls and embassies.
9. Attend and be a part of ethnic activities sponsored in your community. Share your experiences with children and other staff members.

UN BUEN COMIENZO (A GOOD BEGINNING)

A noteworthy effort to provide for both the cultural and special needs of handicapped children who require day-care and their working parents is Un Buen Comienzo, a federally funded model demonstration program located at Rosemount Center in Washington Center in Washington, D.C. This program offers mainstreaming services in day-care for children from four weeks to four years old who have mild to moderate special needs. Special education and early intervention services are provided at the day-care site by a bilingual, multidisciplinary team comprised of a speech pathologist, an infant special educator, an occupational therapist, a family liaison coordinator, and a consulting developmental pediatrician and pscyhologist.

The program is bilingual and multicultural and offers the following services:

1. Screening and assessment for infants at risk and young children with suspected developmental delays. All testing and reports are in Spanish or English.
2. Direct intervention services for children at their day-care sites, provided in their native language (Spanish or English).

Books in children's native languages help them learn important concepts, thus providing feelings of success and accomplishment. What can teachers do to promote language development in all children, regardless of the language they speak?

3. Bilingual communications with parents and providers, including informal discussions, notes, consultations, and formal meetings.
4. Bilingual training programs for parents and day-care providers.

Program personnel plan to publish three manuals about the program. Two of these, for home providers of family day-care, will be available in Spanish and English. The third manual will contain information on replication of this program.

SUMMARY

The important endeavor of meeting the needs of children and families with special needs presents several challenges. The first challenge involves awareness, understanding, and knowledge. Most care-givers will agree that the early identification, care, and education of young children with special needs, regardless of what those needs are, can make a difference in the children's lives and those of their parents. This basic belief, however, needs to be implemented by taxpayers, legislators, and *all* early childhood educators and care-givers. Building public awareness of the needs and challenges involved in meeting children's special needs would be a giant step toward providing children with the best possible education. Everyone must believe that any child who has a special need — regardless of the need, the child's age, and the genetic, environmental, or social circumstance that created the need — has a right to programs that ensure their best developmental outcome.

Awareness, however, is not enough. A second challenge involves resources such as money, time, and talent. Material and human resources are necessary to provide the special programs and program adaptations necessary to meet children's special needs. Care-givers can do many things to adapt programs and mainstream children that do not cost money, but it would be foolhardy to believe that special needs can be met without adequate resources.

A third challenge relates to care-givers themselves. Care-givers must dedicate themselves to their own professional development so that they know and understand their roles and what they can do to help meet children's special needs. Care-givers who are responsible for the care of children with special needs will learn all they need to know to address special needs properly. Care-givers must also be willing to advocate on behalf of special needs children and their parents for programs designed to meet particular needs.

How well care-givers, the early childhood profession, and the public meet these three challenges will determine to a large extent how well the needs of special needs children are met.

PROGRAM VIGNETTE

United Cerebral Palsy Center
Denver, Colorado

Fifteen-month-old Ben Hightower has Down's syndrome. Ten years ago the prognosis for a child like Ben would have been bleak. Today, Ben has a bright future because of changed attitudes, caring parents, and a dedicated team of professionals at the United Cerebral Palsy Center. According to Janet Speirer, coordinator of the Infant Development Program, "Early intervention increases Ben's potential for being educated and employed. We know now that children with Down's syndrome can make great gains as a result of early intervention. Ben started in our program when he was one month old. This has given us a chance to develop a program that will help Ben reach his fullest potential."

Ben's parents, Kathy and Bill, bring him to the center twice a week for one-hour sessions. Kathy and Bill are young professionals who have been able to arrange their work schedules so they can be involved in and share Ben's educational and therapeutic program. Kathy brings Ben on Monday mornings and Bill brings him on Wednesday afternoons.

During these one-hour sessions, Ben and his parents meet with a *transdisciplinary* team. This team is headed by an early childhood educator and includes an occupational therapist, physical therapist, and speech therapist. This team is a key ingredient in the service delivery program. In this approach, each team member trains the others about his or her goals for Ben. During the session, only one team member works directly with Ben and his parent. The other members are present so the team member conducting the session can, when necessary, gain support and clarification concerning activities and information.

"We know that infants cannot take too much stimulation from too many people at one time," says Janet, who is also the early childhood educator for the infant program. "Too much stimulation is counterproductive to learning, and when overstimulated, an infant will "shut down," so we give the parent and child one person to interact with during the session. It is also easier for parents to deal with one team member at a time. However, if there is anything that needs to be clarified, the others are there to help."

When Ben entered the program, he was assessed by the team in order to determine his specific needs and to develop a preliminary program of objectives and activities. One of the instruments used in the assessment process was the Hawaii Early Learning Program (HELP). Following the initial assessment, a *staffing meeting* was held. Ben's parents, the team members, and a social worker attended the meeting. Assessment information was shared and Bill and Kathy stated their views about Ben, his abilities, and what they hoped would be done for him. Goals and objectives were cooperatively projected for Ben's education and development. Following this staffing meeting, an *Individual Program Plan* (IPP) (the same as an IEP) was written. It included goals, objectives, suggested activities, and target dates for attaining objectives. The IPP was approved by Bill and Kathy and is reviewed and updated every six months. Refer back to Figures 8-1 and 8-2 (pp. 278–279) for Ben's diagnosis and language IPP.

During the visits, the team conducts training. The focus of the training is the parent, in keeping with the team's belief that the parents are the first and primary teachers of their children. Janet articulates the staff's philosophy this way: "The parent is the one who needs to integrate knowledge, information about the child, and what we are teaching, in everyday life activities in order for the plan to be effective. We empower parents when we give them a good knowledge base. When parents understand what to do, they can do it in the family setting and the child profits."

During the first forty-five minutes of the session, a team member works with Ben and his mother or father. Today, Kyo Miller, the occupational therapist, conducts the session. The team previously observed that Ben was hitching across the floor instead of crawling. It is normal for some children to hitch, but they don't want Ben to use hitching to replace the normal developmental routine of creeping and crawling. It is important for Ben to learn to support his weight on all fours. Kyo shows Kathy how to do this with Ben and demonstrates activities she can do at home to achieve the team's goal of having Ben assume a quadruped position.

Another IPP goal is to have Ben nest two and three objects. Kyo shows Kathy how to do nesting activities and then offers her suggestions about how to generalize the objective into everyday activities using cans, cups, plastic bowls, and measuring cups.

The final fifteen minutes are devoted to a parenting training session. With a group of four parents, one of the team members discusses such topics as normal child growth and development; language development; selection and use of toys; and how children learn through play.

The team is a professional group, dedicated to offering a full range of educational services with therapeutic support. They view themselves as an integrated team working for the enhancement of the lives of children and parents. "I'm part of the team," says Kyo. "As an occupational therapist, I have to work with Ben as a whole child. Without all of the areas working together — gross motor, fine motor, language, and cognitive — Ben won't develop to his full potential. I'm happy to share my trained skills with the transdisciplinary team in order to promote the maximum development of children."

Judith Burch-Jones, the team speech and language pathologist, believes that language and learning are integrated processes. "My experience tells me that if a child's language is impaired, his learning will be also. If a child doesn't understand language, then his knowledge of the world is limited. Parents of handicapped children sometimes focus too much on the gross motor rather than on language development. Part of my job is to keep reminding parents and my team members about the importance of communication. The most frustrating thing for the handicapped is their inability to communicate. For many, if they could express themselves well they would be happier. It gives a person dignity as an individual when she can express herself."

Play is a central part of the educational and therapeutic programs. The team emphasizes the development of all of the skill areas through play. They make special efforts to show parents how to adapt the environment to help children learn. "If you can't move it is difficult to explore your environment," says Jill Valenti, the physical therapist. "For many of the handicapped, it is physically difficult to be mobile in their surroundings. Therefore, we have to work on helping parents learn how to adapt the environment so it can be brought to children. If a child's learning does come from the environment — and our team believes it does — a handicapped child, because of motor disabilities, may not be able to be involved in the environment. Therefore, it is up to parents — and care-givers — to bring the environment to the child through adaptations. For example, a child who does not have trunk control may not be able to use his hands. By showing the parent how to use a seat insert to improve the child's trunk control, however, we can enable him to use his hands. We have adapted the environment to him. Also, many traditional pull toys have slippery plastic cords, which are difficult for some handicapped children to grasp. A successful adaptation would be substituting plastic links into a pull chain, which enables the child to get a good grip."

One of the basic features of the CP program is working with parents to help them help their children. "When parents understand what to do and are able to do it, then they and their children profit," asserts Janet. She admits, however, that working with parents is no easy task. Parents of handicapped children first have to recognize that their children have a handicap and that there are things that they can do as parents to help them. "For many parents, the most positive step they can take is to come through the door to our program," says Janet. "Once they do we can really start to help them."

The Denver Cerebral Palsy program has a number of unique features. First, it has a dedicated staff. It may sound trite to say that a dedicated staff is a critical ingredient of a good program, but it needs to be said. This program is good because of Janet, Kyo, Judith, and Jill. They are dedicated to helping parents and their handicapped children have better lives now and in the future. In addition, these care-givers, individually and as a team, are able to articulate well what they believe and why they believe it, which is a true mark of the professional.

Second is the use of a transdisciplinary team. The use of such a team is the best way to deliver educational and therapeutic services to parents and children. Parents of the handicapped have to deal with many specialists. It makes sense to have a team of specialists to help, but to work with one specialist at a time.

The third feature is parent involvement. Many programs say they have parent involvement, but often parents are only involved to satisfy program requirements or because care-givers view it as helping *them* in some regard (see Chapter 9.) Not so in this program. Parents are involved with the specific intent of empowering them in their roles as the primary educators of their children. Training sessions are also provided in parent advocacy strategies and how to make the transition between home and school easier for parents and their children.

ENRICHMENT THROUGH ACTIVITIES

1. In the vignette on the Denver Cerebral Palsy program, speech pathologist Judith Burch-Jones said that cognitive development occurs through language. "If you don't have language you don't have learning."
   a) Do you agree or disagree with Judith's view of the relation of cognitive development to language development? Why or why not?
   b) Compare Judith's view of language development to the theories presented in Chapters 2 and 3.
2. Mary Brian visited many child-care centers in search of the one that was right for her daughter. The one she liked most was for children with mild to moderate handicaps. The administrator is planning a program of integrating nonhandicapped children into the preschool child setting. Mary, however, is reluctant to enroll her daughter in a program designed especially for special education.
   a) What are the pros and cons of enrolling a nonhandicapped child in a special education program?
   b) What would you advise Mary to do?
   c) Develop a list of questions Mary might ask the administrator of the program that will help her make her decision.
3. Visit child-care programs and preschools that take care of children from different cultures. Through interviews with care-givers and parents, determine specific ways that culture influences the following, and give examples:
   a) Language development

      b) Eating habits

      c) Discipline

      d) Parent-child relationships

      How can care-givers take these differences into account in programs where there are children from many cultures?

4. List appropriate curriculum topics that can be used with the very young on an annual basis. Show with specific activities and examples how these topics can be made multicultural.

5. List five behavioral differences between toddlers and preschoolers. Are these differences recognized in other cultures? Give specific examples.

6. How can the Match-Up Matrix developed by Mary Wilson help care-givers provide for the needs of handicapped children? What do you think are the most important features of the Match-Up Matrix?

7. Interview care-givers who work with special needs children.

      a) What do they consider to be their biggest challenges?

      b) What special training have they had that they found particularly helpful?

      c) What further training do they think would help them in their work with special needs children?

8. Visit a preschool program for handicapped children. In a three-page paper, describe the curriculum used, the nature of staff-child interactions, and your impression of the program.

9. Interview a care-giver whose main task is providing care for a handicapped infant. Describe this person's major responsibilities. What are the rewards the care-giver receives? What do you learn from your interview?

10. Would you want your child to attend either of the two programs described in this chapter? Why? Why not?

ENRICHMENT THROUGH READING

Adams, Barbara. *Like It Is: Facts and Feelings About Handicaps from Kids You Know.* New York: Walker and Company, 1979.

    A realistic and honest presentation by handicapped children and youths, who tell in their own ways about their various handicaps, their special needs, and their desire to be treated like everyone else. Chapters deal with hearing and speech impairment, visual impairment, orthopedic handicaps, developmental disabilities and mental retardation, learning disabilities, and behavior disorders. Excellent first-person vignettes.

Buscaglia, Leo. *The Disabled and Their Parents: A Counseling Challenge.* New York: Holt, Rinehart and Winston, 1983.

    Buscaglia believes the disabled and their families need reality-based guidance. He challenges professionals to provide better information on the nature and implications of each disability and the complex problems of day-to-day living.

Brown, Tricia, and Ortiz, Fran. *Someone Special Just like You.* New York: Holt, Rinehart and Winston, 1984.

    This picture book with supporting text shows special needs children engaged in many activities that all children like to do. The accounts can help children, teachers, and parents understand that handicaps need not separate children from the experiences that are vital to growing and a happy life. The underlying theme here is normalcy — being accepted and having opportunities to participate in all of life's enriching activities.

Featherstone, Helen. *A Difference in the Family: Life with a Disabled Child*. New York: Basic Books, 1980.

Written by the parent of a seriously disabled child, this book deals with the problems and pleasures of rearing the handicapped. In the introduction, the author states her purpose this way: "In this book I describe the pain and other feelings — both good and bad — that come with membership in a particular sort of family. I focus on the family with a difference, the family of a handicapped child. I am also concerned with families in general and with how they endure any serious trouble." This book is sensibly and sensitively written. It should be required reading for all who work with special needs children and their parents.

Mitchell, Joyce Slayton. *Taking on the World: Empowering Strategies for Parents of Children with Disabilities*. New York: Harcourt Brace Jovanovich, 1982.

An enthusiastic, action-filled manual with step-by-step directions and practical advice on how to be an advocate for children with disabilities. Part One deals with how to take on the worlds of the family, medicine, the school, church, work, and bureaucracy. Part Two deals with empowering strategies and provides advice on how to stabilize, mobilize, and activate.

National Center for Clinical Infant Programs. *Equals in This Partnership: Parents of Disabled and At-Risk Infants and Toddlers Speak to Professionals*. Washington, D.C.: National Center for Clinical Infant Programs, 1984.

In 1984, a conference, "Comprehensive Approaches to Disabled and At-Risk Infants and Toddlers," was held in Washington, D.C. This conference gave people an opportunity to learn about the work and concerns of early childhood professionals and the parents of disabled and at-risk young children. This booklet contains the proceedings of that conference. The main premise is that parents and families, not professionals and consultants, have to be in charge of the education and care of their handicapped children — a refreshing and hopefully contagious point of view. This should be read by all early childhood educators who work with special needs children.

Webb, James T.; Meckstroth, Elizabeth A.; and Tolan, Stephanie S. *Guiding the Gifted Child: A Practical Source for Parents and Teachers*. Columbus: Ohio Psychology Publishing Company, 1982.

The authors provide much useful information about their experiences in working with parents of gifted children. They believe that helping parents help their gifted children is a critical endeavor, especially in places where schools or other programs don't provide services for gifted children. Sections on resources for developing skills in guiding gifted children and on organizations that work with parents are particularly useful.

NOTES

1. James M. Cornell, "Spontaneous Mirror-Writing in Children," *Canadian Journal of Psychology* 39 (March, 1985): 174–179.

2. Nicholas J. Anastasiow, William K. Frankenbure, and Alma W. Fandal, *Identifying the Developmentally Delayed Child* (Baltimore: University Park Press, 1982), xi.

3. Carol D. Mardell and Dorthea S. Goldberg, *Dial — R: Developmental Indicators for the Assessment of Learning — Revised* (Edison, N.J.: Childcraft Education Corporation, 1983).

4. *Federal Register,* vol. 42, no. 163 (August 23, 1977), 42,478.

5. *Federal Register,* vol. 42, no. 250 (December 29, 1977), 65,083.

6. B. A. Hare and J. M. Hare, "Learning Disabilities in Young Children," in *Educating Young Handicapped Children: A Developmental Approach,* ed. S. G. Garwood (Germantown, Md.: Aspen Systems, 1979), 287–288.

7. Education Consolidation and Improvement Act, 1981, sec. 582.

8. Michael Lewis and Linda Michalson, "The Gifted Infant," in *The Psychology of Gifted Children,* ed. Joan Freeman (New York: John Wiley, 1985), 42–47.

9. Lewis and Michalson, "Gifted Infant," 55.

Chapter 9

Involving the Parents of the Children We Care For

Questions to Guide Your Reading and Study

- Why do parents want to be involved in early childhood programs?
- Why should care-givers involve parents in their programs?
- What is parent involvement?
- Why are some parents not involved in early childhood programs?
- How does the concept of readiness apply to parent involvement programs?
- How is parent involvement a developmental process?
- What are the five levels of parent involvement?
- What roles can the community play in parent involvement?
- Why is it important for care-givers to develop positive attitudes toward parents?
- What are the essential steps in conducting successful parent conferences?
- What are the special needs of parents and how do they influence a successful program of parent involvement?
- How can care-givers provide for the special needs of parents?
- How can care-givers involve fathers in their programs?
- Why are home visitations important?
- What are current issues related to parent involvement?

INTRODUCTION

Mark Twain said that everybody talks about the weather, but nobody does anything about it. The same used to be true of parent involvement. Now more programs are not only talking about it, they are doing something about it. More early childhood educators are asking, "Is it possible to operate quality preschool programs without parent involvement?" More and more programs are answering this question with a resounding no and are recognizing the value of parent involvement in all facets of early childhood programs.

Why Parent Involvement?

There are a number of compelling reasons why early childhood educators are incorporating parents into their programs:

Parents Want to Be Involved. For the last decade, parents have demonstrated their desire to be involved in their children's education and welfare through consumer education, civil rights advocacy, the feminist movement, child advocacy, and, currently, through the child abuse reform movement. This almost intuitive desire of parents to be involved will become even stronger and add impetus to care-givers' efforts to find ways to meaningfully involve parents.

Increased Achievement and Social Skills. When parents are involved, children's self-images and achievements increase. Young children who have had a positive preschool setting as well as supportive and involved parents do better on academic and social skills than children who don't have such support.[1] Children see parent involvement as a signal that their parents value education, and then they, too, perceive education and schooling as valuable. Children mirror their parents' values and enthusiasms. When they see their parents involved in the program, they don't get the feeling that their parents are just "dumping them off" and forgetting them.

Parent Support. Parents are more supportive of programs in which they have direct contact and meaningful involvement. If early childhood educators want support for quality programs, one certain way to achieve it is through parent involvement. Parents are the support base of a program, and their involvement ensures a firm foundation.

Parent Rights. Early childhood educators recognize that parents have a right to be involved in programs that affect them. This right is bestowed on parents when programs accept their children and money for services rendered.

Parent Duty. Every parent has a duty to be involved in some way for at least the time their children are in a program. No parent should be ab-

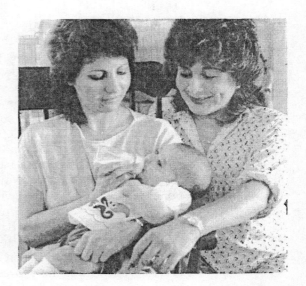

Parents want and need to be involved in the programs that provide services to them and their children. This mother and care-giver have developed a special rapport that enables them to feel good about each other. How does such rapport develop?

solved from the responsibility of being involved, at some level, in a program that provides a major service to them and their children.

Legislation. Specific legislation, especially legislation related to programs receiving federal and state funds, mandates parent involvement. Specifically, P.L. 94-142, the Education for All Handicapped Children Act (see Chapter 8), mandates parent involvement when children receive services supported by federal monies. State laws may also specify parent involvement. The state of Florida Basic Education Act of 1975, for example, encourages parent involvement in the development of educational plans for primary children.

Parent Involvement: A Definition

A definition of parent involvement is helpful, for it provides a common understanding about this important process.

Kevin Swick, parent involvement specialist at the University of South Carolina at Columbia, defines parent involvement as consisting of three parts. First, it is "a partnership between parents and teachers and their 'helpers' in the community." Second, it is "a developmental process that is built over a period of time through intentional planning and effort of every team member." Third, it is "a process by which parents and teachers work, learn, and participate in decision-making experiences in a shared manner."[2] Swick views parent involvement as a developmental process characterized by partnership and shared decision making.

In an earlier work, the author of the present work defined parent involvement as the "process of actualizing the potential of parents; of helping parents discover their strengths, potentialities, and talents; and of using them for the benefit of themselves and the family."[3] The central focus in this definition was on the parent rather than on the child, program, or agency. This definition, however, does not strike a balance between the three participants in the partnership: children, parents, and agency. Consequently, a better definition would be *parent involvement is a process of helping parents use their abilities to benefit themselves, their children, and the early childhood program.* In this definition, parents are still first in the process, children second, and programs last. Although all three parties benefit from a well-planned program of parent involvement, parents should be the major focus of care-givers' efforts. A good program of parent involvement benefits everyone. It is a "win-win" situation.

The locus of control in parent-child-family interactions is the parent. Early childhood educators have to work with and through parents if they want to help children over the long term. When a parent involvement program places the emphasis on what parents can do for the program, instead of vice versa, then the process becomes self-serving. Parent involvement is a two-way street and programs should not look on parents as commodities to be exploited.

Barriers to Parent Involvement

There are a number of reasons why parents are not involved more than they are and why some programs find it difficult to involve parents.

Parents Feel Unwanted. Some child-care programs and preschools don't make parents feel wanted, welcome, or needed. They tend to involve parents only when something is wrong (for example, when a parent is suspected of child abuse) or when the program needs something (for example, help with fund raising). Operated in this manner, parent involvement is a knee-jerk reaction to a specific issue rather than an ongoing process.

Staff Attitudes. Staff attitudes are often a barrier to parent involvement. This barrier may be based on the belief that a quality program can be conducted without parent involvement. Sad to say, early childhood educators have not always encouraged parent involvement. Thankfully, this is changing.

Lack of Meaningful Involvement. Some parents drop out of parent involvement programs because the nature of the involvement is not meaningful or because they cannot participate in a way the staff wants them to participate.

Past Experiences. Parents' past experiences with schools and agencies may turn them away from involvement. Some parents, because of failure in school or a bad experience with a teacher, are reluctant to get involved. As one parent explained, "My education was a disaster. I had some pretty miserable experiences. It was only because the teachers at my child's pre-school encouraged me that I ever thought of getting involved."

Culture. Some parents' cultures may not place a heavy emphasis on parent involvement in the child-care and education processes. First-generation Hispanic parents, in particular, believe that teachers know best. They believe there is no need for them to become involved and are content to leave child care and schooling to the "experts."

Parent Inferiority. Many parents believe care-givers and teachers know more than they do and therefore they are reluctant to get involved. Low-income parents in particular may feel inferior to teachers and care-givers and shy away from involvement.

Personal Problems. Some parents are consumed with problems associated with child rearing and working. They don't have the time or the energy to be involved. They are stressed by the tensions of a career, child rearing, and balancing a budget. Parents want to spend the little free time they do have on themselves, not on their children's programs.

PARENT INVOLVEMENT AND THE CONCEPT OF READINESS

Early childhood educators use the word "readiness" when describing or referring to children's abilities to learn concepts and accomplish developmental tasks. Teachers' concerns for readiness are generally manifested in two ways.

First, good teachers understand the concept of readiness. They know it makes sense to match what children are ready to learn to the tasks they provide for them. Second, they ensure that children will learn by helping them become ready. Good care-givers are guided by the concept of readiness when educating and developing young children.

Levels of Readiness for Parent Involvement

The concept of readiness also makes good sense when conducting a program of parent involvement. In effective parent involvement programs, readiness exists at several levels.

Level 1. The first level involves care-giver attitudes and skills. Not all care-givers are at the same level of readiness when it comes to parent involvement. Some would rather not have any more to do with parents than necessary.

Although most early childhood educators agree that parent involvement is a good idea and believe that it will help children as well as the program, not all know how to involve parents. Some staff may also have serious doubts about the practicality of trying to involve parents, especially given all that they are asked to do during a workday.

The key to overcoming this barrier is staff training. Program directors must be leaders and provide for the staff training, resources, support, and encouragement that make parent involvement more than a desired hope. Care-givers need help and encouragement in developing both a positive attitude and a program for parent involvement. Support from a caring administrator and in-service training can promote and increase the readiness level of teachers to participate in parent involvement.

Level 2. A second level of readiness relates to the center or program. A program is not ready for parent participation if it does not have a plan for involvement. Staff members have to know in their own minds how they want to involve parents before they are really ready for parent involvement.

Other factors that indicate a lack of program readiness include not encouraging parent involvement through word and deed, discouraging parents when they demonstrate an interest, and assuming that parents won't become involved.

Passive readiness. Some programs exhibit a passive readiness for parent involvement. Parent involvement is neither actively encouraged nor actively discouraged. Parents are treated with benign neglect. Encounters with parents are serendipitous.

Passive readiness is also characterized by involving parents mostly in passive ways. These passive ways entail little face-to-face communication, short or infrequent phone calls, and having open houses only once a year.

Active readiness. Active readiness, on the other hand, is characterized by planning and providing a variety of ways for parents to be involved. Examples of active parent involvement include regularly scheduled parent conferences, parent seminars and courses, and home visits.

Level 3. A third level relates to the involvement readiness of parents. Not all parents have the inclination, time, or abilities to be involved in the same ways. A program that demonstrates a high level of readiness provides for the readiness levels of parents. Care-givers must provide a range of activities for parents. Most parents will welcome an opportunity to be involved when their readiness level is matched to parent involvement activities.

PARENT INVOLVEMENT AS A DEVELOPMENTAL PROCESS

Parent involvement is a developmental process for parents, staff, and programs.

Myths of Parent Involvement

One myth of parent involvement is that there have to be many concurrent parent activities. Certainly an effective program of parent involvement has to be planned for, but it should not have so many activities that they have no meaning or purpose. The ability of the staff to involve parents grows over time, and how the staff involves parents also changes over time. At the same time, a staff can only do so much at one time.

Parents' abilities, desires, and opportunities for involvement change over time in response to changing roles and lifestyles. What parents enjoy doing today may be quite different from what they will want to do tomorrow. As parents develop new skills, they want to try new and different things.

Another myth of parent involvement is that all parents must be involved. It is unrealistic to expect that a program will involve all parents. It is not unrealistic, however, to expect that all programs will *try* to involve all parents in some way.

Individualizing Parent Involvement Activities

One way of trying to involve all parents is to individualize involvement opportunities. For a parent who could not attend a parent seminar on nutrition, for example, the staff could make a tape recording of the seminar and give it to the parent.

Parents can also be given activities to do at home. Educators who are serious about parent involvement know that many parents don't have time to volunteer or become involved in the child-care or preschool program. Parents can, however, be involved in the lives of their children and programs by doing activities at home. Care-givers could provide books and tips on how to read to children; show parents how children can learn through games; show parents how the home environment can be used to teach and learn; provide a calendar of center activities with suggestions about how to supplement them in the home, and send parents materials they can use in suggested activities.

LEVELS OF PARENT INVOLVEMENT

Parent involvement can be divided into a hierarchy of five different levels or processes. Care-givers must provide opportunities for involvement at all these levels, which progress from a low to a high level.

Level 1. This is the lowest level of parent involvement. It consists primarily of involving parents as providers of services. The services parents can provide are limited only by their time and desires. One parent, an account executive with a brokerage firm, takes a day off twice a year to help chaperone field trips. Another parent, who is employed in a print shop, keeps the center supplied with surplus paper and poster board.

Level 2. This level is where parents are involved as resources. Most parents have talents that can be used to benefit the program, and themselves as well. Determine parents' talents and use them. A father who is a computer buff may be able to spend some time with the children on the computer. He may also help identify and evaluate software suitable for children.

Level 3. At this level, parents are involved as teachers and aides. Parents are the first teachers of their children. Care-givers should invite them into programs to help teach. At the same time, care-givers can teach parents how to teach and interact effectively with their children.

Level 4. This level involves parents as decision makers. Every program should have a parent advisory committee. Part of the purpose of this committee is to help make policy decisions about the program. Parents' work skills can be used to help make policy decisions. An accountant, for example, can help develop a budgeting and record-keeping system.

An advisory council is an excellent way to involve parents in policy recommendations. In fact, the majority of program policies should come as recommendations from the advisory council. In Head Start, policy councils are mandatory, and 50 percent of the council membership must consist of parents who have children in the program.

Level 5. At this level, parents act as advocates and lobbyists. Parents can and should be involved in advocacy activities regarding their program, legislation, and improving early childhood education. Parents who think they lack the skills to advocate can be taught by other parents. Parents can raise money, write letters, attend meetings, invite legislators as speakers, offer expert testimony, and generally advocate on behalf of programs.

Parents' abilities, then, exist along a continuum, from parents who perceive themselves as possessing few skills and who are reluctant to be involved to parents who are supremely self-confident and ready to be involved immediately.

THE COMMUNITY AND PARENT INVOLVEMENT

Knowledge of the community can help care-givers involve parents. Nationally, we know from census data that families are smaller, more women are heads of families, families are more mobile than ever before, many families lack a support system to help them with problems encountered in everyday living, and more women are below the poverty line than ever before — poverty has been feminized. Such demographic data on families help convey what "typical" families are like in a community and give perspective to the total parent involvement program.

Another kind of information that is crucial to parent involvement and development is knowledge of agencies in the local community. Care-givers can conduct a survey to identify agencies and their services. The data gathered can be used to link parents to those services that can assist them with child rearing and living. The survey results will help care-givers know the availability of counseling services, parenting information, resource people, and agencies that provide such things as food, clothing, and eye glasses. Care-givers can compile a booklet of services and give it to parents.

Effective ways to learn about a community are to live in it, take a walk through it, consult the Yellow Pages and community directories compiled by chambers of commerce, and experience it through guest speakers.

Community agencies and their staffs can help in parent involvement. Some parents respond to church-sponsored activities or to programs held in public libraries better than they do activities in a school-like setting. One of the myths of parent involvement is that it has to occur at the center or preschool.

Getting to know the community is one of the most effective ways care-givers have of truly helping and involving parents. A child-care or preschool program cannot meet all the needs of parents. It makes sense to network with other agencies and solicit their help in helping parents.

GETTING TO KNOW PARENTS

Getting to know parents is an imperative for all who would truly have an effective parent involvement program. Care-givers who don't know parents can't meet their needs. Parent information can be gathered during interviews at the time of registration and enrollment and during home visits, conferences, social events, and open houses. Some of the types of information care-givers should know about parents are described in the following paragraphs.

Attitudes Toward Children

Some parents are overprotective and won't let their children do much on their own. Other parents may be preoccupied with child abuse and, as a result, have children who are afraid of other adults. Still other parents are "benign" and can't wait to get rid of their children. Parents' feelings about their children have implications for how care-givers will care for the children and involve the parents.

Parents' Needs

Parents' needs are identified through conversations, home visits, and events in the program. Some common parent needs are nutrition information and guidance; parenting information, especially as it relates to discipline; help with family problems; child abuse information; and guidance about interpersonal relations.

DEVELOPING POSITIVE ATTITUDES TOWARD PARENTS

Getting to know parents helps care-givers develop positive attitudes toward them. Care-givers need to accept parents as they are, not as they should be or as they want them to be based on some romanticized ideal of family and parents. Relationships between care-givers and parents need to be warm, friendly, and open.

Parents have to feel comfortable with care-givers and the program in order to have effective parent involvement. Some parents' willingness to get involved is a matter of cultural and social factors. Care-givers must avoid any hint of having stereotypical views, but they must also recognize that a parent's propensity to become involved in a program is based in part on socioeconomic status. Care-givers may wish that parents in upper socioeconomic levels were not as involved as they are. Conversely, repeated efforts may be necessary to involve parents from low socioeconomic levels. Variations in willingness to be involved are not related to parents' interest in their children, for all parents are interested in their children. Rather, these differences frequently stem from social and cultural differences and how care-givers respond to these differences. Care-givers need to respond positively to all parents.

To make parent involvement work with a low socioeconomic-level clientele, the program staff must take the initiative and conduct a vigorous program of outreach. This requires that the staff be determined, patient, and responsive to parent attitudes about what they can and are willing to do. What works with one group of clients may not work with another.

PROVIDING PARENTS WITH INFORMATION

Care-givers must satisfy parents' needs for sound child-rearing information. Some parents are uncomfortable in their roles as parents. They have poor parenting skills and need help from care-givers. Some parents are stressed by the tensions of balancing a career and child rearing. Some must deal with not having enough money to adequately care for their children, and others don't know what to do for problem children.

Consequently, many of today's parents hunger for information. Some will get it from care-givers. Some will consult *Family Circle* and *Women's Day*. Some parents are going to get the wrong information, and others are not going to get any advice at all.

When parents won't voluntarily seek advice or are not aware of their need for information, care-givers have to be confident enough to make them aware of the problem. If four-year-old children are watching the Playboy channel on television with their parents, for example, care-givers need to say that this is inappropriate and tell parents to switch channels.

A parent resource room is an ideal way for care-givers to provide parents with information and resource material. It is also a good way and place for parents to meet other parents. A family-parent bulletin board in the resource area keeps parents up to date on center and community happenings. A parent lending library provides professional literature relating to topics of interest and concern.

Parent meetings, which should be held at least once a month, offer parents the opportunity to know each other and to learn about topics of their choice. Parents should be involved in planning their meetings. When parents set the time, select the place, and choose the topics, the meetings will be more successful than they are when these matters are set by care-givers alone.

COMMUNICATING WITH PARENTS

A successful approach to parent involvement can be summed up in three words: communicate, communicate, communicate. One of the most important things care-givers want to communicate to parents is the quality, nature, and activities of the program. A good way to do this is to send home information about what children are and will be doing. Parents prefer to find out about a program and its activities through their children.[4] Care-givers, then, should use children to communicate with parents.

Parents frequently say "My child doesn't bring anything home. What does she do all day?" This is a common response when parents have an academic orientation to and expectation of a program. Care-givers must satisfy this natural desire of most parents to know about the daily activities of their children.

Communication involves bringing parents close to the child's preschool life by telling them face to face about the program and what their children have done throughout the day. Parents believe this direct approach is the most effective method for communicating with them.[5] In response to the question, "When is Harry going to start writing?" for example, tell the parent that Harry is using a snap clothespin to pick up colored rods as a means of developing the manual dexterity needed as a foundation for writing.

Care-givers should not only share problems with parents, but the good things as well. Instead of saying, "Odalys had a terrible day," say, "Odalys shared nicely today, but she wasn't as attentive as usual. Is she worried about something at home?"

In addition to direct conversations, use messages on bulletin boards or chalkboards to tell parents the news about their children and the program. A brief daily written report can also keep parents informed.

Care-givers and parents may be tempted to quickly hand the child over to each other at the beginning and ending of the day. Care-givers, how-ever, should take a few minutes with parents to help them and their chil-dren make the daily transition from and to each other. In the morning, parents can share information with care-givers that will help the child's day go better. At the end of the day, care-givers can share information about the highlights of the child's day. Both these procedures make parents feel wanted and comfortable with the program. These are the kinds of practices that make parents feel that care-givers really do care, and parents are therefore inclined to support the center's program.

A center's need for parent participation must be constantly restated. Care-givers cannot take for granted that parents are welcome to be involved.

PARENT CONFERENCES

Regardless how many daily conversations care-givers have with parents, there should be at least three or four formal conferences a year. These con-ferences help parents see where their children have been and where they are going. Conferences should be built into the yearly calendar but ad-justed to the time preferences of parents. When parents enroll their chil-dren in a program, they should understand that they have a commitment to a specified number of conferences.

How to Conduct Parent Conferences

Some basic points to keep in mind for conducting successful parent con-ferences are:

1. *Plan for the conference.* Gather materials that illustrate all the topics you want to cover. The time spent in planning always pays dividends in the long run.
2. *Set a time limit.* Most parent conferences can be conducted in about fifteen minutes.
3. *Be on time and start on time.* Care-givers should not make parents wait for them to start a conference. If parent conferences are scheduled one after the other, being on time keeps things moving and avoids making everyone wait.

4. *Talk so parents understand you.* Don't use educational jargon or words parents won't understand.
5. *Be positive and provide specific helping suggestions.* Parents expect that care-givers will help guide and direct them with positive, helpful parenting suggestions.
6. *Solicit and consider parents' feelings and ideas.* Remember that parents have feelings too and want to be treated as competent human beings. Parents know a great deal about their children. Use this information to help everyone concerned.
7. *Bring closure to the conference.* Summarize who said what and who is going to do what.
8. *Follow up and follow through.* A parent conference is only as good as the follow-up. If nothing results from a conference, then, in a sense, the conference was a waste of everyone's time.

INVOLVING PARENTS WHO HAVE SPECIAL NEEDS

An effective program of parent involvement meets the special needs of parents and families. These special needs may result from children's handicaps; a death in a family; the family's being in some stage of dissolution; child or spouse abuse; illness; poor language skills, including not knowing English; unfamiliarity with educational customs and practices in the United States; single parenting; and work.

Single Parents

The number of single parents is growing. Because of their single status, single parents are more likely to need child care than any other parents. A good child-care or preschool program may be the most important support service a single parent has — indeed, it may take the place of the second parent for the family.

Don't treat all single parents alike! Some single parents have been and want to be single; others are in a transition stage. A single teenage parent has different needs than a single parent who is a corporate vice president.

Single parents may need help with baby-sitting, parenting, and discipline. They may also need someone to talk to who will listen. Care-givers can fill all these needs.

Working Parents

Working parents may need "before- and after-program" child-care services. Also, frequent closings of programs for holidays that parents don't have in the work place are a real problem for working parents. Care-givers can help parents link up with alternative child-care services when their programs are closed.

Although working parents don't have a lot of time, they should be invited into the classroom and center to help with instructional and other activities. Parents can be involved in special events such as field trips, holiday celebrations, and other special occasions.

Parents of Handicapped Children

Parents of the handicapped may need more time and support from caregivers than other parents do. In particular, care-givers need to explain to parents the adjustments they make in their programs to mainstream the handicapped child. Parents need help adjusting home life and activities to the handicapped child. Special efforts can be made to ensure that the staff is receptive to their questions, suggestions, and concerns. Care-givers can meet the needs of parents of the handicapped by linking parents to support groups, helping parents organize support groups, soliciting the help of experts and resource people, informing parents of their rights, and teaching parents how to work directly with their children.

Language Minority Parents

Language minority parents are parents whose native language is not English and who have no understanding or a limited understanding of the English language. They need to be treated fairly, courteously, and humanely. Some strategies that can be used to involve these parents include teaming the parent up with a bilingual parent; providing a translator at parent meetings and conferences; sending home center information and newsletters in the parents' native language; and conducting special orientation programs designed to familiarize the parent with American educational customs and procedures. Care-givers also need to help language minority parents understand the similarities and differences between their culture's child-rearing practices and those practiced in a particular program.

INVOLVING FATHERS

Care-givers must recognize that fathering and mothering are complementary processes. Definitions of birth, affection, care taking, and masculinity are changing to include a legitimate, positive involvement for fathers in the lives of children. Many fathers are competent care-givers. Some fathers may be uncertain about their roles in parenting and look to care-givers for help, support, and advice.

It is not only fathers' direct roles in parenting that is important, but also their indirect roles. They help provide stability in a relationship, support the mother in her parenting role, and serve as masculine role models for children.

Fathers are assuming greater roles in the child-rearing process. What can care-givers do to support fathers?

There are many kinds of fathers: fathers who are at home while their wives work; divorced fathers with custody of children; fathers with children whose wives are deceased; fathers with children whose wives recently left the family; fathers who dominate in the home and control everything; passive or "shadow" fathers who exert little influence in the home; fathers who are absent from the home because of work, or who visit families only occasionally; and live-in "significant others" who are surrogate fathers. Each has to be involved in a different way.

THE ECOLOGY OF PARENT INVOLVEMENT

Care-givers must be aware of and sensitive to the ecology of parents and families. Families live and move in many environments, including the home environment, the work environment, the neighborhood environment, and the child-care environment. What happens in these environments influences how a parent relates to children and care-givers. An employer's demand that the parent work overtime will influence the relationship of the parent to the child and the center. Child abuse at home will influence how the parent views a center's procedures for protecting the child from abuse.

INVOLVING PARENTS THROUGH HOME VISITS

Little used, but highly praised by those who make them, home visits are an ideal way for early childhood educators to involve all parents, especially those who are hard to involve.

Reasons for Home Visits

Home visits are conducted for a number of reasons:

1. To meet with and learn more about the hard-to-involve parent. A parent may have eight children, one of whom is a baby. This parent may have difficulty coming to the program or volunteering his or her services.
2. To learn more about the home life and environment of the child and family. Information gathered during a home visit is invaluable in that it can provide a basis for providing better programs for parents and children.
3. To bring the child's preschool life closer to the parent.
4. To determine how the program can assist parents in their role as primary teachers of their child.
5. To help parents learn how home life can support the child's education.
6. To provide the parent with specific child development and child-rearing information.

At a minimum, the home of every parent with children in a program should be visited at least once a year. The homes of hard-to-involve parents should be visited more often. The first home visit can be a get-acquainted visit. The next visit can be used to help teach parents how to conduct educational activities in the home and to share child development and child-rearing information. Many programs make special arrangements for home visits by giving care-givers released time, conducting visits in teams of two, and assisting with transportation.

Not surprisingly, teachers who make home visits are more likely than teachers who don't to be favorable toward and positive about parent involvement activities.[6] One of the better ways to motivate staff to encourage parent involvement is to give them opportunities for home visits.

PARENTS AS INVOLVERS OF PARENTS

Parents are often the best involvers of other parents. Parents can help identify dates and topics for parent meetings, organize car pools, provide parenting information, and serve as a support system to other parents.

Parents can also help organize support groups for parents so they can learn from each other. Support groups help parents complement and provide feedback to each other. Through their deliberations and discussions, support groups can provide important information and help to care-givers.

PARENT INVOLVEMENT ACTIVITIES

The following sections list activities that have been successfully used by care-givers to involve parents.

Communicating with Parents

1. *Telephone calls and telephone hotlines.* Telephone calls are an excellent way for care-givers to communicate with parents and for parents to communicate with each other. Hotlines staffed by parents can help allay fears and provide information relating to child abuse and other topics.
2. *Newsletters.* Newsletters are a convenient way to keep parents informed about program events, curriculum information, and activities. All parents should receive newsletters, and those who can and want to should be involved in writing them. When possible and practical, newsletters should be in the parents' native language.
3. *Home-school notebooks.* These are notebooks sent back and forth each day with the children. In them, teachers share events and accomplishments and generally keep parents informed. These notebooks are also a great way to develop responsibility in children, since they are the ones who carry them between home and program.
4. *At-home learning materials and activities.* Many programs make a point of regularly sending home learning activities that parents and their children can do together. A monthly calendar with an activity for each day is one good way to keep parents involved in their children's learning. Also, parent activity guides can be furnished for use during holidays and program recesses.
5. *Suggestion boxes.* Although suggestion boxes are not an ideal way to communicate with parents, they do enable parents who might not otherwise make suggestions to have an opportunity to do so.

Events and Activities

1. *Open houses.* Open houses and parent nights are excellent ways for parents and care-givers to get acquainted with each other. Unfortunately, some programs view open houses as their primary obligation for parent involvement.
2. *Potluck dinners.* Dinners, lunches, and breakfasts are always favorites with parents, especially when they include foods from different cultures.
3. *Fairs and bazaars.* These are frequently used as fund-raising events. They usually have a particular topic or theme, such as raising money for the program.
4. *Performances and plays.* There is a saying among early childhood educators that if you want to get parents to the center or school, have a program in which their children have a part. This may be true, but the purpose of children's performances should not be primarily to get parents to attend.
5. *Special events.* Certain occasions, such as the anniversary of the beginning of a program, are ideal for making special efforts to involve par-

ents and the community. An anniversary celebration is also an ideal way for care-givers to share the year's accomplishments with parents and to tell of plans for the coming year.

Developmental Activities

1. *Parent training programs.* Frequently parents use their lack of knowledge or expertise as an excuse for not participating. A good way to overcome this objection is through training programs specifically designed to train parents for involvement.
2. *Direct participation in classroom and center activities.* Not all parents have the time or the desire to be directly involved in classroom activities, but those who do should be encouraged to do so. Parents must be given guidance and direction in these involvements, however. A care-giver must not say to a parent, "You can read this story to the children" without first demonstrating for the parent how to read a story.

   Involving parents directly in programs as paid aides is also an excellent way to provide employment and training at the same time. Many programs, such as Head Start, actively support such a policy.
3. *Involvement of parents in writing individual educational programs (IEPs) (see Chapter 8).* For parents of special needs children, involvement in writing an individualized education plan is a virtual necessity and may even be mandatory, depending on the nature of the funding. It is a good idea, however, to involve all parents in a discussion of their children's educational program.
4. *Parent advocates.* All programs need advocates most of the time in order to get additional funding and services. Parents are the best advocates a program can have. Program staff must support and train parents for their roles as advocates, however.

Services to Parents

1. *Resource libraries and materials centers.* Care-givers can set aside a special area devoted specifically to providing parents with books and other material relating to parenting and other topics of interest. Some programs furnish their parent resource areas with comfortable chairs and other furniture to encourage parents to also use them for informal meetings.
2. *Child care during meetings and activities.* One reason parents may not be able to attend programs and become involved is that they do not have child care for their other children. Child care for parents while they attend a program, serve as an aide, or are involved in some other significant way makes their participation less stressful and more enjoyable, and it may even be the factor that makes it possible.
3. *Respite care.* Increasing numbers of early childhood programs provide

Special events provide opportunities for parents to be involved in their children's programs. What are the benefits of these parent involvement activities?

respite care for parents, especially those who have special needs children. Respite care enables parents to have periodic relief from the responsibilities of parenting.

4. *Service exchanges.* Some early childhood programs support parents in their operation of service exchange or barter programs. One parent who was a photographer compiled a slide presentation about a program in return for a tuition reduction. Exchanges can also include clothing, equipment, and toys.

5. *Parent support groups.* Parents need support in their roles as parents and family members. Groups designed specifically to help parents can provide the emotional and intellectual support they need. Support groups can provide parenting information, link parents to community agencies, and have speakers address issues of concern to parents.

6. *New parent and family welcoming committees.* A good way to induct parents into any program is by having them welcomed by other parents. Parents are frequently the best involvers of parents.

Decision- and Policy-Making Activities

1. *Hiring and policy-making decisions.* Parents can and should serve on committees that set policy and hire staff. Some agencies, such as Head Start, require that parents be involved in such processes.

2. *Curriculum development and review.* Parent involvement in curriculum planning provides for significant involvement, helps parents learn about and understand what constitutes a quality program, and enables parents to be advocates for the program. When parents know what the curriculum is and why the program operates as it does, they are more confident in their support of it.

Outreach to Parents

1. *Home visits.* Home visits are an ideal way to meet parents in their environment. Home visits also provide care-givers with insights into children's backgrounds and give parents demonstrable proof that care-givers care about them.
2. *Community involvement.* Care-givers must be willing to go into the community to learn about it and to demonstrate that their desire to involve parents is authentic. Parental reluctance about being involved in preschool or child-care programs may be due to cultural factors, lack of time, or a general lack of interest. By conducting meetings in local libraries and churches and by demonstrating to parents a willingness to meet them "on their own turf," care-givers can involve more parents, particularly those who are traditionally viewed as "hard to involve."

ORGANIZATIONS FOR PARENTS

Two organizations exist specifically to assist parents in their quest for better education programs for their children. The first is Parents United (401 North Broad Street, Suite 895, Philadelphia, Penn. 19108), an organization of parents working to help other parents work for better schools. The second is the National Committee for Citizens in Education (410 Wilde Village Green, Columbia, Md. 21044; tel. 1-800-638-9675). This organization seeks to inform parents of their rights and to get them involved in the public schools.

PARENT EDUCATION AND FAMILY SUPPORT PROGRAMS

A major movement in early childhood education is the development of family support programs. Such programs look at the total family and design programs to help all members live better, rather than assisting them in just one area, such as child care. Family support programs are not necessarily new. Head Start, through programs such as Home Base, Parent Child Centers, and the Child and Family Resource Program, makes the family, not just children, the focus of its services. Now, more early childhood programs are recognizing that working only with children leaves the family — one of the critical factors in the child's development — out of the process. In addition, when families are supported in their child-rearing tasks, everyone wins.

Millie Almy, a noted early childhood educator, stresses the need for care-givers to learn how to work and be willing to work with *both* parents and children. She maintains that one of the qualities that characterizes the "good" early childhood teacher is "an interest in, and desire to work with, adults that is parallel to the interest in and desire to work with children."[7]

SUMMARY

A positive and active program of parent involvement in preschool, child-care, and early childhod programs sets the tone and direction for parents' attitudes toward involvement as they and their children progress through the educational process. Parents who are involved early in their children's educational careers are more likely to stay involved and contribute to their own and their children's development. From a parental point of view, involvement helps parents become better parents and improve their understanding of a program's purposes and activities. It increases the possibility that their children will benefit from the early childhood program. From a

Involved parents are supportive parents. Care-givers who want the best for children should make special efforts to involve parents. How can parents and care-givers collaborate to provide good early-childhood programs?

care-giver's point of view, when the education of young children is considered a *shared* responsibility and when parents are viewed as children's first and most influential teachers, parent involvement can be seen as a high-priority goal that has the potential to develop and promote long-lasting positive attitudes toward education and parenting.

Care-givers who are serious about providing the best for children and their parents are active in developing links with parents and the community. They envision parent involvement as an essential cornerstone in building the foundation for future learning. Full collaboration with parents ensures that good programs will become better and that above-average programs will become outstanding.

PROGRAM VIGNETTE

Centers in the Parc
Coconut Creek, Florida

Over fifty years ago, John Dewey, the great American education philosopher, said, "What the best and wisest parent wants for his own child, that must the community want for all its children." This philosophy is the guiding principle of Centura Parc in Coconut Creek, Florida, a housing community designed for parents who want a child- and family-oriented life-style. The community is designed to provide a nurturing atmosphere and educational programs for children and parents, with the goal of meeting the living needs of parents. Children, family, neighborhood, and a sense of community are critical values at Centura Parc.

"One of the most vexing problems facing working couples and single parents is finding child care," says Judith LaVorgna, executive director of the two learning centers — Centers in the Parc — that provide care for eighty children. (Projections call for ten centers and care for a thousand children when the community is fully developed in the 1990s.) "Society places tremendous stress on the American family in meeting their home and work-place needs. Young people with families have a terrible sense of isolation," says Judith. "We are literally creating an old-fashioned neighborhood where neighbors can know each other and kids can walk to school."

Centura Parc is designed so children never have to cross a street to reach any of the learning centers. Homes are designed with rounded counter tops and enclosed patios. "We're selling an infrastructure to support family life," says George Bergman, president of Cenvil Family Centers, the corporation that owns and operates the centers. "We are meeting the very real human need of providing professional care for children within the community in which parents reside. Parents leave the community each morning with their hands free."

Child rearing, family life, and parent involvement and support are the themes of the development. All parents are within two minutes of one of the child-care centers, which enroll children between the ages of six weeks and five years. Enrollment is open only to families residing in the community.

Each of the centers has a parent advisory board that advises and helps the director and staff in the following areas:

- Learning and teaching experiences
- Parent and teacher programs
- Teaching materials and resources
- Assistance in program evaluation
- Assistance in the development of advocacy groups on behalf of children and families

The centers have an open-door policy. Parents are encouraged to observe their children and visit in the program at any time. Parents are kept informed of program information and events through "door notes," a community newsletter, and personal contacts by the staff. Parents are informed of their children's progress with a daily written report for each child, a minimum of two formal parent-teacher conferences a year, and informal teacher contacts.

Staff members believe a successful family support system involves bonding between program, families, and children. "Our parents are not visitors in their own program," says Judith. "Parents and care-givers get to know each other very well. We like to think of parents and care-givers working together to educate children and support the family. Before parents enroll their children in the program, we have a long conference with them in which they share information about themselves, the family, and their children. The more we know, the better we can help and teach. Good child care is not a monologue in which the care-giver does all the talking."

The program also provides parents with many seminars related to child rearing and parenting. In addition, parents have opportunities to talk one on one with experts in child care. Community concerts, picnics, and other family-oriented activities make the centers a focal point for family activities. There is also a wide variety of planned adult programs such as aerobics, nutrition, and money management.

The Centers in the Parc are open all year. They are closed only for six national holidays. Parents have a choice of a full program five days a week, a full program three days a week, and a half-day morning program five days a week. The centers are open from 7 A.M. to 6 P.M. For school-age children, there is before- and after-school care. Baby-sitting services are provided from 6:30 to 11:00 P.M. Monday through Friday and from 7:00 P.M. to 12:00 midnight on Saturday.

Parents help the staff create an atmosphere in which children are respected, loved, and cared for. All child-care programming is based on family concepts. Children are grouped into multi-age "families," and each has a family name. Meals are served family style, and staff members eat with the children.

Parents like the family support concept provided at Centura Parc. As single parent Michelle Messbauer says, "I like the idea of a community with child care. Where I lived before, I had to drive my daughter several miles to a baby-sitter before I went to work. This is a community that is sensitive to children's and families' needs."

The current national trend is toward family strengthening, and early child-hood programs are seeking ways to support families. Centura Parc through Centers in the Parc, provides an example and a prototype for family support and development.

ENRICHMENT THROUGH ACTIVITIES

1. Develop a list of suggestions that would benefit a child-care center in developing a program of parent involvement.
2. The care-givers at Tiny Tot Child Care Center were ecstatic because Barry went down the slide for the first time by himself. How should this be communicated to the parents?
3. At the next meeting of the parent seminar series, you are scheduled to talk on the topic "What Makes a Good Parent?" What would you say?
4. List what you think are the special problems faced by single parents. For each one, tell how a program can help parents deal with the problem.
5. Describe how the staff of an infant-toddler program can help families.
6. Tell how parents could be involved in a program of nutrition education.
7. Should a care-giver have an unlisted phone number? Should care-givers give their phone numbers to parents and encourage them to call?
8. Parents tend to blame care-givers and teachers when their children are "not learning." Whose "fault" is it?
9. Should parents be "surprised" about work their children bring home?
10. In some programs, parent communication consists of sending home a monthly newsletter. Is this sufficient parent-program communication? Why? Why not?
11. Consider all the ways to involve parents discussed in this chapter and select the five you think are the most effective. Tell why you selected the ones you did.
12. Develop a plan for implementing the parent involvement activity you ranked first in activity 11.
13. Would you want to live in a community like Centura Parc? Why? Why not?
14. What do you think are the most serious problems facing parents today? How can care-givers help with these problems?

ENRICHMENT THROUGH READING

Abidin, Richard R. *Parenting Skills: Trainer's Manual.* 2nd ed. New York: Human Sciences Press, 1982.

The twenty-four parenting skills sessions described in this book are designed to give parents the basic skills and knowledge they need for effective child rearing. The program is not designed to provide the "right answers" but to give parents insight and skills to help them reach their own parenting goals. The first sessions deal with helping parents learn how to build meaningful parent-child relationships. Eleven sessions deal with managing behavior and feelings, and the last sessions are devoted to special topics such as communicating with teachers.

Brown, Martha C. *Schoolwise: A Parent's Guide to Getting the Best Education for Your Child*. Los Angeles: Jeremy P. Tarcher, 1985.

Brown has written a book designed to help parents who are frustrated in their attempts to deal with the schools. She asks the very basic question, "How can parents as individuals and as organized groups gain more of a say in their children's schools?" The answers, according to Brown, are (1) be persistent in asking questions about all the things about which you want more information; and (2) do not take educators too seriously when they say the ways of learning are too complex for parents to understand. She provides parent-tested strategies that can help parents become advocates for better schools.

Coletta, Anthony J. *Working Together: A Guide to Parent Involvement*. Atlanta: Humanics Limited, 1977.

Working Together is based on the premise that parent-teacher partnerships should be based on clear communication and reciprocity to help children meet their needs for survival, growth, and happiness. It includes plans for parent participation in the classroom, alternative approaches to teaching parenting skills, suggested home-based activities, and helpful child development guides and checklists.

Duff, Eleanor R., Swick, Kevin J.; and Hobson, Carol F. *Building Successful Parent/ Teacher Partnerships*, Atlanta: Humanics Limited, 1979.

Duff and her colleagues provide authoritative solutions to problems that have led many parents and teachers to become disenchanted with parent involvement programs. This text examines the changing nature of parenting and teaching and provides a comprehensive, workable plan for implementing a successful parent-teacher involvement program in any educational setting.

Ehly, Stewart W.; Conoley, Jane Close; and Rosenthal, David. *Working with Parents of Exceptional Children*. St. Louis: Times Mirror/Mosby College Publishing, 1985.

This is a comprehensive and authoritative book on helping care-givers know more about what to do and how to do it when working with parents of special needs children. Although the main focus is parents of exceptional children, the concepts and processes apply to all parents. The last chapter on the gifted is particularly useful.

Harris, Rosa Alexander. *How to Select, Train, and Use Volunteers in the Schools*. Lanham, Md.: University Press of America, 1985.

Part of parent involvement includes how to involve other members of the community. This book provides a concise blueprint for recruiting, selecting, training, and evaluating a school volunteer program. Included are many useful forms and sample suggestions for implementing and conducting the volunteer program. The ideas presented will work best in a school setting where parents and volunteers are highly motivated to volunteer.

Metzger, Peg; Mandy, Elaine M.; Clayton, Cynthia; Quinn, Richard T.; and Shadle, Carolyn. *Parents Make the Difference*. West Falls, N.Y.: Just Sew Education Publications, 1984.

This short, easy-to-read, informative booklet stresses the role parents play in determining the direction of their children's growth and development. Chapters deal with how parents set the stage for learning and communicating with children. Included is a very helpful quiz, "What kind of parent am I?"

Miller, Shelby H. *Children as Parents: Final Report on a Study of Childbearing and Child Rearing Among 12- to 15-Year-Olds*. New York: Child Welfare League of America, 1983.

With the increase in teenage pregnancy, there is a need for care-givers to know more about the problems of teenage parents — "children as parents" — and how to work with them. This book provides a highly detailed description of the lives of young adolescent mothers from the time they realized they were pregnant to a year and a half after their babies' births. The final chapter of conclusions and recommendations provides insights and suggestions for helping teenage parents be good parents.

Rothenberg, B. Annye; Hitchcock, Sandra; Graham, Melinda; and Harrison, Mary Lou. *Parentmaking: A Practical Handbook for Teaching Parent Classes About Babies and Toddlers*. Menlo Park, Calif.: Banster Press, 1981.

This is a practical, detailed, comprehensive, parent-oriented handbook that provides much useful information for care-givers who work with parents. The topics are well organized, with goals and objectives relating to commonly asked questions. This age-stage approach to studying children examines child-rearing issues and provides solid practical answers for parents' consideration.

Swick, Kevin. *Inviting Parents into the Young Child's World*. Champaign, Ill.: Stipes Publishing, 1984.

Swick has written a practical and useful book for facilitating parent involvement. He believes that "the intricate mechanism of bringing together the dynamic and diverse members of home and school settings is a challenge to all who work with young children." He addresses this challenge in a literate and down-to-earth way. This book belongs in a basic bibliography on how to involve parents.

Tonks, Doris Beckett. *For Parents Only: Are Your Children Flowers or Weeds?* New York: Vantage Press, 1984.

This slim volume is based on the reality that there are no schools for parenthood. It is designed as an aid to help parents understand how and why children react the way they do to various situations. Tonks believes that the family is an important socializing force, and it is to parents and children as a family that she addresses many of her remarks.

Wilson, Gary B. *Parents and Teachers: Humanistic Educational Techniques to Facilitate Communication Between Parents and Staff of Educational Programs*. Atlanta: Humanics Limited, 1974.

Wilson provides an intelligent and effective program of lively and engaging strategies to enable parents and teachers to work together effectively. This manual is ideal for anyone engaged in parent involvement and consists of a series of structured experiences designed to promote increased parent-staff interaction.

NOTES

1. Irving Lazar et al., *The Persistence of Preschool Effects: A Summary Report* (Washington, D.C.: U.S. Government Printing Office, 1976).
2. Kevin J. Swick, *Inviting Parents into the Young Child's World* (Champaign, Ill.: Stipes Publishing, 1984), 115.
3. George S. Morrison, *Parent Involvement in the Home, School, and Community* (Columbus, Ohio: Charles E. Merrill Publishing, 1978), 22.
4. Juleen Cattermole and Norman Robison, "Effective Home/School Communication from the Parents' Perspective," *Phi Delta Kappan* 67 (September 1985).
5. Cattermole and Robison, "Effective Communication."
6. Henry Jay Becker and Joyce L. Epstein, "Parent Involvement: A Survey of Teacher Practices," *Elementary School Journal* 83 (November 1982).
7. Millie Almy, *The Early Childhood Educator at Work* (New York: McGraw-Hill, 1975), 27. Reprinted by permission of the author.

Chapter 10

Issues Relating to the Education and Development of Young Children

---

Questions to Guide Your Reading and Study

- What is child abuse?
- What are the roles of care-givers in reporting and preventing child abuse?
- What are the causes of child abuse?
- What are the characteristics of children suffering from child abuse?
- Why is there so much interest in missing children?
- How can care-givers help prevent child abductions?
- What is infant mortality and how can care-givers help reduce it?
- How have families changed in the last decade?
- What are the implications of changing family patterns for care giving?
- How have children's rights been expanded and clarified?
- What is stress and how does it affect young children?
- What can care-givers do to help children cope with stress?
- Why is good nutrition important early in life?
- How can care-givers promote good nutrition in young children?
- What are the major criticisms of children's television?
- What effects does television have on young children?
- How can care-givers encourage good television viewing habits in young children?

INTRODUCTION

Today, young children are the focus of a great deal of attention, in part because of how modern American society views and treats them. Children are in a paradoxical position. On the one hand, many children enjoy the benefits of one of the highest standards of living in the world. On the other hand, children are abused and stolen; run away from their parents; experience the stresses associated with family breakups and the pressures of hurried or missing childhoods; consume junk foods of questionable nutritional value; and spend increasing amounts of time viewing violent programs on television and playing war games that extol aggressive behavior. On the one hand, the infant mortality rate in the United States is at its lowest ever. On the other hand, twelve other nations have infant death rates lower than that in the United States. On the one hand, many social and economic gains have been made in the past decade. On the other hand, many children do not receive the benefits of these gains.

Why are so many conditions that are detrimental to the best interests of children allowed to continue? Why does a country with such a high standard of living, a country whose leaders maintain that children are its greatest asset, have so many problems in caring for the very young? Although these questions may invite trite or easy answers, in reality they have no simple answers, and the problems that raise them cannot be corrected with "quick fixes." Two concerns should be of critical importance to care-givers and parents. The first is the effects these societal processes are having and will continue to have on children. The second is what care-givers can do to contribute to the solution, to prevent negative factors from interfering with children's healthy growth and development.

CHILD ABUSE

Very young children are raped, tortured, undernourished, beaten, abandoned, and sold to others. All of these abuses, which are chronicled with increasing regularity in newspapers across the country, are cruel and shocking examples of how some adults treat children. These reports are not figments of journalistic imagination. In the world of children, abuse is a stark reminder that not everyone loves children or knows how to properly and humanely care for them. Care-givers cannot ignore the problem and wish that such abusive behavior did not exist or assume that if they do nothing others will come to children's aid and protection. To paraphrase the poet John Donne, no person is an island. When the nation's greatest wealth, its children, are abused and robbed of their humanity and potential, then everyone loses. Abuse of children will continue unless care-givers assume assertive, active roles in identifying, reporting, and preventing abuse of the children they care for.

Care-givers must provide children with love and affection as a means of helping them overcome the effects of abuse and stress. What can care-givers do to encourage parents to obtain the help they need in order to prevent child abuse?

What Is Child Abuse?

Public law 93-247, the Child Abuse Prevention and Treatment Act, defines child abuse and neglect as "the physical or mental injury, sexual abuse, negligent treatment, or maltreatment of a child under the age of eighteen by a person who is responsible for the child's welfare under circumstances which indicate that the child's health or welfare is harmed or threatened."[1]

In addition, individual states have statutes that define abuse and neglect, outline reporting procedures, and specify punishments for abusers. In Florida, for example, chapter 827 of the Florida Statutes protects children from abuse and provides for a central abuse registry. The statute goes beyond the generalities of the federal definition and defines abuse and neglect as "any nonaccidental injury, sexual battery, financial, or sexual exploitation or injury to the intellectual or psychological capacity of a person by the parents or other persons responsible for the child's welfare. Neglect is failure to provide adequate food, clothing, shelter, health care, or needed supervision."[2]

Emotional Abuse. Emotional abuse occurs when adults strip children of their self-esteem. This can entail such behaviors as screaming, belittling, and continual criticism. One parent continually told her five-year-old son he was no good, "just like your daddy," who was in prison. Most parents at one time or another say something to a child that they wish they had not said. But this parent habitually talked to her child in this way.

How Widespread Is Child Abuse?

In 1984, there were 1,131,300 *reported* cases of child abuse and neglect in the United States. This represents a 9 percent increase over 1983 figures.[3]

Although there is no way of truly knowing the real extent of child abuse, most child welfare workers suspect that the reported cases represent only the tip of the iceberg. As the public becomes more aware of and involved in identifying and reporting child abuse, the number of reported cases will increase.

Reporting Child Abuse

State statutes frequently require certain individuals to report cases of abuse. In Florida, for example, all of the following workers must report abuse: physicians, nurses, hospital personnel, medical examiners, mental health professionals, school teachers and other school officials, social workers, day-care workers, foster-care workers, residential or institutional workers, and law enforcement officers.

Everyone, whether or not they have a legal obligation, has a moral obligation to report suspected cases of abuse. Quite often, people will say that they don't want to report abuse because they don't want to get involved or because they are afraid of getting sued. Individuals who in good faith report abuse need not fear criminal prosecution. All states provide immunity for *good faith* reporting, even if social workers who investigate the claim find no evidence to substantiate a case for abuse or neglect.

Implications for care-givers

1. Care-givers must be aware of the official policies and abuse reporting procedures in their states and municipalities.
2. Care-givers should report suspected cases of abuse to administrators, who can assist with gathering information and reporting. Remember, the evidence of abuse does not have to be overwhelming to justify a report. Other professionals, such as social workers attached to a department of social services, will investigate and gather more information. More importantly, care-givers should be willing to report directly to the proper authorities when administrators are indifferent or unwilling to be involved. In many instances, care-givers are children's only hope of help and protection.
3. Care-givers have more contact with children than most other persons except parents. Therefore they have a great deal of knowledge about children and are in positions to help as defenders and protectors of children. In addition, care-givers are important sources of information about children that others, such as social workers, can use in helping parents, families, and children.
4. Care-givers must be sensitive to the rights of parents as well as their needs for information, help, and support. Many abusing parents say they don't want to or didn't mean to abuse their children. The front line in the prevention of child abuse is parent education and support.

What Are the Causes of Child Abuse?

Lack of Parenting Skills and Information. Some parents may abuse their children and not realize they are doing it. They think their behavior is perfectly appropriate. A child who is malnourished because the parent does not provide enough or the right kinds of food at home is really a victim of neglect.

Parents' Attitudes Toward Children. Most instances of sexual abuse begin at home. *Incest* occurs when there is sexual intercourse between a child and a related adult. Most societies and cultures have a taboo against such relationships. Incestuous relationships occur for a number of reasons: the closeness and availability of the child; the power of the parent over the child; the parent's view of the child as property, and the parent's lack of moral conviction that incest is wrong.

Family Stress. Today, families are under more stress than ever before. They are torn apart by divorce. More homes are headed by single female parents. Poverty is being "feminized" — more female heads of households are living below the poverty line. More and more, both parents have to work to have an adequate family income. All of these factors place stress on family life and relationships, which leads in some cases to parents' taking out their frustrations on the closest person available, the child.

Abusers Were Abused Children. Child abusers are likely to have been abused themselves as children. Child abuse, then, is a cyclical process that is difficult to break. Researchers Mary Main and Carole George believe that the cycle of abuse begins very early in life. They examined the way abused and nonabused toddlers responded to upset peers. The abused toddlers responded to their upset peers with fear, threats, and aggression. In particular, three of the abused toddlers alternately comforted and attacked upset peers. The researchers said that care giving and aggression "seemed to stimulate one another, suggesting that these two normally highly distinct behavior patterns have the potential to become enmeshed early in life."[4]

Interactive Causes. Sangrund and his associates think that child abuse results from the interaction of three factors: environmental stress, personality traits of the parent, and the actual characteristics of the child that make him or her vulnerable to scapegoating.[5]

The Child's Role in Abuse. Although it may be uncomfortable for caregivers and parents to think that children have a role in abuse, researchers William Friedrich and Jerry Boriskin point out that "the child is not always a benign stimulus to the parent. For example, although it is not necessarily the fault of the child or the mother that a birth is premature, this characteristic of the child has an effect on its care-giver."[6] In addition to prematurity, they also cite such characteristics as mental retardation, physical handicaps, individual differences, and behavioral styles of children as precipitating abuse. As pointed out in Chapter 2, for example, children have different temperaments. The "difficult" child in particular may contribute to the strain and stress of child rearing, especially for the inexperienced parent.

When care-givers recognize that certain children, because of individual characteristics, are more at risk for abuse, they may be able to help parents obtain the help they need to prevent abuse.

The age and sex of the child also play a role in abuse. Allen R. DeJong and his colleagues reviewed 416 cases of abuse with respect to race, sex, and age. Their analysis reveals that male victims were significantly younger than female victims. White and Hispanic females were older than black female victims. Younger victims, regardless of sex or racial origins, were more likely than older children to be assaulted by someone known to them and to be assaulted at home.[7]

Societal Violence. Child advocates maintain that the violence in society encourages violence in interpersonal relationships. They also maintain that violence fosters a callousness toward and acceptance of violent solutions to problems, especially those related to child rearing.

Characteristics of Abused Children

Shirley O'Brien, a human development specialist, provides the following guidelines to help care-givers identify some of the *general* characteristics of abused children.[8] Keep in mind that these characteristics and signs are not precise and do not in and of themselves absolutely identify abuse. Either individually or in combinations, however, they do provide caregivers with cause for concern and follow-up. Abused children:

- Appear different from other members of the family. Parents may describe them as "different" or "bad."
- Seem afraid of their parents.
- May have welts, bruises, sores, and other skin injuries.
- Have inadequately treated injuries.
- Show overall evidence of poor care.
- Are given inappropriate food, drink, and medication.
- Exhibit behavioral extremes, such as crying all the time or being excessively fearful, unusually aggressive and destructive, or passive and withdrawn.
- May be wary of physical contact.
- May exhibit sudden changes in behavior, such as pants wetting, thumb-sucking, and frequent whining.
- May take over the role of the parent, becoming protective or otherwise attempting to take care of the parent's needs.

- Have learning problems the sources of which cannot be diagnosed.
- Are habitually truant or late.
- Arrive too early or remain late rather than return home.
- Are inappropriately dressed for the weather.

Implications for care-givers

1. Care-givers should know the signs of child abuse.
2. Care-givers need to be aware. Often abuse can be prevented by assisting parents. Care-givers can be alert to signs of stress in a family such as unemployment, fighting, and separation. At such times, if parents are provided with support services, they may be less likely to abuse and children will be less vulnerable to abuse.
3. Know the community agencies that can provide services to parents. There are many special facilities, such as crisis nurseries, that provide shelter for children who have been or may be abused by their parents. The Children's Home Society is another agency that provides temporary relief for children who have been abused. Many agencies also offer adoption services, foster care, training for new parents, and counseling for abusing parents and their families.
4. Be aware of community agencies that can train children in your center to protect themselves against child abuse. Also, be knowledgeable about the commercial programs that teachers may use to train children to protect themselves.
5. Learn about state and national agencies that give parents help and support. Parents Anonymous, a national organization with chapters in every state, offers nurturing and therapeutic services to those who abuse their children or who are at risk of abusing their children. Their national toll-free number, 1-800-421-0353, is available to all who want help.

    The federal government, through its National Center on Child Abuse and Neglect, helps coordinate and develop programs and policies concerning child abuse and neglect. For further information, write to the National Center on Child Abuse and Neglect, P.O. Box 1182, Washington, D.C. 20012.
6. Work to provide what researcher Jay Belsky calls "socialization for parenthood" early in life. By permitting school-age children and teenagers to experience what is involved in the care of young children, it is hypothesized, they will gain a sense of responsibility and sensitivity to childhood.[9] The result of such socialization, it is hoped, will be fewer abusing adults.

MISSING CHILDREN: LOST, STRAYED, AND STOLEN

They stare at you from the grocery bag in which you bring the milk home. They stare at you from the carton as you pour milk on your cereal. They are the faces of missing children. Some have been missing for months, others for years. More and more children are disappearing from homes and the care of their parents. Many are being stolen by one parent or another as a result of disagreements over who should have custody of the children when a family breaks up. In a parental or custodial abduction, an estranged or divorced spouse abducts a child or children.

Adam Walsh Child Resource Center

One of the primary advocates of efforts to keep children from being victims of abduction and abuse is John Walsh, the father of Adam Walsh, a child who was abducted and was later found decapitated. Through the Adam Walsh Child Resource Center in Fort Lauderdale, Florida, Walsh leads efforts to provide more antiabuse education in the schools. He is also one of the most visible spokespersons in the movement to find and rescue missing children. The center's address is 1876 North University Drive, Suite 306, Fort Lauderdale, Florida 33322 (tel. 305-475-4847).

Adam Walsh's death in 1981 helped precipitate heightened public awareness of missing children and their plight, enactment of child protection laws, and the establishment of a national telephone hot line to help track and find missing children. The National Center for Missing and Exploited Children in Washington, D.C., is supported by funds from the Department of Justice. Its purpose is to provide resources and act as a clearing-house for information relating to missing children. The hot line number for this agency is 1-800-843-5678. Anyone who wants to report a missing child or the sighting of a missing child may call this number.

Missing Children Clearing-houses

The first clearing-house for information on missing children was established in Florida in 1983. Since that time, the National Center and approximately thirty other state clearing-houses have been established. By Florida state law, all law enforcement agencies must report information on missing children to the Florida Missing Children's Information Clearing House. This information is then entered into their computerized system. At any one time, there are about 3,747 missing children under the age of eighteen in Florida. Of these, 50 percent are runaways, 48 percent are parental abductions, and 2 percent are stranger abductions.[10] One of the problems encountered by the missing children's movement is the lack of reliable figures on the number of missing children by age category and type of abduction.

Missing Children Act

In 1982, the Missing Children Act was signed into law. It requires the attorney general of the United States to maintain a nationwide computer-linked system for registering all missing persons. The result is the National Crime Information Center, which records all reported missing child cases and compiles data for use in preventing and recovering missing children.

In 1986, child search groups banded together to form the National Association of Missing Children Organizations, a coalition designed to help such groups acquire federal grant monies and to support each other in their common efforts.

Prevention of Child Abduction

Education. There have been and continue to be extensive efforts to develop ways to prevent children from being abducted and to find them when they are. One of the most comprehensive efforts is in the area of education. These efforts are directed at educating parents about what they can do to keep their children safe and how to help children protect themselves from abduction. Figure 10-1 lists the Adam Walsh Child Resource Center's suggestions for helping parents and care-givers protect children from abduction.

Educational programs for children generally involve teaching rules relating to strangers — for example, "Don't talk to strangers." One problem with all such programs is the difficulty of teaching children to be wary of others while at the same time teaching them that the world is an okay place and that people are basically good.

Identification of Children. Identification of children in various ways is another procedure many parents use to make finding their children easier. These identification processes include fingerprinting, photographs, and dental identification by cementing a small identification tag to a child's tooth. Some parents compile a dossier on their children that contains all the information, including a recent photograph, that they would need to furnish law enforcement agencies in the event that their child were missing.

Supporters of efforts to identify children also have their critics. Some say that fingerprinting gives parents a false sense of security. They also maintain that when parents educate their children, they shift to the children their own responsibility for the children's safety. Although children should be taught to protect themselves, it is ultimately the parent's responsibility to protect the child. Also, efforts directed toward finding missing children and preventing abduction and exploitation have come in for their share of criticism. In particular, Dr. Benjamin Spock, noted child expert and peace activist, contends that campaigns to prevent abuse and find missing children needlessly frighten children. Critics contend that missing children's groups give the impression that there is a stranger at every corner waiting to molest or abduct a child.

Current interest in and efforts at preventing the abduction of children are positive steps and long overdue. They have heightened public aware-

FIGURE 10-1
Adam Walsh Child Resource Center Safety Tips

Teach your children:
1. Their full name, address, and phone number.
2. How to dial "0" for the operator.
3. To know whose homes they are allowed to enter.
4. If they become separated from you while shopping to go to the nearest check-out counter and ask the clerk for assistance.
5. To walk with and play with other children.
6. That adults do not usually ask children for directions. If someone should stop in a car asking for directions, the child should then ask for help.
7. If someone is following them, to go to a place where there are other people, to a neighbor's home or into a store. They should then ask for help.
8. They should know in whose car they are allowed to ride. Warn your children that someone might try to lure them into a car by saying you said to pick them up. Tell them never to obey such instructions.
9. Never to open the door when home alone. Teach your children how to phone 911. Make sure they know a neighbor to call if someone tries to get into the house or if there is an emergency.
10. To tell if any adult asks them to keep a "secret."
11. That no one has the right to touch them or make them feel uncomfortable. They have the right to say no.
12. To tell you if someone offers them gifts or money or wants to take their picture.
13. To yell "*HELP,*" not just scream, if they need assistance.

As parents you should:
1. Know your children's friends.
2. Never leave children unattended, especially in a car.
3. Be involved in your children's activities.
4. Listen when your child tells you he or she does not want to be with someone.
5. Notice when a stranger shows your child a great deal of attention and find out why.
6. Have your child's fingerprints taken by a trained person; know where to locate dental records.
7. Be sensitive to changes in your child's behavior or attitudes. Encourage open communication.
8. Take a photograph of your child at least once each year.
9. Avoid buying items with your child's name on them. An abductor could start up a friendly conversation after reading your child's name.
10. Be sure their day-care centers or schools do not release children to anyone but the children's parents or preauthorized persons.

Source: Adam Walsh Child Resource Center, 1876 North University Drive, Suite 306, Fort Lauderdale, Florida 33322.

ness of the risks children face. Federal, state, and local laws designed to protect the nation's children are now in place, and programs and curricula are now available to help parents and other agencies help children.

Implications for care-givers

1. Care-givers should be ever-vigilant in ensuring the safety and well-being of children. This includes taking prudent precautions to see that children are protected and cared for.

2. Care-givers should turn the child over only to the custodial parent, guardian, or surrogate specifically designated by the parent.
3. Give parents information and training sessions about how they can help protect their children from abduction.
4. Insofar as practical, care-givers should cooperate with local law enforcement groups and other agencies that want to provide parents and their children with educational programs and materials. Care-givers should review the materials and programs to make sure they are appropriate for the age and maturity of the intended children.
5. Encourage parents to take responsibility for their children's safety and well-being. Some parents think that as long as they have had their children fingerprinted, they have fulfilled the major portion of their responsibilities.
6. Care-givers must exercise good judgment in their efforts to protect children. They must guard against unduly or carelessly frightening and stressing children to the point where they are afraid of everyone. Care-givers also have to ensure that the self-protection skills and concepts they teach children are appropriate to their emotional and intellectual developmental levels. Care-givers must be cautious of the wildly alarmist statements made by some well-intentioned but overzealous individuals, who would have the public believe that the number of missing children in the United States is "soaring into the millions" and that abuse, abduction, and murder of young children are commonplace.

INFANT MORTALITY

The infant mortality rate is a ratio of the number of deaths per thousand live births for children under one year of age. The rate of infant mortality is considered a barometer of the public's interest in and dedication to infants. The administration of President Jimmy Carter set a national goal of reducing infant deaths in the United States to nine per thousand live births by the 1990s. At the same time, a commitment was made to reduce the number of children born with low birth weight. The nation still has a long way to go to reach these commitments. In 1982, the infant mortality rate in the United States was 11.2; in 1983 it was 10.9, in 1984 it was 10.7, and in 1985 it had dropped to 10.6,[11] the lowest level in the nation's history. In 1984, there were 40,686 infant deaths.[12]

Although the overall infant mortality has been dropping in the United States since 1940, the infant mortality rate for black children has remained *twice* that of white children. In other words, black babies are twice as likely to die in their first year as white babies.

The leading cause of infant mortality is low birth weight, which can be attributed in part to a lack of prenatal care on the part of the mother. Low birth weight infants are more than twenty times as likely to die in their first year.[13] Nearly one out of ten black babies is born to a mother who received no prenatal care or care only in the last trimester of pregnancy. Black babies are more than twice as likely as white babies to be low-birthweight (less than 5.5 pounds).

Implications for care-givers. If society is to meet the goal set for decreasing infant mortality, care-givers must continue to be a key factor in this worthy effort. As part of a comprehensive program of services, care-givers can take the steps described in the following paragraphs.

1. Act as advocates to alert the general public and parents about the high incidence of infant mortality and to solicit their help in supporting agencies and programs such as community health agencies that provide care to pregnant women and young children. Care-givers can also work with religious and community leaders regarding what they can do to help with social and health problems.
2. Through their programs, provide information and resource referrals to expectant parents. This information can stress the need for regular prenatal and postnatal care for the mother and child. Special efforts can be made to target teenagers who are pregnant or at risk of being pregnant. Care-givers, when they know a parent is pregnant, can inquire about the kind and amount of prenatal care they are or are not receiving. They can then use the information they acquire to guide the parent. Books and pamphlets about prenatal care can be included in the parent resource center.
3. In cooperation with other agencies, care-givers can conduct seminars for parents that focus on nutrition, prenatal care, and parenting.
4. Cooperate with other agencies in efforts to educate both women and men. Alpha Phi Alpha, a national black fraternity, for example, is sponsoring Project Alpha, an awareness program for male teens. Started in 1983, this project distributes material with the support of the March of Dimes. The project concentrates on improving knowledge of biological and psychological growth, assisting men in clarifying their life goals, and involving men in community projects. The National Urban League has also launched a campaign to educate teenage males about the consequences of pregnancy.
5. Conduct quality programs that stress health, safety, and good nutritional practices. Care-givers can serve as models for parents and model basic practices that can contribute to good maternal and infant health.

CHILDREN'S RIGHTS

The very young are being redefined according to their civil and legal rights. The civil rights movement, the legal profession, and state legislatures are mainly responsible for this redefinition. The very young now have more rights than at any time in history. Primarily as a result of child abuse cases, children are now testifying in court against abusers, and their testimony is considered admissible.

Children even have rights before birth. Some hospitals have fetal advocates on their staffs who champion the rights of the unborn. Suppose, for example, that a sonogram (a device that uses sound waves to measure the size and position of the fetus) of an expectant parent reveals that the fetus has hydrocephalus or "water on the brain." The pediatrician wants to perform fetal surgery to drain the water. The parent, after due consideration, decides against the surgery. The fetal advocate might try to persuade the parent that the surgery should be performed in the best interest of the fetus.

Today's children have rights before and after birth. In New York City, for example, restaurants and other establishments that sell liquor must display the following sign: "Warning: Drinking alcoholic beverages during pregnancy can cause birth defects." This warning brings into sharp focus the growing effort to define children's rights, the ages at which they acquire these rights, and the extent to which children's rights supersede the rights of adults. This warning illustrates how groups and agencies (in this case, a city government) can advocate for the rights of unborn children. It also points out the growing belief that parents don't have the right to abuse their children at any stage of life.

Children's Defense Fund

When do children's rights supersede the rights of their parents? Today, many groups act as advocates on behalf of children to answer this very important question. One such organization is the Children's Defense Fund (CDF). This agency, founded in 1969, provides a voice for the children of America who cannot vote, lobby, or speak for themselves. Based in Washington, D.C., CDF has state and local offices throughout the country. According to Orlando Bugarin, a fulfillment specialist with CDF, the agency "gathers data and disseminates information on key issues affecting children and monitors the development and implementation of federal policies. We provide information, technical assistance, and support to a network of state and local child advocates. We pursue an annual legislative agenda in the United States Congress and litigate selected cases of major importance." CDF is a private organization supported by foundations, corporate grants, and individual donations.

Needless to say, conflict surrounds most discussions about when children's rights begin and parents' rights end. Opinion is polarized around the extremes of the issues. How the rights of children are ultimately defined will involve many social, political, medical, and legal considerations. Their definition and resolution will radically affect parenting, child care, and early childhood education.

Implications for care-givers. Care-givers — on a personal basis, as a staff group, and through professional organizations — can be strong advocates for children's rights. They are often the front line in the war on those who would either knowingly or unknowingly deprive children of their rights. Care-givers can speak for and on behalf of children when they believe children's rights are violated.

CHANGING FAMILIES

The families that children live in have been undergoing a tremendous change in the past decade, and the likelihood is that these changes will continue. Table 10-1 shows eight ways families have changed in recent years. Table 10-2 provides additional data relating to the status of women, children, and families.

Changes in family patterns such as these tables indicate have implications not only for the children who live in them, but also for care-givers in homes and center programs. Valora Washington and Ura Oyemade identify four changes in family life that have implications for care-givers. These changes are

1. The feminization of poverty.
2. The rise in teenage parenting.

TABLE 10-1

Eight Ways Families Have Changed

	1970	1981	1984	Percentage of Change, 1981–1984
1. Married couples	44,728,000	49,294,000	50,090,000	+1.6
2. Married couples with children	25,532,000	24,927,000	24,339,000	−2.4
3. Male householder (no spouse) with children	341,000	666,000	799,000	+20
4. Female householder (no spouse) with children	2,858,000	5,634,000	5,907,000	+4.8
5. Marriages	2,159,000	2,438,000	2,487,000	+2
6. Divorces	708,000	1,219,000	1,155,000	−5.3
7. Average size per household	3.14	2.73	2.71	−1
8. Average size per family	3.58	3.27	3.24	−1

Source: U.S. Department of Commerce, Bureau of the Census.

TABLE 10-2

Characteristics of Women, Children, and Families (1982–1983)

Individuals living in single-parent families	16.3 million
Families living below the poverty level	7.6 million
Families living below the poverty level as a percentage of all families	12.3 percent
Individuals living below the poverty level	35.3 million
Children under eighteen living in poverty	13.0 million
Children under six living with a single female parent as a percentage of all children under six	20 percent
Number of children with mothers in the work force:	
3-year-olds	1.5 million
4-year-olds	1.4 million
Births by teenage mothers:	
under 15 years old	9,773
15–19 years old	513,758

Source: U.S. Department of Commerce, Bureau of the Census.

3. The rise in the number of mothers of preschool children in the work force.
4. Low-income families' increasing difficulty in achieving economic self-sufficiency.

Although they targeted their recommendations to Head Start, the inferences Washington and Oyemade draw apply to other early childhood programs as well. They have the following suggestions for care-givers:

1. Present both boys and girls with positive male images.
2. Promote positive family relationships.
3. Include sex education and programs of pregnancy prevention in the parent involvement component.
4. Increase parental knowledge of child-rearing and parenting skills.
5. Develop leadership potential among low-income families.
6. Accommodate the schedules of working parents.[14]

Single-Parent Families

Care-givers must be aware of how being reared in a single-parent family influences children. E. Mavis Hetherington, a Stanford researcher, has cautioned, "There is a greater probability of problems in school occurring with children from single-parent families. The achievement-test scores and grades in schools of children being reared in single-parent families tend to be lower than those of children living with two parents."[15]

Implications for care-givers. Given the increase in the number of single-parent families, care-givers must work with children, parents, and families to reduce any negative impacts that single parenting may have on children. Specifically, care-givers can take these three steps:

1. Be an extended family and support system for children and their parents. Care-givers can be involved in family celebrations such as birthdays and other events that help promote family unity. Programs can also conduct activities of a "family" nature such as camping and fishing trips so children can participate in novel experiences. In one program, care-givers and children "camp out" twice a year.
2. Involve senior citizens and other adults in program activities.
3. Make special efforts to provide children with male care-givers and role models.

Care-givers cannot ignore the family status of children and their parents. Neither can they act as though family status and economic conditions have no influence on how they care for children and conduct their programs. Rather, they must get to know parents and adjust their programs to meet the short- and long-range needs of all families. Some care-givers may think such activities go well beyond what is expected of them, but a reorientation to a more comprehensive role for care-givers is needed. No longer can care-givers view themselves *only* as care-givers and *only* as providing care for children. The total family is the focus of what the profession refers to as child-care services.

STRESS IN THE LIVES OF THE VERY YOUNG

Stress has always existed and will continue to exist in everyone's life. To live is to be stressed. Children will experience stress all their lives. Care-givers experience stress in their work of providing for the needs of children. There is no escape from stress except through death. Care-givers must find ways to help children and themselves cope with stress.

What is stress? *Stress* is the body's physical and mental response to stressors. A *stressor*, such as a child's trying to grab another child's toy, causes a physical or mental response in the child, in this case, crying.

Is Stress Bad?

Many people have a tendency to think that stress is bad. This is not so. As author Ruth Arent explains,

> *Good stress* is the pressure or emotional condition that inspires children to finish a lesson, do well in sports, or learn to play a musical instrument. It motivates people to be active, to maintain a positive attitude, to work hard, and to benefit from happy relationships and successes.
>
> *Painful stress* is the emotional condition that one feels when it is necessary to cope with unsettling, frustrating, or harmful situations. It is a disturbing

sense of helplessness, perhaps futility, that one feels when there are a number of problems to solve. It is uncomfortable. It can create uncertainty and self-doubt.[16]

Stressors in Children's Lives and Children's Responses to Stressors

There are many stressors operating in the lives of children. (Some examples are listed in Figure 10-2.) How particular children respond to stressors depends on how they have learned to respond and been taught to respond. Figure 10-3 lists some responses children typically make to stressors.

Implications for care-givers. Care-givers must envision that one of their roles is to help children deal with stress. Care-givers must not act as though stress reduction and management are outside the scope of their responsibilities. Some of the ways care-givers can help children cope with stress are described in the following paragraphs.

1. Learn about children, their families, and the life events that are affecting them. Learning about the stressors that are causing stress in children alerts care-givers and enables them to develop a plan to help reduce stress.
2. Be understanding and loving instead of rejecting and critical. Remember, children (and adults, for that matter) are not perfect. Avoid con-

FIGURE 10-2
Stressors

Physical Stressors

Poor nutrition, too little or too much sleep, illness, inadequate clothing, dirty diapers, a handicapping condition.

Mental and Emotional Stressors

Fear of the parent or care-giver, lack of affection, too demanding a care-giver, too many restrictions in the environment, fear of medical procedures, hospitalization, having a parent hospitalized, death of a parent, illness of a parent, being involved in problems beyond the child's ability to cope with, pressure to work or achieve beyond the child's ability level, pressure for early achievement, adjusting to being left in child care, not being picked up on time by a parent.

Environmental Stressors

Noisy home environment, inadequate learning materials, disruptive home life, new sibling, sibling and peer rivalry, factors of contemporary society (television, crime, violence, war), overprogramming of the child's environment to promote achievement, chaotic family life-style, poor or nonexistent adult influence in the home.

Social Stressors

Not being liked by others, fear of others, fear of nuclear war, being cut off from or rejected by parent or parents as a result of divorce, parents' lack of child-rearing skills.

FIGURE 10-3
Indicators of Stress in Young Children

Physical

Nail biting, rashes, illnesses, overeating, withdrawal, frequent urination, upset stomach, diarrhea, insomnia.

Mental or Emotional

Poor self-image, fears, anxiousness, nervousness.

Social

Withdrawal, aggressiveness toward others, hyperactivity.

stant criticism of children such as this: "Well John, so you spilled your milk again. I might have known. It's just like you to do everything wrong."

3. Communicate with children and their parents. Let them know by word and deed that you are someone whom they can talk with. Encourage children to tell you how they feel and to talk about things that are bothering them.

4. Provide time for children to be children. Give them the opportunity to play and be involved in physical activities. Play is an excellent way for children to reduce stress through activity. Also, play provides opportunities to reduce stress through imagination and make-believe. Children can play out situations that they find stressful. In the play situation they are in control, and they can work out solutions acceptable to them.

5. Teach children stress reduction techniques. These techniques include muscle relaxation, yoga, and breathing exercises. Also provide programs of stress reduction such as medical play.

6. Provide the warmth, comfort, and solace of a caring environment.

7. Give time and attention to children. Children need the time and opportunity to interact meaningfully with others, especially care-givers. This relationship provides solace, a cocoon of love and caring that renders the child more resilient under stress.

8. Help children maintain links to home and preschool or child care. Good ways to do this are to have a picture album of the child and the family for use as a "reading" book, allowing children to bring a favorite toy from home, and encouraging parents to visit the program.

9. Care-givers can control and reduce stress in their own lives. A stressed, anxious care-giver can make children stressed and anxious.

10. Provide opportunities for rest and relaxation. Reading to children is a great way to help them relax.

11. Avoid making environments too stimulating. Some care-givers overdo their efforts to make attractive learning environments, and the result is clutter and overstimulation. Also, place relaxing, stress-reducing materials, such as a fish aquarium, in the environment. Looking at

Sometimes children need to be alone in order to have an opportunity to rest and relax. Such opportunities are ideal ways to reduce stress. What else can care-givers do to help children reduce stress in their lives?

swimming fish is a great way for children and adults to relax and forget their worries. Soft music also aids relaxation.

12. Try to keep children from developing bad habits and stressful lifestyles. When care-givers encourage children to excessive achievement, stress competitiveness, and are impatient and hostile, they lay the groundwork for the adult personality prone to heart attack and cardiovascular diseases.

13. Reduce opportunities for children to experience painful, stress-producing events. It is unrealistic to want to protect children from all of life's pains, but care-givers can do such things as (1) reduce failure and rejection as part of the care-giving and schooling process, and (2) help children feel able, worthy, and wanted.

14. Laughter is a great stress reducer. Teach children how to laugh and give them opportunities to laugh by reading them stories that have comic and laughable situations.

NUTRITION

Dieting and other forms of weight control play major roles in many people's lives. Care-givers who attend aerobics classes and "food for life programs" may be unaware of the nutritional backgrounds of the children they care for. Many citizens take the United States's abundant supply of nutritious food for granted, but many children don't have enough or the right kind of food to eat. Parents, lacking adequate nutritional skills themselves, model poor nutritional practices and pass them on to their children. But if children are to achieve their potential, they must be provided with the proper foods and information that will enable them to grow and learn well. Also, children need to develop lifelong habits of good nutrition to lead healthy lives.

Nutrition and the Care-giver

The nutrition the young child receives starts with the nutrition knowledge and practices of care-givers. In the past decade, a great deal of information has been broadcast regarding dietary habits and their relation to certain diseases. Hardly a day passes without an article in the newspaper outlining the recommendations from one group or another regarding food and its influence on health. For all Americans, the U.S. Department of Health, Education, and Welfare has issued the following nutritional guidelines to help individuals lead healthy lives:

- Eat a variety of foods.
- Maintain your ideal weight.
- Avoid too much fat, saturated fat, and cholesterol.
- Avoid too much sugar.
- Avoid too much sodium.
- If you drink alcohol, do so in moderation.[17]

Although general in nature, these guidelines serve to alert and remind care-givers of what they can do to develop good nutritional practices and maintain good health.

As has been said many times throughout this book, children learn by precept and example. Every day, care-givers model good or bad practices of health and nutrition.

Nutrition in Infancy

Young children are dependent on others for their nutritional needs. Maternal nutrition is important during the prenatal period because normal fetal growth depends largely on an adequate supply of oxygen and nutrients. One consequence for the fetus of poor maternal nutrition is low birth weight. Babies of low birth weight are at risk for more sickness and reduced mental competence. And, as mentioned earlier, low birth weight is a leading cause of infant mortality.

During the prenatal period, the fetus receives nourishment via the mother's placenta. Whereas at one time we thought that the placenta was a barrier between the parent and the fetus and screened out all substances that would interfere with growth and development, we now know that this is not true. Because toxic substances that can adversely affect fetus growth and development do cross the placenta, pregnant women are advised to avoid or severely limit their intake of alcohol, aspirin, caffeine, and nicotine. Throughout all the early childhood years, but particularly during infancy, children are dependent on care-givers for nutritional nourishment as well as emotional, social, and intellectual nourishment.

Breast Feeding. The American Academy of Pediatrics recommends that all mothers attempt to breast feed their babies.[18] The advantages of breast feeding are several.

First, mothers' milk contains nutrients necessary for optimum infant growth and development. Supplementing mothers' milk with vitamins and iron is a normal practice when breast or bottle feeding. Although commercial formulas try to simulate breast milk, there is still no substitute for the real thing.

Second, breast milk has antiinfection properties that protect the child from both viral and bacterial infections, including diarrhea, which is a serious health problem of infants, especially in Third World countries.

Third, as a young mother explained it, "I didn't have to worry about my milk agreeing or not agreeing with my baby."

Fourth, mothers' milk is sanitary and there is little, if any, risk of contamination. Sanitation in infant feeding is of serious concern, especially in Third World countries where safe water supplies may be unavailable and where sanitation is not always a high priority.

Fifth, breast feeding may enhance the mother-infant bond. When breast feeding, a care-giver can't "prop a bottle up." There is automatic mother-infant contact. Breast feeding to promote the mother-infant bond may be more of a factor in the lives of working mothers. As one working mother who breast fed her child said, "Feeding time was a quality time for my son and me. I looked on it as a time to bond with him."

Sixth, breast-fed babies tend to be more "in charge" of their feeding — they do not have to drink all the formula that has been put in a bottle. This control tends to lessen the likelihood of overeating.

Economic factors are frequently cited as an added advantage for breast feeding. The reality, however, is that the costs of formula and mothers' milk are similar when the added nutritional intake to support the mother's lactation is taken into consideration.

Mothers who breast feed should consider two necessities. First, they must have an adequate diet that will maintain their health while nursing. Dietary considerations include sufficient caloric and fluid intake. Second, nursing mothers have to be cautious about the effects of birth control pills, nicotine, caffeine, and drugs on their infants. Nursing babies may be the unintended recipients of medication or other substances secreted through mothers' milk.

Supplements for the Breast-Fed Infant. Breast feeding, supplemented with vitamin D, fluoride, and iron, meets the total nutritional needs for the infant until five or six months of age.[19] Vitamin D is necessary as a precaution against rickets, a condition characterized by bending and distortion of the bones. The iron stores in infants whose nutritional intake is not supplemented are rapidly depleted by the fourth to sixth month. Therefore, the American Academy of Pediatrics recommends that iron supplement be started no later than that age.[20] Fluoride supplement started before two years and continued to age three or four reduces dental caries (decay) by 50 to 80 percent.[21] The American Academy of Pediatrics recommends fluoride supplement beginning shortly after birth. The amount of fluoride in the local water supply determines the amount prescribed as a supplement.

Cow's Milk. There is a great deal of controversy about if and when whole cow's milk can be introduced into the infant's diet as a replacement for breast milk or formula. The American Academy of Pediatrics concludes their examination of this topic by recommending that "Although many mothers will continue to breast feed or formula feed their babies through the first year of life, there is at present no convincing evidence from well-designed research studies that feeding whole cow's milk after six months of age is harmful if adequate supplementary feedings are given."[22]

Introduction of Solid Foods

In previous generations, it was common for mothers to introduce solid foods to infants as early as the first or second week. Today, the American Academy of Pediatrics recommends the introduction of solids at four to six months.[23] Anita Owen recommends introducing solid food in the five- to six-month age range and provides the following rationale:

> The introduction of solid foods beginning at approximately 5–6 months of age seems appropriate to the neuromuscular development of the infant. By this time the protrusion reflex of early infancy has disappeared and the ability to swallow non-liquid foods has become established. At 5–6 months of age the infant is able to sit without support, has head and neck control, and is thus able to communicate disinterest or satiety by leaning back and turning away.[24]

The first solid food introduced is usually infant cereal fortified with iron, calcium, thiamine, niacin, and riboflavin according to standards established by the U.S. Food and Drug Administration. Rice is usually the first cereal introduced because of its demonstrated lack of allergenic properties.

When introducing supplemental foods, it is desirable to introduce only one food at a time to determine the food's effect on the infant and his or her tolerance for it. Once this tolerance is determined, usually in three or four days, other foods can be introduced, at the rate of one new food per week.[25] The usual introduction of foods is in this order: dry cereal, fruits, vegetables, and meats, as shown in Figure 10-4.

FIGURE 10-4
Introduction of Solid Foods

INFANT FOOD	HUMAN MILK (or Commercial Formula) PLUS												
	No Solid Food	rice cereal	Fruit				Vege-tables				Meat			Finger Foods
			applesauce	pears	peaches	any above	carrots	squash	beans	peas	beef	lamb	beef/lamb	beef/lamb	cottage cheese toast
INTERVAL	6 months	1 mo.	1 mo.				1 mo.				1 mo.			2 mo.

AGE (months): B 1 2 3 4 5 6 7 8 9 10 11 12

Source: Anita L. Owen, *Feeding Guide: A Nutritional Guide for the Maturing Infant* (Bloomfield, N.J.: Health Learning Systems, 1980), 36.

At six months, the volume of intake of human milk is greater than at any time in the first year, with the *average* infant consuming thirty-seven ounces.

By about six to seven months, when teething begins, the care-giver can introduce finger foods such as arrowroot biscuit, zwieback toast, toasted bread cut in strips, whole-wheat crackers, cheese, hard boiled eggs, and vegetables. Finger foods represent a first step in self-feeding and are also a good way to make the transition to table foods. By eleven months, the infant is developmentally able to chew most foods.[26] Figure 10-5 provides a list of suggested finger foods.

One trend in feeding children over the last decade reflects a similar trend in adult foods and nutrition. That is, there is more of an emphasis on fresh foods (especially vegetables), natural foods, and foods free of salt and sugar. Many parents prepare their own baby foods, and baby food companies manufacture sugar- and salt-free products.

Jarred baby foods for toddlers are really more of a convenience than a necessity for working parents or rushed parents. After infants have outgrown the need for strained baby foods, they can be fed table foods.

Implications for care-givers. Many of the interactions between care-givers and young children revolve around food and the feeding process. Consequently, there are a number of factors care-givers need to consider.

1. Feeding and all experiences associated with food need to be happy times. Care-givers need to make experiences associated with food as

FIGURE 10-5
Suggested Finger Foods

Apple wedges	Fresh pineapple sticks
Banana slices	Grapefruit sections (seeded)
Berries	Green pepper sticks
Cabbage wedges	Meat cubes
Carrot sticks	Melon cubes
Cauliflowerets	Orange sections
Celery sticks (may be stuffed with cheese or	Pitted plums
peanut butter)	Pitted prunes
Cheese cubes	Raisins
Dried peaches	Tangerine sections
Dried pears	Tomato wedges
Fresh peach wedges	Turnip sticks
Fresh pear wedges	Zucchini sticks

Source: A Planning Guide for Food Service in Child Care Centers, U.S. Department of
Agriculture Publication No. FNS-64 (Washington, D.C.: Government Printing Office, 1981).

pleasant as possible. Eating should be a family affair in which children
eat with other children *and* adults. Children learn to eat and enjoy a
wide variety of foods in part by seeing adults eat. Places where children eat should be bright, clean, and nicely decorated. Tables can be
decorated with vases of flowers and place mats made by the children.

2. Food should never be used as a reward or punishment. Food con-
sumption should not be associated with anger, tension, or ill feelings.
Creating a happy environment and establishing routines associated
with eating help promote meal time and snack time as happy events.

Children should not be punished for not eating. Children who are
involved in the normal activities of a program will be hungry and want
to eat. Also, having many opportunities to eat a wide variety of foods
allows children to expand their food preferences.

Normal infants are capable of determining when they have had
enough to eat. Care-givers should not encourage infants to "finish a
bottle" or force children of any age to eat more than they want. Children should not be pushed to finish the last drop or the last spoonful.

3. Children need to be introduced to a wide variety of foods. Feeding can
be used as learning experiences for children. Parents concerned about
food-induced allergies can guard against them by delaying the introduction of solid foods until four to six months and by introducing one
food at a time. Care-givers can keep daily records of what foods children eat and share this information with parents.

The mouth is a sensory organ, and introducing infants to a wide
variety of solid foods helps meet their need for sensory fulfillment.

4. Nutrition education should begin early. It is taught through precept
and example, through what and how children are fed, and through

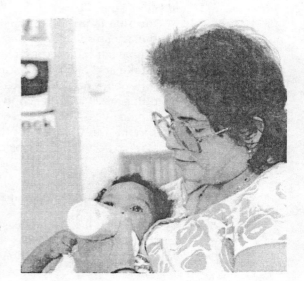

Young children are very dependent on others for their nutritional needs. Parents and care-givers should know and understand what these needs are and how best to meet them. Why is it important for care-givers to educate parents about children's nutritional needs?

the health practices of the care-giver. As a general rule, snack foods and foods high in caloric content should be avoided.

5. Care-givers need to work with parents to help educate them about good nutritional practices such as the importance of breakfast and the nutritional values of foods. Parents, for example, may not know of the sugar or caffeine content in soft drinks. Care-givers can also suggest that a good way to deal with the problem of snacks such as soft drinks and candies is to not buy them.

   Seminars relating to nutrition, e.g., "How to Pack a Nutritious School Lunch" or "Starting the Day the Breakfast Way," provide opportunities to involve the entire family in nutrition education.

   Care-givers need to respect, and where appropriate, accept the cultural basis of foods and feeding as practiced by families. When a cultural practice may have potentially harmful nutritional consequences for the child, however, parents should be so advised. Parents who believe that adding sugar to baby foods and mixing baby foods with milk and formula as a means of having chubby, contented babies must be told that they may be encouraging obesity.

   Nutrition and nutrition-based activities offer many opportunities for introducing children to foods from other cultures. Children can also be involved in the preparation of foods and learn about nutritional value as well as ethnic origin.

7. Programs that provide care for children should have written policies relating to the feeding of young children. Policy statements should address how children are fed; where they are fed; what foods they will be fed; when foods will be introduced; who prepares formula; how

formula is prepared; what food parents furnish; and who gives what dietary supplements.

8. As part of their record keeping, care-givers should note the nutritional intake and habits of children.

9. Independence should be encouraged in nutritional activities, as in other areas. Toddlers and preschoolers should be encouraged to feed themselves. Toddlers can sit at small tables and learn to use forks, spoons, and knives. By two-and-a-half to three years, children can start to serve themselves the amounts of food they will eat.

TELEVISION AND THE VERY YOUNG

Television is a fact in the lives of children and their families. Ninety-eight percent of all homes have television sets. Children spend more time watching television than in any other activity, including going to school, and most children are allowed to watch television with few parental restrictions.[27]

Action For Children's Television (ACT), a nonprofit child advocacy agency, provides some startling information about television viewing habits.

- The average American family watches more than seven hours of television a day.
- Children watch an average of twenty-seven hours of television each week, or almost four hours each day.
- By the time they are eighteen, most children will have spent more time watching television than in school.
- Children see about twenty thousand thirty-second commercials each year, or about three hours of television advertising each week.
- Most of the programs children watch were made for adults.
- Over a million children are still watching television at midnight.[28]

Children ages two to five watch twenty-seven hours, nine minutes of television per week.[29] There is no small amount of controversy over whether television helps or hinders children's learning and views of the world.

Criticisms of Television

There are several general criticisms of television as it relates to children. First, the time children spend watching television is time that could be better spent in other pursuits such as learning activities and interacting with parents.

Second, television is a passive medium requiring little if any involvement or response from children. Since television doesn't ask or require any response from children, all they do is sit and watch. This is the opposite of the type of learning Piaget says children need, that is, active involvement in activities that help promote the development of mental schemes. Instead of watching television, children can be participating in activities, socializing with other children, exercising outdoors, and going places.

Third, much of children's television is prone to violence. Programs give the impression that interpersonal relations are best conducted through hostility and that interpersonal conflicts are best resolved with violence. There is little doubt that violence and aggression as seen on television influence children's behavior.[30] In a summary of research relating to children's television, Parke and Slaby conclude, "Research has demonstrated that television must be considered one of the major socializers of children's aggressive behavior. Two major behavioral effects of heavy viewing of televised violence are: (1) an increase in children's level of aggression; and (2) an increase in children's passive acceptance of the use of aggression by others."[31]

Although television is both a visual and an auditory medium, it is likely that the visual images and actions of television characters serve primarily to attract children's attention. Moreover, the words that characters use to justify their actions may be drowned out by the sound of the actions. Finally, the language that characters use may not be understandable to children viewing their actions. In this sense, the actions of many television characters do indeed speak louder than their words.

Fourth, critics claim children's television programs are one long com-

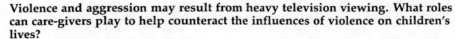

Violence and aggression may result from heavy television viewing. What roles can care-givers play to help counteract the influences of violence on children's lives?

mercial in the form of programs that are built on toys. In essence, children's programs are nothing more than advertisements for the toys they promote.

Fifth, television is often an abused medium in the sense that parents use it as a baby-sitter for their children. It seems easier to put children in front of the television than to interact with them.

Although television is much maligned as an influence on children, it can be a positive influence on children's language development. In particular, language researcher Mabel Rice found that characters on "Sesame Street" and "Mr. Rogers' Neighborhood" speak in short sentences, use the present tense, and limit their observations to the here and now. They present language in ways children understand. On the other hand, cartoons use "garbagese," puns and complex dialogue. According to Rice, young, normal children are quick to pick up language from television, and television programs — the right kind — can be used to enhance language development.[32]

There is little doubt that parents believe that television has a great influence on children. The responses to a questionnaire sent in by the readers of *Better Homes and Gardens* reveal that after themselves, parents believe television has a greater influence on their children than friends, teachers, churches, organized activities, and books.[33]

Television is not going to go away. It will be around for a long time. What are needed are sensible approaches to how to use and control it more effectively. It is unrealistic to think that children should not watch any television.

Implications for care-givers

1. Critics of persons and organizations that would limit or control television maintain that care-givers need to assume a more active role in limiting what children watch and how much they watch. Care-givers should take more of a responsibility for knowing what children are watching by spending a few minutes watching children's programs.
2. Care-givers can discuss the content of television programs with children. Talking about programs can help children differentiate between make-believe and reality.
3. Establish good viewing habits in infants and toddlers. Avoid letting children grow into bad habits such as watching what they want whenever they want.
4. Provide many activities for children to be involved in as alternatives to television. Don't let television be an excuse for not being involved in family activities or other events.
5. Read to children. Reading is an excellent alternative to television.
6. Be an advocate of better television programing for children.
7. Don't use television as a baby-sitter. Limit television viewing in center programs to *planned* educational programs. Care-givers should seriously question the need for a television in a center or preschool.

SUMMARY

A whirlwind of issues — abused and missing children, infant mortality, nutritional needs, childhood stress, television, changing family styles, and children's rights — swirls around young children, their families, and the field of early childhood education. All of our efforts to provide the best for the very young must take all of these into consideration. Care-givers cannot merely wish that these issues and concerns did not exist or assume that by ignoring them they may have the luxury of not being involved in them. Quite the contrary. All of these issues occur within the context of society and affect the growth and development of young children. They also affect the early childhood profession and how children are cared for. Each of these issues has changed how care-givers care for and interact with children. Unfortunately, not all of these changes have been for the better. Consequently, care-givers must act boldy, yet with compassion and understanding, so they can address all of these concerns to develop rational, plausible, and child-appropriate solutions for each of them.

PROGRAM VIGNETTE

Childhaven — The Early Childhood Education Mobile Resource Program
Seattle, Washington

The current interest in child abuse has raised the public's consciousness and created a demand for programs that assist in the detection and prevention of violence committed against children. Early childhood educators in particular are in the vanguard of community and professional efforts to design, develop, and deliver training programs to help abused children and their parents. One such noteworthy effort is conducted by Childhaven, a therapeutic child-care program funded by the United Way, the Washington State Department of Social and Health Services, and other grants and contributions. The 150 children cared for daily by the professional, therapeutic staff are referred by the Children's Protective Services. The children are transported to and from their homes in vans. During the pick-up and delivery of the children, the Childhaven staff can closely monitor the home environment. A variety of educational and support services are offered to the parents.

As part of its outreach services, Childhaven operates a mobile resource program that goes directly to family day-care homes and child-care centers throughout King County to train child-care workers. The program operates two vans, each of which is staffed by two people, a trainer, and a child care worker. The skilled trainer conducts in-service training for the family day-care parent or center staff member while the van's child-care worker assumes the child-care duties in the home or center. This allows the day-care staff to receive uninterrupted training. The training takes place in the van, which is stocked with curriculum materials and aids. Meanwhile, the child-care worker implements a planned program of activities with the children using a box of equipment and materials brought from Childhaven.

In 1975, Childhaven began its program of services because 80 percent of the children in child care in the Seattle area are cared for in family day-care homes. Each training session focused on (1) a child-care topic (such as child development, positive discipline techniques, or setting up the environment), (2) demonstration and modeling of activities, (3) discussion of the concerns of the child-care provider, and (4) a toy lending service. In 1984 the focus of the training was changed to child-abuse prevention, recognition, and training. According to Margo Siegenthaler, program director, "Because of the media attention about child abuse occurring in day-care settings, we felt that day-care providers really needed assistance in how to deal with and respond to the issue of child abuse. Realizing that less than one percent of the abuse actually occurs in child-care settings, we believe that child-care providers are in a unique position to be able to prevent child abuse."

The goals of the Childhaven project are:

1. To increase providers' skills in recognizing abuse.
2. To increase providers' abilities to respond to an abused child, both by offering support to the child and family and making a report to the proper authorities when necessary.
3. To train providers to teach children how to resist abusive situations and report incidents of abuse to a trusted adult when something occurs that doesn't seem right or appropriate.
4. To educate the parents of the children in the day-care setting about child abuse and all the issues surrounding it, thus encouraging them to deal with the subject openly.

Margo believes that, without a program such as the mobile training program, care providers might not otherwise receive the training they need. As she explains, "Day-care licensing in the state of Washington sets only minimal safety standards for day-care facilities. Legally, providers don't have to have training in child development or other child-care topics and usually have had little or no experience in working with groups of children. Also, it is difficult for family child-care providers to get training outside the home, so the mobile resource program has aimed to improve the quality of care by bringing stimulation and support directly to them."

Childhaven trains family child-care providers and the staff of child-care centers in a 50-mile radius of Seattle. To date, approximately 1300 home care providers and staff at 180 child-care centers have been trained. In addition, parents of the children enrolled are also trained at the center and family day-care sites. As Margo points out, "The day-care site is a good place to reach parents. They feel comfortable with the setting and staff. They are willing to participate in training and programs as a natural part of child-care services. We have pretty good success getting parents to come to meetings."

The training consists of two components, one for staff and one for children. The child-care providers are trained in methods of recognizing symptoms of sexual and other abuse, responding to children's needs, and reporting abuse to appropriate agencies and authorities. The providers are taught to incorporate a "personal safety" curriculum into their daily interactions and activities with the children. The children's curriculum, designed primarily for those between the ages of 3–5, includes topics of touching (recognizing), saying "no" (resisting), and telling (reporting). These topics are the three R's of child abuse training. (Child-care providers also are shown how to adapt the material for older or younger children.)

The child-abuse training is conducted during two visits of 1½ hours each. The first visit covers how to recognize if a child has been or is being abused. At this session, most providers bring up concerns about a child in their care. Many are aided in documenting information, which sometimes leads to a report to the state authorities. The second session focuses on how to teach children personal safety skills such as identifying safe and unsafe situations and developing communication skills (being able to say "no").

The activities are designed to help children develop self-esteem by teaching them to identify their feelings and learn appropriate ways to deal with them. Children need to be able to identify how they feel before they can ask for help. For example, the care-givers are shown how to use flannel boards with magazines pictures showing children in different emotional states. Children will be asked, "How does this boy feel?," "Why is he mad?," "What makes you mad (scared, happy, sad, etc.)?" To extend this activity, children are shown pictures depicting various instances of children being touched. They are asked to sort the pictures into the categories of "safe" and "unsafe" touch. One picture may show a smiling boy being hugged by his mother. Other pictures may show a frightened child being hugged by a great big bear or two children fighting. The children are asked, "What is happening here?" "How does this child feel?" "What can he do if he doesn't like being touched in this way?"

The trainers also model activities with puppets and involve the children in role playing. The puppets may hug or fight, or one big puppet may try to get a small puppet to come to a secret hiding place to play a secret touching game. This gives the children practice in using the two rules: (1) say "no" or "stop" when you are being touched in any way that makes you feel uncomfortable, and (2) tell someone you trust if anything happens that makes you feel uncomfortable — even if you are told not to tell.

The care-providers find the program very helpful. One reported that "The program is helpful and informative. I wish I had been involved in a day-care program in which the staff was trained in this manner when I was a child and a victim of sexual abuse." Another reported that she enjoyed the training and would like to see ongoing training two or three times a year. She stressed that "this is a valuable service to day workers in family day-care homes who are short of time for training. It also provides more human contact in the home. This is just what I needed to lessen burnout and help put a little more professionalism in my attitude."

The Childhaven staff conducted a study to determine how training affects attitudes. The Childhaven Child Abuse Opinion Survey, gathered both pre- and post-training information. An analysis of the data revealed that training raised providers' knowledge levels about child abuse from recognizing the symptoms of abuse to dealing with abusive parents and reporting abuse. In addition training enhanced the providers' sensitivity and openness in dealing with children who have been sexually abused.

An outside evaluation of the program revealed that:

- Training makes a significant difference in adult care-givers' knowledge and skills regarding sexual abuse prevention.
- Training significantly increases adult care-givers' use of materials in helping children, while increasing their confidence and feelings of preparedness.
- Training significantly increases children's knowledge and skills.

As is frequently the case, the Childhaven program provides many unexpected insights and revelations in addition to those intended by the planners and implementors. Margo reveals that one-third of the child-care providers who were trained disclosed information regarding their own sexual abuse. As a result, Childhaven was able to provide support, counseling, and referral services for them. For many of these providers, their disclosures represented the first time they were able to share their life events, feelings, and emotions. "We have found that instances of abuse in providers' lives can affect how they care for and relate to children," explains Margo. "The Childhaven staff provides support services which enable these providers to be better care-givers and also to become sources of support to others."

Margo sums up her feelings about the program this way: "Over the years that I have been involved in the program, I have come to have a lot of respect for the hard work and dedication of the care providers. Many of the family day-care providers tend to be isolated from other professionals, so this kind of program helps them keep in touch with the outside world, as well as up to date with information. I would like to see a mobile resource program like this in other parts of the country so that all home care-providers can receive training."

Margo is confident about the future of her program. As she says, "The community wants this kind of program, yet funding is a continual struggle. We receive United Way funding as a base but we are always looking for other sources of support in order to serve the community at a level that will best meet its needs."

There are a number of unique features about the Childhaven Mobile Resource program. First, the mobility of the program directly addresses the training needs of child-care providers by taking the training directly to them. Second, the program is very versatile and adaptable to many training needs. For example, prior to the inception of child-abuse training, the staff delivered training to child-care providers twice a week for a year. Using this approach, they were able to provide in-depth training and support. However, when the staff instituted the child-abuse training program, they were able to train a greater number of providers. There are benefits from both approaches. The year-long training model enables trainers and care-providers to experience a close relationship and significant professional growth. On the other hand, the short-term training enables the staff to reach many more providers. In the future, the program plans to offer either option to child-care providers.

Training and professionalism are two crucial issues facing the child-care community. Programs like Childhaven go beyond mere confirmation of these needs by providing services. In addition, Childhaven meets a critical need of the nation's children. It provides care-givers trained with the skills that will help insulate and protect children from the physical and emotional ravages of child abuse.

ENRICHMENT THROUGH ACTIVITIES

1. List at least five societal trends that have the potential for causing stress in children.
2. List four or more ways care-givers can reduce stress in the very young.
3. Write a lesson plan for teaching four-year-old children one of the stress-reducing techniques identified in number 2 above.
4. Identify six ways care-givers can use television to teach children language processes and cognitive concepts.
5. Write a lesson plan for utilizing television to help promote language development in three-year-old children.
6. List positive and negative examples of sex roles as depicted on television programs.
7. What positive and negative effects does television have on the development of sex roles in children?
8. At the next parent seminar of Happy Days Child Care Program, you have been asked to speak on the topic: "Parents' and Children's Viewing Habits: What Can Parents Do?" What will you say?
9. Watch a "Sesame Street" program. Make a list of concepts and the techniques used to teach them — repetition, fast-paced format, etc. How effective do you think the program is as a teaching program? Why does the program appeal to a wide range of children and adults?
10. In what ways does society in general contribute to the sex typing of children's behavior? How do other cultures contribute to sex typing?
11. Tell why care-givers need to know about the basics of nutrition for young children.
12. Is it important for care-givers to practice principles of good nutrition? Why?
13. Develop lunch-box menus for a two-week period. Explain your choices of foods.
14. Observe the eating habits and food preferences of infants, toddlers, and pre-

schoolers. How are they alike and different? List five implications these differences have for care-givers.

15. A parent tells you that her three-year-old is a "skimpy eater" except for anything sweet, especially cake. What response would you make?
16. List the most common reasons why parents abuse their children.
17. Review a curriculum for "abuse-proofing" young children. Tell why you would or wouldn't use it.
18. Interview the staff of a child-care center to determine what they have done to help reduce the likelihood of child abuse.
19. Why is infant mortality so high in the United States?
    a) Find out the infant mortality rate for your state and compare it to the rate in other states.
    b) Visit a community health agency and determine what they are doing to reduce infant mortality.
20. Of all the issues discussed in this chapter, which one do you feel you as a care-giver could do the most to address? Develop a plan for doing so.
21. Do you agree or disagree that young children have been given too many rights? Give specific examples.

ENRICHMENT THROUGH READING

Arnet, Ruth P. *Stress and Your Child: A Parent's Guide to Symptoms, Strategies, and Benefits.* Englewood Cliffs, N.J.: Prentice-Hall, 1984.

Arnet provides a comprehensive review and discussion of the major factors causing stress in young children. In fact, just about any stressor a parent or care-giver could think of is included. The author also provides many practical suggestions for understanding stress in children and how care-givers can help alleviate situations causing stress. A very readable and worthwhile book.

Blom, Gaston E.; Cheney, Bruce D.; and Snoddy, James E. *Stress in Childhood: An Intervention Model for Teachers and Other Professionals.* New York: Teachers College Press, 1986.

Blom and his colleagues provide a stress-intervention model that teachers and other care-givers can apply without becoming therapists. They also suggest time-efficient interventions adaptable to a teacher's role. Children experiencing stress, as well as their behavioral responses to it, are described in ample variety by means of interesting vignettes. The model is applied to these real-life stress behaviors of children. The tone of the book is practical and encouraging, suggesting that teachers can help children experiencing stress most of the time by using their own skills directly or, when necessary, by referring children to others who have specialized knowledge.

Brenner, Avis. *Helping Children Cope With Stress.* Lexington, Mass.: Lexington Books, 1984.

This book describes the many kinds of stress that affect children. More importantly, it presents many views on how care-givers and parents can help children cope with stress. One of the purposes of the book is to "encourage adults to offer more support to children. It is clear that youngsters can be helped to flourish despite negative experiences in their formative years. Cycles of mistreatment can be broken before puberty. Youngsters need not grow up to repeat the mistakes of their parents." Interesting reading and useful ideas.

Marotz, Lynn; Rush, Jeanettia; and Cross, Marie. *Health, Safety, and Nutrition for the Young Child,* Albany, N.Y.: Delmar Publishers, 1985.

The authors do an excellent job of interrelating the three areas of health, safety, and nutrition. This book focuses on how care-givers can use prevention to help children and their parents. Many useful charts clarify information and make concepts more useful for the reader.

Pelton, Leroy H., ed. *The Social Context of Child Abuse and Neglect.* New York: Human Sciences Press, 1985.

Pelton believes that child abuse has been overly "psychologized." He means that, in their orientation to abuse, too many professionals adopt the medical model of "disease, treatment, and cure." Instead, Pelton says, care-givers must examine the social and economic reasons for abuse and the need for social services to help address the situational context of abuse. This collection of readings especially focuses on the role of poverty in abuse.

Sarafino, Edward P. *The Fears of Childhood.* New York: Human Sciences Press, 1986.

This well-organized book describes what children fear, why fears develop, and what parents and care-givers can do to help children overcome their anxieties. It presents specific ways to prevent fears from developing and gives straightforward practical information on how to help children when fears do arise. Of particular interest is the last section, which contains specific suggestions about children's games and books that can help children cope with their fears.

Thomas, James L., ed. *Death and Dying in the Classroom: Readings for Reference.* Phoenix, Ariz.: Oryx Press, 1984.

This collection of articles and essays provides teachers and care-givers with a resource for investigating issues that relate to death education and dealing with the death of classmates. Although not specifically intended for preschool personnel, the work does provide valuable background information. It can also serve as a resource for teacher-parent seminars.

Townley, Roderick. *Safe and Sound: A Parent's Guide to Child Protection.* New York: Simon and Schuster, 1985.

This book is written for parents with children of all ages. There is much useful information in such chapters as "Physical Abuse: A Quick Checklist for Parents"; "Choosing a Day-Care Center: If You Can't Be at Home and Your Child Is"; and "What to Do If Your Child Disappears." Townley also provides a section, "The Broader Issues," covering such topics as punishment versus rehabilitation for offenders.

Veitch, Beverly, and Harms, Thelma. *Cook and Learn: Pictorial Single Portion Recipes; A Child's Cookbook.* Menlo Park, Calif.: Addison-Wesley, 1981.

This is a compact, attractively illustrated teaching aid to explore learning through cooking with children. The single-portion recipes reflect sound nutritional principles and awareness of foods from many cultures. These cooking experiences help to encourage oral communication, motivate language development, and introduce mathematical relationships.

NOTES

1. *Statutes at Large*, vol. 88, pt. 1 (Washington, D.C.: Government Printing Office, 1976), 5.
2. *Florida Statutes*, chapter 827 (1986).
3. U.S. Bureau of the Census, *Statistical Abstracts of the United States: 1986*, 107th ed. (Washington, D.C.: Government Printing Office, 1986), 161.
4. Mary Main and Carol George, "Responses of Abused and Disadvantaged Toddlers to Distress in Age-Mates: A Study in the Day Care Center," *Developmental Psychology* 21 (May 1985): 407–412.
5. A. Sangrund, R. Gaines, and A. Green, "Child Abuse and Mental Retardation: A Problem of Cause and Effect," *American Journal of Mental Deficiency* 79 (November 1974): 327–330.
6. William N. Friedrich and Jerry A. Boriskin, "The Role of the Child in Abuse: A Review of the Literature," *American Journal of Orthopsychiatry* 46 (October 1976): 581.
7. Allan R. DeJong et al., "Sexual Abuse of Children," *American Journal of Diseases of Children* 136 (February 1982): 129–134.
8. Shirley O'Brien, *Child Abuse and Neglect: Everyone's Problem* (Wheaton, Md.: Association for Childhood Education International, 1984), 17–18. Reprinted by permission of Shirley O'Brien and the Association for Childhood Education International, 11141 Georgia Avenue, Suite 200, Wheaton, MD. Copyright © 1984 by the Association.
9. Jay Belsky, "A Theoretical Analysis of Child Abuse Remediation Strategies," *Journal of Clinical Child Psychology* 7 (Summer 1978): 118.
10. Telephone interview, February 3, 1986, Florida Department of Law Enforcement, Missing Children's Information Clearing House.
11. National Center for Health Statistics, "Birth, Marriages, Divorces, and Deaths for 1985," *Monthly Vital Statistics Report* 34 (December 1985): 1.
12. U.S. Department of Health and Human Services, "Births, Marriages, Divorces, and Deaths for 1984," *Monthly Vital Statistics Report* 33 (March 1985): 5.
13. Children's Defense Fund, *Black and White Children in America: Key Facts* (Washington, D.C.: Children's Defense Fund, 1985), 74.
14. Valora Washington and Ura Jean Oyemade, "Changing Family Trends: Head Start Must Respond," *Young Children* 40 (September 1985): 12–19.
15. B. Frank Brown, "A Study of the School Needs of Children from One-Parent Families," *Phi Delta Kappan* 61 (April 1980): 537.
16. Ruth P. Arent, *Stress and Your Child: A Parent's Guide to Symptoms, Strategies, and Benefits* (Englewood Cliffs, N.J.: Prentice-Hall, 1984), iii.
17. U.S. Department of Agriculture and U.S. Department of Health, Education, and Welfare, "Nutrition and Your Health: Dietary Guidelines for Americans" (Washington, D.C.: Government Printing Office, 1980).
18. American Academy of Pediatrics, "Promotion of Breast Feeding," *Pediatrics* 69 (May 1982): 654–660.
19. Anita L. Owen, *Feeding Guide: A Nutritional Guide for the Maturing Infant* (Bloomfield, N.J.: Health Learning Systems, 1980), 38.
20. Committee on Nutrition, American Academy of Pediatrics, "Iron Supplementation for Infants," *Pediatrics* 58 (November 1976): 756–768.
21. Owen, *Feeding Guide*, 38.

22. Committee on Nutrition, American Academy of Pediatrics, "The Use of Whole Cow's Milk in Infancy," *Pediatrics* 72 (August 1983): 255.
23. Committee on Nutrition, American Academy of Pediatrics, "On the Feeding of Supplemental Foods to Infants," *Pediatrics* 65 (June 1980): 1178.
24. Owen, *Feeding Guide*, 14.
25. Owen, *Feeding Guide*, 16.
26. Owen, *Feeding Guide*, 30.
27. Ross D. Parke and Ronald G. Slaby, "The Development of Aggression," in *Socialization, Personality, and Social Development*, ed. E. Mavis Hetherington, vol. IV of *Handbook of Child Psychology*, ed. Paul H. Mussen (New York: John Wiley, 1983): 595–596.
28. Action for Children's Television, *New Views on TV Viewing* (Newtonville, Mass.: ACT, n.d.).
29. Action for Children's Television, "Viewing Goes Up," *re:act* 13 (1984): 4.
30. Bobbie H. Rowland, Bryan E. Robinson, and Leif Jacobson, "Television Violence: Its Effects on Young Children," *Dimensions* 10 (July 1982): 108–109.
31. Parke and Slaby, "Development of Aggression," 605.
32. "Newsnotes," *Phi Delta Kappan* 67 (February 1986): 472.
33. Kate Keating, "What's Happening to American Families?" *Better Homes and Gardens* 6 (August 1983): 16.

Chapter 11

Becoming a Good Care-giver

Questions to Guide Your Reading and Study

- Why do you want to be a care-giver?
- What personal qualities and characteristics help a person be a good care-giver?
- What role does caring play in care giving?
- What factors cause stress in care-givers' lives?
- What can care-givers do to reduce stress in their lives?
- What does it mean to be a professional?
- Why is it important for care-givers to be a part of the profession?
- What are the developmental stages involved in becoming a good care-giver?
- How does the Child Development Associate program contribute to becoming a good care-giver?
- What are the important features of the initial code of ethics for early childhood educators?
- Are you willing to adopt and live up to the initial code of ethics?

INTRODUCTION

Early childhood education, like the rest of the field of education, is at the center of a heated public discussion about what constitutes quality. This discussion focuses in part on what constitutes quality in programs, care giving, and teaching. It is only proper that questions and discussions about quality should be a part of the American agenda relating to the education and care of children. Addressing issues of quality will help society and the early childhood profession in its search for solutions to problems such as those discussed in Chapter 11.

The quality of programs for educating and developing young children is inseparably linked to the quality of the care-givers involved in them. There is a saying you may have heard before: "Quality in — quality out." When quality care-givers dedicate themselves to developing quality programs, the chance of a quality program resulting, although not assured, is certainly increased. Indeed, without quality care-givers, it is doubtful if there is much of a future for the early childhood profession or children. All who care for and about the very young must not be involved solely in discussions about what constitutes quality. They must also involve themselves in programs and activities of self-development so they may be quality care-givers who can help ensure quality programs for all children.

BECOMING A GOOD CARE-GIVER

Do You Really Want to Be a Care-giver?

Some people, when asked why they want to care for children, respond, "Because I love children." Although it is commendable that people say they love children — children need all the love they can get — citing love as the primary reason for wanting to care for children is not enough. Some care-givers realize too late that there are other considerations involved in being a good care-giver. Children deserve the best care-givers they can have. One way people can be good care-givers is to be happy with themselves and happy in the profession. This is why it is important to think about your important career decision.

Questions to Ask Yourself. Some questions care-givers should ask before they choose a career with children are:

- Why do I want to work with young children?
- What do I enjoy most about working with young children?
- Will I be happy spending the major part of my days — and life — working with and on behalf of children?
- What particular qualities and skills do I have that can benefit children?
- What personal qualities and skills will I have to develop in order to be a good care-giver?

All care-givers must ask themselves these questions: "Why do I want to work with young children?" and "Can I give my best to young children in order to help them develop to their fullest potential?"

- Am I willing to spend extra time and effort improving my knowledge and skills?
- Do I have the temperament and personality that will enable me to work with children, parents, and other care-givers?
- Can I care for children of all cultures, ethnic backgrounds, and socio-economic statuses?
- Can I put the best interests of children ahead of my own self-interests?
- Can I care for special needs children?
- Am I willing to be an advocate on behalf of children?

Care-giver Qualities

In addition to examining their motivations for working with young children, care-givers need to assess what qualities are critical for success in working with children. In a review of research related to effective teaching, Feeney and Chun,[1] identified the following personal qualities as desirable in early childhood educators:

- Love of children
- Warmth
- Kindness
- Ability to foster a happy, creative atmosphere
- Patience
- Aspects of physical health such as energy and coordination

- Self-understanding and serenity
- Genuine respect for children
- A child's-eye perspective (the ability to see naively and with wonder)
- A sense of humor

In addition to the qualities listed, caring, compassion, courtesy, dedication, empathy, enthusiasm, friendliness, helpfulness, honesty, intelligence, and motivation are also helpful. Of all these qualities, caring is the most important. Care-givers who truly care will want to use their talents and intelligence to provide the best for children. And that is what care-giving is all about.

STRESSES ASSOCIATED WITH CARE-GIVING

As experienced care-givers know, there are many pleasures associated with care giving, but there are also many stresses. Indeed, many of the stresses of care giving are the result of the pleasures. In addition to the stresses that come from everyday acts of care giving, there are a number of additional causes of care-giver stress.

1. Most child-care workers and early childhood educators receive low pay. The satisfactions derived from care giving are many. It is regarded as a great and ennobling profession. Unfortunately, care-givers are not paid what they should be. In a recent national survey of its membership,* the National Association for the Education of Young Children found that 50 percent of the teacher aides, 40 percent of the assistant teachers, and 35 percent of the teachers earned between $3.36 and $5.00 per hour.[2] These figures are in keeping with a Child Welfare League of America study, which found that day-care workers who lacked college degrees averaged $6,888 per year and preschool teachers with college degrees averaged $8,833 a year.[3]
2. Physical stress associated with illness. Care-givers face continuous exposure to common children's illnesses.
3. Physical stress associated with walking after children, picking up children, organizing the environment, and conducting activities.
4. Career stress resulting from not having personal and professional goals. Care-givers who have goals and work toward them are happier and more confident than those who have no goals and let life lead them where it may.

---

* The NAEYC cautions that because of the limited sample (3,818), "Readers are encouraged to resist the temptation to generalize these results to specific programs or to the entire population of early childhood employees. Rather, this report may be taken as a gross representation of conditions among a limited sample of NAEYC members and interested others."

What Can Care-givers Do to Reduce Stress?

1. Care-givers can take good care of themselves. Practice good habits related to rest, nutrition, and physical exercise. Being physically fit helps combat fatigue and enables the body to resist the effects of stress.

   Care-givers can practice good habits related to lifting and sitting. Lifting children and sitting on small furniture can contribute to sore backs. A good way to learn about the mechanics involved in lifting is to invite a physical therapist to conduct a seminar on how to lift and sit.

2. Care-givers can reduce stress in their lives through a planned, systematic program of stress reduction. Some good stress reducers are jogging, aerobic dancing, bicycling, swimming, and fast walking. These exercises not only relieve stress, they condition the body, enabling it to deal more effectively with the stress.

3. Care-givers can set goals for their personal and professional lives. Life goals should be set for one- and five-year periods. They should be reviewed annually. As people and circumstances change, goals can be readjusted accordingly. Setting goals and adjusting them as you grow and develop is preferable to having no goals at all.

4. Care-givers can manage their time well in order to achieve personal and professional goals. Many people complain that they don't have the time to attend professional meetings, read professional literature, or engage in other professional activities. By reexamining how time is used in relation to goals, however, time can be allocated from non-productive activities and pursuits to those that help achieve goals. Watching less television and setting time aside to read might be two ways a care-giver could achieve the goal of keeping up with professional literature.

THE DEVELOPMENTAL STAGES OF BECOMING A GOOD CARE-GIVER

Seldom does a person become an outstanding care-giver instantaneously. It takes hard work, study, and dedication. As one enters the profession and begins a care-giving career, one progresses through developmental stages.

Ellen Frede, a teacher trainer who helps teachers implement the High/Scope Cognitively Oriented Curriculum, identifies four stages in the growth of a teacher.[4]

Level I: Mastering the "Nuts and Bolts." At this stage, the teacher focuses on the elements that are easiest to implement and for which expectations are clear. These include the structural elements of the learning environment, such as physical arrangements and the daily routine. Frede says that while this emphasis on the nuts and bolts of teaching provides teachers with immediate success, it can lead to "overstructuring and failure to ask questions about why they are doing what they do." According to Frede, teachers at this level need to be challenged to reflect on a rationale for what they do.

Level II: "Too Much of a Good Thing." In this stage, teachers are comfortable with the structural elements of a program and begin to focus on their teaching styles. Frede says there is a tendency for teachers at this level to overdo a particular teaching strategy that they like and are comfortable with. As a result, teachers can be identified by their teaching styles. Some styles that Frede identifies are "the Questioner," who bombards the children with questions; "the Observer," who observes and writes notes about almost everything; "the Manager," who is concerned about maintaining an orderly environment; and the "Free-Wheeler," who gives children choices but forgets they need limits. Frede believes teachers need help seeing that they may be overgeneralizing in one teaching area.

Level III: "Do It My Way." At this level the teacher believes the only way to teach is his or her own way. Teachers don't necessarily understand that different settings and children require different curriculum implementations. At this level, teachers need opportunities to visit other programs and classrooms to see how other teachers teach.

Level IV: Creative Adaptation. At this level, teachers are able to adapt curricula to different situations, environments, and children. When they reach this level, teachers may want to work with teachers at the other levels and concentrate on other aspects of their own programs, such as parent involvement.

BECOMING A MEMBER OF THE PROFESSION

In previous chapters you read about great men and women who have contributed to the education and development of young children. Just as they have given of themselves to the profession, so must you. Being a care-giver means that you will be involved in the profession in some or all of the following ways.

1. Professional care-givers upgrade themselves through self-enhancement, study, training programs, and college classes. When care-givers have expert care-giving skills and specific training in early childhood education, others recognize them as professionals. Such recognition also upgrades the image of the profession.
2. Share what you do with parents and others in the profession. One of

the best ways to further professionalize the profession is to let parents — the consumers of our services — know what we do and what the profession stands for.

3. Join a professional organization such as the National Association for the Education of Young Children. Be active at the affiliate levels, i.e., in the local and state affiliate organizations. Professional organizations are excellent ways to support the profession, receive support from other professionals, and give support to others.

4. Become an advocate for yourself and the profession. Children, parents, and the profession need strong advocates on their behalf. Advocacy entails using one's time and talents to work on behalf of others. Some methods suggested by the Children's Defense Fund, a national organization involved in advocating for children, are publicity, organizing, educating others, negotiating, using grievance procedures, lobbying, and legal action.[5] There is a constant need to upgrade the profession's salaries, working conditions, and status.

5. Work with colleagues to support them in their efforts to be good caregivers. Cooperative decision making and problem solving can be a stabilizing influence on staff relationships.

6. Participate in professional activities. Each year in April, for example, the National Association for the Education of Young Children sponsors the "Week of the Young Child" to call attention to the critical significance of children's early years. Care-givers can celebrate the week in their programs by calling the week to parents' and others' attention and holding special meetings, seminars, and open houses.

William Ade believes a profession is characterized by certain characteristics: specialized knowledge, service, and the assurance of quality, dependability, and effectiveness.[6] All care-givers have to work to develop these characteristics in themselves and the profession they represent. This means they have to study and participate in training to get the specialized knowledge necessary to provide effective, dependable, quality service.

Lillian Katz, a noted early childhood educator, believes that two important factors in professionalism are the use of advanced knowledge in the formulation of judgments and the adoption of standards for the early childhood profession. As Katz explains:

> Advanced knowledge in early childhood education is derived from developmental psychology as well as from many other fields. Professional judgment involves diagnosing and analyzing events, weighing alternatives, and estimating the potential long-term consequences of decisions and actions based on that knowledge.
>
> One of the major functions of a professional organization is to set standards of performance based on the best available advanced knowledge and practices.[7]

The philosophy of quality early-childhood programs such as at the Park Road Baptist Church is that each child has infinite worth and is an important human being. What are some other beliefs that are essential to good programs?

A major difference between the professional and nonprofessional, according to Katz, is the professional's willingness to maintain professional standards.

In addition to committing themselves to the standards of a professional organization, many programs develop a philosophy to guide their behavior in the local setting. Programs do operate better when staff have a philosophy to guide their daily behavior. The program philosophy should be written cooperatively by the staff rather than imposed by the program director. The staff of the Park Road Baptist Church, for example, wrote and follows the philosophy depicted in Figure 11-1.

PROFESSIONAL TRAINING AND PERSONAL DEVELOPMENT

If care-givers are not sure of themselves, how can they expect young children to be sure of themselves? One key to professional self-assurance is training. The Child Development Associate (CDA) National Credentialing Program initiated in 1971 is a training and credentialing program that helps ensure that key competencies necessary for quality care giving are dem-

FIGURE 11-1
Philosophy of Early Childhood Education

Our Beliefs About Persons

We believe that each person has infinite worth because he is a child of God, a unique human being.

We believe that children are dependable and trustworthy with an innate need to grow and become.

We believe that a positive self-image is essential to the full development of the person.

We believe that the self-concept influences both behavior and learning.

We believe that a child learns to accept himself and others by being accepted and learns to love by being loyal.

We believe that the child develops trust by the consistent caring response to his needs by the adults in his environment.

We believe that joy, delight, wonder, curiosity, love of learning, sense of humor, and creativity are "divine rights" of childhood, which, if carefully nurtured, will carry over to the adult.

Source: Mrs. Marjorie Warlick, "Purpose and Philosophy of Early Childhood Education."

onstrated by practitioners in the profession. The CDA seeks to improve the quality of child care by improving, evaluating, and recognizing the competence of child-care providers and home visitors.[8] The Council for Early Childhood Professional Recognition, a subsidiary of the National Association for the Education of Young Children, administers the CDA program.

Good care-givers provide a variety of equipment, activities, and opportunities for children to explore. What else can care-givers do to facilitate the education and development of young children?

TABLE 11-1

CDA Competency Goals and Functional Areas for Infant/Toddler Care-givers in Center-Based Programs

Competency Goals	Functional Areas
I. To establish and maintain a safe, healthy learning environment	1. *Safe:* Candidate provides a safe environment to prevent and reduce injuries.
	2. *Healthy:* Candidate promotes good health and nutrition and provides an environment that contributes to the prevention of illness.
	3. *Learning environment:* Candidate uses space, relationships, materials, and routines as resources for constructing an interesting, secure, and enjoyable environment that encourages play, exploration, and learning.
II. To advance physical and intellectual competence	4. *Physical:* Candidate provides a variety of equipment, activities, and opportunities to promote the physical development of children.
	5. *Cognitive:* Candidate provides activities and opportunities that encourage curiosity, exploration, and problem solving appropriate to the developmental levels and learning styles of children.
	6. *Communication:* Candidate actively communicates with children and provides opportunities and support for children to understand, acquire, and use verbal and nonverbal means of communicating thoughts and feelings.
	7. *Creative:* Candidate provides opportunities that stimulate children to play with sound, rhythm, language, materials, space, and ideas in individual ways and to express their creative abilities.

(continued)

Table 11-1 shows the CDA competency goals and functional areas for infant and toddler care-givers in a center-based program. Although the six competency goals are the same for all settings (center-based, family, day-care, home visitor), the functional area definitions and sample behaviors change to define the particular skills needed for the specific child-care setting and age group.

A *CDA Assessment* is the process by which a care-giver's competence is evaluated by the CDA National Credentialing Program. The evaluation is conducted by a group of people called the *local assessment team*. This team includes the care-giver (the candidate); an early childhood or child-care professional (the advisor); a member of the local community (the parent or community representative); and a representative of the CDA national program (the CDA representative).[9]

TABLE 11-1 (*continued*)

Competency Goals	Functional Areas
III. To support social and emotional development and provide positive guidance	8. *Self:* Candidate provides physical and emotional development and emotional security for each child and helps each child to know, accept, and take pride in himself or herself and to develop a sense of independence.
	9. *Social:* Candidate helps each child feel accepted in the group, helps children learn to communicate and get along with others, and encourages feelings of empathy and mutual respect among children and adults.
	10. *Guidance:* Candidate provides a supportive environment in which children can begin to learn and practice appropriate and acceptable behaviors as individuals and as a group.
IV. To establish positive and productive relationships with families	11. *Families:* Candidate maintains an open, friendly, and cooperative relationship with each child's family, encourages their involvement in the program, and supports the child's relationship with his or her family.
V. To ensure a well-run, purposeful program responsive to participant needs	12. *Program management:* Candidate is a manager who uses all available resources to ensure an effective operation. The candidate is a competent organizer, planner, record-keeper, communicator, and a cooperative coworker.
VI. To maintain a commitment to professionalism	13. *Professionalism:* Candidate makes decisions based on knowledge of early childhood theories and practices, promotes quality in child-care services, and takes advantage of opportunities to improve competence, both for personal and professional growth and for the benefit of children and families.

Source: CDA National Credentialing Program, *Child Development Associate Assessment System and Competency Standards: Infant/Toddler Care-givers in Center-Based Programs* (Washington, D.C.: CDA National Credentialing Program, 1986), 1.

Early childhood educators are always concerned with developing children in three areas: the physical, the intellectual, and the social and emotional. Teachers and care-givers also have to develop themselves in the six CDA functional areas.

AN INITIAL CODE OF ETHICS FOR EARLY CHILDHOOD EDUCATORS

The late Evangeline Ward, a modern early childhood pioneer, developed the code of ethics in Figure 11-2 to guide care-givers in their work with young children.

FIGURE 11-2
An Initial Code of Ethics for Early Childhood Educators

Preamble
As an educator of young children in their years of greatest vulnerability, I, to the best of intent and ability, shall devote myself to the following commitments and act to support them.

For the Child
I shall accord the respect due each child as a human being from birth on.

I shall recognize the unique potentials to be fulfilled within each child.

I shall provide access to differing opinions and views inherent in every person, subject, or thing encountered as the child grows.

I shall recognize the child's right to ask questions about the unknowns that exist in the present so the answers (which may be within the child's capacity to discover) may be forthcoming eventually.

I shall protect and extend the chlid's physical well-being, emotional stability, mental capacities, and social acceptability.

For the Parents and Family Members
I shall accord each child's parents and family members respect for the responsibilities they carry.

By no deliberate action on my part will the child be held accountable for the incidental meeting of his or her parents and the attendant lodging of the child's destiny with relatives and siblings.

Recognizing the continuing nature of familial strength as support for the growing child, I shall maintain objectivity with regard to what I perceive as family weaknesses.

Maintaining family value systems and pride in cultural-ethnic choices or variations will supersede any attempts I might inadvertently or otherwise make to impose my values.

Because advocacy on behalf of children always requires that someone cares about or is strongly motivated by a sense of fairness and intervenes on behalf of children in relation to those services and institutions that impinge on their lives, I shall support family strength.

Regardless of the careers people decide to dedicate themselves to, it is important for them to be the best they can be. This is doubly important when one chooses a career involving the education and care of young children. To achieve this goal in a career with the very young, there are a number of activities and processes individuals can participate in as they grow in their early childhood careers. The Professional Development Checklist in Figure 11-3 can help beginners and experienced care-givers achieve a level of professionalism that will enable them to have a satisfying and rewarding career.

SUMMARY

A journey through life as a care-giver of young children is fascinating and rewarding for those who are willing to dedicate themselves to making it a

FIGURE 11-2 (*continued*)

For Myself and the Early Childhood Profession

Admitting my biases is the first evidence of my willingness to become a conscious professional.

Knowing my capacity to continue to learn throughout life, I shall vigorously pursue knowledge about contemporary developments in early education by informal and formal means.

My role with young children demands an awareness of new knowledge that emerges from varied disciplines and the responsibility to use such knowledge.

Recognizing the limitation I bring to knowing intimately the ethical-cultural value systems of the multicultural American way of life, I shall actively seek the understanding and acceptance of the chosen ways of others to assist them educationally in meeting each child's needs for his or her unknown future impact on society.

Working with other adults and parents to maximize my strengths and theirs, both personally and professionally, I shall provide a model to demonstrate to young children how adults can create an improved way of living and learning through planned cooperation.

The encouragement of language development with young children will never exceed the boundaries of propriety or violate the confidence and trust of a child or that child's family.

I shall share my professional skills, information, and talents to enhance early education for young children wherever they are.

I shall cooperate with other persons and organizations to promote programs for children and families that improve their opportunities to utilize and enhance their uniqueness and strength.

I shall ensure that individually different styles of learning are meshed compatibly with individually different styles of teaching to help all people grow and learn well — this applies to adults learning to be teachers as well as to children.

Source: Evangeline Ward, "A Code of Ethics: The Hallmark of a Profession," in *Ethical Behavior in Early Childhood Education,* ed. Lillian G. Katz and Evangeline Ward (Washington, D.C.: National Association for the Education of Young Children, 1978), 20–21.

Young children deserve the best care-givers it is possible to have. All who work with young children should dedicate themselves to being the best and doing their best. What can care-givers do to help themselves and others excel?

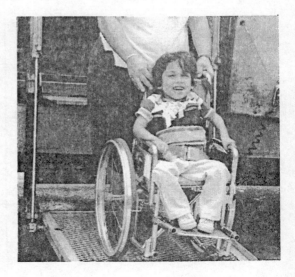

FIGURE 11-3
Fifteen Steps to Becoming a Professional: A Professional Development Checklist

SELF-EVALUATION OF PROFESSIONAL DEVELOPMENT

Desired Professional Outcome	High Level of Commitment and Accomplishment	Satisfactory Level of Commitment and Accomplishment But Need Improvement
1. I have thought about and written my philosophy of teaching and caring for young children.		
2. I have a professional career plan for the next year that includes goals and objectives I will endeavor to meet as a professional.		
3. I engage in study and training programs to improve my knowledge and competence related to teaching and caring for young children.		
4. I am a teachable person. I am willing to change my ideas, thinking, and practices based on study, new information, and the advice of colleagues and professionals.		
5. I have worked or am working on a degree or credential (CDA, AA, BS) in order to enhance my personal life and my life as a professional.		
6. I try to improve myself as a person by engaging in a personal program of self-development.		
7. I practice in my own life and model for others good moral habits and ethical behavior. I encourage others to act ethically.		
8. I act professionally and encourage others to do the same.		
9. I place the best interests of children, parents, and the profession first in decisions about what constitutes quality teaching and care giving.		
10. I know about and am familiar with my profession's history, terminology, issues, contemporary development, and trends.		
11. I consciously and consistently find ways to apply concepts and knowledge about what is best for children to my teaching and care giving.		

FIGURE 11-3 (*continued*)

Low or Little Commitment and Accomplishment — Need Considerable Improvement	Evidence of Commitment and Accomplishment (*Specify what you have done and are doing to meet these professional criteria.*)	Action Plan for Commitment and Accomplishment (*Specify what you plan to do to improve in this area.*)	Target Date for Completing Action Plan or Demonstrating Increased Commitment and Accomplishment

FIGURE 11-3 (*continued*)

Desired Professional Outcome	High Level of Commitment and Accomplishment	Satisfactory Level of Commitment and Accomplishment But Need Improvement
12. I belong to a professional organization and participate in professional activities such as celebrations, study groups, committees, and conventions.		
13. I am an advocate for and on behalf of my profession and the needs and rights of children and families.		
14. I involve parents in my program and help and encourage parents in their roles as children's primary care-givers and teachers.		
15. I seek the advice of and cooperate with other professionals and professional groups in my work with young children, parents, and families.		

good experience for themselves, the children they care for, and the colleagues they work with. The ideas, theories, information, and practical applications presented in this book are intended to assist you in your journey and enhance your appreciation and understanding of quality care giving. In this chapter, the emphasis has been on becoming a good care-giver and professional. In particular, the code of ethics and the Professional Development Checklist can assist you in becoming a quality professional. As a result, you will be a good care-giver and will be able to say at the end of each day, "I did my best," and children and parents will remember you as the best. Good luck in your journey.

ENRICHMENT THROUGH ACTIVITIES

1. Why is it important for care-givers to be part of the profession?
   a) What would you say to someone who said he or she could be a good care-giver without being involved in professional activities?
   b) List five ways care-givers can contribute to the profession.

FIGURE 11-3 (*continued*)

Low or Little Commitment and Accomplishment — Need Considerable Improvement	Evidence of Commitment and Accomplishment (*Specify what you have done and are doing to meet these professional criteria.*)	Action Plan for Commitment and Accomplishment (*Specify what you plan to do to improve in this area.*)	Target Date for Completing Action Plan or Demonstrating Increased Commitment and Accomplishment

2. Interview care-givers who belong to a professional organization. Ask them what benefits they derive from their organization.
3. Cite some instances in which you think care-givers' activities might cause them stress.
4. List ten reasons why you want to be a care-giver.
   a) Share your reasons with friends. Ask them to comment on your reasons.
   b) Compare your reasons with those of a friend. How are they similar or different?
5. Interview care-givers to determine:
   a) Their reasons for becoming care-givers.
   b) Why they are happy being care-givers.
   c) What they dislike about being care-givers.
6. How important to good care giving are the personal qualities and characteristics discussed in this chapter? What other qualities would you include?
7. Recall the care-givers you had as a young child. What qualities and characteristics did they possess that you would want to emulate?
8. Make a list of all possible careers relating to working with young children.
   a) Which of these appeals most to you? Why?
   b) Which of these appeals least to you? Why
9. Write your philosophy of care giving. Share it with your friends and ask them to comment about what you believe.
10. What are things you think people can do to help themselves become better care-givers?

ENRICHMENT THROUGH READING

Kelly, James L., and Kelly, Mary Jean, eds. *The Successful Elementary Teacher*. Lanham, Md.: University Press of America, 1985.

Written for and about beginning teachers, these essays address many of the concerns and problems encountered by new teachers. Chapter topics include intellectual development, motivation, humanizing the classroom, mainstreaming, multicultural education, classroom management, characteristics of good teachers, and the classroom environment. The best chapters in the book are the last two, which cover characteristics of teachers and environments.

Kohl, Herbert. *Growing Minds: On Becoming a Teacher*. New York: Harper and Row, 1984.

Writing with his usual good sense and in his easy-to-read style, Herbert Kohl provides a practical professional guide for growing into the profession of teaching. His main thesis is that regardless of individuals' motivations for entering the profession, they still have to learn how to become good teachers. Competence, Kohl believes, is acquired through careful and steady effort, growth, and experience. He also believes, as have many great educators, that effective teaching focuses on helping children develop the skills to learn how to learn. An excellent book that can be enjoyed and savored by all teachers in any stage of professional development.

Ryan, Kevin; Newman, Katherine K.; Mager, Gerald; Applegate, Jane; Lasley, Thomas; Flora, Randall; and Johnston, John. *Biting the Apple: Accounts of First-Year Teachers*. New York: Longman, 1980.

The authors quote Ashley Montagu: "The largest personal sorrow suffered of human beings consists of the difference of what one was capable of becoming and what one has, in fact become." They believe that events during the first year of teaching or care giving contribute to the gap between care-givers' potential and what they achieve. Their book calls particular attention to the induction phase of teaching and what care-givers and others can do to narrow or eliminate the gap.

NOTES

1. Stephanie Feeney and Robyn Chun, "Effective Teachers of Young Children," *Young Children* 41 (November 1985): 48.
2. "Results of the NAEYC Survey of Child Care Salaries and Working Conditions," *Young Children* 40 (November 1984): 14.
3. Child Welfare League of America, *1977 Salary Study* (New York: Child Welfare League of America, 1977).
4. Ellen Frede, "How Teachers Grow: Four Stages," *High/Scope Resource* (Spring 1985): 10–12.
5. R. Beck, *It's Time to Stand Up for Your Children* (Washington, D.C.: Children's Defense Fund, 1979), 34–37.
6. William Ade, "Professionalism and Its Implications for the Field of Early Childhood Education," *Young Children* 32 (March 1982): 25.

7. Lilian G. Katz, "The Professional Early Childhood Teacher," *Young Children* 39 (July 1984): 3.
8. CDA National Credentialing Program, *Child Development Associate Assessment System and Competency Standards: Infant/Toddler Care-givers in Center-Based Programs* (Washington, D.C.: CDA National Credentialing Program, 1986), 1.
9. CDA National Credentialing Program, *Assessment System and Competency Standards*, 5.

Index